Microsoft®
SQL Server™ 2005
Programming
FOR
DUMMIES®

by Andrew Watt

BICENTENNIAL
1807
WILEY
2007
BICENTENNIAL

Wiley Publishing, Inc.

Microsoft® SQL Server™ 2005 Programming For Dummies®

Published by
Wiley Publishing, Inc.
111 River Street
Hoboken, NJ 07030-5774

www.wiley.com

For general information on our other products and services, please contact our Customer Care Department within the U.S. at 800-762-2974, outside the U.S. at 317-572-3993, or fax 317-572-4002.

For technical support, please visit www.wiley.com/techsupport.

Wiley also publishes its books in a variety of electronic formats. Some content that appears in print may not be available in electronic books.

Library of Congress Control Number: 2006929469

ISBN: 978-0-471-77422-8

Manufactured in the United States of America

10 9 8 7 6 5 4 3 2 1

WILEY

About the Author

Andrew Watt wrote his first computer programs back in 1985. He is an independent consultant, experienced author, and Microsoft MVP (Most Valuable Professional) for SQL Server. His areas of interest and expertise include SQL Server 2005, Windows PowerShell, XML, and Microsoft InfoPath.

Andrew first used SQL Server in version 7.0 and was an active participant in the SQL Server 2005 beta program from August 2003.

Among the books Andrew has written, or co-written, are *SQL Server 2005 For Dummies, Beginning Regular Expressions, Beginning XML (3rd edition), Beginning RSS & Atom Programming, Professional XML (2nd edition),* and *Designing SVG Web Graphics.*

Andrew is often seen answering questions in Microsoft's SQL Server and other newsgroups. Feel free to get involved in the community there. He can be contacted direct at `SVGDeveloper@aol.com`. Due to the volume of e-mail he receives, he can't guarantee to respond to every e-mail.

Dedication

To Jonathan, Stephen, Hannah, Jeremy, Peter, and Naomi. Each a very special human being to me.

Author's Acknowledgments

Every technical book is the product of teamwork, and this book is no exception. I particularly want to thank the technical editor, Damir Bersinic, who came up with many useful comments and good suggestions for additional material, but unfortunately, there wasn't space to accept more than a few of them. It would be nice if somebody invented elastic paper. Until then, books are limited to being of a fixed size.

My thanks to Gavin Powell, who helped out with author review when other authoring commitments for Wiley meant I couldn't slice myself in half.

I would also like to thank my acquisitions editor on this book, Kyle Looper. Thanks are particularly due to Kyle for his patience as time slipped. Isn't that supposed to happen only in science fiction books?

It's been great working with Kim Darosett, my project editor, who has done so much to move the project forward to a successful conclusion. I would also like to thank Heidi Unger, copy editor, whose attention to detail picked up some of those little errors that the rest of us had missed.

Thanks to all the team. It has been a good experience for me working with you all.

Publisher's Acknowledgments

We're proud of this book; please send us your comments through our online registration form located at www.dummies.com/register/.

Some of the people who helped bring this book to market include the following:

Acquisitions, Editorial, and Media Development

Project Editor: Kim Darosett

Senior Acquisitions Editor: Steven Hayes

Copy Editor: Heidi Unger

Technical Editor: Damir Bersinic

Editorial Manager: Leah Cameron

Media Development Manager: Laura VanWinkle

Editorial Assistant: Amanda Foxworth

Sr. Editorial Assistant: Cherie Case

Cartoons: Rich Tennant (www.the5thwave.com)

Composition Services

Project Coordinator: Patrick Redmond

Layout and Graphics: Claudia Bell, Stephanie D. Jumper, Barbara Moore, Ronald Terry

Proofreaders: Aptara, Christy Pingleton

Indexer: Aptara

Anniversary Logo Design: Richard Pacifico

Publishing and Editorial for Technology Dummies

    Richard Swadley, Vice President and Executive Group Publisher

    Andy Cummings, Vice President and Publisher

    Mary Bednarek, Executive Acquisitions Director

    Mary C. Corder, Editorial Director

Publishing for Consumer Dummies

    Diane Graves Steele, Vice President and Publisher

    Joyce Pepple, Acquisitions Director

Composition Services

    Gerry Fahey, Vice President of Production Services

    Debbie Stailey, Director of Composition Services

Contents at a Glance

Table of Contents

Introduction

●●

SQL Server 2005 is Microsoft's premier relational database product. It's the big brother of Microsoft Access — and is designed for serious business or enterprise database use, depending on the edition of SQL Server 2005 that you choose. SQL Server offers you enormous flexibility when creating applications based on a SQL Server database. Unless your application requirements are unusually demanding, you can probably find an edition of SQL Server 2005 that allows you to create the application that you want.

About SQL Server 2005 Programming For Dummies

SQL Server 2005 is an immensely powerful and flexible database program, which means it's almost certain that it can do what you want it to do. But to make it perform as you want it to, you need to get up to speed in the language *Transact-SQL* that is used primarily in SQL Server 2005 to manipulate data.

The Transact-SQL language is enormously flexible. It allows you to manipulate data in a vast number of ways. In this book, I introduce you to many of the core techniques that you need to begin programming SQL Server 2005.

Here are some of the things you can do with this book:

- ✔ Discover how to use the SQL Server Management Studio and the SQLCMD utility to write Transact-SQL code.
- ✔ Create databases and tables using the CREATE DATABASE and CREATE TABLE statements.
- ✔ Retrieve data from a single SQL Server table using the SELECT statement.
- ✔ Retrieve data from multiple SQL Server tables using joins.
- ✔ Insert data into SQL Server using the INSERT statement.
- ✔ Apply constraints to limit values that can be inserted into a column, in order to ensure that your business rules are respected.

- ✔ Create stored procedures using the CREATE PROCEDURE statement.
- ✔ Create DML and DDL triggers.
- ✔ Create functions to modularize custom code.
- ✔ Create indexes to improve performance of queries.
- ✔ Handle errors using the new (to Transact-SQL) TRY . . . CATCH construct.
- ✔ Add logins and users.
- ✔ Specify permissions for logins and users.
- ✔ Encrypt sensitive data.
- ✔ Work with the new XML data type.
- ✔ Work with CLR languages.
- ✔ Create a Windows Forms application in Visual Studio 2005.

Foolish Assumptions

I have to cover a lot of ground in this book to get you up to speed with the basic programming tools and techniques in SQL Server 2005. Therefore, to make the best use of space, I assume that you've already installed SQL Server 2005. There are so many installation permutations for SQL Server 2005 that I could have spent much of this book on that topic alone. If you haven't already installed SQL Server 2005, visit http://msdn2.microsoft.com/en-us/library/ms143516.aspx to find installation instructions.

When you install SQL Server 2005, I assume that you install the database engine. If you don't, you won't be able to do much with the Transact-SQL examples shown in this book.

I also assume that either you or a colleague knows how to administer SQL Server 2005, or at least knows the basics. Failing that, I assume that you have access to somebody who can bail you out if the administrative going gets tough.

Conventions Used in This Book

In this book, all code is set off in a block and appears in a special font, like this:

```
USE pubs
SELECT title, type, pub_id
FROM titles
WHERE pub_id = '1389'
```

New terms are *italicized*. Any text that you need to type appears in **bold**. In addition, many programming terms such as functions, keywords, statements, and the like, as well as URLs, appear in a special monospaced font, like this: www.dummies.com.

What You Don't Have to Read

In much of this book, you can simply dip in and read what you need. For that to work well, you need some basic knowledge of Transact-SQL. If you're completely new to Transact-SQL, I suggest that you read at least Chapter 3 (which describes the toolset) and Chapters 4 through 7, which tell you how to retrieve and manipulate data.

How This Book Is Organized

SQL Server 2005 Programming For Dummies is split into six parts. You don't have to read the chapters sequentially, and you don't even have to read all the sections in any particular chapter. You can use the Table of Contents and the Index to find the information you need and quickly get your answer. In this section, I briefly describe what you'll find in each part.

If you're new to Transact-SQL, I suggest that you make sure to read Chapters 4 through 7, which cover core data retrieval and manipulation techniques.

Part 1: Get Started Using the SQL Server 2005 Development Environment

This part explores some fundamental issues you need to know about databases. In addition, I introduce you to the tools, particularly SQL Server Management Studio, that you use frequently in later chapters of this book.

Part II: Retrieving Data Using Transact-SQL

In this part, you discover the SELECT statement, which you use to retrieve data from a SQL Server 2005 database. You also find out how to use the FROM, WHERE, ORDER BY, and GROUP BY clauses.

This part also delves into the topics of inserting, updating, and deleting data with the INSERT, UPDATE, and DELETE statements.

Part III: Creating Databases and Database Objects with Transact-SQL

This part focuses primarily on creating databases, tables, and views. You find out how to create constraints on a column in a specified table, create a stored procedure, and create DML and DDL triggers. Additionally, I give you the low-down on creating functions, indexes, and handle errors in your Transact-SQL code.

Part IV: Programming SQL Server Security

In this part, I introduce you to SQL Server logins and users. You discover how to grant and deny permissions on database objects to logins and to users, as well as how to encrypt particularly sensitive data so that a casual user can't view it.

Part V: Beyond Transact-SQL Programming

This part goes into detail about how to use the new XML data type to store XML data in SQL Server 2005. You discover how to create an assembly to run on the Common Language Runtime inside the SQL Server 2005 database engine.

Additionally, I show you how to create a simple Windows Forms application based on SQL Server 2005 data in Visual Studio 2005. Finally, I introduce you to SQL Server Management Objects (SMO), a new object model that allows you to create applications to manage SQL Server.

Part VI: The Part of Tens

Chapter 24 focuses on some issues that, if you master them, help you to program like a pro. Chapter 25 points you to additional resources that you can use to build on what you discover in this book about SQL Server 2005 programming.

Icons Used in This Book

What's a *Dummies* book without icons pointing you in the direction of really great information that's sure to help you along your way? In this section, I briefly describe each icon I use in this book.

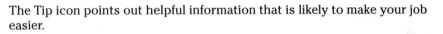

The Tip icon points out helpful information that is likely to make your job easier.

This icon marks a general interesting and useful fact — something that you might want to remember for later use.

The Warning icon highlights lurking danger. With this icon, we're telling you to pay attention and proceed with caution.

When you see this icon, you know that there's techie stuff nearby. If you're not feeling very techie, you can skip this info.

Where to Go from Here

To find out how to use SQL Server Management Studio to create Transact-SQL code, go to Chapter 3.

To discover how to retrieve data from SQL Server 2005, go to Chapter 4 and then follow on through Chapters 5 through 6 to find out about additional data retrieval techniques.

To find out how to insert, update, and delete relational data, go to Chapter 7.

To create databases, go to Chapter 8. To create tables, go to Chapter 9.

To find out how to create a simple Windows Forms application, go to Chapter 22.

Part I

Get Started Using the SQL Server 2005 Development Environment

In this part . . .

You get to discover the sheer joy of writing programs in SQL Server 2005. The fundamentals of SQL Server 2005 are presented to you in a manner typical of a *For Dummies* book, making it easy for you to absorb the basics of using the SQL Server 2005 database software.

Before beginning an in-earnest study of SQL Server 2005, you need a basic grounding of various introductory topics and essential tools you can use to work with SQL Server 2005 easily. The most significant tool in SQL Server 2005 is the Management Studio. The Management Studio organizes many tools into a single Graphical User Interface (GUI). In terms of usability, SQL Server 2005 has come of age with the inclusion and centralization of the new Management Studio software. Almost everything can be managed, monitored, investigated, and maintained from the SQL Server 2005 Management Studio interface.

Chapter 1

The Joy of SQL Server 2005 Programming

In This Chapter

▶ Choosing the right SQL Server edition for your programming goals

▶ Gathering and manipulating data

▶ Enforcing business rules for your database

▶ Ensuring SQL Server security

▶ When Transact-SQL isn't enough

SQL Server 2005 builds on the existing strengths of SQL Server 2000 to help you build applications that retrieve and manipulate data to suit your business needs. SQL Server 2005 continues to support Transact-SQL (T-SQL) as the primary language for the manipulation of relational data but has also added new functionality to allow you to work better with XML and to use .NET languages in your applications.

SQL Server 2005 allows you to flexibly create powerful applications based on its relational tables. Traditionally, you had to use Transact-SQL for those applications, and often that remains the programming language of choice.

When you create applications based on SQL Server 2005, you need to consider the goals of your programming before you do any coding. In this chapter, I discuss how you can define your programming goals and gather and manipulate data in SQL Server 2005. A well-designed SQL Server 2005 application enforces the business rules that your company has defined. If your data is automatically checked for conformity to those rules, you can have increased confidence that the application supports your business objectives.

One of the tasks that many applications carry out frequently is retrieval of data from SQL Server 2005. This process is based on the Transact-SQL SELECT statement. In Chapter 4, I show you the basics of using the SELECT statement. In Chapter 5, you discover how to use joins that select data from multiple SQL Server tables to create a result set for a query.

Security of your data is enormously important. You want to make sure that authorized users have access to the data they need and ensure that unauthorized people do not have access to your data. I discuss security in detail in Part IV.

At times, the conventional approach of using Transact-SQL with relational data isn't enough. Sometimes you want to use a .NET programming language to carry out calculations that Transact-SQL isn't well-suited for. I introduce you to using the Common Language Runtime in SQL Server 2005 in Chapter 21 and show you some techniques you can use in Visual Studio 2005 in Chapter 22. You may also want to store XML (Extensible Markup Language) data, which SQL Server 2005 supports; see Chapter 20 for details.

Deciding Which Version of SQL Server 2005 to Use

When you program with SQL Server 2005, you need to decide early on what you want your application to do. This book can't tell you what the functionality of your application ought to be; you need to decide who will use the application you create and what they need to be able to do with it. Your goals can determine which edition of SQL Server 2005 you need to buy. They can also influence which version of the Windows operating system you need: Not all editions of SQL Server 2005 run on all current Windows operating systems.

If you need detailed installation information about SQL Server 2005, check out SQL Server 2005 Books Online at http://msdn2.microsoft.com/ en-us/library/ms130214.aspx. Detailed information about installing SQL Server 2005, including which editions to install on which operating-system versions, is also available at http://msdn2.microsoft.com/ en-us/library/ms143516.aspx and related pages.

Here is a brief rundown of the various SQL Server 2005 editions:

- ✔ **Express:** If you want to simply teach yourself the basics of Transact-SQL and explore the basics of how you can use Visual Basic.NET or Visual C# in SQL Server 2005, you can use the Express Edition of SQL Server 2005.

  SQL Server 2005 Express Edition has some features that are not included in other editions of SQL Server 2005. In this book, I don't cover features that are present only in Express Edition.

  For production use, you can use SQL Server 2005 Express Edition if your application will run adequately on the limited specification and functionality of Express Edition. Check the Features Comparison Web page at `www.microsoft.com/sql/prodinfo/features/compare-features.mspx` to see if Express Edition meets your needs.

- ✔ **Developer:** The Developer Edition of SQL Server 2005 allows you to explore all the features of any edition of SQL Server 2005. The Developer Edition, which is modestly priced, is technically the same as the Enterprise Edition except that it is not licensed for production use. You can work through the example techniques shown in this book using the Developer Edition.

  Installing the Developer Edition on Windows XP Professional is a cost-effective way to learn SQL Server 2005 programming. It enables you to avoid the much larger licensing costs of Workgroup, Standard, and Enterprise Editions, while allowing you to carry out any SQL Server 2005 programming task.

- ✔ **Workgroup, Standard, and Enterprise:** If Express Edition doesn't meet your production needs, you have a choice of Workgroup, Standard, and Enterprise Editions. Again, a detailed feature-by-feature comparison is available at `www.microsoft.com/sql/prodinfo/features/compare-features.mspx`.

Gathering and Manipulating Data

In most SQL Server–based applications, you use a custom interface for data entry. Because you can create such an input application only after you know how to use Transact-SQL and have some understanding of creating applications with Visual Studio 2005, I often use SQL Server Management Studio's functionality to input data in the chapters of this book.

When it comes to manipulating data in practice, you will use custom applications. However, SQL Server Management Studio is a good teaching tool to help you find out more about the individual parts of Transact-SQL. I have written the chapters in this book in such a way that you can follow the examples by simply reading the text and looking at the figures. However, you learn much more if you open SQL Server Management Studio and run each example. By typing in the Transact-SQL or other code yourself, you are forced to pay much more careful attention to the exact syntax of each command. There is no substitute for actually coding.

Enforcing Business Rules for Your Database

SQL Server 2005 provides several ways for you to enforce the rules that you use when running your business. Constraints provide one way of enforcing some classes of business rules. A *constraint,* as the name suggests, constrains the values that can be inserted into a column. If, for example, you are running a club that allows members of 18 or more, you might constrain an age or date-of-birth column to reflect that rule. I show you how to use constraints in Chapter 10.

Another approach to enforcing business rules is the use of triggers. Typically, these are Data Modification Language (DML) triggers. A DML trigger fires in response to some specified event in a SQL Server database. For example, if somebody changes the data in a particular table, the trigger you have defined may automatically audit who made the changes and when. Having this trigger provides an audit trail that tells you who did what to your database. You find out how to use triggers in Chapter 13.

Ensuring SQL Server Security

Keeping your SQL Server data secure is hugely important. In a worst-case scenario, unauthorized access to your data could cripple your business if stored data is maliciously damaged or competitors are allowed access to confidential information.

SQL Server 2005 security is based on logins (at the SQL Server instance level) and users (at the database level). The permissions you grant or deny to a specified login or user can be applied in a very granular way. I introduce you to logins and users in Chapter 17.

In addition, schemas group database objects in ways that are convenient to allow change of ownership; for example, when an employee leaves the company.

One security concern for Web-facing database applications is *SQL injection.* A malicious user can shape the data entered in a Web form so that SQL Server treats it like Transact-SQL code. One way of minimizing that risk is to use stored procedures to process data entered into Web forms — and treat the data entered by a user as parameters to such stored procedures. If a malicious user attempts to enter malicious input, it likely won't take the form required of a stored procedure parameter, and an error will result. The bonus is that the malicious code isn't executed in a way that may damage your data or compromise its future security. I show you how to create stored procedures in Chapter 12.

When Transact-SQL Isn't Enough

Transact-SQL is an immensely powerful and flexible language for data retrieval and manipulation. But in some situations, you may want to do things with your data that traditional Transact-SQL isn't suited to doing.

In SQL Server 2000, if you wanted to carry out complex calculations, you quite possibly used extended stored procedures that had potential reliability and security concerns. In SQL Server 2005, you can use Visual Basic.NET or Visual C# to create software modules that carry out complex calculations (or any other suitable task) in ways where SQL Server security is more specifically controlled.

SQL Server 2005 provides new functionality that allows you to store XML data directly in a column in a SQL Server 2005 table by using the new xml data type. This functionality complements the existing XML-related functionality where you could break XML into relational data for storage and manipulate retrieved relational data into an XML form.

Chapter 2

Understanding Database Fundamentals

*I*n this chapter, I cover some essential aspects of the SQL Server 2005 database management system. Because this is a book about SQL Server programming, I focus primarily on things that are relevant to programming SQL Server rather than aspects of the database engine that are relevant to administration tasks. However, you need to have some basic understanding of how SQL Server 2005 works to be able to write Transact-SQL code effectively.

Getting to Know the Database Engine

SQL Server 2005 is really a suite of products. The part of the suite that handles the storage and management of data — and that controls security for your data — is the *database engine.* To be able to run the Transact-SQL code that you create later in this book, you must install the database engine when you install SQL Server 2005.

In SQL Server 2005, the database engine supports the traditional storage of data in tables (also called *relations*) and (new to SQL Server 2005) also supports the storage of XML data in a column that uses the new xml data type. In most of this book, I focus on using Transact-SQL to create structures for the storage of relational data and for manipulation of relational data; for example, retrieving data from a database. In Chapter 20, I describe how to use SQL Server to work with XML data.

When you store data in SQL Server 2005 and create an application (or applications) based on that data, you need to carry out several tasks that depend on the database engine:

- ✔ Create a database or databases.
- ✔ Add data to the database or change or delete existing data. Typically, you create a Windows Forms application or an ASP.NET application to carry out the insertion, updating, and deletion operations, depending on your business needs.
- ✔ Deploy the application or applications in ways that allow colleagues or customers to access data relevant to their needs.
- ✔ Assess the performance of the database.

The practical behavior and acceptability of an application based on SQL Server 2005 depends on several administrative activities that are beyond the scope of this book:

- ✔ Backing up your data regularly to minimize the possibility of losing important business data. You need to consider issues such as hardware failure (for example, a hard drive that fails) or external events such as a fire in the building that houses your database server(s).
- ✔ Verifying that data has backed up successfully. Storing backups in a remote location (or locations) ensures that no single disaster can destroy your business while you attempt to get SQL Server up and running again.
- ✔ Ensuring that you can restore backed up data.
- ✔ Replicating data between business sites if it's important that both sites have access to synchronized data.
- ✔ Selecting hardware that supports scalability or high performance; for example, hard-drive size and configuration, and clustering of SQL Server machines.
- ✔ Using database mirroring (new in SQL Server 2005) to allow rapid failover from a failing SQL Server machine to another SQL Server machine that has the database in the same state. That allows your application to continue on the other machine with little or no appearance of a problem to users or customers.

The database engine in SQL Server 2005 is designed to support robust, reliable processing of data. In addition, it's designed to support configurations that ensure high availability and scalability. If you're going to design database applications that support your business's interaction with its customers, the database must be accessible when customers need it. It's bad business to lose orders simply because the database isn't available when your customer wants to place an order. If you have large numbers of customers, SQL Server 2005, in its varied editions, allows you to scale the application across suitable hardware to support very large numbers of users.

Discovering Database Objects

You can think of all the *things* in a SQL Server installation as *objects*. More formally, the `Server` object is the highest-level object in the SQL Server Management Objects (SMO) hierarchy. The `Server` object corresponds to a SQL Server 2005 or SQL Server 2000 instance. SQL Server Management Studio, the management tool that is new in SQL Server 2005, uses SMO to manage SQL Server 2005 and SQL Server 2000 instances and all their contained objects. I describe how you can create a SQL Server Management Objects application in Chapter 23.

Among the objects that are descendants of the `Server` object are the following:

- **Database objects:** Each `Database` object represents a database in a SQL Server 2005, or SQL Server 2000 instance.
- **Login objects:** Each `Login` object corresponds to a login on a SQL Server instance.

Each `Database` object has a hierarchy of objects that relate to it, including

- **Table objects:** Each `Table` object represents a table in the database.
- **User objects:** Each `User` object represents a user of the database.

Just as there are objects that are descendants of the `Server` object, there are objects that are descendants of the `Database` object. When programming for SQL Server 2005, you will likely affect some or all of the following database objects. For each, I mention the SMO object and collection names in Table 2-1.

Table 2-1	SMO Objects
Collection Type	*Object Description*
Assembly	Each `SqlAssembly` object represents an assembly that has been created in the database.
Certificate	Each `Certificate` object represents a certificate for the database.
CompatibilityLevel	The `CompatibilityLevel` property allows you to get or set the compatibility level for the database.
DefaultFileGroup	Gets the default file group used by the database.
Default	Each `Default` object represents a default that you have defined on the database.
DefaultSchema	Gets the default schema for a user.
LogFile	Each `LogFile` object represents a log file defined on the database.
Owner	Gets information about the database principal that is the owner of the database.
Role	Each `DatabaseRole` object represents a role that you have defined on the database.
Schema	Each `Schema` object represents a schema that you have defined in the database.
StoredProcedure	Each `StoredProcedure` object represents a stored procedure in the database.
Table	Each `Table` object represents a table that you created in the database.
Trigger	Each `DatabaseDdlTrigger` object represents a DDL trigger that you have defined in the database.
View	Each `View` object represents a view in the database.

When you create a new database, some of the preceding properties and collections are empty; for example, the `Tables` collection. Others, for example, the `Owner` property, are defined when the database is created (although you can also change it later). When you add a table to a database, for example, a new Table object is added to the Tables collection. You can access and manipulate that table either using Transact-SQL code or using the new SQL Server Management Objects.

On a new install of SQL Server 2005, you have four system databases that you can access:

✔ master   The master database contains system tables that define the behavior of your SQL Server 2005 system. For example, each database that you add is recorded in a system table, and you can access information about those databases by executing a SELECT statement on the sys.databases catalog view. Similarly, information about all system stored procedures is stored in the master database.

✔ model   Each time you create a new database, the model database is used as the template for the database you're creating. It's possible, if you're planning to create multiple databases with the same customizations, to make those customizations once in the model database.

✔ msdb   SQL Agent uses the msdb database to store information about tasks.

✔ tempdb   The tempdb database is the scratch pad for the SQL Server system. A new tempdb database is created each time you start SQL Server 2005. Similarly, the tempdb database is discarded when you shut SQL Server down, so if you use the tempdb database to store temporary data, be aware that the data is lost when you shut down SQL Server. If you might need the data at a later time, store it in some other database.

In addition, in SQL Server 2005 there is a new resource system database that you cannot access. The resource database is used when you, for example, update SQL Server 2005 and apply a service pack.

You might want to explore the master database to improve your understanding of how SQL Server works. Be very careful that you don't make changes that could affect whether your SQL Server installation works. To be on the safe side, be sure that you have a backup that you know how to restore.

In the examples in this book, I suggest that you use three sample databases that you can install with SQL Server 2005 or download separately:

✔ AdventureWorks   The AdventureWorks database replaces the AdventureWorks2000 sample database that you could install with SQL Server 2000. This is a fairly complex sample database with lots of data that is similar to real-life data. It purports to hold data from a cycle company.

✔ pubs   The pubs database is a SQL Server 2000 sample database that I use for some examples. Its simplicity makes it a good teaching tool. The pubs database holds data about books and their authors and publishers.

✔ Northwind   The Northwind database is a SQL Server 2000 sample database that I use in some examples. It's a convenient teaching tool that holds data about a fictional trading company.

See Chapter 3 for details on installing these sample databases.

Introducing SQL Server Data Types

In SQL Server tables, it's crucially important that you store like data with other similar data. For example, never store a name in a column that is intended to store a date.

Setting a column to a value of an inappropriate data type can cause an error. Efficient running of the database engine depends on avoiding such errors. The use of SQL Server data types for each column of data in a SQL Server table is one of the mechanisms available to you to avoid inappropriate data being entered into a column.

The precise details on data types are covered in Chapter 9 where you find out about creating tables. In general, data types are divided into categories, based on their content value:

✔ **Numeric data types:** Can be anything from very small to extremely large numbers. Also included are specific formats such as monetary amounts, float point numbers, numbers with a known number of decimal points, whole numbers, and so on.

✔ **Date and time data types:** Allows the direct input of date and time values. This is usually in a default format, such as mm/dd/yyyy hh:mm, or something similar.

✔ **String data types:** Can be fixed length strings, variable length strings, or even very large text objects. Text objects may or may not be stored in binary format. Strings normally accept alphanumeric data. Alphanumeric characters are letters, numbers, and special characters (anything on your keyboard that is not a letter or a number).

✔ **Binary data types:** Typically used to store large objects, including images, sound files, video, even very large textual values like documents. SQL Server 2005 allows storage of similarly related Microsoft product types, such as directly interpretable storage of Word and Excel documents.

✔ **Unicode data types:** Unicode data simply allows for a lot more available characters. So, using Unicode standards, you can store characters for other languages such as Chinese and Cyrillic characters.

✔ **Other data types:** There are a few other very interesting data types used for specific purposes. These include things like cursors, variant data types, XML, and others:

- A *cursor* is used to programmatically access the results of a SQL statement (a query).

- A *variant* (sql_variant) allows you to store any data type, effectively allowing for an unknown data type.

- *XML* allows direct storage and access as a native XML document. In other words, you can execute standard XML functionality against the stored XML document.

Getting Familiar with SQL Server Naming Rules

SQL Server has rules for how you can name objects in a SQL Server database. The exact rules for identifiers depend on the *compatibility level* you choose for SQL Server. The *compatibility level* indicates the oldest version of SQL Server that you expect your code to work with.

To change the compatibility level of a database, use the sp_dbcmptlevel system stored procedure if you have sufficient permissions.

The name of a SQL Server database object is called its *identifier*. SQL Server has two types of identifiers — *regular identifiers* and *delimited identifiers*. A *regular identifier* follows all the rules in the following list. In SQL Server 2005 (compatibility level is 90), the following rules apply for regular identifiers:

✔ A name begins with lowercase a through z or uppercase A through Z (or in languages other than English, other letters can be used) or the underscore character (_), the "at" character (@) or the hash character (#).

✔ Subsequent characters can be letters (as described in the preceding bullet point), numeric digits, or the at sign, underscore character, hash character, or dollar sign ($).

✔ The identifier must not be a Transact-SQL reserved word.

✔ The identifier must not contain embedded spaces or special characters (that is, any character other than those previously listed).

A regular identifier for a table name might be like this:

```
MyMessages
```

The identifier begins with a letter and all the subsequent characters are letters, so it meets the criteria for a regular identifier.

You must use regular identifiers for the names of variables and of stored procedure parameters.

A *delimited identifier* need not follow the rules for regular identifiers. However, the identifier must be enclosed in paired double quotes:

```
"My Messages"
```

or paired square brackets:

```
[My Messages]
```

I suggest you avoid using delimited identifiers, if at all possible. The longer the code you write, the easier it becomes to incorrectly pair delimiters somewhere in the code with unpredictable error messages, which can be difficult to track down.

The following sample Transact-SQL, `Identifiers.sql`, shows the differences in how you have to write names with no spaces and names that include a space character. The first command creates a new database named `Chapter02`.

```
CREATE DATABASE Chapter02

USE Chapter02

CREATE TABLE MyMessages
(MessageNumber Int Primary Key,
Message varchar(500))

CREATE TABLE [My Messages]
([Message Number] Int Primary Key,
Message varchar(500))

SELECT *
FROM [My Messages]

SELECT     *
FROM My Messages
```

Other naming conventions

The company you work for might have its own naming conventions. SQL Server naming conventions should work without problems with most company naming conventions. If you're starting from scratch, you might want to apply conventions that help to remind you or your colleagues what each database object is, such as preceding a table name with tbl so that the MyMessages table is named tblMyMessages. Similarly, you might prefix a view with vw so that a view of employees might be named vwEmployees.

The USE statement ensures that the subsequent statements run in the correct database. When I create the table MyMessages, there is no space character in the table's name, so I don't have to use delimiters. However, if I call a table My Messages (with a space character), I have to delimit the table name to avoid an error message. Similarly, when I name a column Message Number (with a space character), I need to delimit that name too.

When I retrieve data from the My Messages (with a space) table, I must delimit the table name if I want the SELECT statement to run correctly. If you omit the delimiters, as in the second select statement, you see the following error message:

```
Msg 208, Level 16, State 1, Line 1
Invalid object name 'My'.
```

There are no delimiters in the statement. However, because the name has a space character, the name needs to be delimited to be a legal name. So you can rewrite the query as

```
SELECT *
FROM [My Messages]
```

or

```
SELECT *
FROM "My Messages"
```

Talking Transact-SQL

Relational database management systems, including SQL Server 2005, treat data as sets. The language for manipulating sets is specialized for manipulating data. A specialized, data-oriented language doesn't have to interact with all the functions of the operating system, for example, so limitations in such functionality aren't, generally speaking, a problem.

The Transact-SQL language is the core of programming data in SQL Server 2005. But the world of data is changing. Other languages and approaches are edging into the picture. In particular, in SQL Server 2005, new functionality enables developers to work with XML and with the .NET languages that run on the Common Language Runtime. I introduce programming with the Common Language Runtime in Chapter 21.

More and more data is exchanged between people and between machines. One increasingly used data format for data exchange (among other uses) is XML, the eXtensible Markup Language. I introduce working with XML data in Chapter 20.

Chapter 3

Getting to Know the SQL Server Toolset

To be able to program SQL Server successfully, you need to be able to use the available programming tools effectively. To help you achieve that, this chapter introduces SQL Server Management Studio and the SQLCMD utility, which you can use to write and execute Transact-SQL code. In later chapters of this book, I focus on using Transact-SQL with these tools. For other programming tasks related to SQL Server 2005, you might need to use Visual Studio 2005 or the Business Intelligence Development Studio, which I also introduce very briefly in this chapter.

Note: If you're familiar with SQL Server 2000 tools, please don't skip this chapter. The SQL Server 2005 toolset has undergone major changes.

In addition, you need to be able to configure the SQL Server system so that the code you write will run successfully. For example, the default configuration of SQL Server 2005 does not allow you to connect from a remote client machine to the server machine that is running SQL Server 2005. That's great for security but not for allowing your code to run successfully.

Much of SQL Server 2005 programming is retrieving and manipulating existing data. To that end, you need to install the SQL Server sample databases so that you can work with significantly sized data sets. In the final section of this chapter, I explain how to install the sample databases I reference in later chapters of this book.

SQL Server 2005 tools and variants

For several of the tools I describe in this chapter, Microsoft offers variants of the product for sale or download. For example, SQL Server Management Studio has a variant named SQL Server Management Studio Express, which is intended primarily for use with SQL Server 2005 Express Edition. Several variants of Visual Studio 2005 are also for sale or for download. As a result of that variation and the many possible display configurations for those tools, what you see on-screen may differ slightly from the appearance in screenshots in this chapter.

Exploring SQL Server Management Studio

SQL Server Management Studio is the main graphical tool for the administration of SQL Server. It's also the tool you use to write Transact-SQL code and scripts.

As an important administrative and programming tool for SQL Server 2005 (and any connected instances of SQL Server 2000), SQL Server Management Studio allows you to carry out the following tasks:

✔ Manage existing databases and their contained objects.

✔ Create and modify databases.

✔ Manage security, such as logins and roles.

✔ Review SQL Server logs.

✔ Create and manage replication (publication or subscription).

Launching SQL Server Management Studio

To launch SQL Server Management Studio, follow these steps:

1. **Choose Start➪Microsoft SQL Server 2005➪SQL Server Management Studio. For SQL Server Management Studio Express, select that product on the final step.**

   After you select a version of SQL Server Management Studio, you see a prompt in the Connect to Server dialog box. (See Figure 3-1.)

2. **In the Server Type drop-down list, select Database Engine.**

3. **In the Server Name drop-down list, select the name of the server (plus the instance name, if appropriate).**

For example, to connect to a default (unnamed) instance on the local machine, you can specify a period character or **localhost** in the Server Name drop-down list. To connect to a named instance on a remote server, type **ServerName\InstanceName.**

Note: *Instance* is a term commonly used to describe an instantiation or copy of a database when it is up and running on a computer.

SQL Server Management Studio frequently offers combined, drop-down and text box functionality. You either select a choice from the drop-down list or type in an appropriate value. In general, I refer to this control as a *drop-down list* rather than fully describe it as *drop-down list with text box functionality.*

4. **In the Authentication drop-down list, select Windows Authentication or SQL Server Authentication, as is appropriate for the SQL Server instance you want to connect to.**

   Figure 3-1 shows the Connect to Server dialog box when connecting to a default (unnamed) database engine server instance on the local machine using Windows authentication.

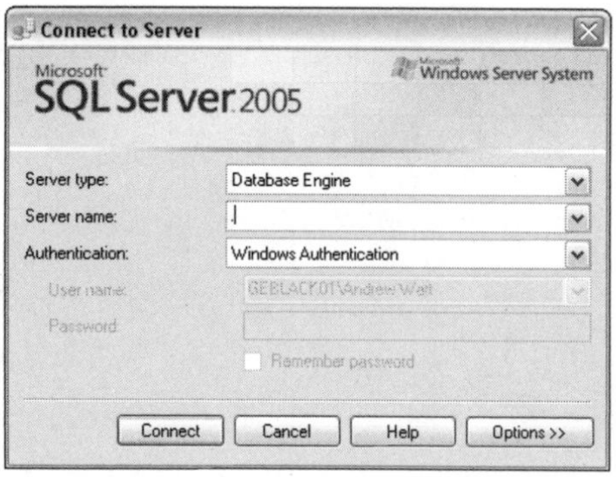

Figure 3-1:
The
Connect to
Server
dialog box.

5. **After you make the appropriate selections in the Connect to Server dialog box, click the Connect button to connect to the specified SQL Server instance.**

When you connect successfully to a SQL Server instance, you see a window similar to Figure 3-2, which I describe in the following list:

- ✔ **Registered Servers:** This pane lists the SQL Server instances available to you. You may add more SQL Server instances for display in this pane.

- ✔ **Object Explorer:** This pane displays the folders representing database objects for the SQL Server instance that you selected using the Connect to Server dialog box.

Windows and SQL Server 2005 authentication

You can connect to SQL Server 2005 using Windows Authentication. What this means is that when you run SQL Server 2005, you can connect automatically using your already verified Windows username and password. SQL Server 2005 will not ask you for a username and password. Windows Authentication prompts you for these when you first turn on your computer. When you want to enhance security, you can also be required to enter a username and password when connecting to SQL Server 2005.

✔ **Summary tab:** In the main area of the SQL Server Management Studio display, the Summary tab displays information similar to the information displayed in the Object Explorer. This is a very similar format to Windows Explorer.

New Query button

Registered Servers

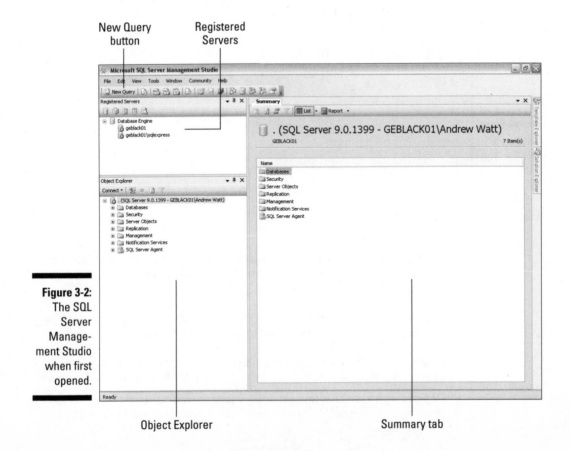

Figure 3-2: The SQL Server Management Studio when first opened.

Object Explorer

Summary tab

If there is a problem connecting to the specified server, you see an error message similar to the one shown in Figure 3-3. If you receive an error, here are some troubleshooting tips to try:

✔ Make sure that you typed the machine name and instance name (if there is one) correctly.

✔ Make sure that you used the authentication appropriate for that SQL Server instance. If the creator of an instance specified that only Windows Authentication can be used, you see an error if you attempt to connect to the server instance using SQL authentication.

✔ Check the Services Console to make sure the SQL Server instance is running. The SQL Server instance might not be configured to accept remote connections. In SQL Server Configuration Manager, described later in this chapter, check that the relevant communication protocols have been enabled.

(You can find the Services Console in the Control Panel under the Administrative Tools section.)

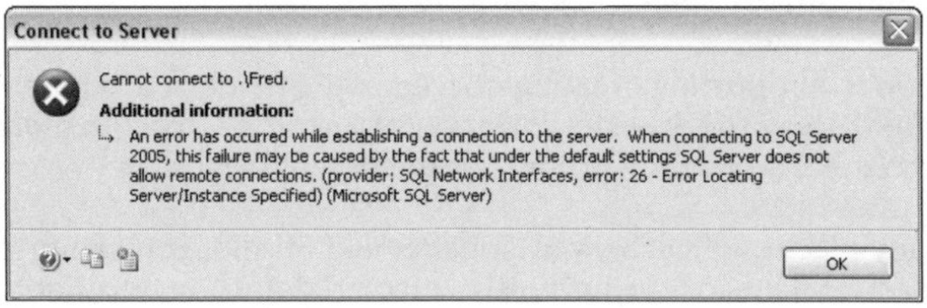

Figure 3-3:
An error message appears when connection to a SQL Server instance fails.

> **Connect to Server**
>
> ❌ Cannot connect to .\Fred.
>
> **Additional information:**
> An error has occurred while establishing a connection to the server. When connecting to SQL Server 2005, this failure may be caused by the fact that under the default settings SQL Server does not allow remote connections. (provider: SQL Network Interfaces, error: 26 - Error Locating Server/Instance Specified) (Microsoft SQL Server)
>
> OK

Discovering what types of queries you can create

When you launch SQL Server Management Studio, by default you see the Standard toolbar shown in Figure 3-4. If the Standard toolbar is not visible, choose View➪Toolbars➪Standard.

Figure 3-4:
The Standard toolbar.

Standard toolbar

To create a new Transact-SQL query, click the New Query button on the Standard toolbar. The buttons to the right of the New Query button (refer to Figure 3-4), enable you to perform the following specialized queries:

- **Database Engine Query:** Create a database engine query.
- **Analysis Services MDX Query:** Create an Analysis Services Multidimensional Expressions (MDX) query.
- **Analysis Services DMX Queries:** Create an Analysis Services Data Mining Expressions (DMX query).
- **Analysis Services XMLA Query:** Create an Analysis Services XMLA query.
- **SQL Server Mobile Query:** Create a SQL Server 2005 Mobile Edition query.

If you hover the mouse pointer over these buttons, a tooltip tells you the purpose of each button.

This book focuses on creating Transact-SQL scripts only. If the Code Editor (described in the next section) opens with an unfamiliar interface, you likely clicked one of the buttons for specialized queries in the SQL Server Management Studio. (Refer to Figure 3-4.)

In addition to supporting creating queries, the Standard toolbar contains buttons to display the Registered Servers pane, the Object Explorer, the Template Explorer, and the Properties pane.

From many places in SQL Server Management Studio, you can press F4 and the Properties pane for the currently selected database or other object appears.

Creating a simple query with the Code Editor

The Code Editor (sometimes called the *Query Pane*) is the area in SQL Server Management Studio where you type Transact-SQL code or customize a Transact-SQL template (which I describe in the next section).

When you click the New Query button to create a new Transact-SQL query, the Summary tab is hidden behind the new query pane. The name for the first query you create is, by default, SQLQuery1.sql. It appears on the page tab toward the top of the screen. You can rename the query before you type its content or when you save the query.

Type the following code to create a simple Transact-SQL query, as shown in Figure 3-5:

```
USE master
SELECT SERVERPROPERTY('Edition')
```

This query returns information about the edition of SQL Server 2005 (or SQL Server 2000) for the SQL Server instance that you've connected to. The first line of the query specifies that SQL Server connects to the `master` database, just prior to executing the query. The `SERVERPROPERTY()` function is used to return information about the edition of SQL Server you're using. Be careful to enclose the argument to the function in paired apostrophes.

To execute the Transact-SQL query, press F5 or click the Execute button on the SQL Editor toolbar. Figure 3-5 shows the result on a Developer Edition machine.

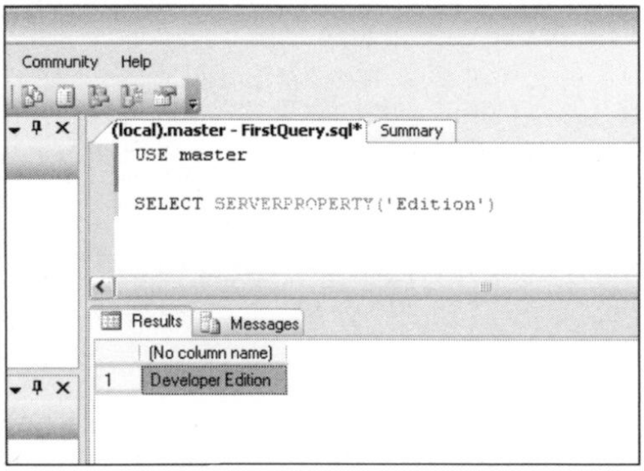

Figure 3-5:
When you execute a Transact-SQL query, the results appear in a grid.

Results appear either in a grid (refer to Figure 3-5) or as text. In addition, you see information about the number of rows affected on the Messages tab.

In Chapter 4, I show you how to use many other aspects of the `SELECT` statement used in this example.

Working with templates

Much of the time you spend writing Transact-SQL code you write your own code from scratch. However, SQL Server Management Studio gives you many prewritten pieces of code where, in effect, you can fill in the blanks. These *code templates* are located in the Template Explorer tool.

The Template Explorer might not be visible when you first open SQL Server Management Studio. To open the Template Explorer, choose View⇨Template Explorer. The Template Explorer opens, by default, on the right side of the SQL Server Management Studio.

TIP

To keep the Template Explorer open, click the horizontal pin that is located toward the top right of the Template Explorer. When the pin is vertical, the Template Explorer stays open.

The Template Explorer provides you with a broad range of templates, as you can see in Figure 3-6. The icons at the top of Template Explorer select templates for the Database Engine (called, simply, *SQL Server* in the tooltip), Analysis Services, and SQL Server Mobile.

To use a template, double-click it in the Template Explorer. The template opens in the Query Pane, as shown in Figure 3-7 for the Create Database template.

SQL Server

Analysis Services

SQL Mobile

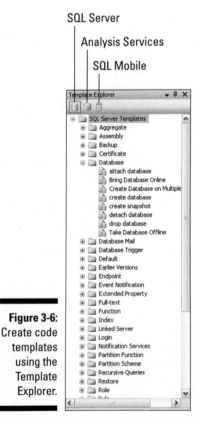

Figure 3-6:
Create code templates using the Template Explorer.

To specify values for a template parameter, choose Query⇨Specify Values for Template Parameters to open the Specify Values for Template Parameters dialog box. Click in the Value column for the parameter that you want to specify. In the Value column, type the desired value for the parameter. For example, in Figure 3-7, you would type the name of a database you want to create.

Creating a query with the Query Designer

In most of this book, I show you how to write code directly using the Transact-SQL language. If at any time you're struggling to get the syntax for a query correct, one option you can use is the Query Designer in SQL Server Management Studio. The Query Designer allows you to build a query graphically, using the tables as pictures. It also includes links between the tables, based on keys linking tables together.

To open the Query Designer, click the Query Designer button on the SQL Editor toolbar in Management Studio. If the SQL Editor toolbar is not visible, choose View⇨Toolbars⇨SQL Editor.

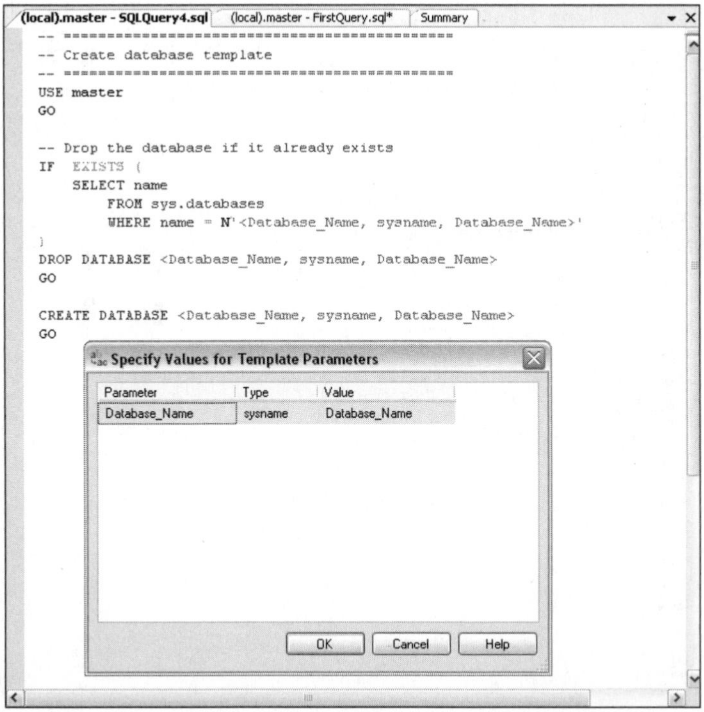

Figure 3-7:
Specify values for a template parameter.

Follow these steps to create a query using the Query Designer:

1. **Click the New Query button to open a new query.**

2. **Select the `AdventureWorks` database in the drop-down list on the toolbar and then click the Design Query in Editor button (shown in Figure 3-8).**

   The Query Designer opens, as shown in Figure 3-9.

   For more on the `AdventureWorks` sample database, see "Installing the SQL Server Sample Databases," later in this chapter.

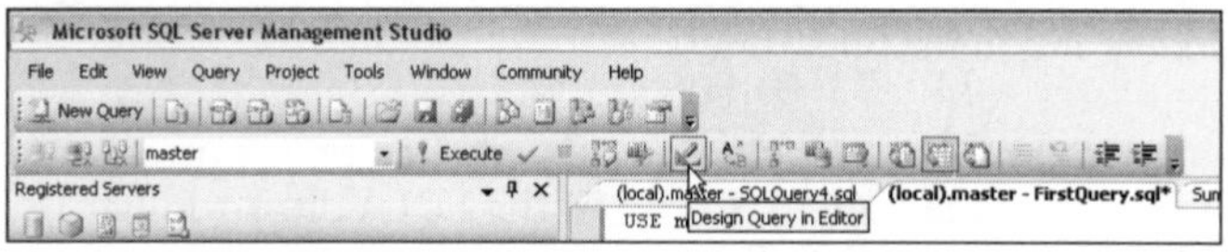

Figure 3-8:
The SQL Editor toolbar and the button to open the Query Designer.

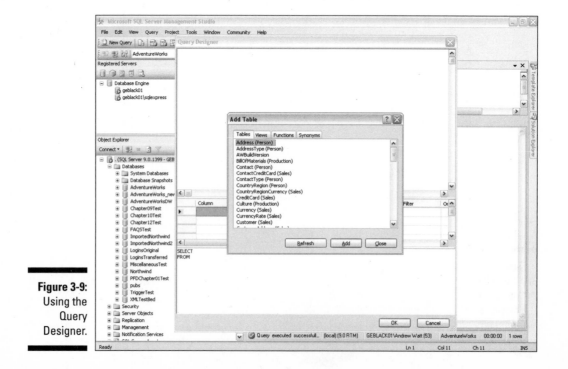

Figure 3-9:
Using the Query Designer.

3. **Select one or more tables and views from the Add Table dialog box. You then select columns in one or more tables and views.**

   Figure 3-10 shows three tables added to the design surface. Their relationships appear visually. Notice, in the lower part of the figure, that the Transact-SQL code has been created for you.

4. **Click OK to close the Query Designer.**

5. **Click the Execute button on the SQL Editor toolbar to execute the query.**

Evaluating the execution plan of a query

To see the estimated execution plan of a query, right-click the Query Editor surface and select Display Estimated Execution Plan. Figure 3-11 shows the estimated execution plan for a query similar to the one created in the Query Designer in Figure 3-10.

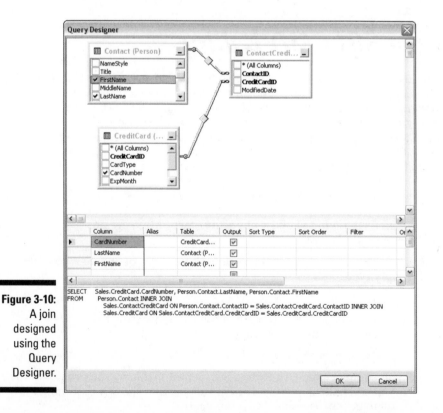

Figure 3-10: A join designed using the Query Designer.

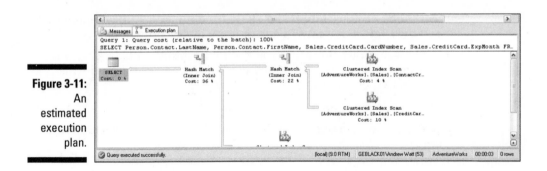

Figure 3-11:
An
estimated
execution
plan.

If a query is not performing well, or you simply want to ensure good performance, inspect the various parts of the execution plan. Pay particular attention to actions that have a high percentage showing. Of course, the percentages add to 100. If, for example, a table scan is present and takes up a significant percentage of the estimated execution plan, this condition strongly suggests that you need to create an index.

Using the SQLCMD Utility

The SQLCMD utility is a new command line tool in SQL Server 2005 that allows you to execute Transact-SQL statements interactively or to execute prewritten Transact-SQL scripts. How useful you find SQLCMD depends on how good your understanding of Transact-SQL is. Everything you do with SQLCMD depends on the correct crafting of Transact-SQL statements. You can either write the code yourself or execute Transact-SQL scripts that somebody else has written.

To check whether SQLCMD is installed, follow these steps:

1. **Open a command shell by choosing Start⇨All Programs⇨Accessories⇨ Command Prompt.**

2. **If you're connecting to a local default instance of SQL Server 2005, simply type**

   ```
   SQLCMD
   ```

   at the command line. Alternatively, when connecting to a named instance on a remote server type, type

   ```
   SQLCMD -S serverName\instanceName
   ```

   If you connect successfully to a SQL Server instance, the prompt in the command shell changes to 1>. This means that the SQLCMD utility is ready to accept Transact-SQL commands.

To signal that you have finished entering Transact-SQL statements, type **GO** on the command line. When you press the Enter key, the Transact-SQL commands are executed:

```
USE master
SELECT * FROM Information_schema.tables
GO
```

The switches you use when starting the SQLCMD utility are case-sensitive.

To display help for the SQLCMD utility, type

```
sqlcmd -?
```

Getting to Know the SQL Server Configuration Manager

Strictly speaking, SQL Server Configuration Manager is an administrator's tool. But the default settings of SQL Server 2005 after installation might stop your code from working at all, so it's important that you have some understanding of how to use it, at least in a development setting. In this section, I briefly describe the SQL Server Configuration Manager and show you how to make some frequently needed configuration tweaks.

To start SQL Server Configuration Manager, choose Start⇨All Programs⇨ Microsoft SQL Server 2005⇨Configuration Tools⇨SQL Server Configuration Manager. Figure 3-12 shows SQL Server Configuration Manager with the nodes (the + signs) in the left pane expanded.

You use SQL Server Configuration Manager to manage services related to SQL Server. In Figure 3-12, the SQL Server 2005 Services node is selected. In the right pane, you can see information about each of the services associated with the instance of SQL Server 2005.

Right-clicking a service displays options to Start, Stop, or Restart a service, as appropriate to the existing state of the service. If you select Properties when right-clicking a service, the Properties dialog box appears. You can configure the behavior of the service, including whether it starts automatically.

To configure network protocols, select a SQL Server instance under the SQL Server 2005 Network Configuration node in the left pane. You see the current configuration in the right pane, as shown in Figure 3-13. To connect remotely to the chosen SQL Server 2005 instance, you need to enable TCP/IP or Named Pipes, depending on your situation.

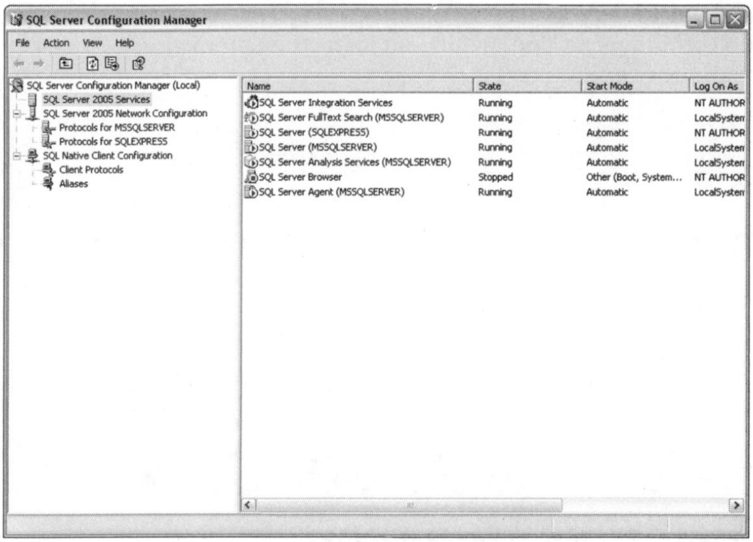

Figure 3-12:
Open SQL
Server
Configu-
ration
Manager to
view
information
about
associated
services.

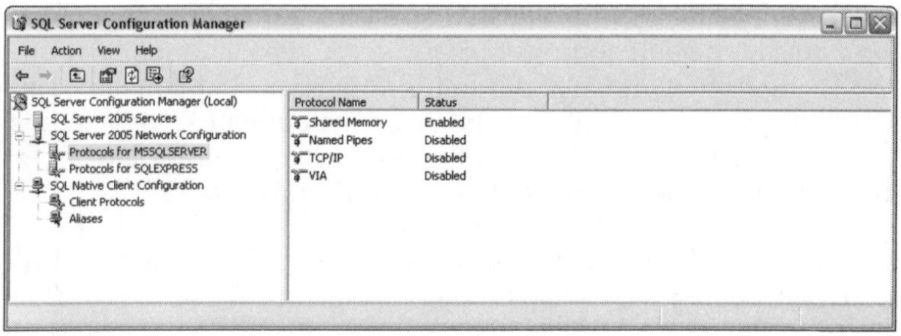

Figure 3-13:
Configuring
network
protocols.

To change the setting for a network protocol, right-click the network protocol of interest and select Enable or Disable, as appropriate.

Using Other SQL Server Programming Tools

In this section, I briefly describe two more specialized programming tools that you may use when programming SQL Server 2005.

Visual Studio 2005

The addition of the Common Language Runtime to the SQL Server 2005 database engine means that developers who use Visual Studio can develop or make use of database objects using .NET languages such as Visual C# and Visual Basic 2005.

I show you how to use Visual Studio 2005 to create a database project in Chapter 22.

The Business Intelligence Development Studio

The Business Intelligence Development Studio (BIDS) is a powerful developer tool for SQL Server 2005, but most of its capabilities lie outside the scope of this book. Using BIDS, you can create projects for SQL Server Integration Services, SQL Server Analysis Services, and SQL Server Reporting Services. The SQL Server business intelligence paradigm is as follows:

- ✔ Integrate (using Integration Services)
- ✔ Analyze (using Analysis Services)
- ✔ Report (using Reporting Services)

I cover using the Business Intelligence Development Studio in the next section.

Accessing SQL Server Books Online (BOL)

SQL Server 2005 is, really, a suite of programs whose scope is enormous. There is no way that a printed book of this size can cover every nuance of every aspect of SQL Server. Even a single aspect, such as SQL Server programming, has so many possible uses and constraints that you need access to comprehensive information.

SQL Server 2005 Books Online, often abbreviated to BOL, is the main, installable, official documentation portal for information about SQL Server 2005. Specifically, BOL offers a great deal of useful reference information and further detail on the Transact-SQL language and many other topics covered in this book.

There is also a version of Books Online available online. At the time of writing, the current version is located at `http://msdn2.microsoft.com/en-us/library/ms130214.aspx`.

If you want to install SQL Server 2005 Books Online, you must make an explicit choice when installing SQL Server. If you want to install only SQL Server 2005 Books Online, select the Advanced option for feature installation and navigate the tree of installation options to specify that you want to install BOL. If you don't install BOL initially, you can run the Setup utility again and elect to install BOL at that time.

To start SQL Server Books Online, choose Start➪All Programs➪Microsoft SQL Server 2005➪Documentation and Tutorials➪SQL Server Books Online. Figure 3-14 shows the initial appearance when you launch Books Online.

The exact appearance might vary slightly. In Figure 3-14, notice the buttons for Contents, Index, and Help Favorites. When you click the Contents button, you see a hierarchy of nodes arranged by topic, as shown in Figure 3-15.

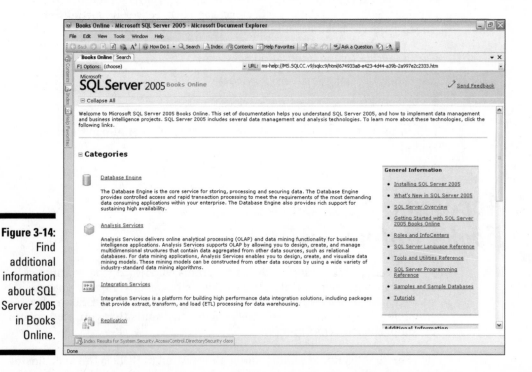

Figure 3-14: Find additional information about SQL Server 2005 in Books Online.

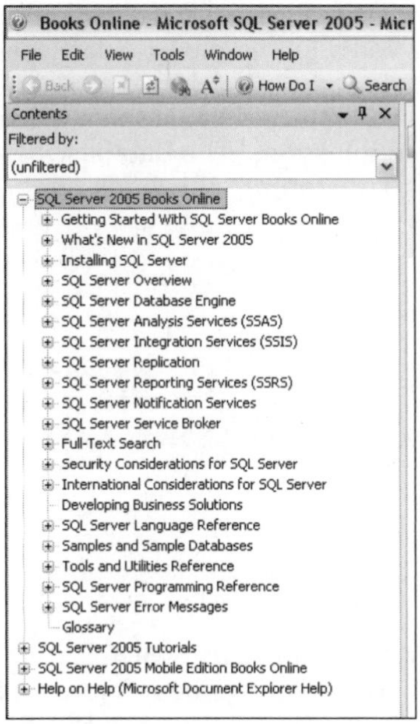

Figure 3-15:
View the
Contents of
SQL Server
Books
Online.

A drop-down list near the top of the Contents pane allows you to filter the displayed information by SQL Server component technology. The available filter options are

✔ SQL Server 2005

✔ SQL Server Analysis Services

✔ SQL Server Data Mining

✔ SQL Server Database Engine

✔ SQL Server Express

✔ SQL Server Integration Services

✔ SQL Server Mobile

✔ SQL Server Notification Services

✔ SQL Server Replication

✔ SQL Server Reporting Services

For the purposes of this book, the SQL Server Database Engine filter is the one you're most likely to find useful. If you're using this book to program SQL Server Express Edition, you might find the SQL Server Express option helpful, too.

Buttons on the Standard toolbar, shown in Figure 3-16, allow you to carry out several, useful tasks. Here are a few you might find particularly useful:

✔ **How Do I:** This button allows you to access help topics written specifically to answer frequently asked questions. The Database Services option is particularly relevant to the topic of this book.

Figure 3-16:
The
Standard
toolbar in
SQL Server
Books
Online.

Standard toolbar

✔ **Search:** Use this button to search the contents of SQL Server Books Online. You can filter the search by selecting one or more topic areas. Particularly relevant to the topics of this book are the SQL Server Database Engine and Transact-SQL filter options in the Technology drop-down list.

✔ **Sync with Table of Contents:** The button to the left of the Ask a Question button allows you to synchronize with the Contents pane. This can be very useful when you find an interesting help page after carrying out a search and want to view related help pages. This button is grayed out if you have not selected a Help topic.

Installing the SQL Server Sample Databases

There is no perfect substitute for working with real data. But because real data is often commercially confidential data, you might find it necessary to work with sample data. The SQL Server 2005 installation discs come with a new, sample database, AdventureWorks, which is much more like real-life data than the sample databases that were used with SQL Server 2000 — the Northwind and pubs databases.

I use all three Microsoft sample databases in this book. If you have already installed the AdventureWorks, Northwind, and pubs sample databases, you can skip the rest of this section.

AdventureWorks

To install the AdventureWorks database, select the Advanced button when running Setup. Navigate down the tree of installation options and select the AdventureWorks sample databases for installation.

You also need to carry out a second step to be able to use the sample databases. Choose Start⇨All Programs⇨Microsoft SQL Server 2005⇨Documentation and Tutorials⇨Samples⇨Microsoft SQL Server 2005 Samples. When the installer starts, follow the on-screen instructions.

If you follow along with the example Transact-SQL code in this book, you can potentially be making various changes to the AdventureWorks database. I suggest that you make a copy of the AdventureWorks database to work on. To do that using SQL Server Management Studio, follow these steps:

1. **Open Object Explorer, if necessary, in SQL Server Management Studio by choosing View⇨Object Explorer.**

2. **Expand the node for the relevant SQL Server 2005 instance and then expand the Databases node.**

3. **Right-click the AdventureWorks node and choose Tasks⇨Copy Database.**

   The Copy Database Wizard runs.

4. **Click Next.**

5. **On the Select a Source Server screen, specify the location of the server and the authentication method to use. Click Next.**

6. **Select a destination server and click Next.**

7. **On the Select a Transfer Method screen, select a method to use to copy the database. (Because this is only sample data, you can use the faster detach and attach method.) Click Next.**

8. **On the Select Databases screen, enable the check box for the AdventureWorks database. Click Next.**

9. **On the Configure Destination Database screen, name the copy AdventureWorks_new. Click Next, click Next, and click Finish.**

The package you create using the Copy Database Wizard runs and creates a copy of the AdventureWorks database. Use the copy of the database when trying out Transact-SQL code so that the original stays intact.

Northwind and pubs

The Northwind and pubs databases, unlike the AdventureWorks database, aren't on the SQL Server 2005 discs. To download the installers for the Northwind and pubs databases, go here:

```
www.microsoft.com/downloads/details.aspx?FamilyID=06616212-0356-46A0-8DA2-
          EEBC53A68034&displaylang=en
```

The file you want is SQL2000SampleDb.msi.

Run the installer to install the Northwind and pubs databases in your SQL Server 2005 installation.

After you successfully install the sample databases, you're ready to try out the various forms of the SELECT statement that I describe in Chapter 4.

Part II
Retrieving Data Using Transact-SQL

The 5th Wave   By Rich Tennant

"We're here to clean the code."

In this part . . .

This part discusses how to read and change data in a database. Reading data from a database is called *querying*. A query quite literally *queries* the data, asking a question of the database. Changing data in a database uses specialized statements for adding new data, or changing and deleting existing data.

A query is made up of various parts, the principal parts being the SELECT clause and the FROM clause. In other words, you SELECT columns FROM tables. You can refine queries using a WHERE clause to filter out data, an ORDER BY clause to sort data, and a GROUP BY clause to summarize data. You can also merge data by reading from more than one table at once. This is known as a *join* because it joins data from two tables into a single query. Other more advanced types of queries include *subqueries*, which are queries called from other queries. You can change data in the database using the INSERT, UPDATE, and DELETE statements.

Chapter 4

Retrieving Data Using the SELECT Statement

*T*he most common action on a database is retrieving data. Retrieving data from a database is why you store data in the first place. You want to make use of the data in different ways, and storing it in a relational database management system such as SQL Server 2005 allows you to access your data in many useful ways.

The Transact-SQL SELECT statement is the statement you use to retrieve data. The SELECT statement is powerful and flexible. In this chapter, I show you how to use the SELECT statement and show you several commonly used clauses — the FROM clause, the WHERE clause, the GROUP BY clause, and the ORDER BY clause.

The simplest use of the SELECT statement is to retrieve data from a single table. In real life, you don't do that very often from a relational database, but it's a useful way to explore the clauses that you can use in the SELECT statement. To retrieve data from multiple tables using the SELECT statement means you have to use *joins*. A *join* is the term for selecting data from two (or more) tables based on some specified criterion. I show you how to use joins in Chapter 5.

I use Transact-SQL keywords, such as SELECT, in uppercase letters. You
don't need to do that, but I find it convenient because it helps me easily see
the structure of a complex query.

Exploring Your Database's Objects

To work with any Transact-SQL statement, you need to understand the characteristics of objects in your databases. You need to know which database
contains the data you want to access. You also need to know which table or
view contains the desired data. In addition, to focus data retrieval on relevant
columns, you also need to know the column names so that you can specify
them when you create a SELECT query.

To view the databases on a SQL Server 2000 or 2005 instance using SQL
Server Management Studio, follow these steps:

1. **Open SQL Server Management Studio.**

   Choose Start⇨All Programs⇨Microsoft SQL Server 2005⇨SQL Server
   Management Studio.

2. **If the Registered Servers pane isn't visible, choose View⇨Registered
   Servers to display it.**

3. **Click the Database Engine icon on the toolbar in the Registered
   Servers pane.**

4. **If the desired SQL Server instance is displayed in the Registered
   Servers pane, skip to Step 10. If not, right-click Database Engine to
   register a new SQL Server instance. In the context menu, choose
   New⇨Server Registration, as shown in Figure 4-1.**

   The New Server Registration dialog box, shown in Figure 4-2, opens.

5. **Enter the name for the SQL Server instance in the Server name drop-
   down list.**

   To connect to the default instance on the local machine, type a single .
   (period character). To connect to a named instance on the local machine,
   type .*InstanceName*. To connect to a default instance on a remote
   machine, type the server name. To connect to a named instance on a
   remote machine, type *ServerName\InstanceName*.

6. **Specify the authentication method in the Authentication drop-down
   list.**

7. **If desired, edit the text automatically entered in the Registered Server
   Name text box.**

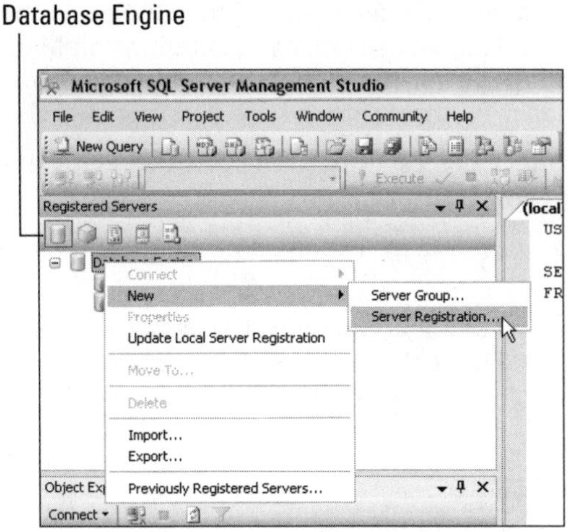

Database Engine

Figure 4-1:
Registering
a new SQL
Server
instance
in the
Registered
Servers
pane.

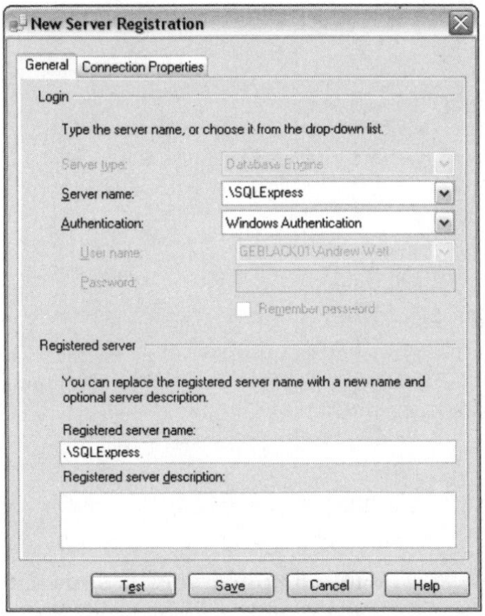

Figure 4-2:
Specifying
information
about a new
registered
server.

8. **Click the Test button to check that you can connect to the desired SQL Server instance.**

   If you get an error message, check to make sure that you have typed the server name and/or instance name correctly.

If you're trying to connect to a newly installed SQL Server instance and you're having problems, open SQL Server Configuration Manager. Verify that the network protocols for the instance are enabled using SQL Server Configuration Manager on the server where you installed the instance.

9. **When you can connect successfully to the desired SQL Server instance, click the Save button.**

   The SQL Server instance is then displayed in the Registered Servers pane.

10. **Right-click the desired instance name in the Registered Servers pane and choose Connect⇨Object Explorer in the context menu, as shown in Figure 4-3.**

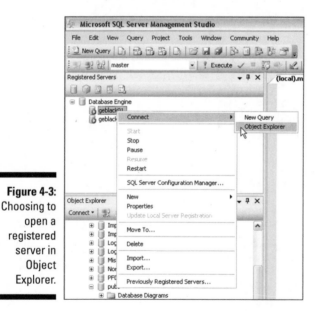

Figure 4-3: Choosing to open a registered server in Object Explorer.

The Object Explorer opens. The initial appearance is shown in Figure 4-4.

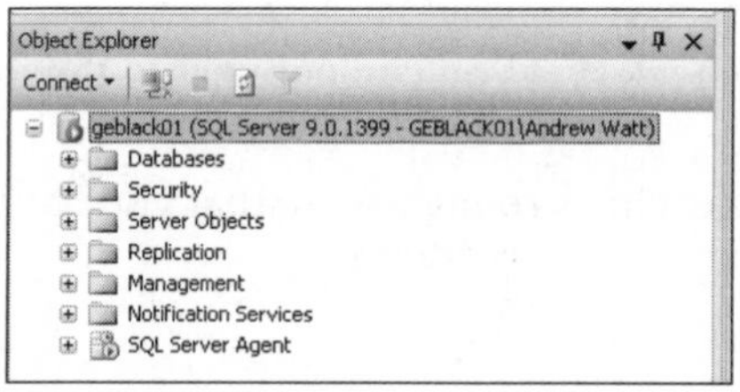

Figure 4-4: The initial appearance of the Object Explorer.

11. To explore the database objects, navigate to the column names by expanding the nodes (the + signs) in the following order: Databases⇨ [*database name*]⇨Tables⇨[*table name*]. Explore the table objects as desired.

For example, for the pubs database, follow this path to explore the columns in the Publishers table: Databases⇨Pubs⇨Tables⇨dbo.publishers folder⇨ Columns. You should see an appearance similar to Figure 4-5. You might need to scroll up or down in the Object Explorer to see all the information shown in Figure 4-5.

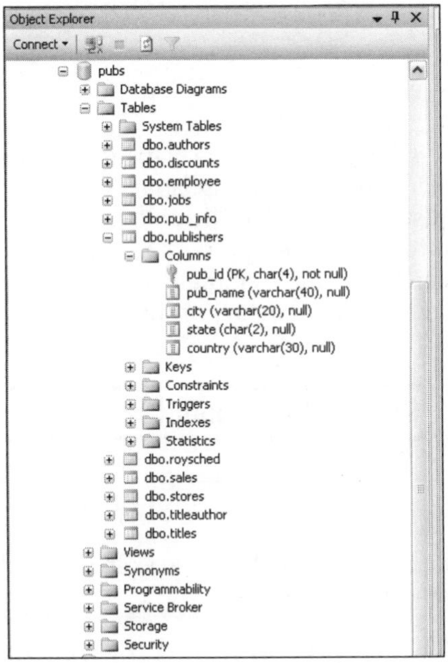

Figure 4-5:
Displaying information about the columns of the Publishers table in the pubs database.

In the example in the next section, the aim is to retrieve the name and country of the publishers in the pubs database. Before you can do this retrieval, you need to inspect the information about columns in the dbo.publishers table to determine the names of the relevant columns.

This technique is also useful when you come to insert, update, or delete information from SQL Server 2005 databases. In that case, you often need to know the *data type* of the data in the columns you work with.

Introducing the SELECT Statement

The SELECT statement is the Transact-SQL statement that retrieves, or selects, data from a SQL Server database.

The following summarizes the forms that the SELECT statement can take:

```
SELECT [ALL | DISTINCT]
[TOP expression]
[<select_list>]
[FROM <table_source>]
[WHERE <search_condition>]
[GROUP BY group_by_expression]
[HAVING search_condition]
[ORDER BY order_by_expression]
```

The paired square brackets ([ ]) contain optional clauses. As you can see in the preceding partial definition, almost everything, apart from the SELECT statement itself, is optional. This illustrates how flexible the SELECT statement can be. It also shows you that you need to think carefully about how you use the SELECT statement because you have so many options available to you. Table 4-1 describes the function of each part of the SELECT statement.

Table 4-1	SELECT Statement Clauses
Clause	*What It Does*
FROM	Specifies one or more tables to read data from.
WHERE	Applies one or more filters rows accessed, retrieving only wanted rows (or removing unwanted rows).
ORDER BY	Resorts rows into a specific order.
GROUP BY	Summarizes (or aggregates) rows into fewer rows, based on some aggregate, such as a SUM function to add rows together for duplicated values.
HAVING	Works similar to the WHERE clause, applying a filtering mechanism to rows. The HAVING clause applies to aggregated rows returned from the GROUP BY clause. The WHERE clause applies to rows returned from SELECT and FROM clauses.

In the remainder of the chapter, I explain in detail how to use the FROM, WHERE, ORDER BY, GROUP BY, HAVING and WITH clauses, in tandem with the SELECT statement.

Using the FROM Clause

A simple use of the SELECT statement is to select one or more columns from a single SQL Server table. The following Transact-SQL code retrieves the name and country of publishers stored in the dbo.publishers table of the pubs database:

```
USE pubs

SELECT pub_name, country
FROM dbo.publishers
```

In the first line, the USE statement specifies which database the following Transact-SQL code is to execute relative to. If you don't specify a database in a USE statement, the code executes against the most recently used database or the default database. If you include a USE statement in your Transact-SQL code, it removes any ambiguity about the database that it will execute against. Unless you want to create a general-purpose Transact-SQL script, I suggest you use the USE statement routinely.

Using a USE statement regularly makes sure that your Transact-SQL code runs against the specified database.

The next line of code

```
SELECT pub_name, country
```

specifies that you select two, named columns, pub_name and country. All other columns are ignored.

The FROM clause

```
FROM dbo.publishers
```

specifies that the columns selected in the select list of the SELECT statement come from the dbo.publishers table.

To execute the code, press the F5 key or click the Execute button. Figure 4-6 shows the results of executing the code.

In Figure 4-6, the results are displayed in a grid. If you prefer the results to be displayed as text, choose Tools⇨Options, and the Options dialog box opens. Choose Query Results⇨SQL Server and select Results to Text in the Default Destination for Results drop-down list shown in Figure 4-7.

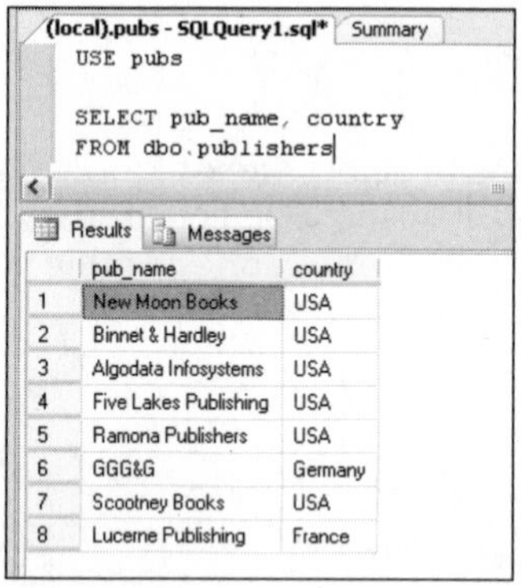

Figure 4-6:
Using the SELECT statement to select specified columns from a single table.

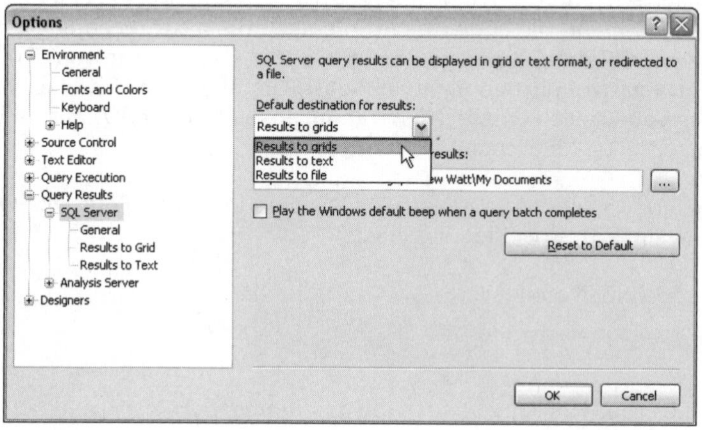

```
(local).pubs - SQLQuery1.sql*   Summary
    USE pubs

    SELECT pub_name, country
    FROM dbo.publishers
```

	pub_name	country
1	New Moon Books	USA
2	Binnet & Hardley	USA
3	Algodata Infosystems	USA
4	Five Lakes Publishing	USA
5	Ramona Publishers	USA
6	GGG&G	Germany
7	Scootney Books	USA
8	Lucerne Publishing	France

Figure 4-7:
Modifying the destination for query results.

To select all the columns in a table, use the * wildcard as the value of the select list. The following code displays all columns in the dbo.publishers table:

```
USE pubs

SELECT *
FROM dbo.publishers
```

Using the * wildcard allows you to quickly display all columns from a table. Once you see what columns are available, you can choose a more specific select list.

The select list can be any of the following:

- ✔ Database table
- ✔ Database view
- ✔ Derived table
- ✔ Joined table

I show you how to use joins in Chapter 5.

In many situations, using the FROM clause as the only clause in a SELECT statement returns potentially enormous amounts of unwanted data. You often need to filter the data returned from a query. That's when you use the WHERE clause, which I describe in the next section.

The WHERE Clause

The WHERE clause filters data returned by a SELECT statement. The WHERE clause allows you to use many comparison operators, logical operators, and other keywords to filter data in a wide range of ways.

To filter data on publishers so that only publishers based in the USA are displayed, add a WHERE clause:

```
USE pubs

SELECT pub_name, country
FROM dbo.publishers
WHERE country = 'USA'
```

Figure 4-8 shows the results returned by the query. Notice that only USA-based publishers are displayed.

The value of the WHERE clause tests the value of the country column for equality. For each publisher, the value of the country column is tested against the value 'USA'. If it equals 'USA', the row is included in the resultset.

By default, SQL Server ignores case in WHERE clause filters. However, this can be changed. This is not the case for other relational databases, and ignoring case could cause serious confusion in many circumstances. For example, *US* could mean *United States* or *us,* as in a group of people talking about themselves.

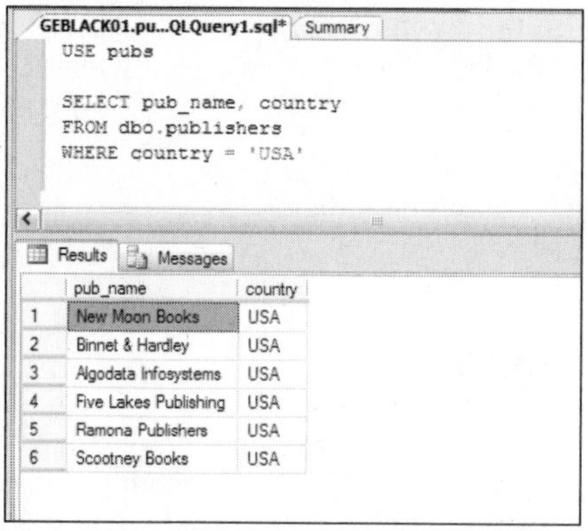

Figure 4-8:
Filtering
results
using a
simple
WHERE
clause.

The following sections explain how you use operators and keywords to filter data in a WHERE clause.

Using comparison operators

Table 4-2 lists which comparison operators you can use in a WHERE clause.

Table 4-2	Comparison Operators
Operator	*What It Tests For*
=	Equality
<>	Inequality
! =	Inequality (an alternative way of writing <>). Inequality is extremely inefficient because searching for what is not there requires scanning through everything.
>	The left expression being greater than the right expression.
<	The left expression being less than the right expression.
>=	The left expression being greater than or equal to the right expression.
<=	The left expression being less than or equal to the right expression.

The operators that test for some type of inequality can be used with character- or numeric-value data types. For example, to display publishers for which the `country` comes alphabetically before H, use the following command:

```
USE pubs

SELECT pub_name, country
FROM dbo.publishers
WHERE country < 'H'
```

To retrieve information about publishers for whom the `pub_id` is greater than 9000, use the following query:

```
USE pubs

SELECT *
FROM dbo.publishers
WHERE pub_id > 9000
```

Figure 4-9 shows the results of executing the two preceding queries.

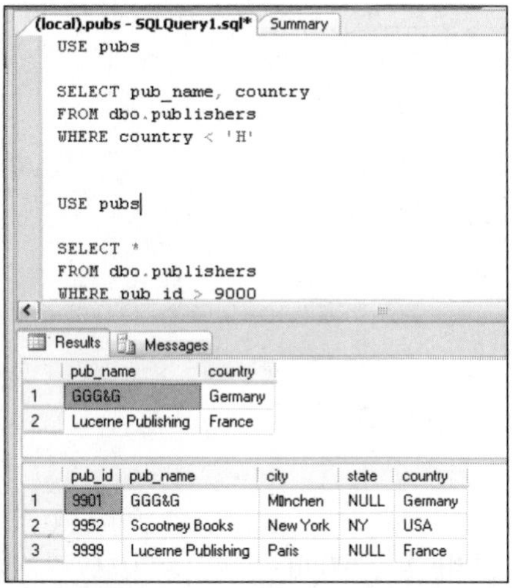

Figure 4-9: Using comparison operators other than for equality.

Combining comparison operators with AND, OR, or NOT

You can combine comparison operators using the logical operators in Table 4-3.

Table 4-3 Logical Operators

Operator	*What It Does*
AND	Returns a row only if both conditions are true.
OR	Returns a row if either condition is true.
NOT	Negates the tested condition.

To retrieve information on publishers where the value in the `country` column is either `USA` or `Germany`, you can use the `OR` operator in the following query:

```
USE pubs

SELECT *
FROM dbo.publishers
WHERE country = 'USA' OR country = 'Germany'
```

Figure 4-10 shows the results of executing the preceding query.

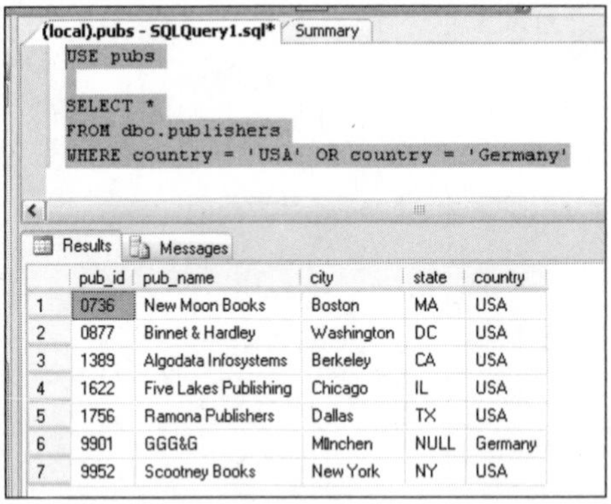

	pub_id	pub_name	city	state	country
1	0736	New Moon Books	Boston	MA	USA
2	0877	Binnet & Hardley	Washington	DC	USA
3	1389	Algodata Infosystems	Berkeley	CA	USA
4	1622	Five Lakes Publishing	Chicago	IL	USA
5	1756	Ramona Publishers	Dallas	TX	USA
6	9901	GGG&G	M nchen	NULL	Germany
7	9952	Scootney Books	New York	NY	USA

Figure 4-10: Using an OR operator in a WHERE clause.

I use the `AND` logical operator in the following example. To retrieve information about publishers whose `pub_id` is greater than `1000` and whose state is greater than `N`, use the following command:

```
USE pubs

SELECT *
FROM dbo.publishers
WHERE pub_id > 1000 AND state > 'N'
```

Figure 4-11 shows the results of executing the preceding query with and without the WHERE clause, to illustrate the effect of using the WHERE clause and including the AND logical operator.

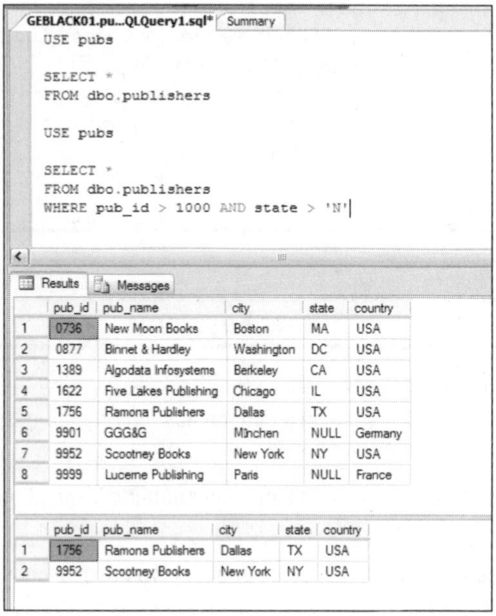

Figure 4-11:
Using
the AND
operator in
a WHERE
clause.

In Figure 4-11, each row in the resultset has a value greater than 1000 in the pub_id column and a value greater than N in the state column. In the second row, the value NY in the state column is greater than N because it would follow N in an alphabetically sorted list. If the WHERE clause is removed from the query, a lot more rows would be returned because the restricting filter is removed.

Using other keywords with the WHERE clause

In addition to the operators already described in this section, you can use other keywords in the FROM clause, as shown in Table 4-4.

What is an escape character?

Some specialized characters are interpreted as commands. For example, an asterisk (*) character is often used to represent any character. So, a * character is called a wildcard character. If a string in a column contains a * character, you don't want the database engine to interpret the * in your string as a wildcard, but to simply return * as a part of the string. The way to prevent interpretation is to *escape* the wildcard character, which prevents database engine interpretation and simply treats the * character as a literal value. The term *escape sequence* is applied to multiple characters when they are all escaped at once, such as three consecutive asterisks (***).

Table 4-4	Other Keywords
Keyword	*What It Does*
BETWEEN	Tests whether the value in a column lies between two, specified values. The range is inclusive.
CONTAINS	Tests whether the value in a column contains a specified sequence of characters.
ESCAPE	Escapes a wildcard character, enabling you to search for a literal occurrence of a wildcard character.
FREETEXT	Tests for meaning — rather than a literal match — in a character-based column.
LIKE	Uses wildcards to test similarity to a column value.

The CONTAINS and FREETEXT keywords depend on a table being full-text indexed. I show you how to do that after the next example.

BETWEEN

The following example illustrates use of the BETWEEN keyword. Notice that the resultset contains values that are exact matches for the values specified. In other words, the range is inclusive.

```
USE pubs

SELECT *
FROM dbo.publishers
WHERE pub_id BETWEEN 9901 AND 9999
```

Figure 4-12 illustrates the results of running the preceding query.

Figure 4-12:
Using the
BETWEEN
keyword in
a WHERE
clause.

CONTAINS

The following example returns information about publishers whose country contains the character sequence 'USA'.

```
USE pubs

SELECT *
FROM dbo.publishers
WHERE CONTAINS (country, 'USA')
```

In the dbo.publishers tables, this means that rows for publishers from the United States are returned, as shown in Figure 4-13.

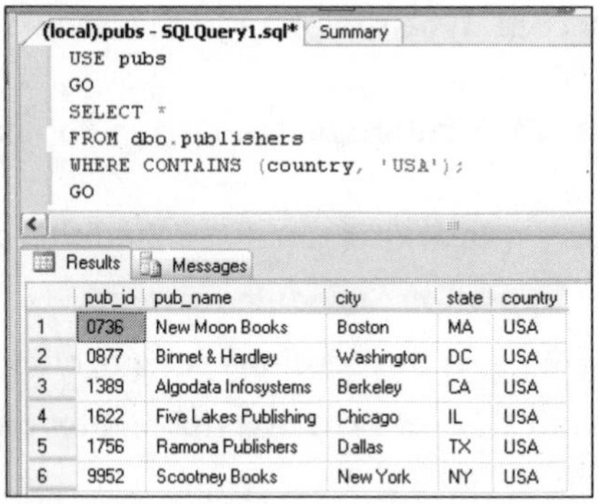

Figure 4-13:
Using
CONTAINS
in a WHERE
clause.

Before you can run the preceding query, you must enable full-text searching for the table. To do that, follow these steps:

1. **In Object Explorer, right-click the dbo.publishers table. Choose Full-Text Index⇨Define Full-Text Index.**

   The Full-Text Indexing Wizard opens.

2. **Click Next on the splash screen. Click Next on the Select and Index screen.**

3. **On the Select Table Columns screen, enable the check box for the** country **column, as shown in Figure 4-14. Click Next.**

   The aim is to be able to use full-text search in the country column.

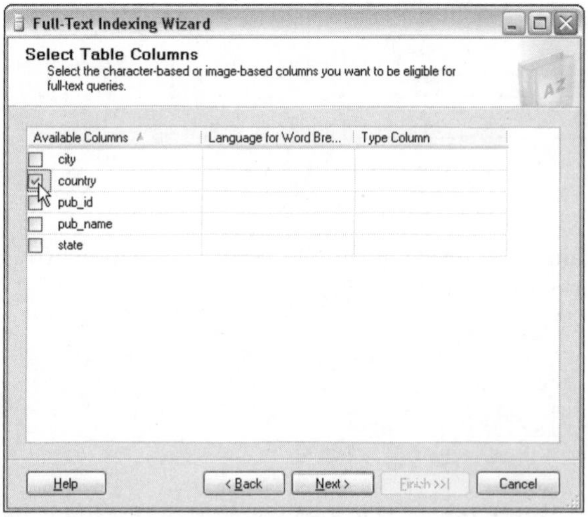

Figure 4-14:
Select the column(s) to create a full-text index on.

4. **Click Next on the Select Change Tracking screen.**

5. **On the Select a Catalog screen, type** Chapter4 **in the Name text box. Click Next.**

6. **Click the New Catalog Schedule button on the Define Population Schedules screen.**

7. **Click OK on the New Full-Text Indexing Catalog Schedule screen.**

8. **Click Next on the Define Population Schedules screen.**

9. **On the Full-Text Indexing Wizard Descriptions screen, click Finish.**

10. **When the Full-Text Indexing Wizard Progress dialog box completes successfully, click Close.**

Now, execute the preceding query. You should see a resultset, as shown in Figure 4-13.

LIKE

Another option in the WHERE clause is to use the LIKE keyword, which allows you to look for values using wildcard matching. The available wildcards are listed in Table 4-5.

Table 4-5	Wildcards
Wildcard	**What It Matches**
%	A string of zero or more characters
_	A single character
[ ]	One of the characters inside the square brackets — characters inside the square brackets are a *character class*
* [^]	Any character not inside the square brackets

The following query matches publishers where the city begins with B. The LIKE keyword is used, and B% means B followed by zero or more other characters. In other words, words that begin with B.

```
USE pubs

SELECT *
FROM dbo.publishers
WHERE city LIKE 'B%'
```

Figure 4-15 shows the results of executing the preceding query.

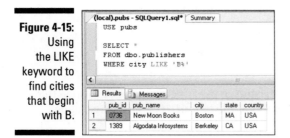

Figure 4-15:
Using
the LIKE
keyword to
find cities
that begin
with B.

The following query finds publishers where the state begins with M or N.

```
USE pubs

SELECT *
FROM dbo.publishers
WHERE state LIKE '[MN]%'
```

Figure 4-16 shows the results of executing the preceding query.

Figure 4-16:
Using a
character
class in the
WHERE
clause.

So far, I have accepted a `resultset` in the order that SQL Server happens to return it. Often, you will want to take some control over how rows are ordered in a `resultset`. The ORDER BY clause, which I describe next, gives you control over that.

The ORDER BY Clause

The ORDER BY clause specifies how you want results ordered in a `resultset`.

The following query specifies that the `resultset` is to be ordered by the value of the `pub_id` column. The default ordering is ascending.

```
USE pubs

SELECT *
FROM dbo.publishers
ORDER BY pub_name
```

Figure 4-17 shows the results of executing the preceding query. Notice that the rows are ordered alphabetically by the value of the publisher name.

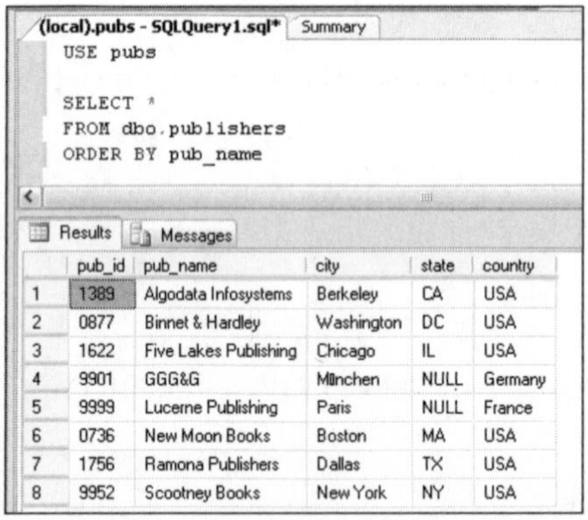

Figure 4-17:
Using
ORDER BY
to order a
resultset.

To display a `resultset` in descending order, use the following query:

```
USE pubs

SELECT *
FROM dbo.publishers
ORDER BY pub_name DESC
```

You can specify multiple columns by which you want a `resultset` ordered.

The GROUP BY Clause

The `GROUP BY` clause specifies how data in a `resultset` is to be grouped. The `GROUP BY` statement is used together with aggregates in Table 4-6.

Table 4-6	Aggregates
Aggregate	*What It Does*
AVG	The average (arithmetic mean) of values in a column
MAX	The maximum value in a column
MIN	The minimum value in a column
SUM	The sum of values in a column

To explore how to use aggregates, use the `AdventureWorks` database. The following query returns information about two specified order numbers (for convenience of display) whose sales order ID is specified in the `WHERE` clause. It doesn't use either an aggregate function or the `GROUP BY` clause. I show you that in the following example.

```
USE AdventureWorks

SELECT SalesOrderID AS "Order Number", LineTotal AS "Line
        Total"
FROM Sales.SalesOrderDetail
WHERE SalesOrderID BETWEEN 43660 AND 43661
```

Figure 4-18 shows the results of executing the preceding query.

I chose to display the column titles in English rather than just use the column names. The `AS` keyword supports that user convenience.

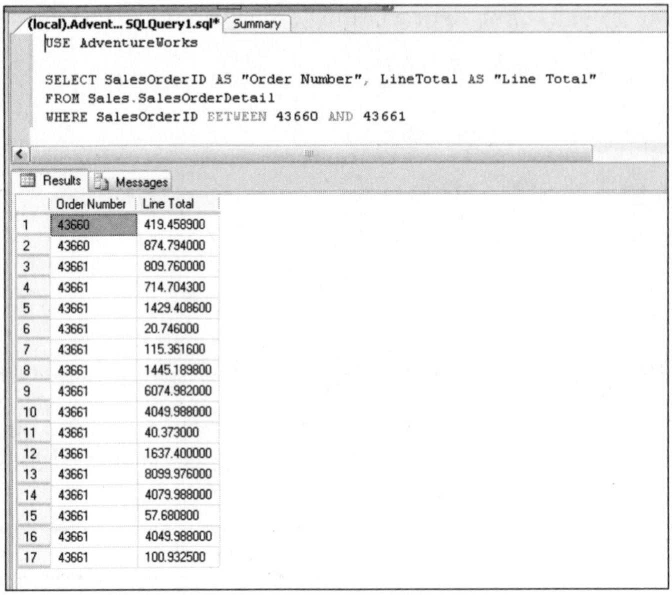

Figure 4-18:
Displaying
line totals
for two
specified
orders.

In the following query, I use the SUM() function and the GROUP BY clause to add the line totals together for the specified orders.

```
USE AdventureWorks

SELECT SalesOrderID AS "Order Number", SUM(LineTotal) AS
        "Sub Total"
FROM Sales.SalesOrderDetail
WHERE SalesOrderID BETWEEN 43660 AND 43661
GROUP BY SalesOrderID
ORDER BY SalesOrderID
```

Notice the SUM() function in the SELECT line. Notice that the GROUP BY and ORDER BY clauses each use the SalesOrderID. Figure 4-19 shows the results returned by the preceding query.

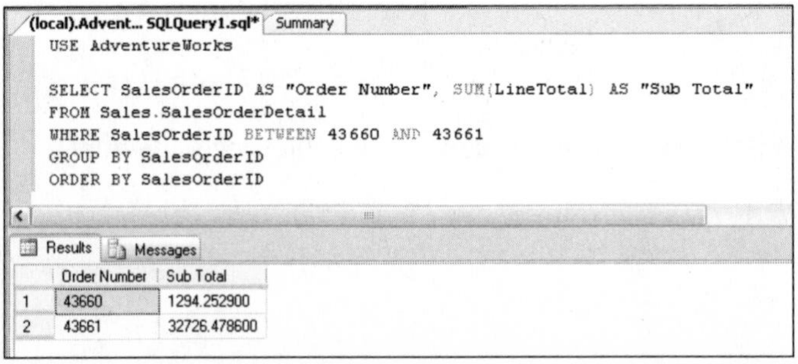

Figure 4-19:
Using the
SUM()
function and
the GROUP
BY clause.

A HAVING clause can be used to restrict the results of the preceding query based on the resulting SUM function. This is a different filtering mechanism to that of the WHERE clause filter:

```
USE AdventureWorks

SELECT SalesOrderID AS "Order Number", SUM(LineTotal) AS
          "Sub Total"
FROM Sales.SalesOrderDetail
WHERE SalesOrderID BETWEEN 43660 AND 43661
GROUP BY SalesOrderID HAVING SUM(LineTotal) > 10000
ORDER BY SalesOrderID
```

I don't cover all options of the SELECT statement in this chapter. There are options including those for creating multi-dimensional analytical reports and returning XML. XML is covered in Chapter 20. Multi-dimensional queries are too detailed for this book and can be found be reading about the Analysis Service. In Chapter 5, I show you how to use the syntax for creating joins in SELECT statements.

Chapter 5

Creating Joins

. . . .

In This Chapter

▶ Retrieving data from multiple tables

▶ Joining with code or a GUI interface: Transact-SQL or SQL Server Management Studio

▶ Streamlining the code with aliases

▶ Exploring one-to-many and many-to-many relationships

▶ Working with outer joins and cross joins

. . . .

*T*he simple use of SELECT statements on columns in a single table that you see in Chapter 4 is pretty limited in its usefulness for retrieving real-world data from a relational database. By definition, all but the simplest relational databases contain data with relationships between data in two or more tables. This circumstance means that in most queries you need to retrieve and display data from two or more tables. The simple form of the SELECT statement you see in Chapter 4 doesn't solve that need.

The need to retrieve data from multiple tables is due to the design of relational database tables. When designing a table, you do it in a way that avoids repeating data. That's a good thing because if some data changes (say, a customer address), you don't have to dive into every place that the address occurs to change it. That would be a maintenance nightmare if you held all the data about orders in a single table and that customer had made dozens of orders. You would have to make multiple changes of the same data, with the risk of introducing data inconsistencies.

To avoid such problems, a database in a relational database management system uses *relations* between tables. A relation in relational database terminology is, in actuality, a table. But in the context of relational database modeling, it means the table and how it relates to other tables, using relationships between those tables.

To retrieve data from multiple tables, you use a *join,* which is a SQL standard term used to describe various methods of merging rows from two tables. This chapter describes three broad types of joins:

- ✔ **Inner join:** An intersection between two tables where only matching rows are returned.

- ✔ **Outer join:** Includes an intersection plus rows in one table, which are not present in both tables.

- ✔ **Cross join:** A Cartesian product merging rows from two tables, regardless of any matching values. A Cartesian product joins every row in one table to every other row in the second table, regardless of any matching values.

Understanding the Need for Joins

A relational database is used to store data in separate tables. For example, in the pubs database, information about publishers and book titles is stored in the dbo.publisher and dbo.titles tables. Figure 5-1 shows the columns contained in the dbo.publishers table. Notice the key symbol beside the name of the pub_id column and the PK inside the parentheses to the right of the column name. Together, these visual cues indicate that the pub_id column is the primary key for the dbo.publishers table. A *primary key* is a column, or group of columns, that uniquely identifies a row in a table.

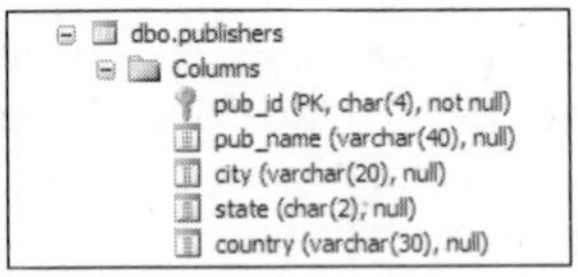

Figure 5-1:
The
columns
of the dbo.
publishers
table.

In Figure 5-2, you see the data from the dbo.publishers table. Notice that each value in the pub_id column is different. If you attempt to add a row with a duplicate value in the pub_id column using the INSERT statement (which I tell you about in Chapter 7), SQL Server displays an error. You're not allowed to add a duplicate value to that column because it is the *primary key.* A primary key is a special constraint placed on a table for two reasons:

✔ **A primary key must be unique.** It ensures that every row can be uniquely identified and found individually, later on. If you have a table of customers with two customers of the same name in two separate cities, then neither could be uniquely identified, and you wouldn't know who to bill.

✔ **A primary key is used to validate relationships between relations (tables).** This is called *referential integrity,* which ensures that all rows in all tables in a database are valid.

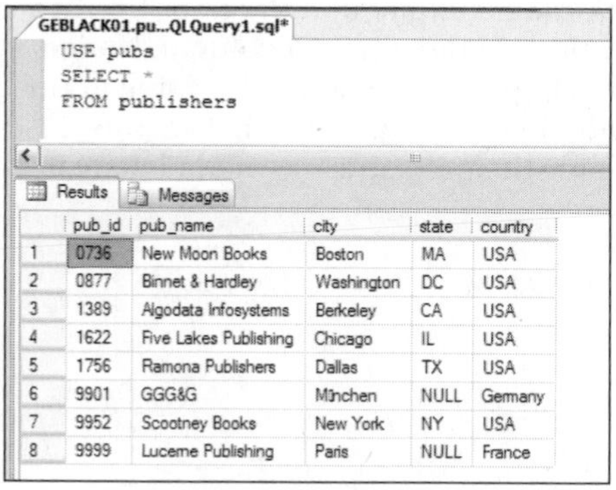

Figure 5-2:
The data
in the dbo.
publishers
table.

As you can see in Figure 5-2, the dbo.publishers table contains information about different publishers, but it doesn't list any of the titles that they publish. To find information about titles, you need to examine the dbo. titles table. Figure 5-3 shows the columns in the dbo.titles table. Notice that the title_id column has the visual cues that tell you that the title_ id column is the primary key for the dbo.titles table. Notice, too, the pub_ id column in the dbo.titles table. It has a key symbol to the left of the column name and has FK inside the parentheses to the right of the column name. These visual cues indicate that the pub_id column is a *foreign key*.

A foreign key is, quite literally, foreign to the table it is created in. Like a primary key, a foreign key is also a referential integrity constraint. However, a foreign key is placed on the child table of a parent-child relationship. A foreign key is thus used to identify a row in a table, as being directly related to the primary key, of a row in another table. The dbo.publishers table uniquely identifies each row by its pub_id column. So, a table of titles will have a foreign key pub_id, which relates each title back to its respective publisher.

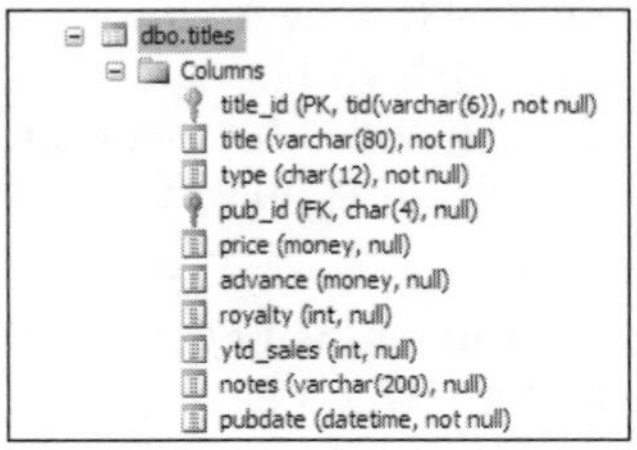

Figure 5-3:
The
columns
of the
dbo.titles
table.

Figure 5-4 shows some of the data contained in the dbo.titles table. Pay particular attention to the values in the pub_id column. Notice, for example, that in several rows from the dbo.titles table, the value in the pub_id column is 1389, which is the same value you find in the pub_id column in the dbo.publishers table for the publisher Algodata Infosystems.

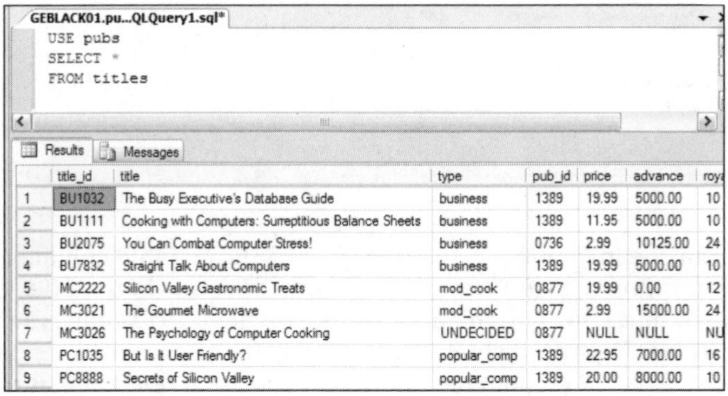

Figure 5-4:
The data
in the
dbo.titles
table.

The presence of the value 1389 in the pub_id column in the dbo.titles table indicates that the publisher for each of those titles is Algodata Infosystems.

If you want to ask a question such as, "Which titles are published by Algodata Infosystems?" you know from your understanding of the dbo.publishers and dbo.titles tables that you can execute a simple SELECT statement like this:

```
USE pubs
SELECT title, type, pub_id
FROM titles
WHERE pub_id = '1389'
```

The results from this query show the title and type for each book published by Algodata Infosystems, as shown in Figure 5-5.

```
GEBLACK01.pu...QLQuery1.sql*
   USE pubs
   SELECT title, type, pub_id
   FROM titles
   WHERE pub_id = '1389'
```

Figure 5-5:
Data on
titles
published by
Algodata
Infosystems.

	title	type	pub_id
1	The Busy Executive's Database Guide	business	1389
2	Cooking with Computers: Surreptitious Balance Sh...	business	1389
3	Straight Talk About Computers	business	1389
4	But Is It User Friendly?	popular_comp	1389
5	Secrets of Silicon Valley	popular_comp	1389
6	Net Etiquette	popular_comp	1389

The data in the pub_id column isn't in a user-friendly form. If you include the preceding query in an application, an end user doesn't know what a pub_id of 1389 means. The data that would be meaningful to her — the name of the publisher — is in another table, in this case the dbo.publishers table.

To present information in a way that makes sense to an end user, you need to retrieve and display data from the two tables you have looked at. You can do this by creating a join between the two tables.

You can create joins in the FROM clause or in the WHERE clause of a SELECT statement. Microsoft recommends that you use the technique that uses the FROM clause. That is the syntax I show you for each type of join that I demonstrate in this chapter.

Creating an Inner Join

Inner joins are the kinds of joins that you're likely to use most often. An *inner join* is an intersection between two tables where rows are joined based on one or more matching column values. Inner joins allow you to answer questions like, "Which books does Algodata Infosystems publish and what categories are they in?" You need to retrieve information from the dbo.publishers and dbo.titles tables to answer those questions. The publisher name is contained in the pub_name column of the dbo.publishers table. You can retrieve that information using a SELECT statement like this:

```
SELECT pub_name
FROM dbo.publishers
```

Similarly, to retrieve the book title and category information, you need data from the title and type columns in the dbo.titles table. You can also retrieve that information with a SELECT statement:

```
SELECT title, type
FROM dbo.titles
```

Now, you need to find a way to combine these two SELECT statements so that only the information about titles published by Algodata Infosystems is displayed. To do that, you can modify the preceding code by adding a WHERE clause so that the code reads as follows:

```
SELECT pub_name
FROM dbo.publishers
WHERE pub_id = '1389'
```

and

```
SELECT title, type
FROM dbo.titles
WHERE pub_id = '1389'
```

If you combine these to form the following query, you get close to a solution, but a new problem arises.

```
USE pubs
SELECT pub_name, title, type
FROM publishers, titles
WHERE pub_id = '1389'
```

As you can see in Figure 5-6, the column name pub_id is ambiguous because it occurs in both the dbo.publishers and dbo.titles tables.

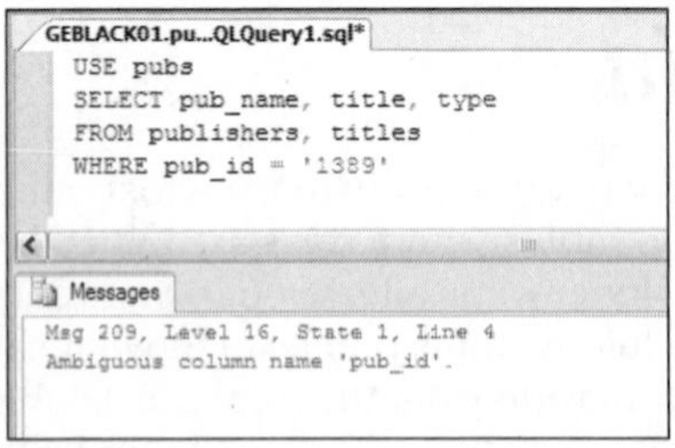

Figure 5-6:
An attempt
to retrieve
data from
two tables.

To remove that ambiguity, you need to identify which table the pub_id column is in. You do that by adding the table name and a period (.) before the column name. You have to *disambiguate* the pub_id column. It's also a good idea to disambiguate the columns that you want to display, although in this example, the column names are enough. Apart from the pub_id column, no other column name is used in both tables. The following code gets the answer to your question, as you can see in Figure 5-7.

```
USE pubs
SELECT publishers.pub_name, titles.title, titles.type
FROM publishers, titles
WHERE publishers.pub_id = '1389'
AND publishers.pub_id = titles.pub_id
```

Figure 5-7:
A join
using the
deprecated
WHERE
clause
syntax.

The code supplies the answer to the question, but unfortunately, it uses the _deprecated_ (no longer supported) syntax for a join: a WHERE clause. The recommended method is to use the FROM clause, as I describe next. However, I think it's useful to see the WHERE clause syntax because it shows you the logic that you use to create a join.

Now, look at the syntax needed to answer the original question, "Which titles does Algodata Infosystems publish and what categories are they in?"

```
USE pubs
SELECT publishers.pub_name, titles.title, titles.type
FROM publishers
INNER JOIN titles
ON publishers.pub_id = titles.pub_id
WHERE publishers.pub_id = '1389'
```

Notice the inner join with the titles table in the fourth line. That, taken together with the FROM clause on the third line, specifies the two tables in this inner join. The ON clause in the fifth line specifies the criterion for the join. In this case, the value of publishers.pub_id equals titles.pub_id.

Figure 5-8 shows the result of executing the preceding code.

The join based on a WHERE clause works and produces in the example the same results as the recommended FROM clause syntax, as you have just seen. So why is the other method, using the FROM clause, the recommended syntax?

```
GEBLACK01.pu...QLQuery1.sql*
USE pubs
SELECT publishers.pub_name, titles.title, titles.type
FROM publishers
INNER JOIN titles
ON publishers.pub_id = titles.pub_id
WHERE publishers.pub_id = '1389'
```

	pub_name	title	type
1	Algodata Infosystems	The Busy Executive's Database Guide	business
2	Algodata Infosystems	Cooking with Computers: Surreptitious Balance Sh...	business
3	Algodata Infosystems	Straight Talk About Computers	business
4	Algodata Infosystems	But Is It User Friendly?	popular_comp
5	Algodata Infosystems	Secrets of Silicon Valley	popular_comp
6	Algodata Infosystems	Net Etiquette	popular_comp

Figure 5-8: Creating an inner join using the recommended FROM clause syntax.

The method using the FROM clause is more portable, if you need to write code that isn't confined to SQL Server 2005. Also, there have been hints from Microsoft that the old syntax (the WHERE clause syntax) might be dropped in a future version of SQL Server. The choice of which syntax to use is yours in SQL Server 2005. However, I suggest that you use the inner join syntax.

Using aliases for table names

Before going on to look at more complex inner joins, I want to point out a syntax convention that you're likely to find frequently in other developers' code and that you might prefer to the code I show earlier in the chapter.

Compare this version of the code (which you see in the preceding section):

```
USE pubs
SELECT publishers.pub_name, titles.title, titles.type
FROM publishers
INNER JOIN titles
ON publishers.pub_id = titles.pub_id
WHERE publishers.pub_id = '1389'
```

with the following version:

```
USE pubs
SELECT p.pub_name, t.title, t.type
FROM publishers AS p
INNER JOIN titles AS t
ON p.pub_id = t.pub_id
WHERE p.pub_id = '1389'
```

If you run the code, you get the same results because the two versions of the code mean the same. Notice that instead of using the name of the table I use an *alias* for each table name, which is simply a shorthand way of referring to a database object. The alias for the `publishers` table is defined in this line:

```
FROM publishers AS p
```

And the alias for the titles table is defined on this line:

```
INNER JOIN titles AS t
```

You can choose any alias you like to replace table names — provided you stick to legal SQL Server names and avoid using a Transact-SQL keyword as an alias.

Notice in the two preceding lines of code that I use the AS keyword. SQL Server allows you to omit that. So an alternative way to specify the alias for the `publishers` table is

```
FROM publishers p
```

My personal preference is to include the AS keyword, but either syntax is supported in SQL Server.

The choice of whether to use aliases is yours. Using aliases can be helpful when you write complex queries. The alias makes the code shorter and (hopefully) easier to read.

Creating an inner join with SQL Server Management Studio

You can create a join using Transact-SQL just as I showed you in the preceding examples. SQL Server Management Studio also allows you to graphically create a query, which includes an inner join.

With SQL Server Management Studio open, follow these steps:

1. **Click the Design Query in Editor button shown in Figure 5-9 to open the Query Designer.**

   When the Query Designer opens, the Add Table dialog box appears, as shown in Figure 5-10.

2. **In the Add Table dialog box, select the `publishers` table and then click Add.**

3. **Select the `titles` table and click Add.**

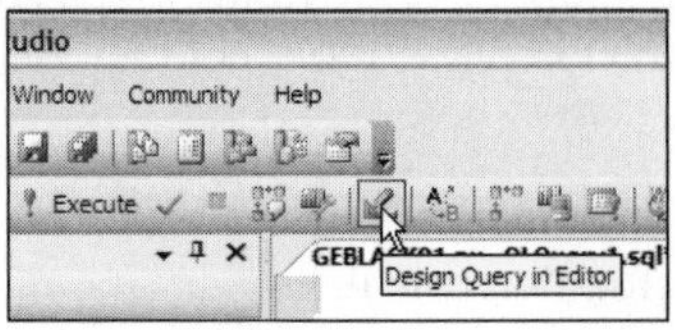

Figure 5-9:
Clicking to
launch the
Query
Designer.

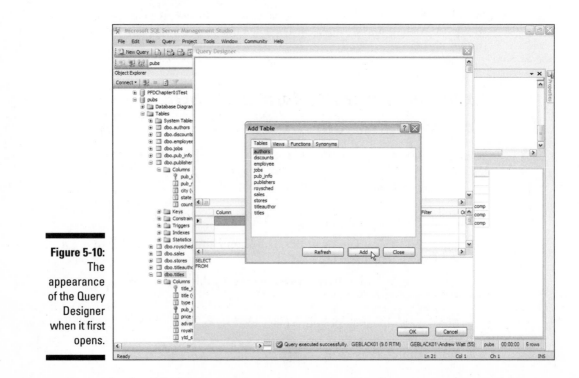

4. Click the Close button to close the Add Table dialog box.

The Query Designer now looks similar to Figure 5-11. I moved the
table graphics in the design area to show the relationship between the
publishers table and the titles table. You can see in Figure 5-11
that the relationship between the publishers and titles tables
uses the pub_id column. Notice that on the publishers table end of
the connector, there is a key symbol, and on the titles table end of the
connector, there is a ∞ symbol. The ∞ symbol represents the fact that
one publisher is likely to have published multiple titles.

Notice in the lower part of Figure 5-11 that the Query Designer has
created the basic syntax for an inner join.

Figure 5-10:
The
appearance
of the Query
Designer
when it first
opens.

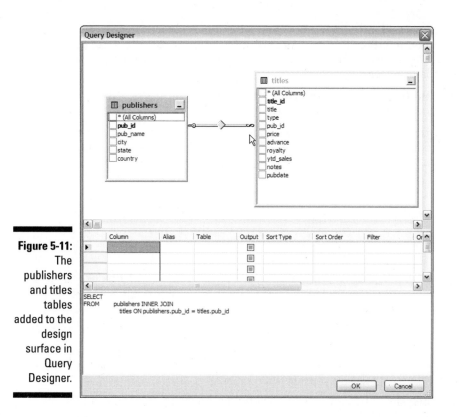

5. **Now you need to select which columns to include from each table. Select the `pub_name` check box in the `publishers` table graphic and select the title and type check boxes in the `titles` table graphic.**

   You might realize that you're selecting the same columns as you selected using Transact-SQL when you created the example using code.

   The Query Designer creates the following code for you:

   ```
   SELECT publishers.pub_name, titles.title, titles.type
   FROM    publishers INNER JOIN
           titles ON publishers.pub_id = titles.pub_id
   ```

   Notice that the code the Query Designer creates for you doesn't use aliases.

   At this point, if you execute the code, the titles published by all publishers will be returned. You need, in effect, to add a WHERE clause to the T-SQL that the Query Designer created for you. You can add that clause manually if you wish, by editing the code or using the Query Designer, as instructed in the following step.

6. **To add a filter using the Query Designer, select the `pub_id` check box in either the `publishers` table graphic, or select the `pub_id` check box in the `titles` table graphic. (You can select both, but it is unnecessary.)**

7. **In the grid part of the Query Designer, type `'1389'` in the Filter column for the `pub_id` row.**

8. **Deselect the Output columns for both `pub_id` rows because you don't want to display the values of the `pub_id` columns in the output.**

   The Query Designer produces the following code:

   ```
   SELECT    publishers.pub_name, titles.title, titles.
             type
   FROM      publishers INNER JOIN
                  titles ON publishers.pub_id = titles.
             pub_id
   WHERE     (publishers.pub_id = '1389')
   ```

   If you filtered on both tables, your WHERE clause will look like the next piece of code. You don't have to filter both tables; it is allowed but is unnecessary and inefficient:

   ```
   WHERE (publishers.pub_id = '1389') AND (titles.pub_id
         = '1389')
   ```

   The round brackets are also unnecessary for this particular query, but the Query Designer adds them anyway.

   See Figure 5-12 for what you should see when you have completed designing the query.

9. **Click the OK button.**

   The query now appears in the query window in SQL Server Management Studio.

10. **Click the Execute button to execute the code.**

    As you can see in Figure 5-13 the code produces the same results as the Transact-SQL code that you coded by hand earlier in this chapter.

The choice is yours — using Transact-SQL code throughout, using only the Query Designer, or using the Query Designer to produce code that you then edit by hand. Any of the three approaches can give you syntactically correct queries.

Joining more than two tables

Strictly speaking, any single join involves two tables, but there can be more than one JOIN statement in a FROM clause so that, effectively, you can join more than two tables. This capability allows you to use inner joins to answer more complex questions that involve retrieving data from multiple tables.

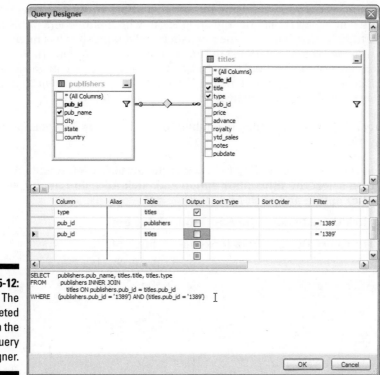

Figure 5-12:
The completed query in the Query Designer.

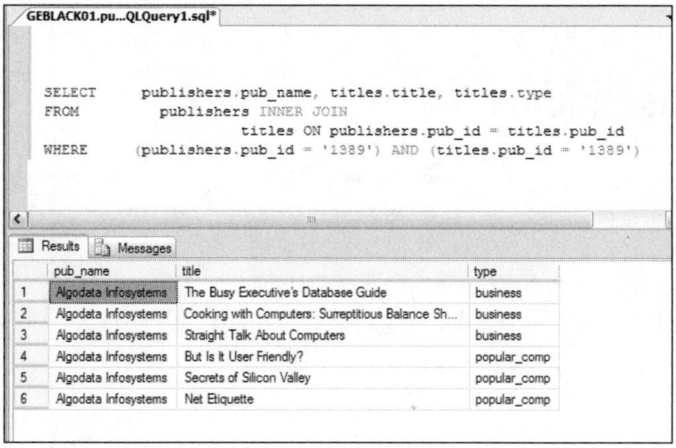

Figure 5-13:
The results returned by the query you created in the Query Designer.

Think about how you would find out which authors wrote which books. This is more complicated than the question about which publishers published which titles. A title has only one publisher, and a publisher has many titles. This is a *one-to-many* relationship (one publisher to many titles). But one author can write many books, and a book can have more than one author. This is a *many-to-many* relationship. You can't directly represent that in two SQL Server 2005 tables. You need to add another table.

To create a join of more than two tables, open the Query Designer and follow these steps:

1. **In the Add Table dialog box, select the authors option and click Add, then select the titleauthor option and click Add, and finally, select the titles option and click Add.**

2. **Click Close to close the Add Table dialog box.**

   The Query Designer now looks like Figure 5-14.

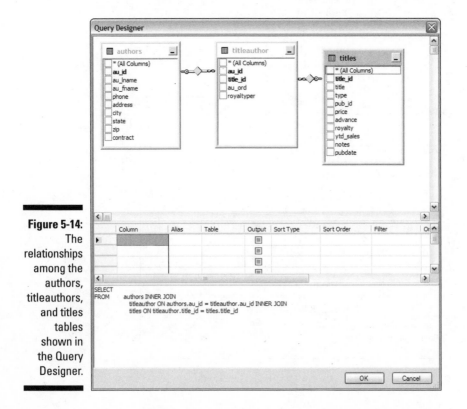

Figure 5-14: The relationships among the authors, titleauthors, and titles tables shown in the Query Designer.

Figure 5-14 shows a one-to-many relationship between the `authors` and `titleauthor` tables, using the `au_id` columns in each table. Additionally, there is another one-to-many relationship the `titles` and `titleauthor` tables. Both one-to-many relationships together represent a many-to-many relationship between authors and titles. So you can create a three-table join (a join of two table joins), for the three related tables depicted in Figure 5-14.

Notice in the lower part of Figure 5-14 that the Query Designer has created nested `INNER JOIN` statements for you:

```
SELECT
FROM   authors
 INNER JOIN titleauthor
ON authors.au_id = titleauthor.au_id
 INNER JOIN titles
ON titleauthor.title_id = titles.title_id
```

3. **You now need to specify which columns in the tables you want to display. Select the `au_lname` and `au_fname` columns in the `authors` table (they represent author last name and author first name) and select the `title` and `pubdate` columns in the `titles` table.**

The columns you select depend on the question you want to answer. For this example, you want to display all authors and titles together with the publication dates.

Figure 5-15 shows the selections made and the automatically generated code.

4. **Click OK to close the Query Designer.**

5. **In the query window in SQL Server Management Studio click Execute to run the code.**

As you can see in Figure 5-16, the query displays author information with their titles and the publication dates of those titles.

When you create an inner join, the "side" doesn't matter. The first table is the "left" table, and the second table is the "right" table. The following code, which reverses the left and right tables, produces the same results:

```
SELECT       titles.title, titles.pubdate, authors.au_lname,
             authors.au_fname
FROM         authors
INNER JOIN titleauthor
 ON authors.au_id = titleauthor.au_id
INNER JOIN titles
 ON titleauthor.title_id = titles.title_id
```

Side isn't important for inner joins, but it is important for outer joins, which I describe next.

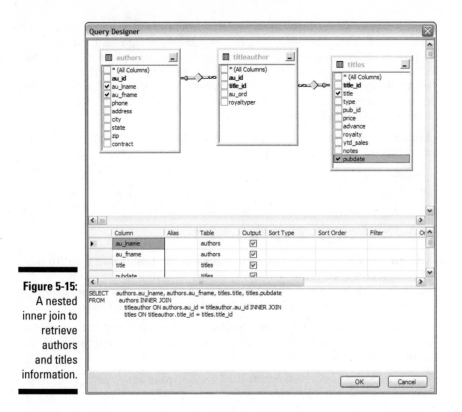

Figure 5-15:
A nested inner join to retrieve authors and titles information.

Creating an Outer Join

An *outer join* finds rows in one table of a join that are not in the other table — in addition to the intersecting rows from both tables. There is an exception to this rule called a *full outer join,* which finds the intersection, plus rows in both tables not in the other. A full outer join is not the same as a Cartesian product because any outer join still includes at least the intersection.

Side is important when you create an outer join. The table whose name comes before the JOIN keyword is the left table. The table whose name comes after the JOIN keyword is the right table.

In a left outer join, all values in selected columns in the left table are displayed. If the right table has a corresponding value, it's displayed too. If there is no corresponding value, a NULL value is displayed in the results.

In a right outer join, all values in the selected column(s) in the right table are displayed. If the selected column(s) has a corresponding value(s) in the left table, it's displayed. If there is no corresponding value, a NULL value is displayed.

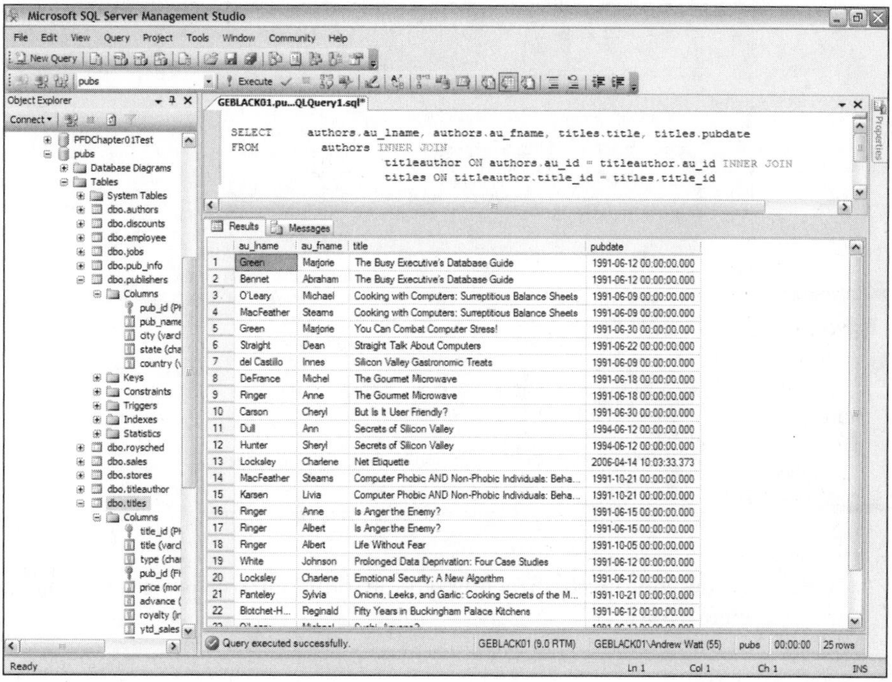

Figure 5-16:
Displaying
information
about
authors,
titles, and
publication
dates.

To show you how outer joins work, I use the `stores` and `discounts` tables from the `pubs` database. First, look at the data in each table. Execute the following two Transact-SQL commands:

```
SELECT *
FROM stores
SELECT *
FROM discounts
```

Figure 5-17 shows the results of executing the two preceding commands.

Before creating an outer join, create an inner join to see what is returned. (See the preceding section for more on inner joins.) Open the Query Designer, add the `stores` and `discounts` tables to the design surface. Check the `stor_name` column in the `stores` table and the `discount` column in the `discounts` table.

The following code is created for you:

```
SELECT      stores.stor_name, discounts.discount
FROM        discounts
INNER JOIN  stores
ON discounts.stor_id = stores.stor_id
```

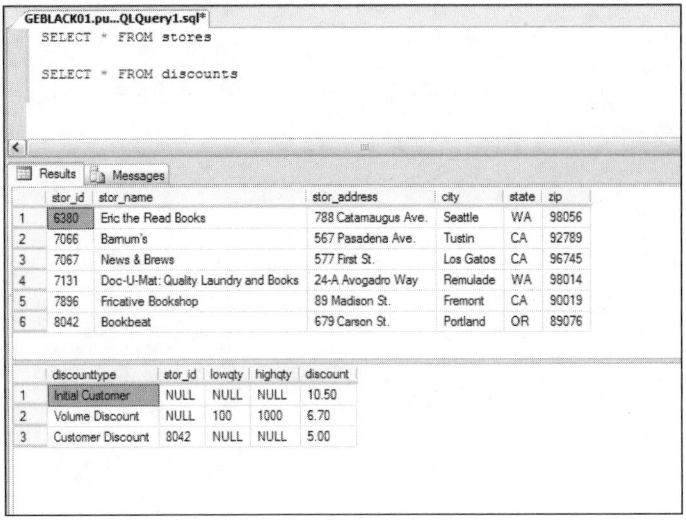

Figure 5-17:
The data
in the
stores and
discounts
tables.

When you run the preceding code, only one row is returned, as shown in Figure 5-18.

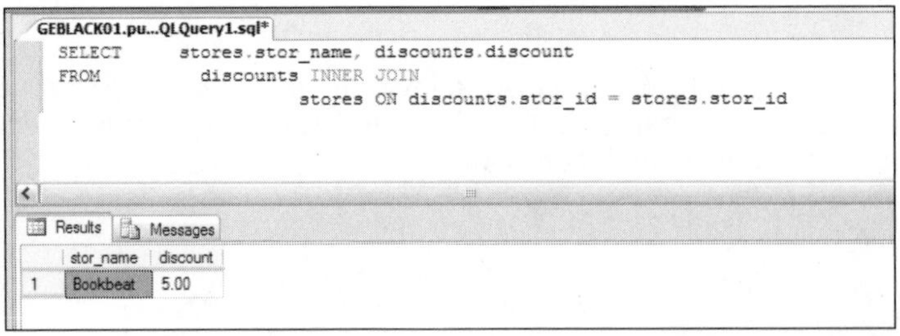

Figure 5-18:
Only one
row is
returned by
an inner
join.

Notice that the `discounts` table is mentioned before the `INNER JOIN` keywords in the preceding code. This is important when you look at the outer join in a moment.

You can see in Figure 5-17 that there are five stores and three levels of discount, but in Figure 5-18, only one row is displayed. The inner join returns only one row. That row is the only row that has both a store name and a discount. One way of describing this is that an inner join is *exclusive* — it excludes all rows that don't both necessary pieces of data, in this case a store name (stored in `stores.stor_name`) and a discount (specified in `discounts.discount`).

Edit the code in the SQL Server Management Studio query window so that it reads like this:

```
SELECT      stores.stor_name, discounts.discount
FROM        discounts
LEFT OUTER JOIN stores
ON discounts.stor_id = stores.stor_id
```

The preceding code answers the question, "Which stores have each of the specified discount levels?"

Execute the code in SQL Server Management Studio. Figure 5-19 shows the results. Notice that the discount column has a value in each row. Remember, the discounts table is on the left, so all rows are populated with a value from that table. Two of the three rows have NULL values for the stor_name column.

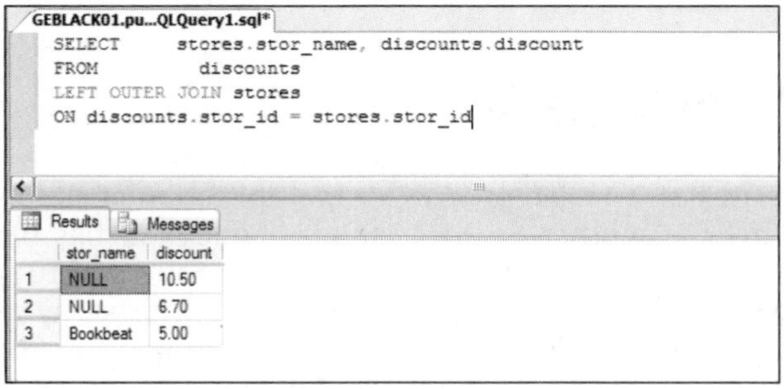

Figure 5-19: Discount levels that have stores where they are applied.

The results tell you that only the 5.00 discount has a store that benefits from it. The other two discount levels have no corresponding stores.

If you change the left outer join to a right outer join, you can answer the question, "Which stores have a discount?" or in other words, "What discount, if any, does each store have?"

Simply change LEFT to RIGHT and you create a right outer join.

```
SELECT      stores.stor_name, discounts.discount
FROM        discounts
RIGHT OUTER JOIN stores
ON discounts.stor_id = stores.stor_id
```

Execute the code in the query window in SQL Server Management Studio. The results are shown in Figure 5-20.

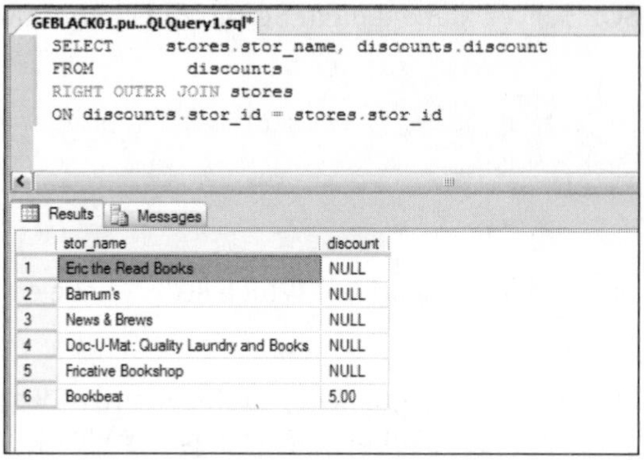

```
GEBLACK01.pu...QLQuery1.sql*
SELECT      stores.stor_name, discounts.discount
FROM        discounts
RIGHT OUTER JOIN stores
ON discounts.stor_id = stores.stor_id
```

	stor_name	discount
1	Eric the Read Books	NULL
2	Barnum's	NULL
3	News & Brews	NULL
4	Doc-U-Mat: Quality Laundry and Books	NULL
5	Fricative Bookshop	NULL
6	Bookbeat	5.00

Figure 5-20:
Finding
what
discount
stores have.

If you reverse the order of the table names, you find that the results change for both the left outer join and the right outer join.

Creating a Cross Join

A *cross join* creates a Cartesian product or multiplication of all rows in one table, with all rows in another. So, for example, if one table has 10 rows and another 100 rows, a cross-join query produces the product of 10 and 100, which is 1,000 rows. The data from each table is not necessarily related in all query row results. As a result, a cross join isn't something you use often. Cross joins are often used for generating test data — and sometimes for data-warehouse analytics.

A cross join generates more rows than are in either table used in the cross join. To create a cross join on the `stores` and `discounts` tables, use this syntax:

```
SELECT stores.stor_name, discounts.discount
FROM    discounts
CROSS JOIN stores
```

When you execute the code in the query window in SQL Server Management Studio, you see results similar to Figure 5-21.

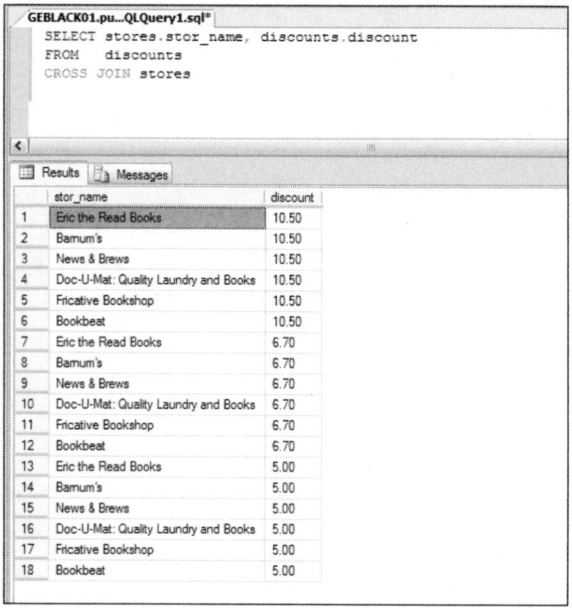

Figure 5-21:
A cross join
on the
stores and
discounts
tables.

As you can see in Figure 5-21, there are 18 rows returned. Look back at Figure 5-17 and you see that there are six rows in the `stores` table and three rows in the `discounts` table. It is no coincidence that 18 = 3 * 6. A cross join displays every combination of the values in a row in one table with every combination of the value(s) in a row in the other table. This is also known as a *Cartesian product.*

You can use a cross join to create large quantities of test data by creating relatively small amounts of data in two tables. The cross join creates all possible combinations of rows from each table. Cross joins can cause serious performance problems and are best avoided.

Chapter 6

Creating Advanced Queries

. . . .

In This Chapter

▶ Nesting queries with subqueries

▶ Specifying a condition with the EXISTS keyword

▶ Type casting data types with CAST

▶ Converting data types with CONVERT

▶ Expressing temporary results with common table expressions

. . . .

*I*n Chapters 4 and 5, I show you how to use the Transact-SQL SELECT state-ment to retrieve data from one or more tables in a SQL Server database. In this chapter, I show you how to use nested subqueries to allow you to answer questions that you couldn't easily answer using the techniques in earlier chapters.

I also describe converting data types and type casting of data types. Con-verting a data type changes a value from one data type to another — if it is possible. A *typecast* is where you express one data type as another.

Finally, I show you how to use a common table expression using the WITH clause. A common table expression effectively creates a temporary table in memory as an expression (a SELECT statement contained within a WITH clause).

Using Subqueries

A *subquery* is a Transact-SQL query that is nested inside another Transact-SQL query. To identify the nested subquery, you enclose that Transact-SQL statement inside paired parentheses.

You can write many subqueries as joins — and vice versa. Substituting sub-queries for joins can sometimes help to alleviate the complexity in joins with many more than two tables. This practice is recommended only in highly nor-malized, highly granular, and extremely active OLTP database environments.

Utilizing subqueries in multiple table joins can make the overall join query easier to write and easier to decipher when a problem is encountered. However, execution performance may not necessarily be a benefit.

This example uses the Northwind database. Suppose you want to find out which items were ordered on the last day that an order was placed. If you know the date of the last order, you can put that date into the query as a literal value. If you don't know when the last order was placed, you can find it simply by using the MAX() function with the order date, assuming that the Northwind database is the current database.

```
SELECT Max(OrderDate) FROM Orders
```

Figure 6-1 shows the result of executing the preceding statement.

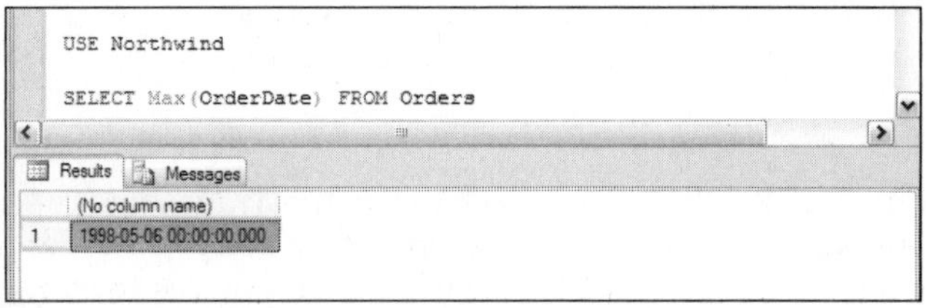

Figure 6-1:
Finding the
date of the
most recent
order in the
Orders table.

After you find the most recent date that has an order, you can edit the date into the query:

```
SELECT DISTINCT [Order Details].ProductID,
          Orders.OrderDate
FROM Orders
JOIN [Order Details]
  ON Orders.OrderID = [Order Details].OrderID
WHERE Orders.OrderDate = '1998-05-06'
ORDER BY ProductID
```

Notice that the name of the Order Details table has a space in it, so you must delimit the table name when you use it in the query. You should see that 27 rows are returned, indicating that 27 products were ordered on the date of the most recent order.

In practice, it isn't convenient to hand-edit code before running it. You saw earlier that the MAX() function allows you to find the most recent order date. Using a subquery, you can find the date of the most recent order and use that value in the WHERE clause of the SELECT statement:

```
SELECT DISTINCT [Order Details].ProductID,
          Orders.OrderDate
FROM Orders
JOIN [Order Details]
  ON Orders.OrderID = [Order Details].OrderID
WHERE Orders.OrderDate = (SELECT MAX(OrderDate) FROM
          Orders)
ORDER BY Orders.OrderDate
```

When you execute the preceding code, you get the same results as you see when you hand code the date in the WHERE clause. Figure 6-2 shows part of the results.

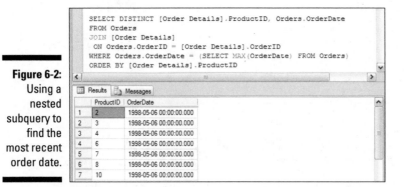

Figure 6-2:
Using a
nested
subquery to
find the
most recent
order date.

Suppose you want to identify the products ordered in the last seven days. Modify the query as follows. Now, the subquery is used in an expression inside the SELECT statement.

```
SELECT DISTINCT [Order Details].ProductID,
          Orders.OrderDate
FROM Orders
JOIN [Order Details]
  ON Orders.OrderID = [Order Details].OrderID
WHERE Orders.OrderDate > ((SELECT MAX(OrderDate) FROM
          Orders) - 7)
ORDER BY [Order Details].ProductID
```

Notice the nested parentheses in the WHERE clause. The outer parentheses ensure that the expression

```
(SELECT MAX(OrderDate) FROM Orders) - 7
```

is treated as an expression to be evaluated as a whole. It finds the date seven days before the most recent order date. If the value of the OrderDate column is greater than that date, the date is in the last seven days. Figure 6-3 shows the results.

```
USE Northwind

SELECT DISTINCT [Order Details].ProductID, Orders.OrderDate
FROM Orders
JOIN [Order Details]
 ON Orders.OrderID = [Order Details].OrderID
WHERE Orders.OrderDate > ((SELECT MAX(OrderDate) FROM Orders) - 7)
ORDER BY [Order Details].ProductID
```

	ProductID	OrderDate
1	1	1998-05-05 00:00:00.000
2	2	1998-05-05 00:00:00.000
3	2	1998-05-06 00:00:00.000
4	3	1998-05-06 00:00:00.000
5	4	1998-05-06 00:00:00.000
6	6	1998-05-06 00:00:00.000
7	7	1998-05-05 00:00:00.000
8	7	1998-05-06 00:00:00.000
9	8	1998-05-06 00:00:00.000

Figure 6-3: Using a nested subquery inside an expression.

Examining the EXISTS Keyword

The EXISTS keyword allows you to specify a condition that depends on a subquery. The syntax is

```
EXISTS subquery
```

and returns TRUE if the subquery contains any rows.

One use of the EXISTS keyword is in the WHERE clause of a SELECT statement. If you want the subquery always to return at least one row (which means that EXISTS returns TRUE), you can use a literal value in the SELECT statement in a subquery. Statements such as

```
SELECT 1
```

or

```
SELECT NULL
```

always cause EXISTS to return TRUE.

For example, the following code returns TRUE from the EXISTS keyword, so the outer SELECT statement returns data about department IDs and names.

```
USE AdventureWorks_New
GO
SELECT DepartmentID, Name
FROM HumanResources.Department
WHERE EXISTS (SELECT 1)
ORDER BY DepartmentID ASC
```

The preceding code assumes that you've created a copy of the
AdventureWorks database called AdventureWorks_New.

You can also use the EXISTS keyword to apply a test in a WHERE clause to a
column that you don't want to be returned. You can use the EXISTS keyword
to answer questions such as which customers have placed any order. To find
out which customers of AdventureWorks Cycles have placed an order, you
can execute the following code (it assumes that AdventureWorks_New is
the current database):

```
SELECT CustomerID, TerritoryID
FROM Sales.Customer
WHERE EXISTS
   (SELECT SalesOrderID
    FROM Sales.SalesOrderHeader
    WHERE Sales.SalesOrderHeader.CustomerID =
              Sales.Customer.CustomerID)
```

Figure 6-4 shows the results of executing the preceding code.

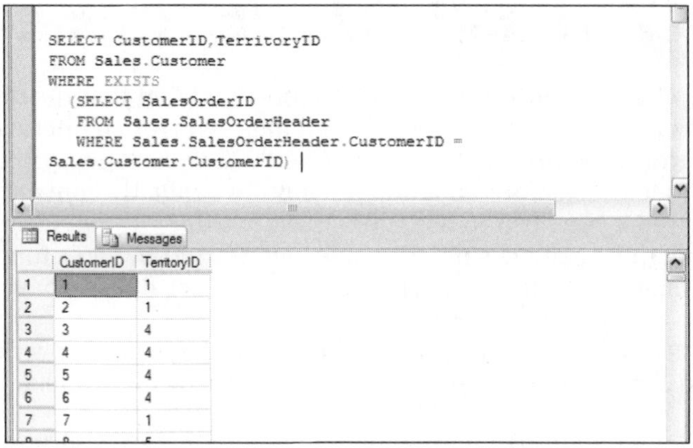

Figure 6-4:
Finding
which
customers
have placed
an order.

```
SELECT CustomerID, TerritoryID
FROM Sales.Customer
WHERE EXISTS
   (SELECT SalesOrderID
    FROM Sales.SalesOrderHeader
    WHERE Sales.SalesOrderHeader.CustomerID =
Sales.Customer.CustomerID) |
```

	CustomerID	TerritoryID
1	1	1
2	2	1
3	3	4
4	4	4
5	5	4
6	6	4
7	7	1

If a customer ID doesn't appear in the Sales.SalesOrderHeader table, the
customer hasn't placed an order. To find customers who've never placed an
order, simply use the NOT keyword before the EXISTS keyword:

```
SELECT CustomerID,TerritoryID
FROM Sales.Customer
WHERE NOT EXISTS
   (SELECT SalesOrderID
    FROM Sales.SalesOrderHeader
    WHERE Sales.SalesOrderHeader.CustomerID =
            Sales.Customer.CustomerID)
```

Many times, when you use the EXISTS keyword, you can retrieve the same data using a join. For example, the following join finds all customers who have placed an order:

```
SELECT DISTINCT Sales.Customer.CustomerID,
            Sales.Customer.TerritoryID
FROM Sales.Customer
JOIN Sales.SalesOrderHeader
 ON Sales.Customer.CustomerID =
            Sales.SalesOrderHeader.CustomerID
ORDER BY Sales.Customer.CustomerID
```

Because you can retrieve the same data using a pretty straightforward join, why bother learning how to use the EXISTS keyword? The answer is that the EXISTS keyword is likely to give better performance than the join. On large queries or a heavily loaded SQL Server instance, the improved performance can be important.

Using the CAST and CONVERT Functions

Inevitably, when you write Transact-SQL code, you find that the data type retrieved from a column isn't the required data type for an operation that you want to perform. Unfortunately, SQL Server 2005 doesn't always carry out data type conversions for you automatically. To explicitly convert or type cast a data type, you need to use the CAST() and/or CONVERT() functions. The two functions behave similarly; however, the CONVERT() function has some datetime conversion functionality that CAST() doesn't have.

The CONVERT() function is not ANSI-compliant. If you need to write code that can be used on more than SQL Server, use the ANSI-compliant CAST() function.

To use the CAST() function, use this general syntax form:

```
CAST (expression AS datatype)
```

To use the CONVERT() function, use this general syntax form:

```
CONVERT(datatype, expression)
```

You can specify a maximum length for the data type and specify a style for an output date (if applicable) using the following form:

```
CONVERT(datatype [length], expression [, style])
```

If you don't specify a value for *length,* the CONVERT() function assumes a length of 30 characters.

As an example, try to output the contact ID for a contact using the following code:

```
USE AdventureWorks_New

SELECT 'The first contact has a contact ID of ' +
        ContactID
FROM Person.Contact
WHERE ContactID = 1
```

When you execute the code, SQL Server attempts to automatically convert the literal string in the first line of the code to the int data type. Not surprisingly, that attempted data-type conversion fails. The error message displayed is

```
Msg 245, Level 16, State 1, Line 3
Conversion failed when converting the varchar value 'The
        first contact has a contact ID of ' to data
        type int.
```

Notice that the failed automatic data type conversion is trying to do something appropriate — convert a string to an integer. To get the code to do what you want, you need to convert the int data type of the ContactID column to a varchar data type. To do that using the CAST() function, use the following code:

```
SELECT 'The first contact has a contact ID of ' +
  CAST(ContactID AS varchar(30) )
FROM Person.Contact
WHERE ContactID = 1
```

Figure 6-5 shows the results of executing the preceding code.

To achieve the same using the CONVERT() function, execute the following code:

```
SELECT 'The first contact has a contact ID of ' +
        CONVERT(varchar(30), ContactID)
FROM Person.Contact
WHERE ContactID = 1
```

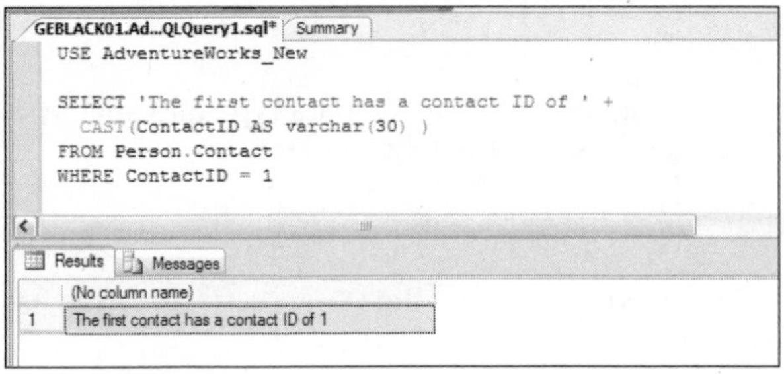

Figure 6-5:
Using the
CAST()
function
gives you
the desired
result.

```
GEBLACK01.Ad...QLQuery1.sql*  Summary
    USE AdventureWorks_New

    SELECT 'The first contact has a contact ID of ' +
        CAST(ContactID AS varchar(30) )
    FROM Person.Contact
    WHERE ContactID = 1

    Results    Messages
        (No column name)
    1    The first contact has a contact ID of 1
```

If you execute the preceding code, you see the same result as shown in
Figure 6-5.

When you use dates with text messages, you see error messages due to data-
type conversion issues. If you want to retrieve some data on a specific order
in the SalesOrderHeader table in AdventureWorks, you can do that using
the following code:

```
SELECT OrderDate, SalesOrderID
FROM Sales.SalesOrderHeader
WHERE Sales.SalesOrderHeader.SalesOrderID = 44000
```

You can also display the order date with some explanatory text; for example,
using the following code, you see an error message:

```
SELECT 'The order date for order 44000 is ' + OrderDate
FROM Sales.SalesOrderHeader
WHERE Sales.SalesOrderHeader.SalesOrderID = 44000
```

SQL Server's attempt at automatic data-type conversion tries to convert the
explanatory string to the data type of the OrderDate column, which is
datetime. That attempted data-type conversion fails, and the following error
message appears:

```
Msg 241, Level 16, State 1, Line 1
Conversion failed when converting datetime from character
        string.
```

If you use the CAST() function to display the datetime with a message, you
can use the following code:

```
SELECT 'The order date for order 44000 is ' +
        CAST(OrderDate AS varchar(30))
FROM Sales.SalesOrderHeader
WHERE Sales.SalesOrderHeader.SalesOrderID = 44000
```

Alternatively, you can use the basic form of the CONVERT() function:

```
SELECT 'The order date for order 44000 is ' +
        CONVERT(varchar(30), OrderDate)
FROM Sales.SalesOrderHeader
WHERE Sales.SalesOrderHeader.SalesOrderID = 44000
```

As you can see in Figure 6-6, both the CAST() and CONVERT() functions display the same results.

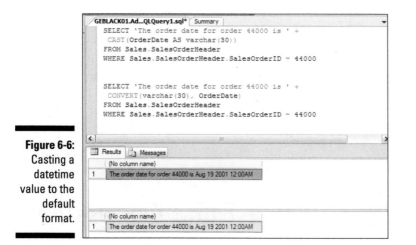

Figure 6-6:
Casting a datetime value to the default format.

For some purposes, the default display format for a date might be acceptable to you. In some situations, however (for example, if you're displaying dates for customers in the United Kingdom or Japan), the default display format will probably not be acceptable to them. The CONVERT() function gives you control over how the date is displayed, but the CAST() function doesn't.

To customize how the date and time are displayed, you use the style codes as the final argument to the CONVERT() function. When you execute the following code, you see styles 103 and 113, which are European-style date display formats:

```
SELECT 'The order date for order 44000 is ' +
        CONVERT(varchar(30), OrderDate, 103)
FROM Sales.SalesOrderHeader
WHERE Sales.SalesOrderHeader.SalesOrderID = 44000

SELECT 'The order date for order 44000 is ' +
        CONVERT(varchar(30), OrderDate, 113)
FROM Sales.SalesOrderHeader
WHERE Sales.SalesOrderHeader.SalesOrderID = 44000
```

Figure 6-7 shows the results of executing the preceding SELECT statements. The full list of style codes is shown in SQL Server Books Online (http://msdn2.microsoft.com/en-us/library/ms130214.aspx).

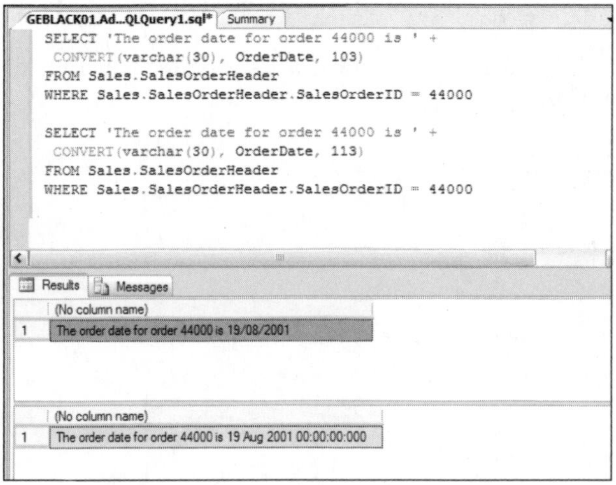

Figure 6-7:
European-style formatting for a date with and without time data.

Working with Common Table Expressions

A new feature in SQL Server 2005 is support for common table expressions. A *common table expression* is a temporary result set that is used for some purpose and is written as a WITH clause. To write a common table expression, use this general form of syntax:

```
WITH expression_name [(column_names)]
AS
(common_table_expression_definition)
```

The preceding statement is then followed by, for example, a SELECT statement that selects data from the temporary result set created using the WITH statement.

The following code shows a simple use of a common table expression. The code assumes that the AdventureWorks database is the current database.

```
WITH DirReps(ManagerID, DirectReports) AS
(
    SELECT ManagerID, COUNT(*)
    FROM HumanResources.Employee AS e
```

```
      WHERE ManagerID IS NOT NULL
      GROUP BY ManagerID
)
SELECT ManagerID, DirectReports
FROM DirReps
ORDER BY ManagerID
```

Figure 6-8 shows some of the data returned when the preceding code is executed.

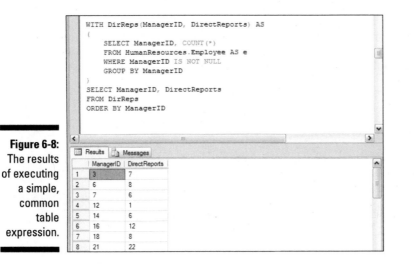

Figure 6-8:
The results of executing a simple, common table expression.

Notice in the `WITH` clause that two columns, `ManagerID` and `DirectReports`, are defined in the CTE (Common Table Expression) named `DirReps`. In effect, you create a temporary table called `DirReps`, which has two columns, named `ManagerID` and `DirectReports`.

The definition of the common table expression is contained inside parentheses:

```
SELECT ManagerID, COUNT(*)
    FROM HumanResources.Employee AS e
    WHERE ManagerID IS NOT NULL
    GROUP BY ManagerID
```

The data from the `ManagerID` column of the `HumanResources.Employee` table goes in the `ManagerID` column of `DirReps`. The data in the `DirectReports` column of `DirReps` is a count of employees that have a particular manager.

Now that you have a temporary table called `DirReps`, you can select data from it using a `SELECT` statement as you would from any ordinary table.

```
SELECT ManagerID, DirectReports
FROM DirReps
ORDER BY ManagerID
```

The preceding code simply selects the data in the two columns in the `DirReps` table.

One useful aspect of common table expressions is that you can use them *recursively;* that is, the definition of a common table expression can refer to the common table expression itself. One example is to find hierarchies in tabular information. For example, in the `HumanResources.Employee` table, you can look for the direct reports of a particular manager using the following code:

```
WITH DirectReports(ManagerID, EmployeeID, EmployeeLevel)
         AS
(
    SELECT ManagerID, EmployeeID, 0 AS EmployeeLevel
    FROM HumanResources.Employee
    WHERE ManagerID IS NULL
    UNION ALL
    SELECT e.ManagerID, e.EmployeeID, EmployeeLevel + 1
    FROM HumanResources.Employee e
        INNER JOIN DirectReports d
        ON e.ManagerID = d.EmployeeID
)
SELECT ManagerID, EmployeeID, EmployeeLevel
FROM DirectReports
ORDER BY ManagerID
```

When you execute the preceding code, you see results similar to those shown in Figure 6-9. Notice in Figure 6-9 that employee `109` has a `NULL` value for his manager's ID. The value is `NULL` because employee `109` is the boss and has no manager.

The `WITH` clause defines a temporary table, named `DirectReports`, that has three columns: `ManagerID`, `EmployeeID`, and `EmployeeLevel`. Notice that the literal number `0` is the initial value for `EmployeeLevel`.

The definition for the `DirectReports` table is a little more complex than previously and includes two `SELECT` statements and a reference to the `DirectReports` table in a join:

```
WITH DirectReports(ManagerID, EmployeeID, EmployeeLevel) AS
(
    SELECT ManagerID, EmployeeID, 0 AS EmployeeLevel
    FROM HumanResources.Employee
    WHERE ManagerID IS NULL
    UNION ALL
    SELECT e.ManagerID, e.EmployeeID, EmployeeLevel + 1
    FROM HumanResources.Employee e
        INNER JOIN DirectReports d
        ON e.ManagerID = d.EmployeeID
)
SELECT ManagerID, EmployeeID, EmployeeLevel
FROM DirectReports
ORDER BY ManagerID
```

Results | Messages

	ManagerID	EmployeeID	EmployeeLevel
1	NULL	109	0
2	3	4	3
3	3	9	3
4	3	11	3
5	3	158	3
6	3	263	3
7	3	267	3
8	3	270	3
9	6	2	2
10	6	46	2

Figure 6-9: Using a common table expression to show a hierarchy.

```
SELECT ManagerID, EmployeeID, 0 AS EmployeeLevel
    FROM HumanResources.Employee
    WHERE ManagerID IS NULL
    UNION ALL
    SELECT e.ManagerID, e.EmployeeID, EmployeeLevel + 1
    FROM HumanResources.Employee e
        INNER JOIN DirectReports d
        ON e.ManagerID = d.EmployeeID
```

Notice the WHERE clause that specifies that the initial value of ManagerID is NULL. In the second SELECT statement, notice that the value of EmployeeLevel is incremented by 1 and that the INNER JOIN references DirectReports recursively. The result is that a table containing all employees and their manager IDs is created.

You can use the DirectReports table defined in the common table expression to explore the hierarchical organization structure. For example, if you want to know which employees are on employee level 2 (that is, their manager reports directly to employee 109), you can do that easily using the following code:

```
WITH DirectReports(ManagerID, EmployeeID, EmployeeLevel)
        AS
(
    SELECT ManagerID, EmployeeID, 0 AS EmployeeLevel
```

```
     FROM HumanResources.Employee
     WHERE ManagerID IS NULL
     UNION ALL
     SELECT e.ManagerID, e.EmployeeID, EmployeeLevel + 1
     FROM HumanResources.Employee e
         INNER JOIN DirectReports d
         ON e.ManagerID = d.EmployeeID
)
SELECT ManagerID, EmployeeID, EmployeeLevel
FROM DirectReports
WHERE EmployeeLevel = 2
ORDER BY ManagerID
```

When you create the definition of common table expressions, it's possible to potentially create infinite loops. When writing common table expression definitions, you have an option to limit the maximum number of times recursion takes place. It's used in the following form:

```
SELECT columns_from_CTE
FROM CTE
OPTION (MAXRECURSION 3)
```

The preceding code limits the maximum number of recursions to three.

Chapter 7

Manipulating Data

· ·

In This Chapter

▶ Making a copy of a database

▶ Adding data using INSERT

▶ Deleting data using DELETE

▶ Changing data using UPDATE

· ·

*I*n Chapter 4, I show you how to retrieve data from a single table using a SELECT statement. In Chapter 5, I show you how to retrieve data from multiple tables using joins. In this Chapter, I show you how to modify data contained in a table.

Part of Transact-SQL is called the Data Modification Language, DML, because you can use certain Transact-SQL statements to modify data. The Data Modification Language consists of the INSERT, DELETE, and UPDATE statements, which are covered in detail in this chapter.

Copying a Database

I use the pubs database in this chapter to illustrate the use of the INSERT, DELETE, and UPDATE statements. Because you might later use the pubs database to test results from chapters in this book, I suggest you first make a copy of the pubs database and work on it. By working on a copy you can always go back to an unchanged original.

To copy a database (such as the pubs database), open SQL Server Management Studio and follow these steps to use the Copy Database Wizard:

1. **In the Object Explorer, right-click the pubs database and choose Tasks⇨Copy Database, as shown in Figure 7-1.**

   The Copy Database Wizard opens.

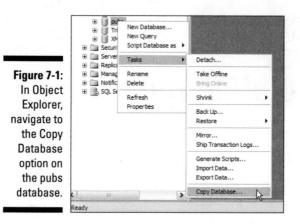

Figure 7-1:
In Object
Explorer,
navigate to
the Copy
Database
option on
the pubs
database.

2. **Click Next.**

   The Select a Source Server screen appears, as shown in Figure 7-2.

3. **Select the server containing the database you want to copy.**

   If you're already connected to a SQL Server 2005 instance, you might
   simply need to click Next on the Select a Source Server screen. If the
   desired SQL Server instance isn't displayed, click the button with an
   ellipsis (...) to the right of the Source Server text box. Then in the SQL
   Servers dialog box, choose the desired server instance and click OK to
   return to the Select a Source Server screen.

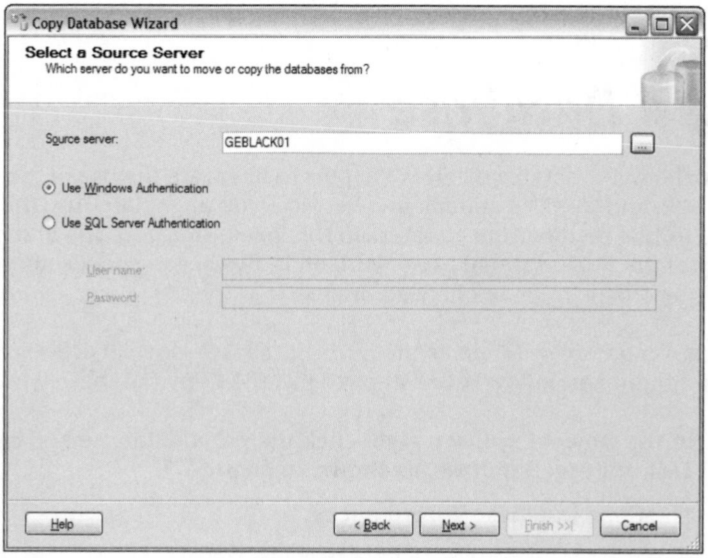

Figure 7-2:
The Select
a Source
Server
screen in
the Copy
Database
Wizard.

Alternatively, you can type the desired SQL Server instance name in the Source Server text box. For a default instance, type the name of the server. For a named instance, type the server name followed by a back slash followed by the instance name.

Figure 7-2 shows the default instance where I've selected the server name GEBlack01.

4. Click Next.

The Select a Destination Server screen opens, as shown in Figure 7-3.

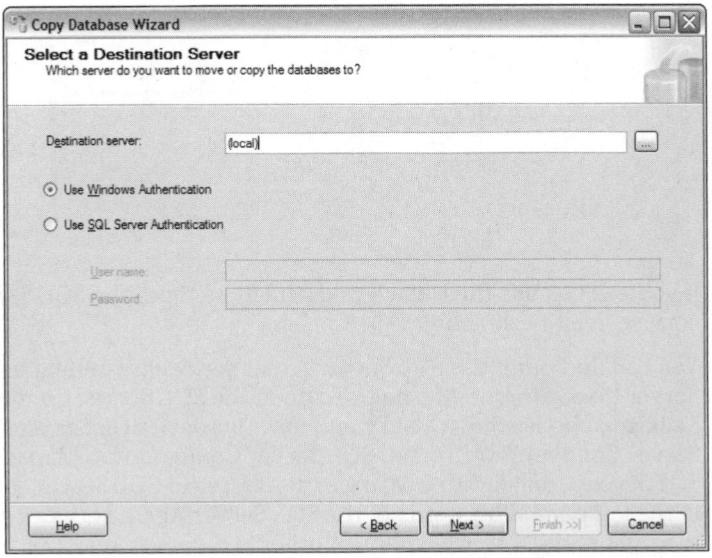

Figure 7-3:
The Select a Destination Server screen in the Copy Database Wizard.

5. In the Destination Server text box, select a destination for the copy of the database and click Next.

By default, if you're connected locally to a SQL Server instance, the (local) option is offered. If that isn't the destination you want either, type in the name of the desired SQL Server instance or click the ellipsis button and make a selection from the available SQL Server instances that are listed in the SQL Servers dialog box.

The Select the Transfer Method screen appears, as shown in Figure 7-4.

6. Choose one of the following options for transferring the data:

- **Use the Detach and Attach Method:** This is the faster option of the two. Because you're using a test database for the example, select this option.

- **Use the SQL Management Object Method:** If you copy a production database that must stay online, use this method.

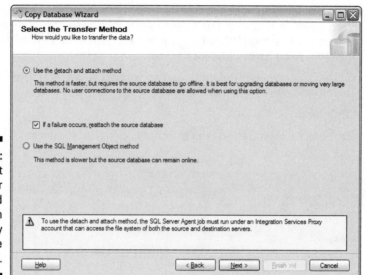

Figure 7-4:
The Select
the Transfer
Method
screen in
the Copy
Database
Wizard.

If you elect to use the Detach and Attach method, the SQL Server Agent service must be running.

You can find out if the SQL Server Agent service is running using the SQL Server Configuration Manager. To open the SQL Server Configuration Manager, choose Start➪All Programs➪Microsoft SQL Server 2005➪SQL Server Configuration Tools➪SQL Server Configuration Manager. After SQL Server Configuration Manager starts, select SQL Server 2005 Services in the left pane. The status of the SQL Server Agent service appears in the right pane, with the status of other SQL Server services. You can also check a service in the Windows operating system using various methods. One of those methods is the Services icon, which is located in the Control Panel under Administrative Tools.

 7. **After you select a transfer method, click Next.**

 The Select Databases screen appears.

 8. **Make sure that the database is selected in the Copy column and click Next.**

 The Configure Destination Database screen appears, as shown in Figure 7-5.

 9. **The default options are likely to be acceptable. Review these and make any changes, if you wish. Click Next.**

 For the example, I accept the default name for the copy of pubs_new.

 The Configure the Package screen opens.

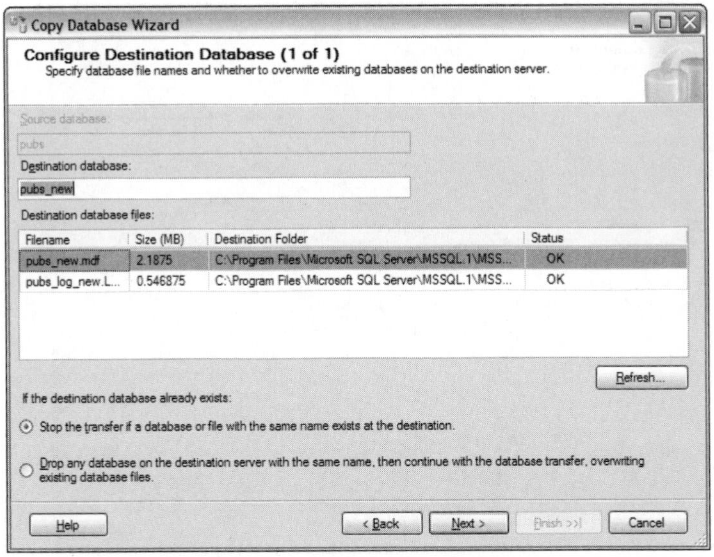

Figure 7-5:
The
Configure
Destination
Database
screen in
the Copy
Database
Wizard.

10. **Accept the default options and click Next.**

    The Schedule the Package screen opens.

11. **Make sure that the Run immediately option is selected and click Next.**

    The Complete the Wizard screen appears.

12. **Review the information in that screen, which shows the intended operation, and then click Finish to begin the copy operation.**

    The Performing Operation screen appears.

    If the copy completes successfully, you see the screen shown in Figure 7-6.

    If the SQL Server Agent service is not running, you will see the error shown in Figure 7-7.

    If the error occurs, first ensure that you start the SQL Server Agent service. Then click the Back button in the Performing Operation screen. The Complete the Wizard screen appears. Click Finish to retry the copy operation.

13. **Click the Close button to dismiss the Performing Operation screen.**

14. **Confirm that the database is available in SQL Server Management Studio. In the Object Explorer, right-click the Databases node and select Refresh from the context menu.**

    The pubs_new database appears. If you chose a different name, check that the name you chose is displayed.

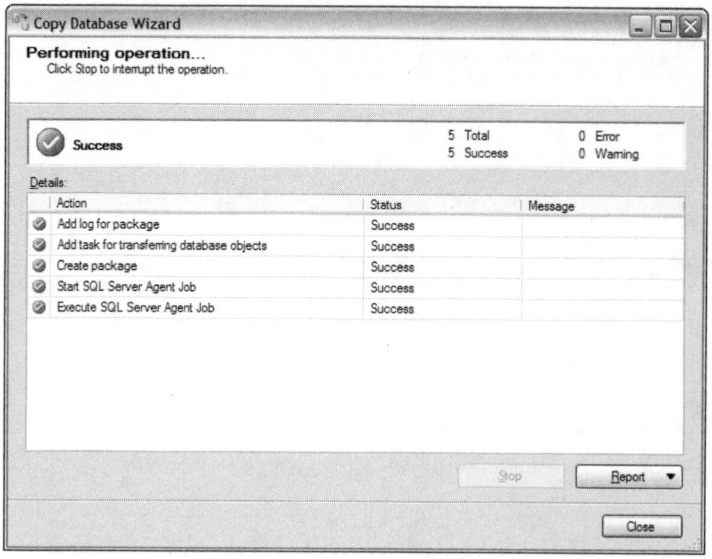

Figure 7-6:
The screen you see if copy of the database is successful.

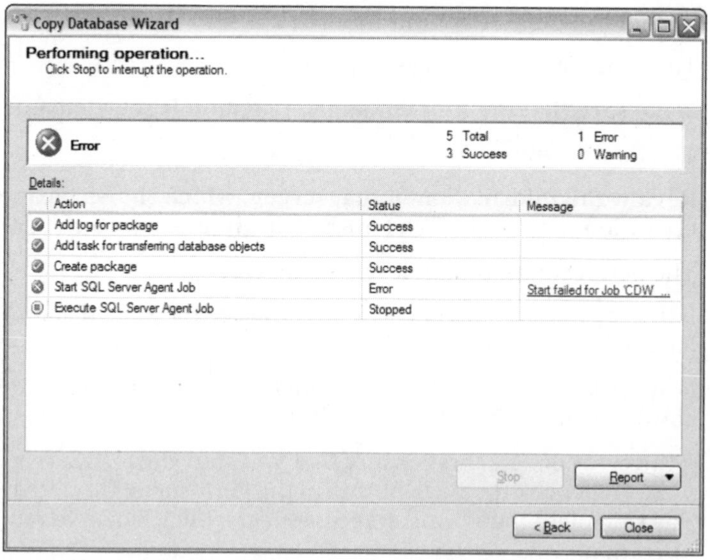

Figure 7-7:
The error you see if the SQL Server Agent service isn't running.

You're now ready to try out the Data Modification Language Transact-SQL statements on the copy of the pubs database.

Adding Data Using INSERT

You use the INSERT statement to put new data into a table. Specifically, the INSERT statement adds a row to a table.

The INSERT statement takes the following general form:

```
INSERT [<columnName> [, <columnName2>]
VALUES (<value> [, <value2>])
```

When you insert data into a table, you need to match data types for the columns in the tables that you want to insert data into. In other words, you can't try to add a string into an integer data type because the string can't be converted to a number. You can, however, add a number into a string because a number can be interpreted as a sequence of alphanumeric characters.

You can review column information in the Object Explorer by expanding the Databases node, then expanding the node for the database of interest (in this case, the pubs_new database, which is a copy of the pubs database), expand the Tables node, and then expand the node(s) for the individual tables that you want to add data to.

Writing a basic INSERT statement

The INSERT statements I show you next add a listing for this book to the pubs database. You need to add data to the authors, publishers, titleauthor, and titles tables. You can't add data first to the titles table because its pub_id column is a column key. If you try it, you see the following error message:

```
Msg 547, Level 16, State 0, Line 2
The INSERT statement conflicted with the FOREIGN KEY
constraint "FK__titles__pub_id__07020F21". The conflict
occurred in database "pubs_new", table
"dbo.publishers", column 'pub_id'.
The statement has been terminated.
```

This error happens because there is no value in the pub_id column in the publishers database. You can't specify a row that contains a column that is a foreign key if the relevant primary key hasn't been defined. See Chapter 5 for explanations of primary and foreign keys.

To add information about Wiley Publishing to the publishers table, use this code in SQL Server Management Studio query pane:

```
INSERT
INTO publishers
VALUES ('9945', 'Wiley Publishing', 'Foster City', 'CA',
           'USA')
```

When you run the code, you see this message:

```
(1 row(s) affected)
```

Notice that the values are enclosed in paired apostrophes and separated by commas. Optionally, after the name of the table, you can list the columns that you want to insert data into. In this case, you inserted data into all columns, so you didn't need to specify the column names. Data is inserted into columns in the order that they're displayed in Object Explorer. So for example, the value 9945 is inserted into the pub_id column because it's the first column specified.

There is a check constraint (I describe constraints in Chapter 10) on the publishers table. You must use a value that has four digits and begins with 99. To see the constraint, expand the Constraints node in the pubs_new database in Object Explorer.

To insert a new title into the titles table, type and execute this command in the query pane, which adds some real and some fictional data about this book:

```
USE pubs_new
INSERT
INTO titles
VALUES('WI234', 'SQL Server 2005 Programming for Dummies',
          'business', '9945', '29.99', '5000.00', '10',
          NULL, 'Not yet published.', '2006-10-16')
```

You can confirm successful inserts into both tables using an inner join. (See Chapter 5 if you need information on using inner joins.) The code looks like this:

```
SELECT publishers.pub_name, titles.title, titles.price
FROM publishers
INNER JOIN titles
ON publishers.pub_id = titles.pub_id
WHERE publishers.pub_name = 'Wiley Publishing'
```

As you can see in Figure 7-8, you have successfully inserted data about an additional publisher and title.

Figure 7-8:
Retrieving
information
on the
newly
added title
using an
inner join.

```
GEBLACK01.pu...QLQuery2.sql*

SELECT publishers.pub_name, titles.title, titles.price
FROM publishers
INNER JOIN titles
ON publishers.pub_id = titles.pub_id
WHERE publishers.pub_name = 'Wiley Publishing'
```

	pub_name	title	price
1	Wiley Publishing	SQL Server 2005 Programming for Dummies	29.99

Inserting data from another table

There is a form of the INSERT statement that allows you to load data in bulk from another table. The command takes the general form:

```
INSERT [<columnList>]
INTO <sometable>
SELECT <some_columns>
FROM <another_table>
```

The values to insert are retrieved from another table using a SELECT statement. Again, the column list for the INSERT statement is optional. If it is omitted, then the SELECT statement must match the sequence of column names and data types for all columns in the INSERT targeted table.

The following example shows how to add multiple rows from a table in another database:

```
USE pubs_new
INSERT INTO titles
SELECT *
FROM TitleData.dbo.TitlesToAdd
```

SQL Server identity columns

A SQL Server identify column is a specialized sequence counter, sometimes known as an auto counter. These types of columns are typically used to contain *surrogate keys*. It's called a surrogate key because it replaces the primary key on a table. One of the reasons for using surrogate keys is for better performance because integer surrogate keys perform better than strings. Another reason repeats an example mentioned earlier in this book. What happens when you have two customers with the same name? You have to be able to tell them apart. One solution is a surrogate key.

Figure 7-9 contains three Transact-SQL statements and two sets of results. The first `SELECT` statement displays the single value in the `titles` table in the `pubs_new` database before the preceding `INSERT` statement is executed.

The `INSERT` statement is executed, and the `SELECT` statement is executed again. Notice in Figure 7-9 that there are now three new rows in the titles table whose results are displayed in the grid.

Figure 7-9: Using a SELECT statement to INSERT data from another table.

Inserting data into a table with an identity column

If you want to insert data into a row where one column is an identity column, you typically allow SQL Server to automatically provide a value for the identity column.

The following code creates a simple table, `MessageTable`, that contains an `ID` column and a `Message` column:

```
USE master
CREATE DATABASE Messages
CREATE TABLE MessageTable(
ID int identity,
Message varchar(100)
)
```

The preceding script creates a table with an identity column called `ID`. The table has just been created, so it doesn't have any rows yet.

In the following `INSERT` statements, two techniques are demonstrated, both allowing you to insert a row into the new table. The first `INSERT` statement does not specify a column name because there is only one column that is not an identity column. In the second use of the `INSERT` statement, you explicitly provide the name of the column that doesn't take an identity value.

```
INSERT
INTO MessageTable
VALUES ('Hello World')
INSERT
INTO MessageTable (Message)
VALUES('Roses are red.')

SELECT *
FROM MessageTable
```

Figure 7-10 shows the results of executing the preceding code. Notice in the lower grid that two rows have been added to the `MessageTable` table, one row by each of the `INSERT` statements.

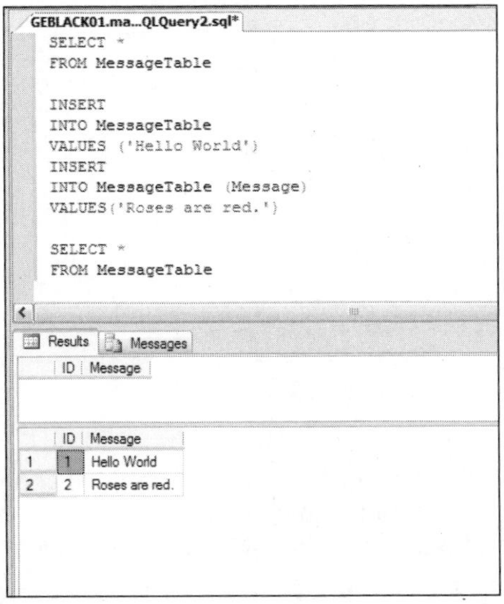

Figure 7-10: Inserting data into a table with an identity column.

By default, you can't insert a value into an identity column. If you attempt it, you get the following error message:

```
Msg 544, Level 16, State 1, Line 4
Cannot insert explicit value for identity column in table
        'MessageTable' when IDENTITY_INSERT is set to
        OFF.
```

To allow inserting data into the ID column of the MessageTable table, run this Transact-SQL code:

```
SET IDENTITY_INSERT Messages.dbo.MessageTable ON
```

After you run the code, you can insert an explicit value into the identity column:

```
INSERT
INTO MessageTable (ID, Message)
VALUES ('-50', 'Inserted the ID value from T-SQL.')
```

Figure 7-11 shows that the preceding code adds a row to the MessageTable table.

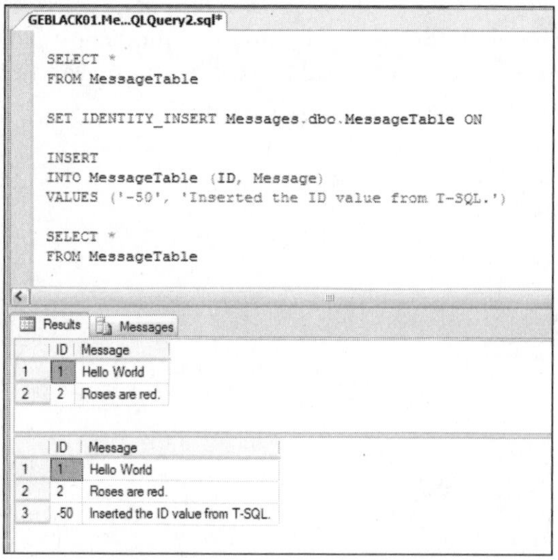

Figure 7-11: Setting IDENTITY_INSERT to ON to allow insert into an identity column.

At times, you might want to disallow any inserts on a table. If you want to prevent anyone adding data to a table, you can use an INSTEAD OF trigger to prevent the INSERT operation. I describe INSTEAD OF triggers in Chapter 13.

Removing Data Using DELETE

A DELETE statement, as its name implies, removes one or more rows from a table. To delete rows from a table, you must have delete permissions on the table. If the DELETE statement has a WHERE clause, you also need select permissions on the table.

Be careful when trying out the DELETE statement. If you're working with a database that you haven't backed up, you're risking losing data! I suggest you make a copy of a database (as described in the earlier section, "Copying a Database") when you're trying out the DELETE statement. Or you can create a table that contains data of no lasting value.

The simplest form of the DELETE statement has a FROM clause, which specifies the table that data is to be deleted from. The following Transact-SQL code deletes all rows from the MessageTable table:

```
USE Messages
DELETE
FROM MessageTable

SELECT *
FROM MessageTable
```

Figure 7-12 shows that all data has been deleted from the MessageTable table.

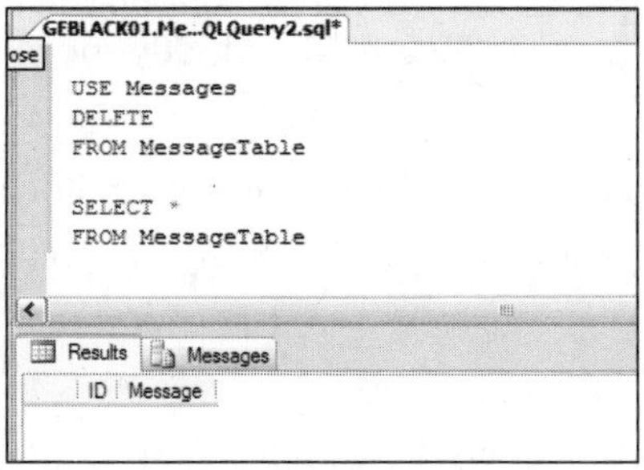

Figure 7-12:
Deleting all data from a table.

Typically, you won't want to delete all data in a table. More likely, you'll want to delete data about a specific employee, order, and so on. To make selective deletions, use the WHERE clause with a DELETE statement.

To add three rows to the MessageTable table, use the following Transact-SQL code. Notice that I turn IDENTITY_INSERT off (see the SET ... OFF command that follows), before executing three INSERT statements, each of which relies on SQL Server 2005 to create the value in the ID column.

```
SET IDENTITY_INSERT Messages.dbo.MessageTable OFF
INSERT
INTO MessageTable
VALUES ('Hello World')
INSERT
INTO MessageTable (Message)
VALUES('Roses are red.')
INSERT
INTO MessageTable (Message)
VALUES ('Inserted the ID value from T-SQL.')
```

In the preceding script, the SET command can be used to change general settings. Now, you have three rows in the `MessageTable` table. Figure 7-13 shows the data.

```
GEBLACK01.Me...QLQuery2.sql*

   SELECT *
   FROM MessageTable

 Results   Messages
     ID  Message
 1    6  Hello World
 2    7  Roses are red.
 3    8  Inserted the ID value from T-SQL.
```

If you run the data on your own machine, check the values in the ID column. Depending on which previous operations you carried out on the table, the values might differ from those shown in Figure 7-13. Modify the following code accordingly, if necessary.

To delete the row with the message `Hello World`, use the following code:

```
DELETE
FROM MessageTable
WHERE ID = 6
```

Notice in the final line of the code that you don't enclose the value in paired apostrophes because it's an `int` value. Figure 7-14 shows the data in the `MessageTable` before and after the preceding code is executed.

You can delete a set of rows by using a comparison operator other than = in the WHERE clause. The next example uses the > operator in the WHERE clause.

Run the following statement to add a third row back into the `MessageTable` table:

```
INSERT
INTO MessageTable
VALUES ('Hello World')
```

Check the values you see in the ID column. On my machine, the values are 7, 8, and 9. Delete two rows using the following Transact-SQL code:

```
DELETE
FROM MessageTable
WHERE ID > 7
```

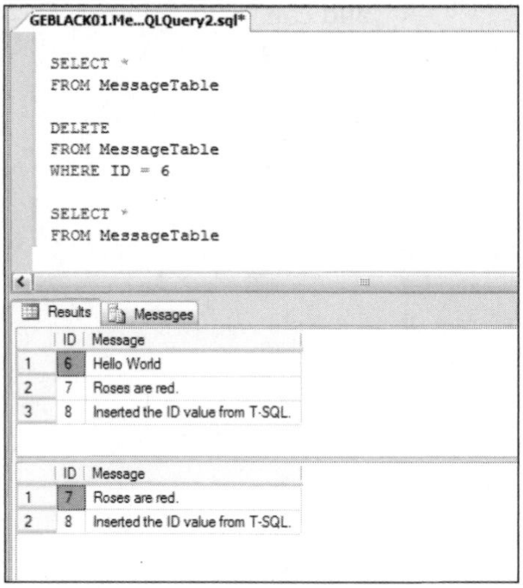

Figure 7-14:
Using a
WHERE
clause in a
DELETE
statement.

Figure 7-15 shows the data in the MessageTable table before and after running the preceding code.

Most real-life databases have references between tables. You can't delete a row containing a primary key if a foreign key in another table references it.

For example, in the pubs_new database, the titles table contains a pub_id column that references the pub_id column of the publishers table. If you attempt to delete the information about Wiley Publishing using the command

```
USE pubs_new
DELETE
FROM Publishers
WHERE pub_id = '9945'
```

you see the following error message:

```
Msg 547, Level 16, State 0, Line 2
The DELETE statement conflicted with the REFERENCE
constraint "FK__titles__pub_id__07020F21". The conflict
occurred in database "pubs_new", table "dbo.titles",
column 'pub_id'.
The statement has been terminated.
```

If you want to delete data about Wiley Publishing from the publishers table, you must first delete rows in other tables, in this case the titles table, which contains a foreign key that references that pub_id in the publishers table.

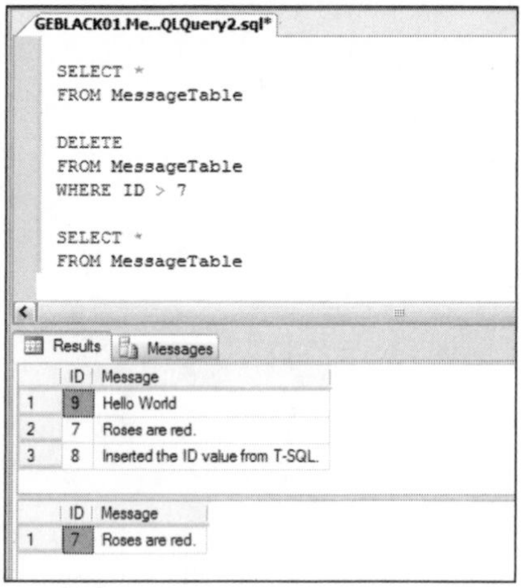

Figure 7-15:
Using the
WHERE
clause to
delete a set
of rows.

Changing Data Using UPDATE

An UPDATE statement allows you to change existing data. To execute an UPDATE statement, you need update permissions on the table. If the UPDATE statement contains a WHERE clause, you also need select permissions on the table.

The UPDATE statement takes the following general form:

```
UPDATE <tableName>
SET <columnName> = <value> , [<columnName2> = <value2>]
[FROM <sourceTableName>]
[WHERE <condition>]
```

If you've been running all the examples in this chapter, there is only a single row in the MessageTable table with the message Roses are red. To change the message so it reads Roses are very red., execute the following code.

```
UPDATE MessageTable
SET Message = 'Roses are very red.'
WHERE ID = '7'
```

Figure 7-16 shows the data before and after running the preceding code.

You can update multiple columns at once. For example, take a look at the title highlighted in Figure 7-17. To begin with, the type of this book is set to *business,* and the year-to-date sales are NULL. The following UPDATE statement changes two column values:

```
UPDATE titles
SET type = 'programming', ytd_sales = 1000
WHERE title = 'Microsoft SQL Server 2005 for Dummies'
```

The change performed by this UPDATE statement is also shown in Figure 7-17, by the inclusion of both the before and after images of the query result.

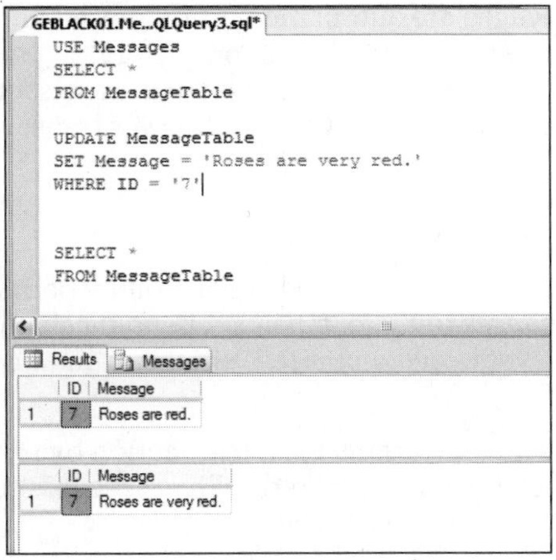

Figure 7-16: Changing the value of a message using an UPDATE statement.

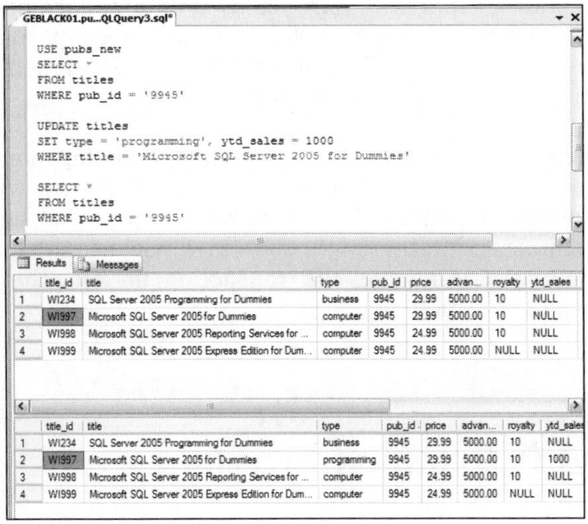

Figure 7-17: Using an UPDATE statement to change values in multiple columns.

Transactional Control

SQL Server database is a little unusual in that database changes are automatically committed unless otherwise forced. Other relational databases do not have automated commit of database changes as the default, but SQL Server does.

All SQL Server database changes are automatically committed until a BEGIN TRANSACTION command is issued. At that point, only COMMIT TRANSACTION or ROLLBACK TRANSACTION commands can terminate the transaction cleanly. Essentially, three commands are involved with SQL Server transactional control:

- ✔ BEGIN TRANSACTION   Begins a transaction.

- ✔ COMMIT TRANSACTION   Terminates a transaction by permanently storing any *pending changes* to the database. A pending change is a change that has not as yet been committed, either automatically or explicitly.

- ✔ ROLLBACK TRANSACTION   Terminates a transaction by undoing a change to the database by applying stored rollback records to quite literally "undo" what has just been changed.

The preceding commands allow for creation of explicit transactional control, or explicit transactions, explicitly controlled by programming code in sequences of Transact-SQL commands. Without the preceding commands, all DML or DDL commands, changing data in the database or metadata respectively, will automatically commit database changes.

If any errors are encountered during a transaction containing one or more changes to the database, then all changes at and after the error will be rolled back, depending on the locations of commit and rollback operations. In the following simple script, the row is not added because the ROLLBACK TRANSACTION command terminates the transaction, undoing the change just made by the INSERT statement:

```
BEGIN TRANSACTION
    INSERT INTO REGION(REGION_ID, REGION)
        VALUES(100, 'A New Region')
    ROLLBACK TRANSACTION
```

Part III
Creating Databases and Database Objects with Transact-SQL

The 5th Wave   By Rich Tennant

"We take SQL Server security here very seriously."

In this part . . .

This part covers the fundamentals of database model design, plus various database objects, including embedding programs into a database.

Database modeling uses a technique called *normalization* to design tables and the relationships between those tables. In general, the purpose of normalization is to reduce repetitive data, thereby saving space, and also to ensure that the integrity of data is maintained. A database with good data integrity is one with no data errors.

A database consists of two different types of data. The first type is the data consisting of information like customer names and addresses. The other type of data is the *metadata* (the data about the data). Metadata forms the storage structures for storing and manipulating data — the most obvious of those structures being the tables in a database. All other things in a database are also by definition database objects, no matter what their role in the grand scheme of things with respect to data and metadata. In fact, the most basic and important of all database objects is the database itself, which contains all other database objects, such as tables, indexes, views, stored procedures, and so on.

Constraints restrict values entered and enforce the validity of relationships between tables. They are not essentially independent objects but rather parts of table objects. A view stores a query that can be read just like a table. An index is a physical copy of a small part of a table's data. An index is organized in a way that promotes very rapid searching into a database's tables.

Different types of procedural objects are used to embed programming into a database. These procedural database objects are stored procedures, functions, and triggers, all of which are discussed in this part.

In addition to stored database programs, SQL Server 2005 has added programming functionality allowing for automated trapping and response when an error occurs in an embedded piece of program code.

Chapter 8

Designing, Creating, and Altering Database Objects

*T*o efficiently retrieve data from a database, you need to design it appropriately and create it to reflect the high-quality design that you define. In this chapter, I discuss how you should approach the design of a relational database and how to use T-SQL statements that allow you to create a database and modify its structure.

A database that's a good business tool results when you carefully consider its purpose and who uses it. It's far better to create a database properly at the beginning than to throw something together that you keep tinkering with and that's never really what you want or need.

Examining the Key Phases to Designing a Database

To work effectively with a relational database, you first have to design it effectively. To design an effective and efficient database, you need to plan carefully. The level of detail of planning and design varies according to the size and complexity of the project, as well as client requirements. This section gives a brief summary of some of the important tasks that you're likely to need to think about.

A full-blown database design and development process can include the following phases:

- Definition
- Requirements
- Evaluation
- Design
- Implementation
- Documentation and testing
- Delivery
- Maintenance

Each of these phases is described in detail in the following sections.

Definition

In this phase, you begin to define the purpose and scope of a database project. This is a key phase. Getting it right can save you a lot of time and money later. At the end of this phase you should have a document that defines the problem that a database is intended to solve, defines the purpose of the database, and estimates the resources needed to execute the project successfully.

In the definition phase, an important fundamental question is "What is the database for?" You can break that fundamental question down into the following subquestions, each of which is important for you to consider carefully:

- What is the business aim of the database?
- Who will use the database?
- What information will users need to retrieve in order to carry out their business tasks?

When you design a fairly simple database, you might be able to hold the key points in your head, but I strongly recommend that you document your thinking right from the beginning, even when you're designing a fairly simple database system. Creating documentation for a simple system gives you useful experience of approaching questions systematically that you can later apply to the planning and design of a more extensive system. Often, as you actually write the documentation, you become aware of gaps or ambiguities. The earlier you identify those, the less costly they are.

Requirements

In this phase, you need people skills and time. You, or a colleague, need to spend time with users who represent all likely users of the proposed system. You need to understand how they work and what *their* specific information needs are. You need to document these needs and define a data model that allows you to meet those needs.

Meeting with prospective users of the system during the requirements phase can be time consuming, and sometimes, frustrating. It's not uncommon for people to already be very busy throughout their working day, and finding time to meet with the designers and developers of a new database system is often low on their priority list. Current users also often just use the current system without having thought much about how it can be improved and how their needs for information change as the business changes.

Finding the right people to talk to is a good investment of your time. Make sure that you speak to power users and ordinary users. Make sure that you identify and document the order that pieces of information become available to users. Knowing that can be important for how you design the user interface. Also, keep in mind the varying levels of computers skills of different groups of users. An approach that seems straightforward to a power user might add a lot of hassle later in the project if ordinary users find it clumsy.

Evaluation

If the company you're working for hasn't chosen a database management system, you need to make that decision based on the needs and user model defined in the requirements phase. Review the project scope and feasibility. Create job descriptions for team members for all but small projects. Document choices made about software and project scope, resources, and how long you have to complete a project (the *timescale*).

Design

In the design phase, you map a model of user requirements into a model that you can later implement in a relational database management system. A commonly used approach creates an *entity-relationship* model. An entity-relationship model is depicted in an entity-relationship diagram (ERD), which is graphical representation of a relational database. An ERD shows all the tables in a database, plus relationships between all those tables. When you create an entity-relationship model, you need to consider the following aspects:

- ✔ Entities
- ✔ Attributes
- ✔ Identifiers
- ✔ Relationships

Entities

An *entity* in the context of the entity-relationship model is something or some-one that the user needs to know about or keep track of. For example, in a sales order system, it is obvious that you need to keep track of each order. So an order is almost certainly one entity that you need to include in the entity-relationship model. In effect, an entity is the same as a table.

Attributes

For each entity that you identify, you also need to decide which *attributes* of the entity you need to record data about. An *attribute* is simply a column or field in a table (or entity). For example, a first attempt at identifying the attributes of an order might include the following attributes:

- ✔ Order date
- ✔ Customer name
- ✔ Customer address
- ✔ Items ordered

As you list the attributes of entities that you've provisionally identified, you might find that some attributes of an existing entity would be better repre-sented as new entities. For example, in the preceding list of attributes, you notice that you need information about customers. So customer is added to the list of entities that you have identified. Similarly, you might recognize that you need information about items ordered and create additional entities such as order details or line items.

You need to consider whether an attribute that you identify is sufficiently *atomic* (broken down into its simplest form), to be appropriate. In the preced-ing list, if customers are individuals, you might want to split the customer name into two attributes: customer first name and customer last name. Similarly, the customer address probably should be broken out into multiple attributes such as customer street, customer city, customer state, customer postal code, and customer country.

You need to think about attributes in the light of business processes that you identify in the requirements phase. For example, for a retail store that doesn't deliver goods, storing customer address information as a single address might work fine. For an online or mail order retailer, almost certainly you'll need to record a billing address and a delivery address. Sometimes, the information might be the same in each, but often it will differ. You need to allow for all likely scenarios when deciding on the entities and attributes you specify.

Identifiers

In a relational database, each row must have a unique identifier. That *identifier* is used to distinguish a particular row from all other rows. In some situations, some characteristic or characteristics of an entity might be enough to provide a unique identifier. In many situations, there's no obvious combination of columns that can form a unique identifier, and you need to create an additional column (or, occasionally, columns) to specify a unique identifier. For example, in the list of attributes of an order shown earlier, there's no obvious unique identifier. So, you need to add another attribute, typically an order ID.

Relationships

In an entity-relationship model, you need to think carefully about the relationships between entities. The kinds of relationships determine how you will design relationships between tables when you come to implement the entity-relationship model.

The following kinds of relationships exist:

- **One-to-one:** A one-to-one relationship exists when one entity relates to a defined other entity, such as a book and a publisher. In other words, a book has a single publisher. Sometimes, as in this example, you need to think carefully about what you mean by an entity such as a book. For example, the hard cover edition of a book might be published by one publisher and the paperback edition by a different one. Similarly, the publisher for the United States edition of a book might be different from the publisher of the same content in the United Kingdom. In effect, a "book" is actually an edition of a book. Another example of a one-to-one relationship is the relationship between an individual U.S. citizen and the corresponding Social Security number.

- **One-to-many:** A one-to-many relationship exists when one entity relates to many entities of another kind. For example, a publisher is likely to publish many books, or an author is likely to write many books.

- **Many-to-many:** A many-to-many relationship is common and exists when many instances of one entity might relate to many instances of a different entity. For example, a book might have multiple authors, and an author might have written multiple books.

  When a many-to-many relationship exists, you can't implement that relationship between two tables in a relational database. You need to add an additional table, which often contains two keys that express a relationship with the two tables that represent the two entities between which a many-to-many relationship exists.

Chapter 5 shows how the pubs database implemented a many-to-many relationship. Information about each author is stored in the `authors` table of the `pubs` database, and information about each title is stored in the `titles` table. The `titleauthor` table contains two columns, one that expresses a relationship to the `authors` table and the other the relationship to the `titles` table. Figure 8-1 shows the relationship between these tables in the SQL Server Management Studio Query Designer.

Figure 8-1:
The relationship between the authors, titleauthor, and titles tables in the pubs database.

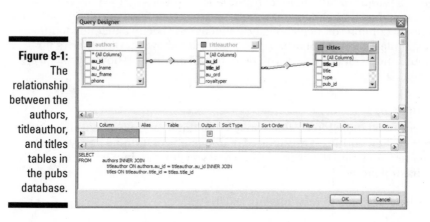

An entity-relationship model is often represented as a set of diagrams where entities are represented as rectangles and relationships as lines between the relevant entities. If you're interested in finding out more about creating entity-relationship diagrams, check out *Beginning Database Design* by Gavin Powell (Wiley).

Be careful that you don't become confused by the terms *relation* and *relationship*. The term *relation* is often used to refer to a table in a relational database. The term *relationship* is used to refer to the logical connection between two entities, tables, or relations.

Implementation

In this phase, you create a database and table structure that implements the model you created in the design phase. You create tables to correspond to the *relations* with columns that correspond to the *attributes*. If you're creating a database application on top of the database and table structure, you might be able to create the program code in parallel with the process of creating the database structure.

It is a poor decision to attempt to omit the preceding phases and start with implementation. Implementation is coding your software. Design is figuring out how to build your coding. So implementing first is akin to trying to put the cart before the horse.

In the implementation phase, you're dealing with how you create databases and, principally, how you create tables, define the data they're to contain, and define how they're related to each other. I show you how to create a database later in this chapter. In Chapter 9, I show you how to create tables.

Documentation and testing

Once you've built the database and table structure and, if appropriate, the database application, you need to test that the behavior corresponds to the design. Also, test that all the requirements defined earlier have been implemented. Testers not on the development team need to put the application through its paces. Often, subtle, or not-so-subtle, mistaken assumptions come to light during user testing. These problems might require you to revisit earlier phases to refine requirements or implementation. In addition, you'll probably create documentation to be used by end users of a database application — for example, online help or printed documentation.

Delivery

You install the database application in preparation for it to go live. This, too, might need careful planning. For example, if you're replacing a current business-critical process, consider whether a staged process of going live might be best and how much user training is needed before going live and in the days or weeks after the new application is installed.

Maintenance

You might need to correct bugs that come to light during real-world use that you didn't notice during predelivery testing. The client might need additional functionality. Depending on the scope of desired change, you might need to treat the updates as a new project using all of the phases listed here.

Normalizing Data

Unless you have knowledge of relational databases, you're likely to instinctively create data structures (entities, tables, and relationships) that differ significantly from the *normalized* forms generally found in a well-designed relational database management system.

There are three kinds of *normal form* that you're likely to use frequently when designing your databases:

- ✔ First normal form
- ✔ Second normal form
- ✔ Third normal form

Descriptions of what each of these normal forms require are often wordy and difficult to understand if the concepts are new to you. I find it is easiest to explain these concepts by providing an example and showing how you can normalize the database structure in order to ensure the integrity of data. What does that mean? It means you break your data structures down into the simplest parts so that errors can't be caused.

Normal forms are denoted in a number of ways, including First Normal Form, First normal form, 1st Normal Form, 1st normal form, 1NF, and probably a few other methods as well. Do not be alarmed or confused. This terminology all means the same thing.

First normal form

Suppose you're running a help desk and you want to log information about calls. Your first attempt at the design of a simple logging system has a single entity with the following attributes:

- ✔ CallID
- ✔ CallDate
- ✔ CallSubject
- ✔ Company
- ✔ CompanyAddress
- ✔ CompanyPhone
- ✔ ContactName

The CallID column is used to hold a unique identifier for each call. The CallDate and CallSubject are straightforward. However, if you use a single table to express this entity and you receive many calls from a single company, you will end up with multiple copies of the data containing the company address. That can cause problems with data consistency if different help desk staff enter the address in different ways. In other words, you always want the company details to be the same. Different data entry staff could spell a company's name differently or type a phone with or without hyphens and brackets. To a database, the phone numbers would be different, and thus you have two companies when in fact there is only one company. That is a data integrity problem. It's an error!

For a relation to be in *first normal form,* the following criteria must be satisfied:

- ✔ Each cell must contain a single value or be empty.

- ✔ All the cells in one column must be of the same kind.

- ✔ Each column must have a unique name.

- ✔ The ordering of columns doesn't matter. (It does matter, for example, when using the INSERT statement.)

- ✔ The ordering of rows doesn't matter.

- ✔ No two rows are permitted to be identical.

The requirement for unique column names is needed to avoid ambiguity. Think about what would happen if you had two identically named columns. A SELECT statement that included the duplicated name might mean that data was to be retrieved from one column or the other, maybe both. There would be no way to remove the ambiguity.

Table 8-1 shows what data in different columns might look like for the example call logging system.

Table 8-1			Sample Column Values		
CallID	Call Date	Call Subject	Company Name	Company Address	Contact
377777	20061128	Using XQuery in T-SQL	ABCD Company	234 Any Street, Anycity, Anystate, 12345, USA	Jane Allwood

The sample values for the CompanyAddress and ContactName columns are not atomic, so they don't satisfy the requirements of first normal form. Each value is better split into two or more parts:

- ✔ CompanyAddress   The value in the CompanyAddress column has street, city, state, postal code, and country components. To be able to select or search effectively on those components of the current value, you need to split the CompanyAddress into the following columns:

> - CompanyStreet
> - CompanyCity
> - CompanyState
> - CompanyPostalCode
> - CompanyCountry
>
> ✔ ContactName   The value in the ContactName column consists of two parts — the first name and last name of the contact. So, split that information into two columns:
>
> - ContactFirstName
> - ContactLastName

Suppose you also want to be able to track who handles each call and whether the problem has been resolved. You need to add information about the employee and about call status. The revised draft of the table now looks like this:

> ✔ CallID
>
> ✔ CallDate
>
> ✔ CallStatus
>
> ✔ CallSubject
>
> ✔ Company
>
> ✔ CompanyStreet
>
> ✔ CompanyCity
>
> ✔ CompanyState
>
> ✔ CompanyPostalCode
>
> ✔ CompanyCountry
>
> ✔ CompanyPhone
>
> ✔ ContactFirstName
>
> ✔ ContactLastName
>
> ✔ EmployeeLastName
>
> ✔ EmployeeFirstName

Second normal form

To be in *second normal form,* a relation needs to satisfy all the criteria of first normal form (see the preceding section), and each nonkey attribute must depend on the primary key. In the preceding list, several of the attributes depend on nonkeys. For example, CompanyStreet depends on the company, not the CallID, which is the unique identifier for a call.

To achieve second normal form, you can split the attributes across several tables (relations). The Call table contains the following attributes:

- ✔ CallID
- ✔ CallDate
- ✔ CallStatus
- ✔ CompanyID
- ✔ ContactFirstName
- ✔ ContactLastName
- ✔ EmployeeFirstName
- ✔ EmployeeLastName

Each of the columns in the Call table depends on the CallID, which is the primary key. The CompanyID is a foreign key that relates to a primary key, CompanyID, in the Company table shown following.

The Company table contains the following attributes:

- ✔ CompanyID
- ✔ Company
- ✔ CompanyStreet
- ✔ CompanyCity
- ✔ CompanyState
- ✔ CompanyPostalCode
- ✔ CompanyCountry
- ✔ CompanyPhone

Third normal form

A relation is in *third normal form* if it satisfies all the requirements of second normal form and, in addition, has no transitive dependencies.

A *transitive dependency* happens when some object depends on another object, which, in turn, depends on something else. So for example, if A depends on B and B depends on C, then A indirectly depends on C, or is *transitively dependent* on C.

In the `Company` table, the `CompanyCity`, `CompanyState`, `CompanyPostalCode`, and `CompanyCountry` are interdependent. If you want to ensure third normal form for the company and address data, you can split the attributes into two tables. In practical terms, you might well want to keep the company name and address data in a single table. It's a judgment call with no absolutely right or wrong answer.

Designing Relationships

Once you've decided to put related data in separate tables in order to achieve normalization (as described in the preceding section), you have to specify the kind of relationship that exists between tables.

There are three essential types of relationships that you need to consider:

 ✔ One-to-one
 ✔ One-to-many
 ✔ Many-to-many

You express relationships using *keys*. There are two types of keys — *primary key* and *foreign key*. A *primary key* is used in a row to uniquely identify that row in that table. A *foreign key* has the same set of values as a primary key in another table.

I discuss primary keys and secondary keys in more detail in Chapter 5.

Creating Databases

Creating a database in SQL Server 2005 is pretty straightforward. You can use the T-SQL `CREATE DATABASE` statement or you can design a new database in SQL Server Management Studio.

The most basic form of the `CREATE DATABASE` statement is

```
CREATE DATABASE <database name>
```

The database name used in the `CREATE DATABASE` statement must be unique in the SQL Server instance and must obey the rules for SQL Server identifiers. I introduce the rules for SQL Server identifiers in Chapter 2.

The optional arguments to the `CREATE DATABASE` statement are listed in Table 8-2.

Table 8-2	Optional Arguments for CREATE DATABASE
Argument	*What It Specifies*
ON	The location of the files that will be used to create the database.
PRIMARY	The location of the primary file(s).
LOG ON	The location of the database log files.
COLLATE	The default collation for the database.
FOR ATTACH	Use existing files to create the database.
FOR ATTACH_REBUILD_LOG	Use existing files to create the database and rebuild any missing logs.
NAME	A logical name for the database files
FILENAME	The physical name (the drive location) for the database files.
SIZE	The initial size of the file. If absent, the size of the new database is the size of the model database for that SQL Server instance.
MAXSIZE	The maximum size to which the database files are allowed to grow.
UNLIMITED	The file can grow until the hard drive is full or until a 2TB limit is reached for log files or 16TB limit is reached for database files.

Every database you create in SQL Server 2005 has a primary (database) file and a transaction log file.

If you simply create a database without specifying any of the options described in Table 8-2, then default characteristics, names and, locations are supplied. To view the default size in MB of a database, execute the following code:

```
USE master
CREATE DATABASE SimpleTest
SELECT name, size, size*1.0/128 AS [Size in MBs]
FROM sys.master_files
WHERE name = N'SimpleTest';
```

Figure 8-2 shows the results on one SQL Server 2005 instance. Depending on the size of the data model database in the SQL Server instance where you create a new database, the default size might vary from that shown. Any new database you create is based on the model database in that SQL Server instance.

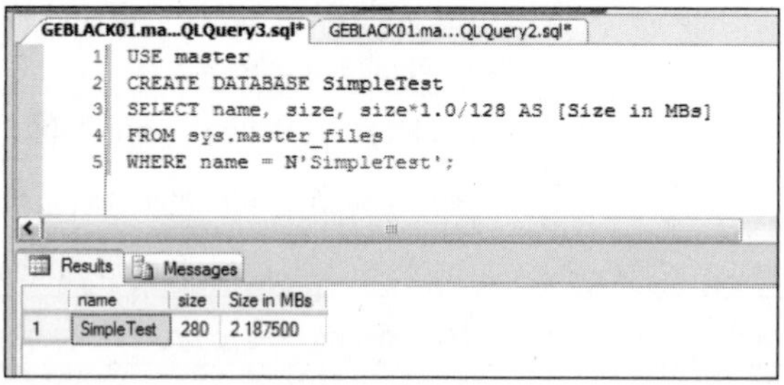

Figure 8-2:
The default
size of a
new
database.

Several characteristics of a new database are also defined by default. You can view these characteristics by right-clicking the Databases node in Object Explorer and selecting Refresh. Right-click the newly created database and select Properties. In the Database Properties dialog box, you can view the properties of the newly created database. Figure 8-3 shows several options that have been defined by default.

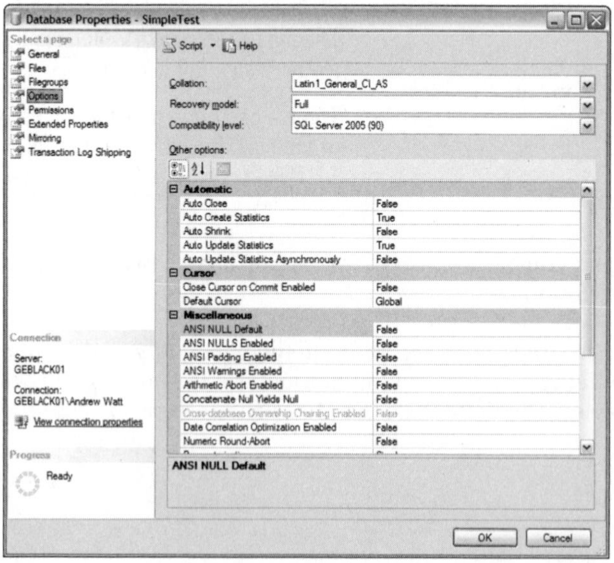

Figure 8-3:
Default
settings in a
newly
created
database.

Altering Databases

The ALTER DATABASE statement allows you to alter characteristics of a database whether it's newly created or contains large amounts of data.

When you intend to alter the characteristics of a database, I strongly recommend that you back up the database before you start. See Chapter 7 for details.

To execute the ALTER DATABASE statement on a database, you must have ALTER permissions on that database.

The general form of the ALTER DATABASE statement is

```
ALTER DATABASE <database name>
```

Followed by one or more arguments that specify which characteristic(s) of the database are to be altered. Available arguments are listed in Table 8-3.

Table 8-3	Optional Arguments for ALTER DATABASE
Argument	*What It Specifies*
MODIFY NAME	A new name for the database.
COLLATE	The collation for the database.
ADD FILE	Adds a file to the database.
ADD LOG FILE	Adds a log file to the database.
REMOVE FILE	Removes a file from the database.
MODIFY FILE	Modifies a file.
SIZE	The initial size of a new file or the new size of an existing file. (The new size must be larger than the existing size.)
MAXSIZE	The maximum size to which a file can grow.
OFFLINE	The file is offline, and all objects in the file group aren't accessible.

Dropping Databases

Dropping a database is something you ought to need to do very infrequently. When you do want to drop a database, you must be very sure that you really mean to delete the database. If you don't have relevant backups when you execute the DROP DATABASE statement, the database is deleted, and you can't expect to be able to recover the data. There is no Undo option. So, at the risk of belaboring the point, use this command with great care.

The following T-SQL commands create a new database called Disposable:

```
USE master
CREATE DATABASE Disposable
```

Confirm that the Disposable database has been created by opening Object Explorer. Expand the Databases node, right-click, and select Refresh. The Disposable database should be visible among any other databases on the relevant SQL Server instance.

To delete the database you have just created, run the following command:

```
DROP DATABASE Disposable
```

Chapter 9

Designing, Creating, and Changing Tables

....

In This Chapter

▶ Naming tables and columns

▶ Choosing data types for columns

▶ Using the CREATE TABLE statement

▶ Creating relationships using Transact-SQL

▶ Creating tables using SQL Server Management Studio

▶ Using the ALTER TABLE statement

....

*I*n this chapter, I show you an approach to the design of database tables and show you how to create tables using the T-SQL CREATE TABLE statement. In addition, I show you how to alter the structure of a SQL Server table using the ALTER TABLE statement.

You must carry out tasks such as naming tables and columns and selecting data types for those columns before you start coding. It's important that you make these decisions, particularly decisions on selection of data types, carefully.

Choosing a Naming Scheme for Tables and Columns

In Chapter 8, I discuss the phases that are useful when designing databases. In this section, I look more closely at issues relating to table design.

It's helpful to choose a consistent naming scheme both for tables and columns. A consistent naming scheme in all tables in a database makes it easier to write queries because table names and column names are easier to remember.

When you name tables, use one of the approaches in the bullet list that follows for column names. Generally, I find that naming tables is straightforward because I can use a single noun rather than a compound of two or more nouns as the table name. So table names such as Orders and Customers leave little cause for debate, although some designers prefer orders and customers (that is, they use all lowercase letters).

SQL Server by default, does not care about case (it is case insensitive), so the convention matters more than anything else. And convention is often a personal preference or a standard within a specific end-user organization.

Naming columns can be a negotiable, if not problematic exercise. My personal preference is to avoid abbreviations in column names — except for obvious ones like ID in a CallID column, for example — and to use an initial uppercase letter for each word in a column name that contains more than one word.

Commonly used naming conventions include the following:

✔ Use lowercase letters for all column names. Some column names in the pubs database use this approach. It does have the advantage of consistency, but one disadvantage is that long column names can become difficult to read.

✔ Use lowercase letters for the first word in a column name, but start each later word using an uppercase letter — for example, lastName.

✔ Use an uppercase letter to begin each word in a column name — for example, LastName. This is the approach I prefer. This approach is widely used in the AdventureWorks database.

✔ Use underscore characters to separate words in a column name — for example last_name or Last_Name. This is used in several column names in the pubs database.

✔ Abbreviate one or more of the words in a column name. I suggest you avoid this approach because many such abbreviations are nonstandard and make it more difficult to remember column names. Abbreviations are used in several column names in the pubs database.

In some situations, you choose the naming scheme that is an enterprise standard. In other projects, you have complete freedom to choose one of the options listed here. Whatever approach you choose, it helps later writing of queries if you adopt one approach and stick to it in all column names. In other words, be consistent throughout the naming of your database objects.

I recommend that you avoid the use of space characters in a compound name. If you use space characters, you need to use paired square brackets to delimit the name in Transact-SQL queries. Writing complex T-SQL queries can be difficult enough without adding an extra burden of ensuring the correct use of multiple pairs of square brackets. Make life easy for yourself.

Choosing Data Types for Columns

Choosing a data type for each column can be straightforward in many situations. However, carefully consider the possible values that are in use now and how future business changes might impact on values that you'll need to store at some future date. It's good practice to give careful thought to the data type of each column when you create the table.

As described in Chapter 2, a data type is a way of forcing data in a specific column to be of a specific kind and format. For example, a numeric data type only accepts numbers, whereas a string data type accepts alphanumeric characters. Alphnumeric characters include both numbers and letters.

SQL Server 2005 supports an extensive range of data types that you can use in the tables that you create. Specifying a data type for each column in a SQL Server table is mandatory. It avoids the possibility that the wrong type of data is inserted into a column. For example, if one column of a table should accept only numeric values, but all columns in a database consist of varchar(30), you have no way to prevent character data being entered into the column. When some later processing expects numeric data in that column, errors are likely.

When choosing the correct data type for a column, avoid, for example, truncating data where you specify a data type of varchar(30) but some values are greater than 30 characters in length.

I briefly describe the data types available for use in SQL Server 2005 in the following sections.

Exact numeric data types

Table 9-1 briefly describes exact numeric data types.

Table 9-1	Exact Numeric Data Types	
Data Type	*Size in Bytes*	*Description*
bigint	8	Includes the range -2^{63} ($-9,223,372,036,854,775,808$) to $2^{63}-1$ ($9,223,372,036,854,775,807$).
bit	1 byte can store from 1 to 8 bit values.	An integer value that stores the values 0, 1, or null. SQL Server 2005 optimizes storage of bit data types by storing each group of up to 8-bit columns as a single byte.
decimal	Depends on the scale sion of the number.	Stores numeric values with and preci-fixed precision and scale. The *precision* is the total number of decimal digits that can be stored (both to the left and right of the decimal point). The *scale* is the maximum number of decimal digits that can be stored to the right of the decimal point. The precision must be in the range 1 to 38. Possible values when maximum precision is used is in the range $-10^{38}+1$ through $10^{38}-1$. I list in a following table the storage needs for values of the decimal data type of varying precision. The decimal data type is functionally equivalent to the numeric data type.
int	4	Includes the range -2^{31} ($-2,147,483,648$) to $2^{31}-1$ ($2,147,483,647$).
money	8	Used to represent currency. Values in the range $-922,337,203,685,477.5808$ to $922,337,203,685,477.5807$ can be represented.
numeric	Depends on the scale and precision of the number.	Possible values when maximum preci-sion is used are in the range $10^{38}+1$ through $10^{38}-1$. The numeric data type is functionally equivalent to the decimal data type. In other words, the numeric data type is a synonym for the decimal data type.
smallint	2	Includes the range -2^{15} ($-32,768$) to $2^{15}-1$ ($32,767$).

Data Type	Size in Bytes	Description
smallmoney	4	Used to represent currency. Values in the range −214,748.3648 to 214,748.3647 can be represented.
tinyint	1	Includes the range 0 to 255.

The number of bytes used by each value of decimal data type are shown in Table 9-2.

Table 9-2	Storage Requirements of Approximate Numeric Data Types
Precision	**Bytes for Storage**
1–9	5
10–19	9
20–28	13
29–38	17

Approximate numeric data types

Table 9-3 briefly describes approximate numerics. An *approximate numeric data type* stores a value to base 2 that is a close approximation, in most circumstances, to the desired number to base 10.

Table 9-3	Approximate Numeric Data Types	
Data Type	**Size in Bytes**	**Description**
float	4 or 8	Represents floating point numbers in the range −1.79E+308 to −2.23E−308, 0 and 2.23E−308 to 1.79E+308. A float value has a mantissa in the range 1 to 53. That is equivalent to a precision of 7 or 15 digits.
real	4	Represents floating point numbers in the range −3.40E + 38 to −1.18E − 38, 0 and 1.18E − 38 to 3.40E + 38. A real value is equivalent to float(24).

Values of the `float` data type use either 4 bytes or 8 bytes for the storage of each value. The number of bytes used for storage depends on the number of digits in the mantissa of the floating point value which is to be stored. The *mantissa* is the part of the floating point number after the decimal point. Where the number of bits used to store the mantissa is in the range 1 through 24, a `float` value can represent 7 digits and uses 4 bytes. When the number of bits used to store the mantissa is in the range 25 through 53, a `float` value can represent 15 digits and uses 8 bytes of storage.

Date- and time-related data types

Table 9-4 briefly describes data types relating to the representation of date and time. The data type you choose depends on the range of dates that you need to represent and the size of the smallest time interval that you need to represent.

Table 9-4	Data and Time Data Types	
Data Type	*Size in Bytes*	*Description*
datetime	4	Represents a date and time of day in the range January 1, 1753, through December 31, 9999, to an accuracy of 3.33 milliseconds.
smalldatetime	2	Represents a date and time of day in the range January 1, 1900, through June 6, 2079, to an accuracy of 1 minute. Values entered are rounded to the nearest minute.

Non-Unicode character data types

Table 9-5 briefly describes data types available for the storage of character data.

Table 9-5	Character Data Types
Data Type	*Description*
char(n)	Stores fixed-length character data. The value in parentheses specifies the number of characters that can be stored and the number of bytes used to store each value. The value in parentheses is in the range 1 through 8,000.

Data Type	Description
`text`	Deprecated in SQL Server 2005. Use `varchar(max)` instead for storage of variable-length, non-unicode data.
`varchar(n)`	Stores variable-length character data. The value in parentheses specifies the maximum number of characters that can be stored and the number of bytes used to store each value. The value in parentheses is in the range 1 through 8,000 and `max`. Where the value in parentheses is `max`, the maximum number of characters that can be stored is $2^{31}-1$.

Unicode character data types

Table 9-6 briefly describes data types available for the storage of Unicode character data.

Table 9-6	Unicode Character Data Types
Data Type	**Description**
`nchar(n)`	Stores fixed-length character data. The value in parentheses specifies the number of bytes used to store each value, which is twice the number of characters that can be stored because each Unicode character requires 2 bytes for storage. The value in parentheses is in the range 1 through 8,000.
`ntext`	Deprecated in SQL Server 2005. Use `nvarchar(max)` instead for storing variable-length, Unicode character strings.
`nvarchar(n)`	Stores variable-length character data. The value in parentheses specifies the number of bytes used to store each value which is twice the numberß of characters that can be stored because each Unicode character requires 2 bytes for storage The value in parentheses is in the range 1 through 8,000 and `max`. Where the value in parentheses is `max` the maximum number of characters that can be stored is $2^{31}-1 / 2$.

Binary data types

Table 9-7 briefly describes the data types available for storage of binary data.

Table 9-7	Binary Data Types
Data Type	**Description**
binary(n)	Stores fixed-length binary data. The values allowed in parentheses are in the range 1 through 8,000 and represent the number of bytes that can be stored.
Image	Deprecated in SQL Server 2005. Use `varbinary (max)` instead.
varbinary(n)	Stores variable-length binary data. The values allowed in parentheses are in the range 1 through 8,000 and `max`. When the value in parentheses is in the range 1 through 8,000, that's the number of bytes used to store each value. When the value in parentheses is `max`, up to $2^{31}-1$ bytes can be stored.

Miscellaneous data types

In Table 9-8, I briefly describe some miscellaneous data types available for use in SQL Server 2005.

Table 9-8	Miscellaneous Data Types
Data Type	**Description**
cursor	A data type for storage of variables or stored procedure OUTPUT parameters that contain a reference to a cursor.
sql_variant	A data type for storage of values of various SQL Server 2005-supported data types, except `text`, `ntext`, `image`, `timestamp`, and `sql_variant`. The data type of the value stored in each row may differ. Also, because the maximum storage for a `sql_variant` value is 8,016 bytes, storage of `varchar(max)`, `nvarchar(max)`, and `varbinary(max)` values is not supported, but `varchar(n)`, `nvarchar(n)`, and `varbinary(n)` are supported.
table	A special data type used to store a result set for later processing. A result set is the result of execution of a query.
timestamp	Stores an automatically generated binary number often used to time stamp rows. Each value requires 8 bytes of storage.

Data Type	Description
`uniqueidentifier`	Stores a 16-byte GUID (Globally Unique Identifier).
`xml`	Stores XML data in Native XML format, Native implying the stored xml column is directly interpretable as an XML document. This is new in SQL Server 2005. The stored binary representation cannot exceed 2GB in size.

The CREATE TABLE statement

Use the CREATE TABLE statement to create a table and define the structure of its columns. You see in Chapter 8 that when you use the CREATE DATABASE statement, several characteristics of a new database are specified because the model database is used to create the new database. There is no such facility for the CREATE TABLE statement, so you need to specify the columns in the table and specify the data type for each column.

As an alternative to the CREATE TABLE statement, you can create a table using the graphical user interface in SQL Server Management Studio's Object Explorer. It's important that you understand the CREATE TABLE statement because you might sometimes need to define aspects of a table that aren't easily specified using the graphical user interface. In addition, in larger projects, you'll likely use or edit CREATE TABLE statements.

A simple use of the CREATE TABLE statement is

```
CREATE TABLE <table_name>
( <column_definitions>
 )
```

The table name must adhere to the naming rules for identifiers. Each column definition consists, at a minimum of the column name followed by the data type of the column. Column definitions are separated by a comma. I suggest you define each column on a separate line, which aids readability of your code.

When using the CREATE TABLE statement, precede it by a USE <database_name> statement to ensure that the table is created in the intended database. Failing to include the USE statement will, in time, lead to you creating one or more tables in the wrong database, often the master database.

To create a database Chapter9Test and create a Messages table in it, execute the following code:

```
USE master
CREATE DATABASE Chapter9Test
GO
USE Chapter9Test
CREATE TABLE Messages
( MessageID int,
Message varchar(100)
)
```

Figure 9-1 shows the appearance in Object Explorer after creating the Chapter9Test database and adding the Messages table to it. I have expanded several nodes to aid clarity. Notice that the column definitions you specified in the T-SQL code are expressed in Object Explorer.

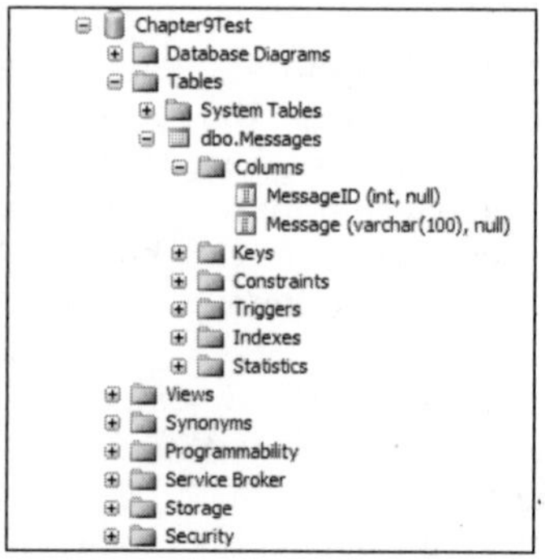

Figure 9-1:
The newly created Chapter9-Test database shown in Object Explorer.

Optionally, you can specify a database name and a schema name when creating a table using the CREATE TABLE statement. So, for example, if you're in the dbo role, you can omit the code

```
USE Chapter9Test
```

in the preceding example and write the CREATE TABLE statement as

```
CREATE TABLE Chapter9Test.dbo.Messages
( MessageID int,
Message varchar(100)
)
```

Typically, when creating a table, you need to express a relationship between two tables using primary key and foreign key constraints. I describe how to create these in the next section. Often, you want to specify additional constraints when creating tables. I describe more about constraints in Chapter 10.

I describe later in this chapter how to create tables using SQL Server Management Studio.

Creating Relationships Using Transact-SQL

In a real-life relational database, you almost always have relationships between tables. In the design phase of your database project, you should define the tables you want to create, for example, using an entity-relationship model. When doing this, you should recognize which columns (attributes) you plan to use as primary keys or foreign keys.

To illustrate how to create two tables that have a relationship between them, I show you how to create tables for publishers and their titles. You can represent the needed data in two tables, Publishers and Titles. To create a simple version of a Publishers table, execute the following code:

```
USE Chapter9Test
CREATE TABLE Publishers (
PublisherID int identity PRIMARY KEY Not Null,
PublisherName varchar(50) Not Null,
PublisherCity varchar (40) Not Null
)
```

Figure 9-2 shows the appearance you should see in Object Explorer, after you've expanded the relevant nodes.

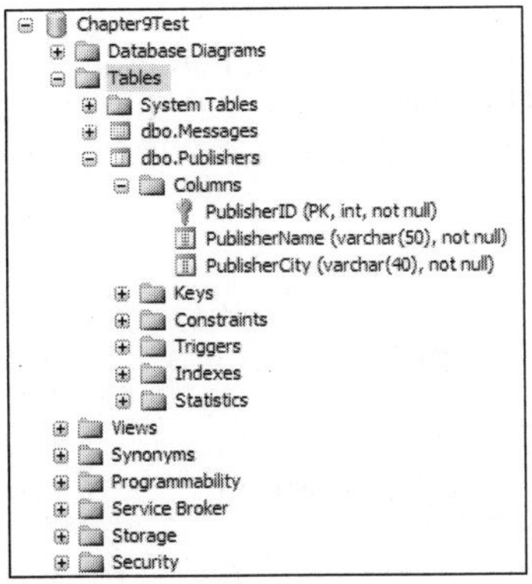

Figure 9-2: The newly created Publishers table.

Notice, in Figure 9-2, the key symbol to the left of the PublisherID column. That indicates that the PublisherID column is the primary key for each row in the Publishers table.

Notice that when defining the PublisherID column, it's defined both as identity and as PRIMARY KEY. The identity keyword specifies that the value in the PublisherID column is to be generated automatically. The

PRIMARY KEY keyword specifies that the PublisherID column is to be the primary key for each row in the Publishers table. You can demonstrate that the values in the PublisherID column are generated automatically by executing the following code:

```
INSERT INTO Publishers
VALUES ('Sample Publisher', 'New York')
```

then selecting the data you just added by executing this code:

```
SELECT *
FROM Publishers
```

Figure 9-3 shows the results.

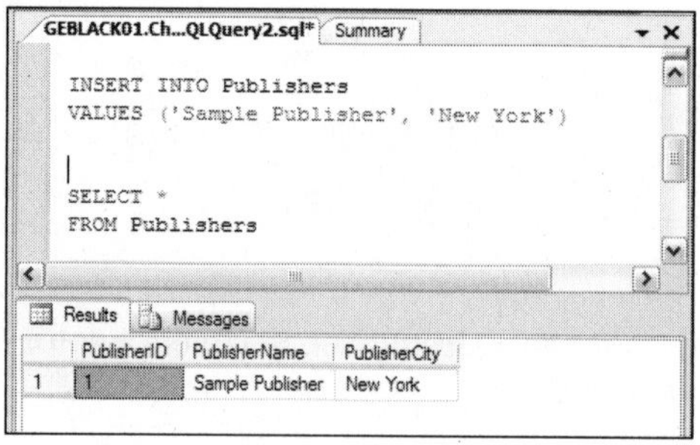

Figure 9-3:
The value of
an identity
column is
generated
automat-
ically.

Now that you've created the Publishers table, you can create a Titles table that references a publisher ID. For the purposes of this example, I assume that each book has a single author. To do that, run the following code:

```
USE Chapter9Test
CREATE TABLE Titles
(
TitleID int PRIMARY KEY Not Null,
Title varchar (100) Not Null,
PublisherID int FOREIGN KEY REFERENCES dbo.Publishers,
Author varchar(100) Not Null
)
```

Figure 9-4 shows the appearance of the newly created Titles table in Object Explorer. Notice the key symbol to the left of the TitleID column. Also, notice PK in parentheses indicating that the TitleID column is the primary key.

Notice, too, the key symbol to the left of the PublisherID column and the FK in parentheses indicating that the PublisherID column is a foreign key.

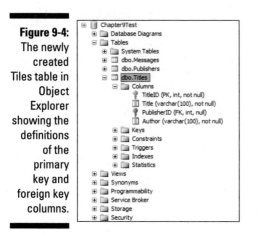

Figure 9-4:
The newly
created
Tiles table in
Object
Explorer
showing the
definitions
of the
primary
key and
foreign key
columns.

You can demonstrate in a couple of ways that the PublisherID column in the Titles table that you've just created is working correctly. One way is to add a value to the Titles table and then use a join to retrieve the relevant data. First, insert a row in the Titles table:

```
INSERT
INTO Titles
VALUES ('001', 'Some sample title', 1, 'John Smith')
```

Then, confirm successful insertion of the row:

```
SELECT *
FROM Titles
```

Next, execute the INNER JOIN:

```
SELECT Publishers.PublisherName, Titles.Title,
        Titles.Author
FROM Publishers
INNER JOIN Titles
ON
Publishers.PublisherID = Titles.PublisherID
```

Figure 9-5 shows the results of executing the two preceding SELECT statements.

If the relationship between the Titles and Publishers tables has been implemented correctly, you're unable to insert a value for the PublishersID column in the Titles table that isn't present in the PublishersID column of the Publishers table. Remember that the Publishers column has a single row with the value in the PublisherID column of 1. Execute the following statement to attempt to insert a row in the Titles table that contains an invalid value in the PublisherID column:

```
INSERT
INTO Titles
VALUES (
'2', 'A second title', 2, 'Jane Doe'N
)
```

```
SELECT *
FROM Titles

SELECT Publishers.PublisherName, Titles.Title, Titles.Author
FROM Publishers
INNER JOIN Titles
ON
Publishers.PublisherID = Titles.PublisherID
```

	TitleID	Title	PublisherID	Author
1	1	Some sample title	1	John Smith

	PublisherName	Title	Author
1	Sample Publisher	Some sample title	John Smith

Figure 9-5:
Confirming
successful
creation
of the
relationship.

When you attempt to run that code, the following error message is displayed, indicating that the primary key-foreign key relationship was successfully implemented when you created the `Titles` table.

```
Msg 547, Level 16, State 0, Line 1
The INSERT statement conflicted with the FOREIGN KEY
        constraint "FK__Titles__Publishe__0BC6C43E".
        The conflict occurred in database
        "Chapter9Test", table "dbo.Publishers", column
        'PublisherID'.
The statement has been terminated.
```

Creating Tables Using SQL Server Management Studio

You can use the graphical tools in SQL Server Management Studio to create databases and tables. In this example, I show you how to create a database, `Chapter9Test2`, and create `Publishers` and `Titles` tables in it, which implement the primary key-foreign key relationship shown in the preceding section.

The choice of whether you use the graphical tools or Transact-SQL to create database objects is yours in many situations. In practice, if you're working frequently with SQL Server 2005, it's likely that you need to master both techniques.

Creating the database

To create the Chapter9Test2 database in SQL Server Management Studio, follow these steps:

1. **Open SQL Server Management Studio.**

   Choose Start⇨All Programs⇨SQL Server 2005⇨SQL Server Management Studio.

2. **If Object Explorer isn't visible, choose View⇨Object Explorer.**

3. **Right-click the Databases node. From the context menu, select the New Database option.**

   The New Database dialog box shown in Figure 9-6 opens.

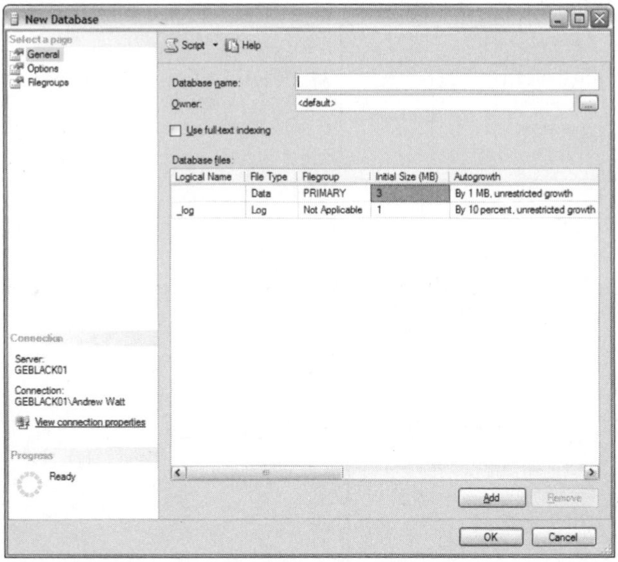

Figure 9-6:
The New Database dialog box.

4. **In the Database Name text box, type** Chapter9Test2. **Click OK.**

To verify that the database has been created successfully, right-click the Databases node in Object Explorer and select Refresh. The Chapter9Test2 database should be among the databases displayed.

Creating the tables

To create the Publishers table, follow these steps:

1. **Expand the Chapter9Test2 database node in Object Explorer and expand the Tables node inside it.**

2. **Right-click the Tables node and select the New Table option.**

3. **In the dialog box that opens, enter values in the Column Name and Data Type columns as you see in the minitable that follows. (Keep in mind that this minitable is not how it looks on your screen, as shown in Figure 9-7.)**

Column Name	Data Type
PublisherID	Int
PublisherName	varchar(50)
PublisherCity	varchar(40)

   To toggle the check box in the Allow Nulls column, press the spacebar.

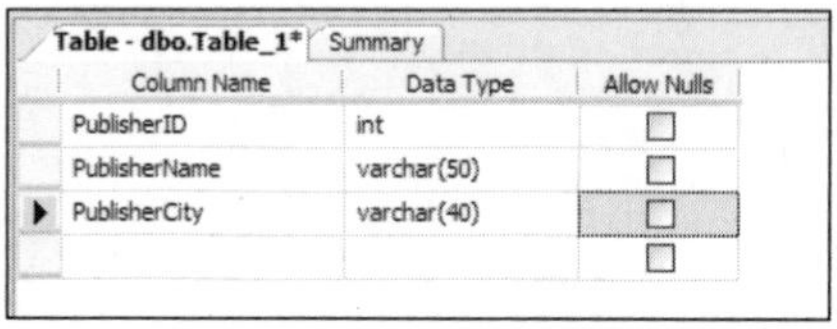

Figure 9-7:
Defining the columns in the Publishers table.

4. **Right-click the tab of the table design pane and select the Save option, as shown in Figure 9-8.**

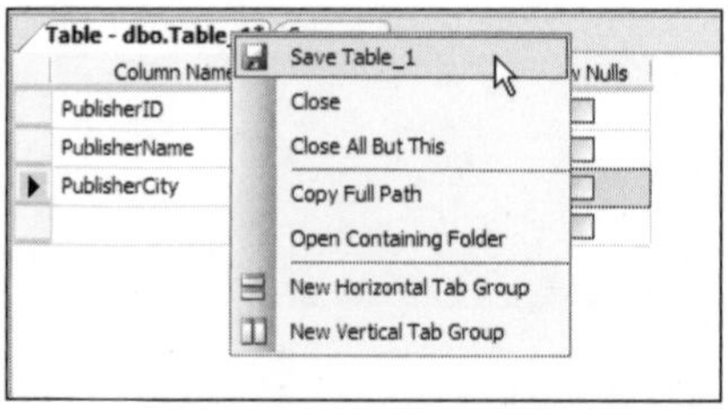

Figure 9-8:
Selecting to save the table design.

The Choose Name dialog box opens, as shown in Figure 9-9.

5. **In the Enter a Name for the Table text box, type Publishers. Click OK.**

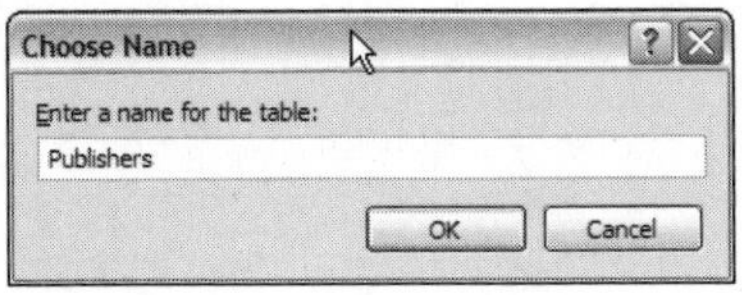

Figure 9-9:
The Choose
Name
dialog box.

Figure 9-9:
The Choose
Name
dialog box.

6. **Right-click the `Tables` node in Object Explorer and select Refresh.**

   The `Publishers` table is displayed.

7. **Right-click the `Publishers` node and select Modify.**

8. **Right-click the arrow button at the top left of the table designer. (See the position of the cursor in Figure 9-10.)**

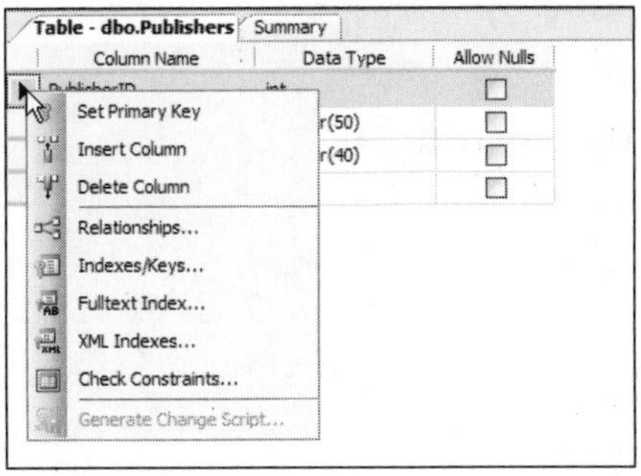

Figure 9-10:
Making a
column the
primary key.

9. **Select the Set Primary Key option.**

   The `PublisherID` column should now have a key symbol to the left of its name in the table designer, as shown in Figure 9-11.

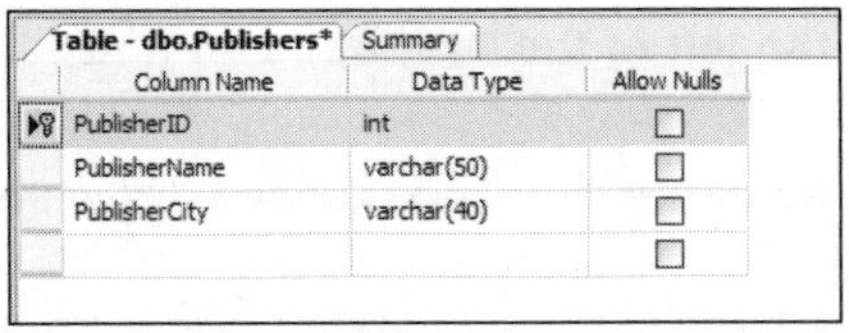

Figure 9-11:
The key
symbol
identifies
the primary
key column.

10. **Right-click the tab for the table designer and select Save.**

    In Object Explorer, right-click the `Tables` node in `Chapter9Test2`. Expand the `Columns` node and confirm that the `PublisherID` column is now the primary key, as shown in Figure 9-12.

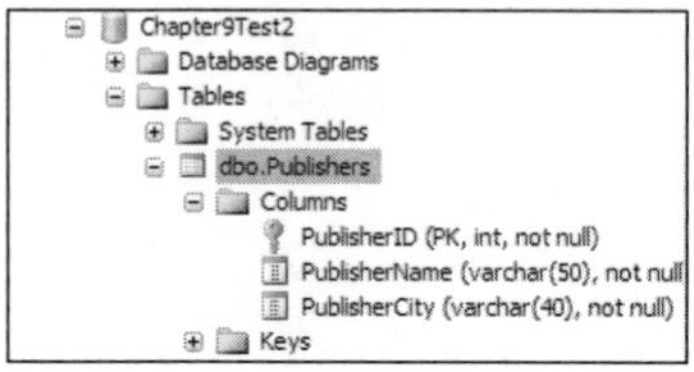

Figure 9-12:
The column
definitions
in Object
Explorer.

To create the `Titles` table, follow these steps:

1. **Right-click the `Tables` node and select New Table.**

2. **In the table designer, enter data as it is in the minitable that follows. (Keep in mind that this minitable is not how it looks on your screen, as shown in Figure 9-13.)**

Column Name	Data Type
TitleID	Int
Title	Varchar(100)
PublisherID	Int
Author	Varchar(100)

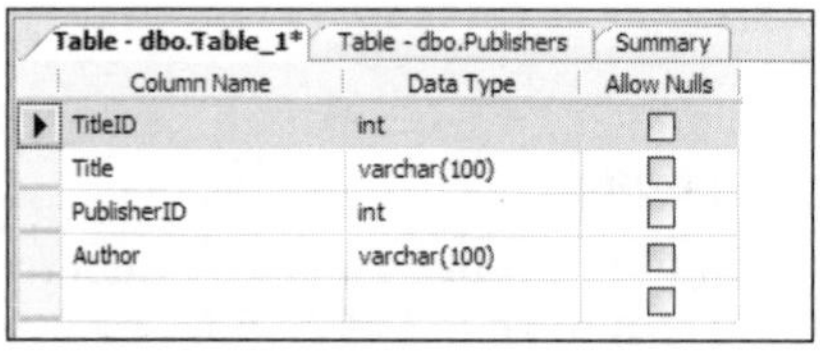

Figure 9-13:
The
definition
of the Titles
Table in
the table
designer.

3. **Right-click the arrow to the left of the `TitleID` row and select the Set Primary Key option.**

4. **Right-click the arrow to the left of the `PublisherID` row and select the Relationships option.**

   The Foreign Key Relationships dialog box, shown in Figure 9-14.

5. **Click the ellipsis (. . .) to the right of the `Tables and Columns Specification` node, shown by the cursor position in Figure 9-14.**

   The Tables and Columns dialog box opens.

6. **Click the Primary Key Table drop-down list and select the `Publishers` table, as shown in Figure 9-15.**

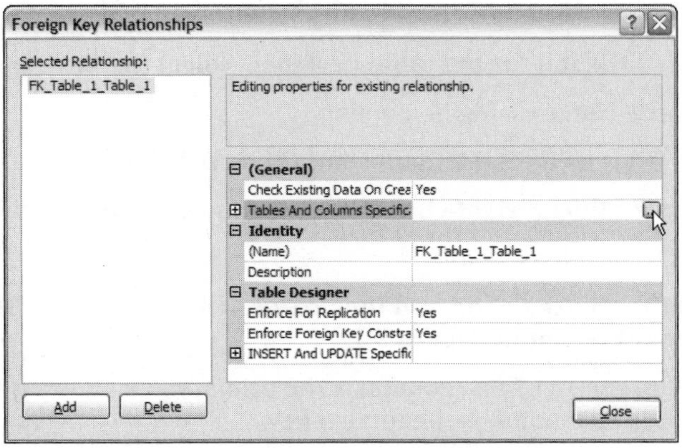

Figure 9-14:
Click the
ellipsis to
the right
of the
Tables and
Columns
Specifica-
tion node.

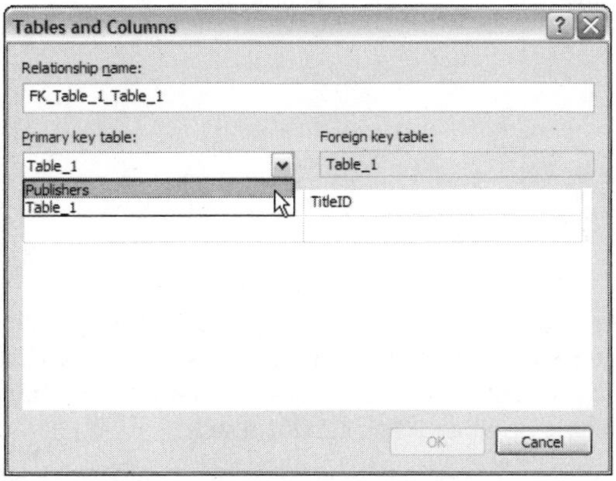

Figure 9-15:
Select the
Publishers
table as
the primary
key table.

7. **Select the `PublisherID` column in the two drop-down lists shown in Figure 9-16 and click OK.**

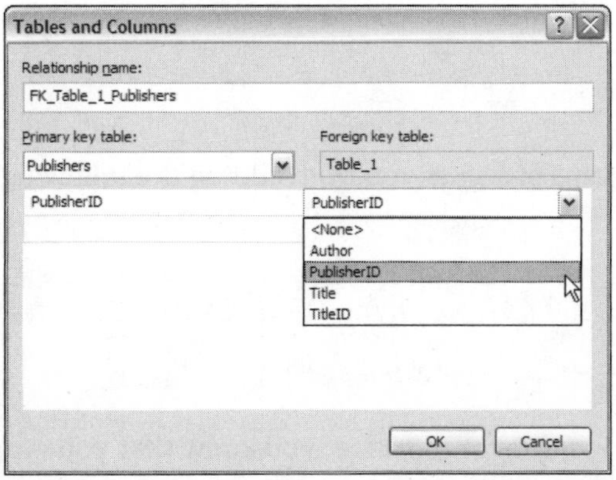

Figure 9-16:
Specifying
columns.

8. **Click Close to close the Foreign Key Relationships dialog box.**

9. **Right-click the tab for the table designer. Select the Save option.**

   The Choose Name dialog box opens.

10. **Specify** Titles **as the table name and then click OK.**

11. **In Object Explorer, right-click the** `Tables` **node and select Refresh.**

    The `Titles` table is visible.

12. **Expand the** `Titles` **node and the** `Columns` **node inside it. The appearance should resemble Figure 9-17.**

    Notice that the `TitleID` column is the primary key and that the `PublisherID` column is the foreign key.

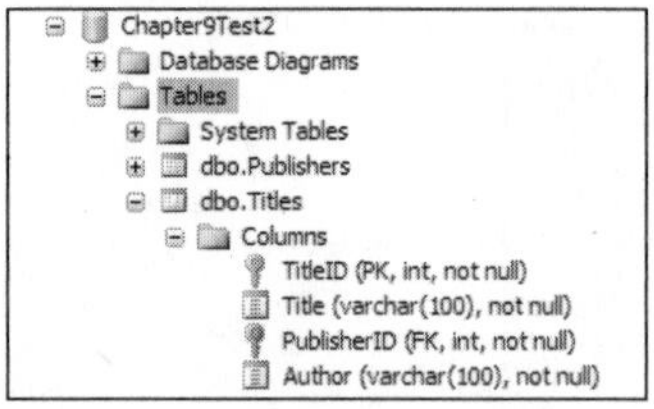

Figure 9-17:
Specifying
the foreign
key column.

In the next section, you can verify the relationship between the `Publishers` and `Titles` tables. The next sequence of commands inserts a single row into each of the `Publishers` and `Titles` tables. Also, remember that for this example, you're using the `Chapter9Test2` database:

```
USE Chapter9Test2
INSERT
INTO Publishers
VALUES (
1, 'A publisher', 'New York')

INSERT
INTO Titles
VALUES (
'1', 'A title', 1, 'Janice James')
```

The foreign key constraint prevents you from adding the following invalid row to the `Titles` table:

```
INSERT
INTO Titles
VALUES (
'2', 'A second title', 2, 'James Caroll')
```

When you see the following error message, you know that you correctly defined the relationship.

```
Msg 547, Level 16, State 0, Line 1
The INSERT statement conflicted with the FOREIGN KEY
constraint "FK_Titles_Publishers". The conflict
occurred in database "Chapter9Test2", table
"dbo.Publishers", column 'PublisherID'.
The statement has been terminated.
```

The ALTER TABLE Statement

So far in this chapter, you have seen tables created with the called CREATE TABLE statement. You have also seen creation of tables in the SQL Server Management Studio. Altering a table in SQL Server Management Studio is just as easy as creating a new one. To alter a table in the Management Studio, you simply right-click the table name in the Object Explorer and then select the Modify option.

The ALTER TABLE statement allows you to change tables from the command line, as a new query in the query window, or even using a tool such as SQLCMD (which is described briefly in Chapter 3).

What specifically does the ALTER TABLE statement let you do?

✔ Change default column settings.

✔ Set a new identity column or alter an existing identity column.

✔ Add one or more new columns.

✔ Define, add, and drop constraints for a column or the entire table, or both (see Chapter 10).

Speaking of changing constraints, the ALTER TABLE statement also allows you to add and change primary and foreign key settings. From a metadata perspective, referential integrity keys are in fact constraints. The very basic syntax for the ALTER TABLE statement is of one of the following forms:

✔ You can change an existing column:

```
ALTER TABLE <table_name>
(
    ALTER COLUMN <column name>
        <default or identity settings>
)
```

✔ You can add one or more columns where the [, ...] means that one or more new columns can be added in the same ALTER TABLE statement:

```
ALTER TABLE <table_name>
(
    ADD <column name> <optional constraint>
    [. ... ]
)
```

✔ You can drop an existing column:

```
ALTER TABLE <table_name>
(
    DROP COLUMN <column name>
)
```

✔ You can drop a constraint from an existing column without dropping the column itself:

```
ALTER TABLE <table_name>
(
    DROP CONSTRAINT <constraint name>
)
```

✔ One of the most important things is that you can change a data type, default values, NULL settings, and again-identity columns. Obviously, if a column contains values, such as strings, you will not be allowed to change the column to a numeric data type unless all string values are numbers:

```
ALTER TABLE <table_name>
(
    <column name> <data type>
        DEFAULT <value>
        NULL
        NOT NULL
        IDENTITY ...
)
```

✔ And lastly, you can change referential integrity:

```
ALTER TABLE <table_name>
(
    <column name> <data type> PRIMARY KEY
    <column name> <data type> UNIQUE
    <column name> <data type> REFERENCES
        <table name> <optional column list>
)
```

In short, you can change a great deal using the ALTER TABLE statement. You see some use of the ALTER TABLE statement in Chapter 10. However, when doing this kind of thing yourself, I strongly recommend creating and changing tables using the GUI tools in the Management Studio. It's there to make your life easier.

Chapter 10

Applying Constraints

· ·

· ·

A *constraint* constrains or restricts the values that a column can be set to. Beyond building of tables, defining columns, and data types, applying constraints creates another way to ensure the integrity of the data in your database. Constraints help to expand the implementation of business logic into a database model.

In general, a constraint can be classified as either table level or column level. A table-level constraint applies to a table as a whole, usually because it has to be applied at the table level. A column-level constraint is applied to a specific column.

First, I discuss the different types of constraints in general, when using SQL Server 2005. Then I go into detail about how to use them.

Understanding the Types of Constraints

Several types of constraints assist in achieving data integrity:

✔ NOT NULL   Specifies that a column can't contain a NULL value. If NOT NULL is omitted for a column, then the default setting is NULL. Even so, a column can be explicitly set as NOT NULL or NULL.

✔ UNIQUE   Restricts a column value to be unique across all rows in a table. UNIQUE does allow NULL values and will default to NULL.

However, only one row can have a NULL value because more than one NULL column, in more than one row, is no longer unique and violates the constraint.

✔ PRIMARY KEY   A primary key is a special type of unique constraint in that it can be linked to one or more foreign key columns, in one or more tables, and even a foreign key in the same table. Primary keys implement referential integrity. Unique keys are just that — unique! Also, a primary key can span multiple columns when a primary key is a composite of more than one column in a table. In this case, it becomes a table-level constraint. See Chapter 9 for more details on primary keys.

✔ REFERENCES   This is a foreign key constraint, which helps to enforce referential integrity. A foreign key can also be a composite column (table-level) constraint, when its referenced primary key is a composite key. See Chapter 9 for more details on foreign keys.

✔ CHECK   Specifies a condition that values in a column must satisfy. Check constraints can even be applied to enforce expressions, which span multiple columns. In some database engines, check constraints can even span multiple tables, which is excessive.

✔ DEFAULT   Specifies a default value for a column when the column is not specified in an INSERT statement.

I introduce PRIMARY KEY constraints in Chapter 9, where I show you how to create them using Transact-SQL and using the table designer in SQL Server Management Studio.

Creating NOT NULL Constraints

One of the simplest forms of constraint is the NOT NULL constraint. It is a type of a check constraint because it checks that a column value is set to something and not specifically set to NULL. The NOT NULL constraint specifies whether a column can contain NULL values. Whether a NOT NULL constraint is appropriate depends on the business setting for the data. For example, if you have an Employee database, it is likely that a valid value in the DepartmentID column is required. For such a database, a NULL value is inappropriate. In other settings, for example, a call center, you're likely to want to record as much information as possible about a caller, but because you can't guarantee that every caller will give every potentially relevant piece of data, it might make good business sense to allow NULL values where it simply isn't possible to get data.

You can create a NOT NULL constraint using Transact-SQL or using the table designer in SQL Server Management Studio.

Assume you've already created a database called `Chapter10Test` using the following Transact-SQL statements:

```
USE master
CREATE DATABASE Chapter10Test
```

To create a simple `Employee` table with a `DepartmentID` column that doesn't allow `NULL` values, use the following Transact-SQL code:

```
USE Chapter10Test
CREATE TABLE Employee
(EmployeeID int identity,
 DepartmentID int NOT NULL,
 LastName varchar(30),
 FirstName varchar(30)
)
```

Notice that the definition of the `DepartmentID` column is that the data type is an `int`, and there is a `NOT NULL` constraint specified.

If you attempt to insert a row into the `Employee` table with no value specified for the `DepartmentID` column, an error is raised. The following code attempts to insert such a row into the `Employee` table:

```
INSERT
INTO Employee
(LastName, FirstName)
VALUES ('Smith', 'John')
```

When you execute the code, you expect to see an error message like the following:

```
Msg 515, Level 16, State 2, Line 1
Cannot insert the value NULL into column 'DepartmentID',
        table 'Chapter10Test.dbo.Employee'; column does
             not allow nulls. INSERT fails.
The statement has been terminated.
```

Each time the `INSERT` statement for a row fails due to the `NOT NULL` constraint, the next successfully inserted row skips a value for the identity column `EmployeeID`.

Figure 10-1 shows the column definitions for the `Employee` table in Object Explorer in SQL Server Management Studio. Notice that both the `EmployeeID` and `DepartmentID` columns have a `NOT NULL` constraint specified.

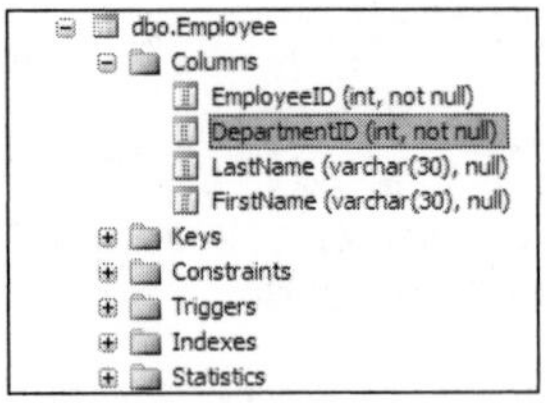

Figure 10-1:
The column
definitions
in the
Employee
table
showing two
NOT NULL
constraints.

```
⊟  dbo.Employee
  ⊟      Columns
            EmployeeID (int, not null)
            DepartmentID (int, not null)
            LastName (varchar(30), null)
            FirstName (varchar(30), null)
  ⊞      Keys
  ⊞      Constraints
  ⊞      Triggers
  ⊞      Indexes
  ⊞      Statistics
```

The NOT NULL constraints for the EmployeeID and DepartmentID columns
were created using different syntax:

```
CREATE TABLE Employee
 (EmployeeID int identity,
  DepartmentID int NOT NULL,
```

The EmployeeID column is set as IDENTITY column, whose value is supplied by SQL Server 2005. Its value is an INT data type. The column can't contain a NULL value, although you don't explicitly express that in the column
definition. In the definition of the DepartmentID column, you explicitly
specify a NOT NULL constraint on the column.

Alternatively, you can create an Employee2 table containing NOT NULL
constraints using the table designer in SQL Server Management Studio. To
create the table, right-click the Tables node in the Chapter10Test database node in Object Explorer. From the context menu, select New Table. The
table designer opens. Create column definitions in the table designer with the
data in the minitable that follows. See Figure 10-2 for an idea of what your
screen should look like when you're done.

Column Name	Data Type	Allow Nulls
EmployeeID	Int	No
DepartmentID	Int	No
LastName	varchar(30)	Yes
FirstName	varchar(30)	Yes

Notice that the Allow Nulls check boxes for the EmployeeID and
DepartmentID columns are not checked. In other words, a NOT NULL
constraint is applied to those columns, meaning that NULL values are not
allowed in those columns. To specify the EmployeeID column as IDENTITY,
use the (Is Identity) drop-down list shown in the lower part of Figure 10-2.

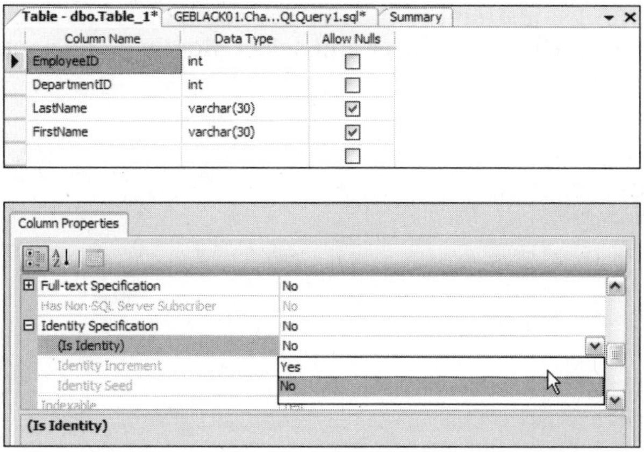

Figure 10-2:
Creating a
table in
the table
designer.

The preceding examples show you how to apply a NOT NULL constraint when first creating a table, but sometimes you might want to add a NOT NULL constraint to a column in a table after you create the table.

In Transact-SQL, you use the ALTER TABLE statement to add a NOT NULL constraint to an existing table. The following statement applies a NOT NULL constraint to the LastName column in the Employee table you create earlier in this section. See the end of Chapter 9 for syntax details of the ALTER TABLE statement.

```
USE Chapter10Test
ALTER TABLE Employee
ALTER COLUMN LastName varchar(30) NOT NULL
```

Notice that you use both the ALTER TABLE and ALTER COLUMN statements. In the ALTER COLUMN statement, although you don't change the column data type, varchar(30), you specify it again before adding the NOT NULL constraint. Figure 10-3 shows that the NOT NULL constraint now applies to the LastName column.

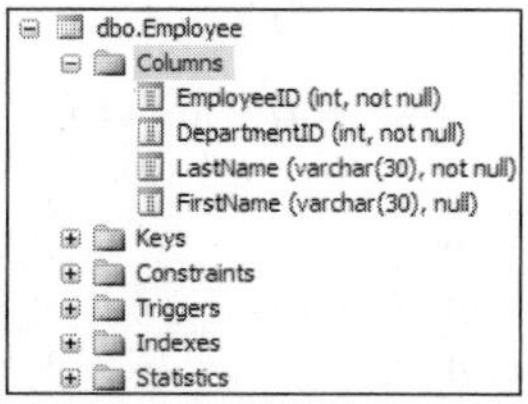

Figure 10-3:
Adding a
NOT NULL
constraint
to the
LastName
column.

To add a NOT NULL constraint to the Employee2 table, right-click the Employee2 node in Object Explorer and select Modify in the context menu, as shown in Figure 10-4.

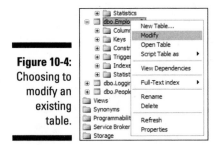

Figure 10-4:
Choosing to
modify an
existing
table.

Click the Allow Nulls check box for the LastName column. That deselects the check box so that NULL values are no longer allowed. Save the table by right-clicking the tab and selecting Save Employee2 from the context menu. Confirm that there's now a NOT NULL constraint on the LastName column by clicking the Employee2 table and its Columns table to display the column definitions.

Creating DEFAULT Constraints

A DEFAULT constraint provides a value for a column in an INSERT statement when no value for that column is specified. For example, when adding new employees to an Employees database, you might want to default to specifying their start dates as the current date. You can use a DEFAULT constraint to do that.

The following statements specify a new Employees database in which you create an Employees table.

```
USE master
CREATE DATABASE Employees
```

Then, create the Employees table. Notice the use of the keyword DEFAULT in the definition of the StartDate column in the Employees table.

```
USE Employees
CREATE TABLE Employees
(EmployeeID int IDENTITY,
 LastName varchar(30),
 FirstName varchar(30),
 StartDate datetime
  DEFAULT GetDate())
```

If you examine the column definitions in Object Explorer, you'll see no indication that a DEFAULT constraint exists, as shown in Figure 10-5. The GetDate() function returns the current date and time.

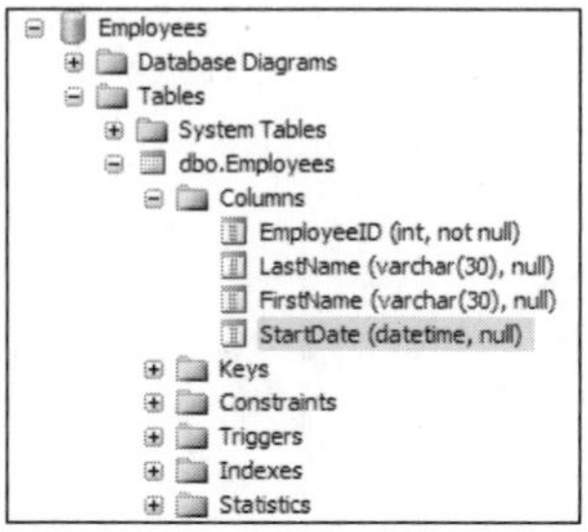

Figure 10-5:
The column
definitions
don't show
a DEFAULT
constraint.

Figure 10-5:
The column
definitions
don't show
a DEFAULT
constraint.

You can confirm the existence of a DEFAULT constraint by showing that a default value is supplied when you execute an INSERT statement. The following statements insert two rows into the Employees table. In the first row, you specify the value for the StartDate column explicitly. In the second row, you use the DEFAULT constraint to supply the value in the StartDate column.

Figure 10-6 shows the successful use of the DEFAULT constraint.

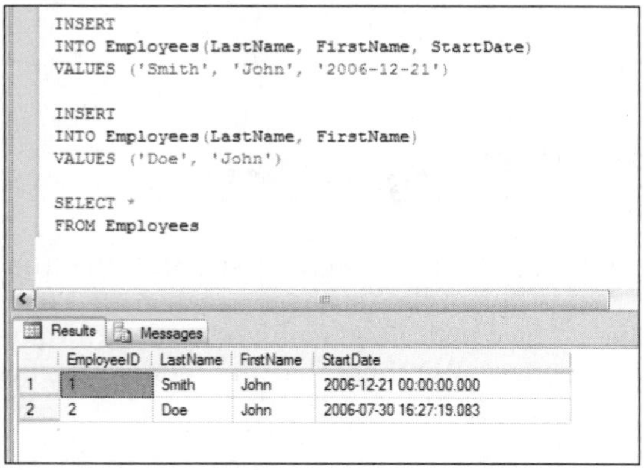

Figure 10-6:
Successful
use of a
DEFAULT
constraint.

If you want to directly examine the constraints specified on the Employees table, run the statement

```
sp_helpconstraint Employees
```

which executes the sp_helpconstraint system stored procedure. It returns a list of all constraint types, their names (whether user-defined or system-supplied), the columns on which they've been defined, and an expression that defines the constraint. Figure 10-7 shows the result of executing the preceding statement.

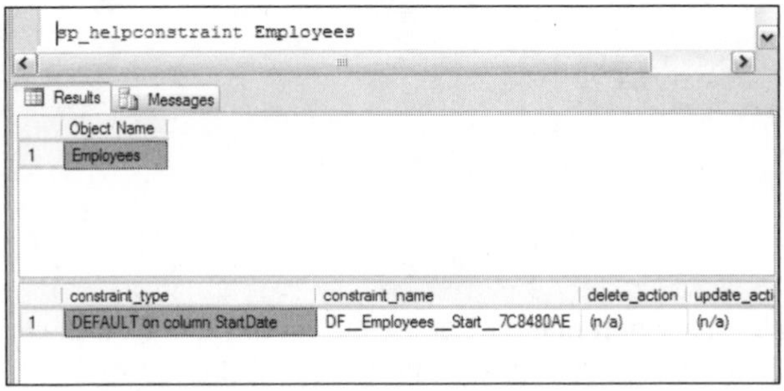

Figure 10-7:
Using the
sp_help-
constraint
stored
procedure
to display
constraints
defined for
a table.

In SQL Server 2005, the syntax that uses sys.default_constraints is preferable. The following code displays the same results as those shown in Figure 10-7:

```
USE Employees
SELECT *
FROM sys.default_constraints
```

Creating UNIQUE Constraints

A UNIQUE constraint is an entity constraint that specifies that the value in a column on which a UNIQUE constraint has been created can't be inserted into a table if the value in the constrained column matches a value in the same column for any existing row in that table. In other words, the value must be unique.

A UNIQUE constraint differs from a PRIMARY KEY constraint in the following ways:

✔ A table may have more than one UNIQUE constraint. Only one PRIMARY KEY is allowed per table.

✔ If there's no NOT NULL constraint, a column with a UNIQUE constraint may contain a NULL value.

✔ The column to which a UNIQUE constraint is applied isn't considered to be the unique identifier for the table. A column to which a UNIQUE constraint is applied is an *alternative identifier* for the table.

To specify a UNIQUE constraint on a column, use the UNIQUE keyword when defining the column. The following example shows a simple Contacts table that includes a MobilePhone column on which you define a UNIQUE constraint.

```
USE Chapter10Test
CREATE TABLE Contacts(
ContactID int IDENTITY,
LastName varchar(30),
FirstName varchar(30),
Company varchar(50),
MobilePhone varchar(14) UNIQUE
)
```

You can't directly verify the existence of the UNIQUE constraint from the column definitions in Object Explorer. Use the sp_helpconstraint stored procedure to display the constraints defined for the Contacts table using this command:

```
sp_helpconstraint Contacts
```

Figure 10-8 shows the UNIQUE constraint defined on the Contacts table.

Figure 10-8:
Using the sp_helpconstraint stored procedure to reveal a UNIQUE constraint.

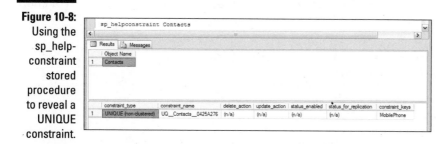

You can also demonstrate the existence of the UNIQUE constraint by attempting to add duplicate data to the Contacts table. The following command adds a row to the Contacts table with a value for the MobilePhone column of 1234567890.

```
USE Chapter10Test
INSERT INTO Contacts
VALUES ('Jones', 'Alfred', 'Acme Consulting',
        '1234567890')
```

Because this is the first row inserted into the Contacts database, it inserts correctly. If you attempt to insert another row with the same value in the MobilePhone column, it fails.

```
INSERT INTO Contacts
VALUES ('Clark', 'Aloysia', 'Example Consulting',
        '1234567890')
```

The UNIQUE constraint prevents the row from being inserted. The following error message is displayed.

```
Msg 2627, Level 14, State 1, Line 1
Violation of UNIQUE KEY constraint
        'UQ__Contacts__0425A276'. Cannot insert
            duplicate key in object 'dbo.Contacts'.
The statement has been terminated.
```

You might see several naming conventions for UNIQUE constraints. The preceding error message uses UQ as a prefix. You might also see AK, meaning *alternative key*.

To add a UNIQUE constraint to an existing table, use the ALTER TABLE statement. The following statements add a database called AddUnique.

```
USE master
CREATE DATABASE AddUnique
```

The following statements create a table, Contacts, in the AddUnique database. Notice that there's no constraint applied to the MobilePhone column.

```
USE AddUnique
CREATE TABLE Contacts(
ContactID int IDENTITY PRIMARY KEY,
LastName varchar(30),
FirstName varchar(30),
MobilePhone char(14)
)
```

However, there is a constraint — a PRIMARY KEY constraint — on the ContactID column. If you execute

```
sp_helpconstraint Contacts
```

the information about the PRIMARY KEY constraint is displayed. To add the UNIQUE constraint, execute the following code:

```
USE AddUnique
ALTER TABLE CONTACTS
ADD CONSTRAINT UQ_ContactsMobPhone
UNIQUE (MobilePhone)
```

Once you execute the code, you can check that the UNIQUE constraint has been added by again executing this statement:

```
sp_helpconstraint Contacts
```

Figure 10-9 displays the information returned by the sp_helpconstraint stored procedure.

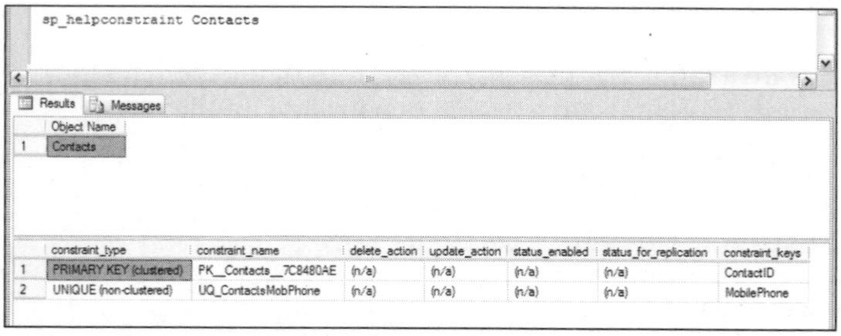

Figure 10-9:
The UNIQUE
constraint
added to the
previous
PRIMARY
KEY
constraint.

In SQL Server 2005, the newer syntax is preferable:

```
SELECT *
FROM sys.key_constraints
```

Figure 10-10 shows the results.

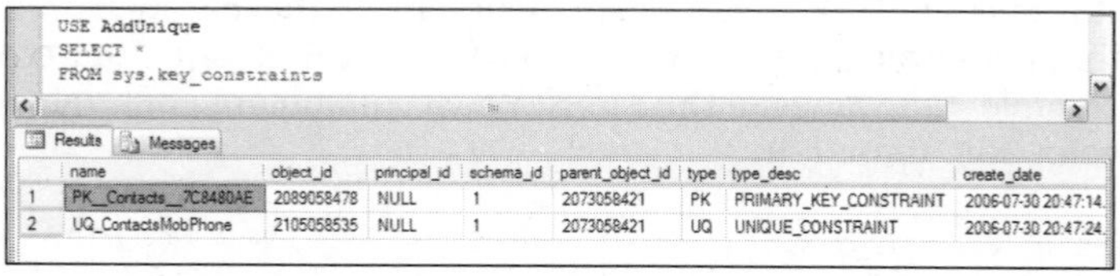

Figure 10-10:
Using
sys.key_
constraints
to display
information
about
UNIQUE
constraints.

Creating CHECK Constraints

The CHECK constraint allows you to limit the values that can be inserted into a column. CHECK constraints can be used to implement a wide range of business or other rules to limit the range of values that can be inserted into a column. For example, if you choose to design a table that contains information about events, you might want to store dates in separate columns, such as EventYear, EventMonth, and EventDay. Each of those columns has a range of values that are meaningful, and any value outside such a range can safely be excluded from insertion into the Events table.

First, create a database, Events, by executing the following code:

```
USE master
CREATE DATABASE Events
```

Next, create a table, Events, in the Events database. The EventYear and EventMonth columns have CHECK constraints applied.

```
USE Events
CREATE TABLE Events(
EventID int IDENTITY PRIMARY KEY,
EventTitle varchar(50),
EventYear int
  CONSTRAINT ck_Year CHECK (EventYear BETWEEN 2000 AND
          2050),
EventMonth int
  CONSTRAINT ck_Month CHECK (EventMonth BETWEEN 1 AND 12),
EventDay int
)
```

Notice that the data type for the EventYear column is specified in the normal way:

```
EventYear int
```

The CONSTRAINT clause specifies the constraint. First, the name of the constraint is specified, ck_Year. Then, inside parentheses, an expression is created that constrains the int values allowed in the EventYear column. In this example, the values in the EventYear column are constrained to be between 2000 and 2050.

```
CONSTRAINT ck_Year CHECK (EventYear BETWEEN 2000 AND
          2050),
```

You can confirm that the CHECK constraints have been added using the following code:

```
SELECT *
FROM sys.check_constraints
```

Figure 10-11 shows the results of executing the preceding code.

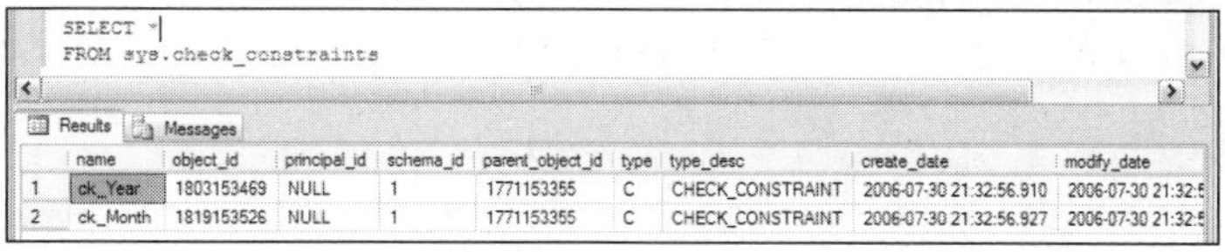

Figure 10-11:
Confirming
that CHECK
constraints
have been
created.

Notice that I didn't add a CHECK constraint to the EventDay column. The allowed values for that column must lie between 1 and 31.

To add a CHECK constraint to the EventDay column, execute the following code:

```
USE Events
ALTER TABLE Events
ADD CONSTRAINT ck_Day
CHECK (EventDay BETWEEN 1 AND 31)
```

Notice that the ALTER TABLE statement is used to specify the table where the alteration is to be made. The ADD CONSTRAINT statement specifies the constraint to be added. First, the name of the constraint, ck_Day, is specified. Then, the constraint is specified to be a CHECK constraint. Finally, the expression in parentheses specifies that the values of the EventDay column must be between 1 and 31.

To confirm that a new CHECK constraint has been successfully added, execute the following command:

```
SELECT *
FROM sys.check_constraints
```

Figure 10-12 shows that the ck_Day CHECK constraint has been added to the ck_Year and ck_Month CHECK constraints that already existed.

You can also create CHECK constraints using the table designer in SQL Server Management Studio.

To create a table, Events2, that is the same as the Events table created using Transact-SQL, follow these steps:

1. **Open SQL Server Management Studio.**

2. **Open Object Explorer and navigate to the node for the Events database, created earlier using Transact-SQL.**

3. **Right-click the Tables node and select New Table from the context menu that appears.**

4. In the table designer, create definitions for the columns so that the appearance is the same as shown in Figure 10-12.

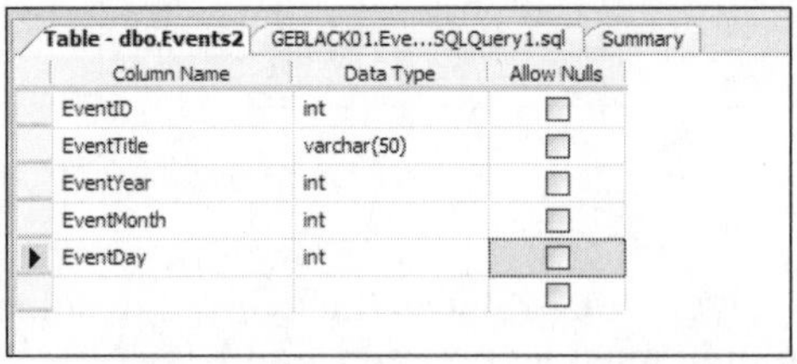

Figure 10-12:
Specifying
the columns
in the
Events2
table.

Figure 10-12:
Specifying
the columns
in the
Events2
table.

5. Right-click the tab and select the Save option. Name the table Events2.

6. At this stage, no CHECK constraints are defined. Right-click the arrow to the left of EventYear in the table designer, as indicated by the position of the mouse cursor in Figure 10-13.

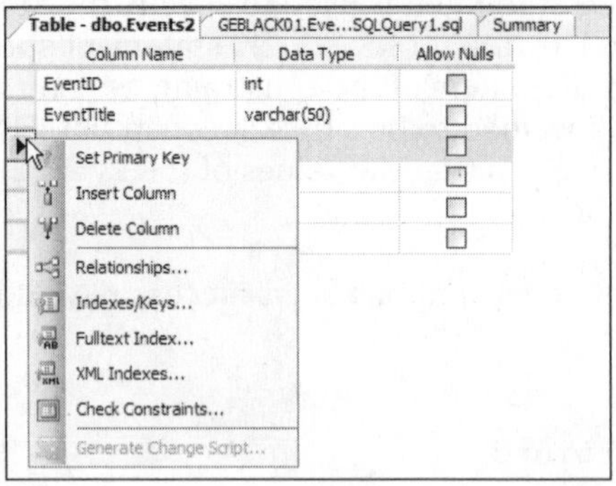

Figure 10-13:
The context
menu for
EventYear.

7. Select the Check Constraints option in the context menu that appears. The Check Constraints dialog box, shown in Figure 10-14, appears.

8. In the Check Constraints dialog box, click Add.

The Check Constraints dialog box now looks like Figure 10-15.

9. Click the ellipsis (. . .) in the Expression text box. The ellipsis appears once you click in the text box in the Expression row.

The Check Constraint Expression dialog box shown in Figure 10-16 appears.

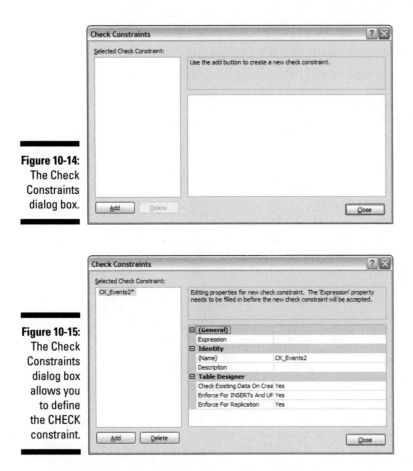

Figure 10-14:
The Check
Constraints
dialog box.

Figure 10-15:
The Check
Constraints
dialog box
allows you
to define
the CHECK
constraint.

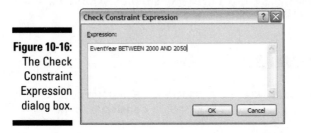

Figure 10-16:
The Check
Constraint
Expression
dialog box.

10. **Create the CHECK constraint expression like this:**

```
EventYear BETWEEN 2000 AND 2050
```

Type the preceding code into the Check Constraint Expression editor, as
shown in Figure 10-16. Click OK to close the Check Constraint Expression
dialog box.

11. **Edit the name of the CHECK constraint to ck_Year.**

12. **Click Close to close the Check Constraints dialog box.**

The newly created CHECK constraint ck_EventYear is saved.

To confirm successful creation of the ck_EventYear CHECK constraint, execute the following code:

```
USE Events
SELECT *
FROM sys.check_constraints
```

Figure 10-17 shows that the ck_EventYear CHECK constraint has been successfully added.

Figure 10-17:
The ck_
EventYear
CHECK
constraint
has been
successfully
added.

```
USE Events
SELECT *
FROM sys.check_constraints
```

	name	object_id	principal_id	schema_id	parent_object_id	type	type_desc	create_date	modify_date
1	CK_EventYear	21575115	NULL	1	5575058	C	CHECK_CONSTRAINT	2006-07-30 22:12:32.940	2006-07-30 22
2	ck_Year	2105058535	NULL	1	2073058421	C	CHECK_CONSTRAINT	2006-07-30 21:49:13.427	2006-07-30 21
3	ck_Month	2121058592	NULL	1	2073058421	C	CHECK_CONSTRAINT	2006-07-30 21:49:13.427	2006-07-30 21
4	ck_Day	2137058649	NULL	1	2073058421	C	CHECK_CONSTRAINT	2006-07-30 21:49:22.490	2006-07-30 21

To add the ck_EventMonth and ck_EventDay CHECK constraints, follow the steps listed for the creation of the ck_EventYear CHECK constraint.

You can't repeat the name of an existing CHECK constraint in a table.

Removing Constraints

To remove an existing constraint, use the ALTER TABLE statement. The following statement deletes the ck_EventYear CHECK constraint in the Events database:

```
ALTER TABLE Events2
DROP CONSTRAINT ck_EventYear
```

You can confirm the deletion of the CHECK constraint by executing the following code:

```
USE Events
SELECT *
FROM sys.check_constraints
```

Figure 10-18 shows the results.

Using Advanced Constraints

So far in this chapter, and when covering referential integrity constraints in Chapter 9, you have seen only column-level constraints. There are one or two slightly more complex constraints to examine.

Earlier in this chapter, you find out how to create a table called `Employees`. You can use the `ALTER TABLE` statement to add a column to that table:

```
USE Employees
ALTER TABLE Employees
    ADD
    (
        TermDate datetime
        CHECK (TermDate IS NULL OR TermDate >= StartDate)
    )
```

If you try to execute the preceding statement, it won't work because the check constraint accesses two separate columns in the same table and is therefore a table-level constraint. It is not a column-level constraint because it is not applicable to a single column.

So you can add the new column first:

```
ALTER TABLE Employees ADD TermDate datetime
```

And then add the constraint at the table level (for the entire table):

```
ALTER TABLE Employees ADD CHECK
    (TermDate IS NULL OR TermDate >= StartDate)
```

If you add a new employee, then the termination date must either be NULL or greater than or equal to the starting date.

Now examine another type of table-level-only constraint and add a department number to the table:

```
ALTER TABLE Employees ADD DepartmentID int NOT NULL
```

Now you have a table with column that looks like this:

```
DepartmentID int NOT NULL,
EmployeeID int IDENTITY,
LastName varchar(30),
FirstName varchar(30),
StartDate datetime DEFAULT GetDate()
TermDate datetime
```

Each row in the table is now identified uniquely (as the primary key), by the composite of the DepartmentID and EmployeeID columns. You can re-create the table like this:

```
DROP TABLE Employees
CREATE TABLE Employees
(
    DepartmentID int NOT NULL,
    EmployeeID int NOT NULL,
    LastName varchar(30),
    FirstName varchar(30),
    StartDate datetime DEFAULT GetDate(),
    TermDate datetime,
    CHECK(TermDate IS NULL OR TermDate >= StartDate),
    PRIMARY KEY(DepartmentID, EmployeeID)
)
```

Chapter 11

Creating Views

. . . .

In This Chapter

▶ Getting a handle on what a view is

▶ Understanding the need for views

▶ Creating a view

▶ Using views for security

▶ Updating through views

▶ Indexing a view

. . . .

In this chapter, I show you how to create views. I discuss scenarios in which creating views is helpful, either to provide customized views for differing groups of users, or to provide a simpler way for, say, power users to work with table data.

You create views for several reasons. Certain groups of users might like to see only part of an extensive data set. Security considerations might require that some data is available to only certain users, for example, depending on their job role or security clearance.

Views allow you to provide an interface that might be significantly simpler than the structure of underlying tables. Views enable you to provide a simple view that allows non-experts to make use of the data without having to spend time figuring out how to manipulate data in multiple tables by using joins, for example.

What Is a View?

A *view* stores a query and does not store data. It has the following characteristics:

✔ A view allows reuse of an existing query where the underlying data may not remain the same because it is stored in tables.

✔ A view allows access to data to be restricted to certain user groups.

✔ A view can even read data from tables in multiple databases, with some restrictions.

✔ A view takes data from heterogeneous data sources, such as different database vendor software using an ODBC driver.

One way of looking at a view is that it's a way of storing a query so that you can use it again easily. Another way of looking at a view is that it's a filter on the underlying data in the table or tables from which the view's data is retrieved. The filter might be of columns (if you select only some of the columns in the original tables) or of rows (if you use a WHERE clause to filter rows by a specified criterion or multiple criteria).

Understanding the Need for Views

In earlier chapters, I cover several techniques that allow you to select data from one or more tables. As you apply queries to your business data, you'll likely find that some queries are appropriate for reuse. Creating a view is one option that allows you to reuse a query. You simply refer to the view by name and retrieve all its data, or filter in some way the data that the view represents. In effect, executing a SELECT statement on a view also runs the original SELECT query used in the view definition.

You might want to create a view for any of the following reasons:

✔ To focus on specific data, perhaps for security reasons.

✔ To simplify manipulation of data for some users, such as power users.

✔ To provide backward compatibility.

✔ To export data.

A view allows you to control the display of data so that selected columns in the underlying table aren't displayed. In the next section titled "Creating a View," I show you an example of how you might use a view to display confidential data only to selected users.

Some power user might be comfortable working with simple Transact-SQL queries. Suppose you create a view using the following code:

```
CREATE VIEW VistaCardholders
AS
SELECT      Person.Contact.LastName,
            Person.Contact.FirstName,
            Person.Contact.MiddleName,
            Sales.CreditCard.CardType,
            Sales.CreditCard.CardNumber,
                    Sales.CreditCard.ExpYear
```

```
FROM          Sales.CreditCard INNER JOIN
                      Sales.ContactCreditCard ON
              Sales.CreditCard.CreditCardID =
              Sales.ContactCreditCard.CreditCardID INNER JOIN
                      Person.Contact ON
              Sales.ContactCreditCard.ContactID =
              Person.Contact.ContactID
WHERE CardType = 'Vista'
```

A power user interested in Vista credit card information could create simple queries, such as

```
SELECT *
FROM VistaCardHolders
WHERE ExpYear = 2006
```

without having to work with joins, which might be beyond the capabilities of a nonspecialist. The power user can find focused information by the simple use of WHERE and ORDER BY clauses.

If you have legacy applications that access data assuming a particular schema, you might want to create a view that uses the old schema. One example is where you have normalized data previously held in a single table. A view can use a join to display the data as if it still was stored in a single table. Taking that approach minimizes the changes that you need to make to keep your application working correctly.

If you want to export data to, say, Microsoft Excel, a view can contain exactly the data you want to export. Use the bcp utility to export the data contained in the view.

One of the considerations that you might need to take into account is performance. Views are always a little more inefficient than the SELECT statement that exists in the view definition. In simple situations, the difference in performance is likely to be negligible. When a view contains calculated columns or aggregates, a view might be significantly slower. In that scenario, you might consider creating an index on the view. I describe creating an index on a view later in this chapter.

Creating a View

To create a view, you use the CREATE VIEW statement to create a named version of a query. The view is stored in SQL Server, and you can access information about a view's characteristics in SQL Server Management Studio's Object Explorer.

You can name a view in such a way that it's clear that it's a view. Or you could name it as if it were a table. From an end-user perspective, reading a view appears and behaves just as a table would. For clarity, it can be useful to indicate in the view's name that it's a view. You might see conventions such as vMyView, vwMyView, or MyView_vw to indicate that the object is a view.

The CREATE VIEW statement creates a new view. The general form of simple use of the CREATE VIEW statement is as follows:

```
CREATE VIEW <view_name>
AS
SELECT <select_statement>
```

The SELECT statement part of the CREATE VIEW statement can be any T-SQL query. Suppose that the human resources department of a company wants to identify all employees who are at least 60 years old in 2007.

In the AdventureWorks_new database (this is a copy of the AdventureWorks database so that I can, for example, INSERT or UPDATE data), I can find the desired employees using the following SELECT statement:

```
USE AdventureWorks_new
SELECT EmployeeID, NationalIDNumber, BirthDate
FROM HumanResources.Employee
WHERE BirthDate < '1948-01-01' AND BirthDate >
           '1946-12-31'
```

In the AdventureWorks_new database, there is only one such employee, as you can see in Figure 11-1.

Figure 11-1:
Finding
employees
who become
60 in 2007.

You can create a view, SixtyIn2007, which uses the preceding SELECT statement, as in the following statements.

```
USE AdventureWorks_new
CREATE VIEW SixtyIn2007
AS
SELECT EmployeeID, NationalIDNumber, BirthDate
FROM HumanResources.Employee
WHERE BirthDate < '1948-01-01' AND BirthDate >
           '1946-12-31'
```

To see the data in the newly created view, execute this statement:

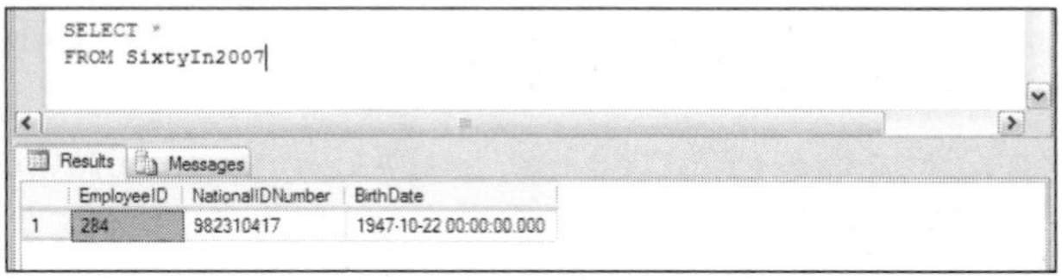

```
SELECT *
FROM SixtyIn2007
```

Figure 11-2 shows that the same data is returned as when you execute the `SELECT` statement that is used in view definition in the `CREATE VIEW` statement.

Figure 11-2:
Selecting
data from
a view.

Figure 11-2:
Selecting data from a view.

You can access information about the view in Object Explorer in SQL Server Management Studio. Expand the `AdventureWorks_new` node (or relevant node if you named your copy of `AdventureWorks` differently), and then expand the `Views` node. The `dbo.SixtyIn2007` node should be visible. Expand that and expand the `Columns` node it contains. The appearance should be similar to Figure 11-3.

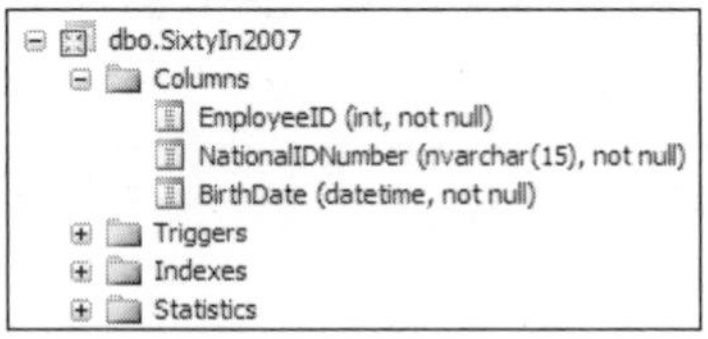

Figure 11-3:
The columns
in the
SixtyIn2007
view in
Object
Explorer.

Notice that the three columns in the `SixtyIn2007` view are the columns specified in the `CREATE VIEW` statement that created the view. Notice, too, that the metadata for those columns is the same as the metadata for the corresponding columns in the `HumanResources.Employee` table in the `AdventureWorks_new` database.

You can use a join when creating a view definition. Suppose you want to create a list of contacts who hold Vista credit cards. Creating this list requires that you use a join that involves three tables. To use the Query Designer in SQL Server Management Studio to create the query, follow these steps:

 1. **Click the New Query button in SQL Server Management Studio and connect to the relevant SQL Server instance.**

 2. **In the query pane that opens, right-click and select Design Query in Editor from the context menu.**

    The Add Table dialog box opens.

 3. **In the Add Table dialog box, add the `Contact`, `ContactCreditCard`, and `CreditCard` tables to the design surface by clicking each table in the list of tables and then clicking the Add button.**

 4. **When you have added the three tables, click the Close button in the Add Table dialog box.**

 5. **Select the `LastName`, `MiddleName`, and `FirstName` columns from the `Person.Contact` table.**

 6. **Select the `CardType`, `CardNumber`, `ExpYear`, and `ExpMonth` columns from the `Sales.CreditCard` table.**

    You don't select any columns from the `Sales.ContactCreditCard` table. You simply make use of the `ContactID` and `CreditCardID` columns to express the many-to-many relationship between the `Person.Contact` and `Sales.CreditCard` tables.

 7. **Click in the Sort Order column opposite ExpYear and choose 1.**

 8. **Click in the Sort Order column opposite ExpMonth and choose 2.**

 9. **Click in the Filter column opposite ExpYear and type `=2007`.**

 10. **Click in the Filter column opposite CardType and type `=Vista`. Click in a blank cell.**

    The appearance should now resemble Figure 11-4. You type `=Vista`, but because it's treated as Unicode characters, SQL Server displays `=N'Vista'`.

 11. **Click OK to close the Query Builder.**

 12. **In the query pane, you see the completed query.**

    Press F5 to execute the query you created. Figure 11-5 shows part of the results of executing the query.

The query you created in Query Builder is shown here.

```
SELECT     Person.Contact.LastName,
           Person.Contact.MiddleName,
           Person.Contact.FirstName,
           Sales.CreditCard.CardType,
           Sales.CreditCard.CardNumber,
                      Sales.CreditCard.ExpYear,
           Sales.CreditCard.ExpMonth
```

```
FROM         Person.Contact INNER JOIN
                   Sales.ContactCreditCard ON
             Person.Contact.ContactID =
             Sales.ContactCreditCard.ContactID INNER JOIN
                   Sales.CreditCard ON
             Sales.ContactCreditCard.CreditCardID =
             Sales.CreditCard.CreditCardID
WHERE        (Sales.CreditCard.ExpYear = 2007) AND
             (Sales.CreditCard.CardType = N'Vista')
ORDER BY Sales.CreditCard.ExpYear,
             Sales.CreditCard.ExpMonth
```

A power user might want to work with information on Vista credit cards that expire in 2007. A convenient way is to create a view VistaExpireIn2007. The following CREATE VIEW statement does that:

```
USE AdventureWorks_new
GO
CREATE VIEW VistaExpireIn2007
AS
SELECT       Person.Contact.LastName,
             Person.Contact.MiddleName,
             Person.Contact.FirstName,
             Sales.CreditCard.CardType,
             Sales.CreditCard.CardNumber,
                   Sales.CreditCard.ExpYear,
             Sales.CreditCard.ExpMonth
FROM         Person.Contact INNER JOIN
                   Sales.ContactCreditCard ON
             Person.Contact.ContactID =
             Sales.ContactCreditCard.ContactID INNER JOIN
                   Sales.CreditCard ON
             Sales.ContactCreditCard.CreditCardID =
             Sales.CreditCard.CreditCardID
WHERE        (Sales.CreditCard.ExpYear = 2007) AND
             (Sales.CreditCard.CardType = N'Vista')
ORDER BY Sales.CreditCard.ExpYear,
             Sales.CreditCard.ExpMonth
```

You think you've created a view that works nicely because you know from Figure 11-4 that the SELECT statement works. However, when you run the preceding code, you see the following error message:

```
Msg 1033, Level 15, State 1, Procedure VistaExpireIn2007,
          Line 9
The ORDER BY clause is invalid in views, inline functions,
          derived tables, subqueries, and common table
          expressions, unless TOP or FOR XML is also
          specified.
```

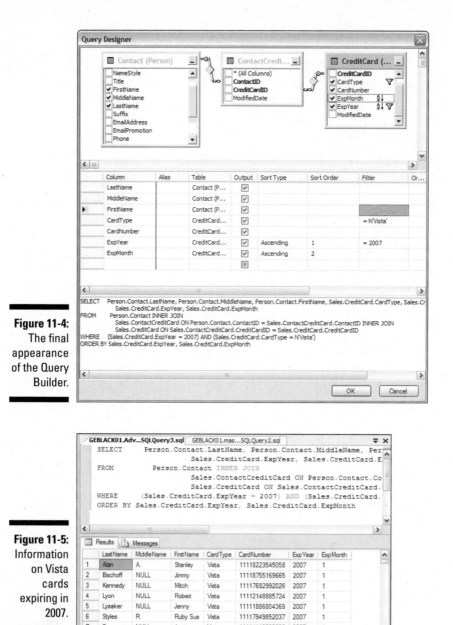

Figure 11-4:
The final
appearance
of the Query
Builder.

Figure 11-5:
Information
on Vista
cards
expiring in
2007.

The error message indicates that you can't use an ORDER BY clause in a view definition. If you comment out the ORDER BY clause, you can successfully create the VistaExpireIn2007 view by executing the following CREATE VIEW statement:

```
USE AdventureWorks_new
GO
CREATE VIEW VistaExpireIn2007
AS
SELECT       Person.Contact.LastName,
             Person.Contact.MiddleName,
             Person.Contact.FirstName,
             Sales.CreditCard.CardType,
             Sales.CreditCard.CardNumber,
                     Sales.CreditCard.ExpYear,
             Sales.CreditCard.ExpMonth
FROM          Person.Contact INNER JOIN
                      Sales.ContactCreditCard ON
             Person.Contact.ContactID =
             Sales.ContactCreditCard.ContactID INNER JOIN
                      Sales.CreditCard ON
             Sales.ContactCreditCard.CreditCardID =
             Sales.CreditCard.CreditCardID
WHERE        (Sales.CreditCard.ExpYear = 2007) AND
             (Sales.CreditCard.CardType = N'Vista')
```

Confirm the successful creation of the `VistaExpireIn2007` view in Object
Explorer by right-clicking Views and selecting Refresh. You should see an
appearance similar to Figure 11-6.

If you can't use an `ORDER BY` clause in a view definition, how can you order
the results? You must use an `ORDER BY` clause when you select from the
view. You need to avoid simply using the original table names:

```
ORDER BY Sales.CreditCard.ExpYear,
         Sales.CreditCard.ExpMonth
```

Figure 11-6:
The column
metadata
for the
columns in
the Vista-
ExpireIn2007
view.

The `ExpYear` and `ExpMonth` columns are now columns of the `VistaExpire
In2007` view so you can order columns using the following code:

```
SELECT *
FROM VistaExpireIn2007
ORDER BY ExpYear, ExpMonth
```

The limitation on using an ORDER BY clause is one of several criteria that you must consider when creating a view. Also consider the following:

✔ You can create a view only in the current database. The view can, however, reference data in other databases.

✔ The name for the view must obey SQL Server rules for naming identifiers.

✔ The name of a view must be unique in a schema.

✔ You can associate INSTEAD OF triggers with a view but not AFTER triggers.

✔ The query that defines the view can't include the ORDER BY clause unless you use the TOP keyword in the SELECT statement.

✔ You can't create a full-text index on a view or issue a full-text query against a view. However, a view definition can include a full-text query on an underlying table.

✔ You can't create a view on a temporary table.

I describe triggers in Chapter 13.

The requirement for uniqueness of a view's name means that it must be different from the names of all existing tables and views. You can't give a view the name of an existing table.

Using Views for Security

SQL Server allows you to specify an access control list for individual columns, but management of that is very difficult. This can be problematic where confidential data is held in a table with some data that is legitimately public.

Views are convenient for controlling access to data. For example, if you have a table that contains data about employees, their departments, and salaries, the names of staff and their departments are likely to be generally available. However, you want to ensure that display of salary data is carefully controlled. By using a view to allow access to, say, an employee directory with information about department and contact information, but that contains no salary information, the chances of confidential information being inappropriately disseminated is reduced.

Suppose you use the following commands to create a single table of `Employee` information. In reality, the data (and more) is likely to be spread across multiple tables:

```
Use Chapter11Test
CREATE TABLE Employee
(EmployeeID int identity PRIMARY KEY,
LastName varchar(30),
FirstName varchar(30),
Department varchar(30),
Salary money)
```

The answer to the problem is to create a view from which users can retrieve widely accessible data.

```
CREATE VIEW PublicEmployeeData
AS
SELECT LastName, FirstName, Department
FROM Employee
```

Access to that view can be made available to all employees. A query such as this one doesn't cause security problems because there's no confidential data in the view:

```
CREATE VIEW PublicEmployeeData
AS
SELECT LastName, FirstName, Department
FROM Employee
```

At the same time, you grant permissions on the `Employee` table only to, for example, human resources staff and senior managers, so those who need access to confidential salary data can have it:

```
SELECT *
FROM Employee
```

In some business reporting scenarios, the salaries of some staff are intended to be public, at least for shareholders. You might need to add a column to the `Employee` table and create two views to accommodate that kind of scenario.

Updating through Views

Views allow you to retrieve data from single or multiple database tables. Views also allow you to run inserts or updates on those tables in some situations. In practice, you can safely assume that you can insert data into a view or update data in a view when it is drawn from a single table. However, if a view contains only some of the columns in the underlying table, you might be able to insert data only if default values are specified for the columns not included in the view.

If you want to insert data or update data in a view created from multiple tables, you can't insert data into the underlying tables. To carry out an INSERT or UPDATE, you need to use an INSTEAD OF trigger. I describe INSTEAD OF triggers in Chapter 13. For the moment, it's enough that you realize that an INSTEAD OF trigger is a piece of code that runs *instead of* the code that you try to execute.

Indexing a View

When a view isn't indexed, it exists as a list of column names and data types. Therefore, when you create a SELECT statement to retrieve information from the view, the SELECT statement used in the view definition is run again against the underlying tables. If the original SELECT statement is complex — for example, using calculated columns or aggregates — retrieving data from a view might be slow and not produce the performance that you desire.

An index can significantly improve the speed of some categories of query. However, the existence of an index means that if updates or inserts are frequent, inserts and updates will be slower because the index also has to be updated to reflect changes in the data.

To index a view, you create a unique clustered index on it. Creating an index on a view has several criteria that you must meet in addition to the criteria that apply to creating any index:

- ✔ The user who executes the CREATE INDEX statement is the view owner.
- ✔ Several SET options must be ON when the CREATE INDEX statement is executed. (ANSI_NULLS, ANSI_PADDING, ANSI_WARNINGS, CONCAT_NULL_YIELDS_NULL, QUOTED_IDENTIFIER)
- ✔ The NUMERIC_ROUNDABORT option must be OFF (the default).
- ✔ The IGNORE_DUP_KEY option must be OFF.
- ✔ The view can't contain columns of the text, ntext, or image data types.
- ✔ If the SELECT statement in the view definition specifies a GROUP BY clause, the key of the unique clustered index can reference only columns specified in the GROUP BY clause.

I describe how to create indexes in Chapter 15.

Chapter 12

Using Stored Procedures

S tored procedures allow you to create routines that can be executed in SQL Server 2005. Stored procedures also enable you to carry out tasks related to administering a SQL Server database, and they can provide a more secure way of executing Transact-SQL in response to user input in, for example, a Web application. You can write stored procedures in Transact-SQL and in .NET languages.

A *view*, which I introduce in Chapter 11, is a named reusable SELECT statement. A *stored procedure,* like a view, is a named piece of code that runs in SQL Server. However, a stored procedure is much more flexible because it can contain any Transact-SQL statements, or it can be written in a .NET language, such as Visual Basic .NET.

Getting to Know Stored Procedures

A *stored procedure* is a routine that allows you to reuse a code module in a SQL Server context. Anything you can do with Transact-SQL or with a .NET language, you can use in a stored procedure. Some limitations exist, however. For example, you can use only .NET code that is relevant to the SQL Server context that you're executing in.

A stored procedure can

✔ Accept input parameters.

✔ Return one or more output parameters.

✔ Call other stored procedures.

✔ Perform operations in a database.

✔ Return a status value to a calling procedure or batch to indicate whether the operation is successful.

SQL Server 2005 supports two broad kinds of stored procedures:

✔ System stored procedures

✔ User-defined stored procedures

System stored procedures are stored in the `resource` database. The `resource` database is new in SQL Server 2005. It isn't displayed in the `System Databases` node of Object Explorer in SQL Server Management Studio. Instead, the objects that are physically persisted in the `resource` database are displayed as system objects in all SQL Server databases. If you installed SQL Server 2005 on drive C:, the `resource` database is located at `C:\Program Files\Microsoft SQL Server\MSSQL.1\MSSQL\Data\ Mssqlsystemresource.mdf`.

To get access to system stored procedures for which you have permissions, you can use any system or user-defined database in the Object Explorer in SQL Server Management Studio. To view information about system stored procedures by using the Northwind database, follow these steps:

1. **In Object Explorer in SQL Server Management Studio, expand the `Databases` node and then expand the `Northwind` node.**

2. **Expand the `Programmability` node and then expand the `Stored Procedures` node.**

   You see a folder for System Stored Procedures and several user-defined stored procedures, as shown in Figure 12-1.

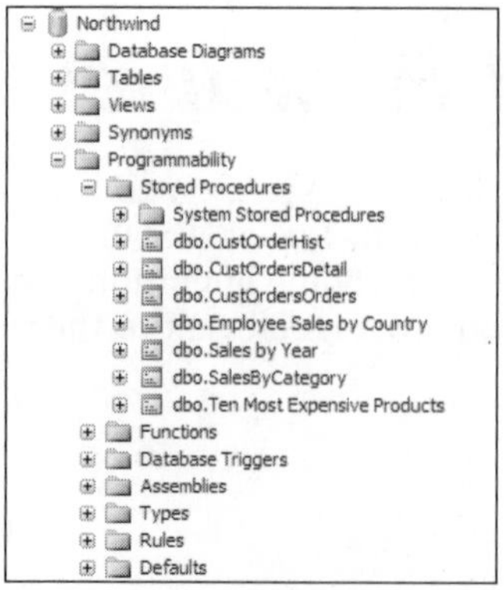

Figure 12-1: Stored procedures in the Northwind database.

3. **To view system stored procedures, expand the System Stored Procedures node, as shown in Figure 12-1.**

   An extensive list of stored procedures is displayed.

SQL Server Management Studio allows you to filter system stored procedures to make finding system stored procedures easier. To filter stored procedures, follow these steps:

1. **Right-click System Stored Procedures. In the context menu that appears, choose Filter⇨Filter Settings, as shown in Figure 12-2.**

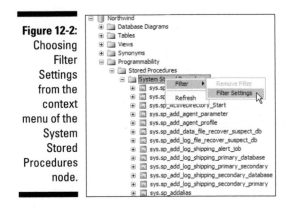

Figure 12-2: Choosing Filter Settings from the context menu of the System Stored Procedures node.

The Object Explorer Filter Settings dialog box, as shown in Figure 12-3, opens.

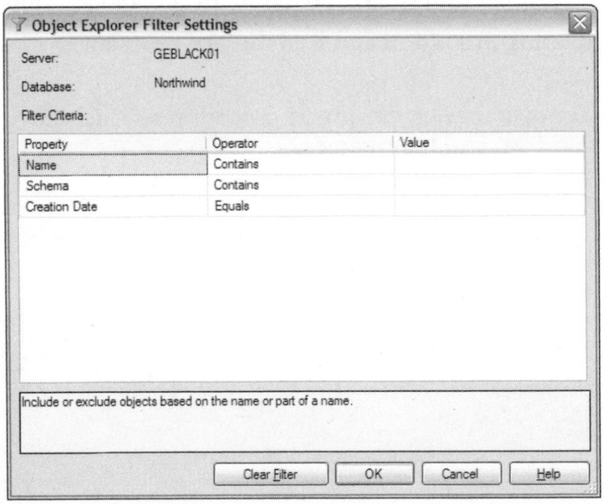

Figure 12-3: The Object Explorer Filter Settings dialog box.

2. **To specify a filter on a system stored procedure Name row, choose an operator, as shown in Figure 12-4, and then type in a sequence of characters in the Value column.**

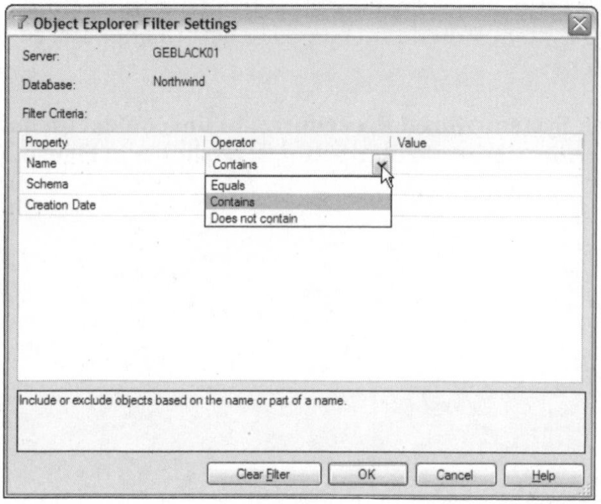

Figure 12-4: Specifying an operator for the stored procedure name.

The operator choices are Contains (the default), Equals, and Does Not Contain.

3. **To specify a filter on the Schema row of a stored procedure, specify an operator in the drop-down list and then type a sequence of characters in the Value column.**

4. **To specify a filter on date, specify an operator in the Creation Date row drop-down list and then type a date in the Value column.**

5. **After completing Steps 4, 5 and 6 (if they're relevant to your choice), click OK.**

   Figure 12-5 shows the system stored procedures, which have the character sequence `login` in their names.

Notice in Figure 12-5, to the right of the `System Stored Procedures` node, the text `(filtered)` appears, indicating that the system stored procedures have been filtered before display.

You can use the same technique to define a filter on user-defined stored-procedures. In that case, in Step 1, right-click the `Stored Procedures` (rather than the `System Stored Procedures`) node.

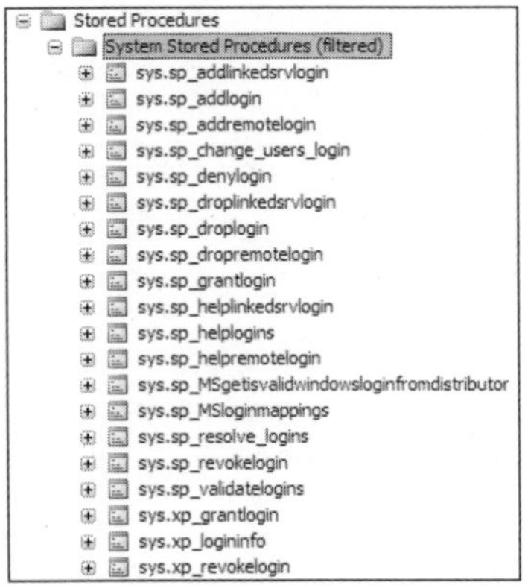

Figure 12-5:
System
stored
procedures
that include
login in
their names.

A *user-defined stored procedure* can

✔ Accept input parameters.

✔ Return tabular or scalar values.

✔ Return messages to a client machine.

✔ Invoke DML (Data Modification Language) or DDL (Data Definition Language) statements.

✔ Return output parameters.

Three types of user-defined stored procedures are supported in SQL Server 2005, one of which is deprecated:

✔ Transact-SQL stored procedures

✔ CLR stored procedures

✔ Extended stored procedures (this is deprecated but still supported)

Transact-SQL stored procedures are enormously flexible. You can use a Transact-SQL stored procedure to, for example, insert a row in a table or to execute a SELECT statement. You can use many Transact-SQL constructs in a stored procedure, but you can't use the following constructs in a Transact-SQL stored procedure:

✔ CREATE AGGREGATE

✔ CREATE DEFAULT

✔ CREATE FUNCTION

- ✔ ALTER FUNCTION
- ✔ CREATE PROCEDURE
- ✔ ALTER PROCEDURE
- ✔ CREATE RULE
- ✔ CREATE SCHEMA
- ✔ CREATE TRIGGER
- ✔ ALTER TRIGGER
- ✔ CREATE VIEW
- ✔ ALTER VIEW
- ✔ SET PARSEONLY
- ✔ SET SHOWPLAN_ALL
- ✔ SET SHOWPLAN_TEXT
- ✔ SET SHOWPLAN_XML
- ✔ USE *databaseName*

To use a database object in a stored procedure, you must create it (assuming it doesn't already exist) in the stored procedure before you use it.

Other Transact-SQL stored procedure factors to keep in mind are

- ✔ If you create a temporary table in a stored procedure, the temporary table is deleted when you exit the stored procedure.
- ✔ If a stored procedure calls another stored procedure, the called stored procedure can access any objects created in the calling stored procedure.
- ✔ If you execute a remote stored procedure, it can't take part in a transaction, so it can't be rolled back.
- ✔ The maximum number of parameters for a stored procedure is 2100.
- ✔ Available memory is the only limit on the maximum number of local variables used in a stored procedure.
- ✔ The maximum size of a stored procedure is 128MB, assuming available memory.

CLR stored procedures let you create routines in managed code by using languages, such as Visual Basic .NET or Visual C#. CLR stored procedures offer security and reliability advantages compared to extended stored procedures, which they're intended to replace.

Extended stored procedures let you create reusable external routines in a language, such as C. Avoid using extended stored procedures in new code. Support for extended stored procedures will be removed in a future version of SQL Server. Use CLR stored procedures instead of extended stored procedures.

To run a stored procedure, use the EXECUTE statement. To run a stored procedure named spGetCustomers, use this command:

```
EXECUTE spGetCustomers
```

You can use EXEC as an abbreviation for EXECUTE, so typing

```
EXEC spGetCustomers
```

also executes the spGetCustomers stored procedure.

Functions are another type of code routine that can execute in SQL Server. (Functions are described in detail in Chapter 14.) A stored procedure differs from a function in these aspects:

✔ Stored procedures don't return values in place of their name.

✔ Stored procedures can't be used directly in an expression.

Why Use Stored Procedures?

A stored procedure allows you to save a piece of Transact-SQL code for re-use. Modularizing code in that way is efficient and assists in code maintenance.

A stored procedure offers the following advantages compared with storing Transact-SQL code on client machines:

✔ Stored procedures are registered at the server.

✔ Stored procedures can have permissions assigned to them.

✔ Stored procedures can have certificates associated with them.

✔ Stored procedures can reduce network traffic.

✔ Maintenance of stored procedures is more efficient because any changes have to be made only on the server, rather than by distributing updated code to multiple client machines.

You can assign permissions on a stored procedure to a user without giving that user any permissions on the objects on which the stored procedure acts (depending on how data inside the stored procedure is accessed). Therefore, you have tight security control over what such users can do in the database.

Parameterized stored procedures offer protection against *SQL injection attacks.* A SQL injection attack occurs when an end user substitutes malicious code for dynamic Transact-SQL code.

Creating a Stored Procedure

You create a stored procedure by using the CREATE PROCEDURE statement. The general form of a CREATE PROCEDURE statement is as follows:

```
CREATE PROCEDURE <stored_procedure_name>
AS
<Transact-SQL statement(s)>
```

You can use PROC as an abbreviation for PROCEDURE, as in:

```
CREATE PROC <stored_procedure_name>
AS
<Transact-SQL statement(s)>
```

You may see either of the preceding forms in existing code that creates stored procedures.

In order to successfully create a stored procedure, you need to be sure several criteria are satisfied:

- ✔ The CREATE PROCEDURE statement must be the only statement in a batch.
- ✔ You must have CREATE PROCEDURE permissions on the database.
- ✔ You must have ALTER permissions on the schema in which the stored procedure is going to be created.
- ✔ The name of a procedure must follow the SQL Server rules for naming of identifiers.
- ✔ You can create a stored procedure only in the current database.

In the first bullet point in the preceding list, I mention that the CREATE PROCEDURE statement must be the only statement in a batch. If you attempt to execute the following code, you see an error message.

```
USE Chapter12
CREATE PROCEDURE spGetCustomers
AS
SELECT CompanyName, City, Region, Country
FROM Northwind.dbo.Customers
```

The following is the error message you will receive:

```
Msg 111, Level 15, State 1, Procedure spGetCustomers, Line
        5
'CREATE/ALTER PROCEDURE' must be the first statement in a
        query batch.
```

To enable successful execution of the CREATE PROCEDURE statement, add a GO keyword, which signals the end of a batch. Therefore in the following commands, the CREATE PROCEDURE statement is the first statement in a new batch that follows the GO keyword.

```
USE Chapter12
GO
CREATE PROCEDURE spGetCustomers
AS
SELECT CompanyName, City, Region, Country
FROM Northwind.dbo.Customers
```

To check that you successfully created the stored procedure spGetCustomers, expand the Stored Procedures node in the Chapter12 database in Object Explorer. Figure 12-6 shows the appearance you should see if you successfully created the spGetCustomers stored procedure.

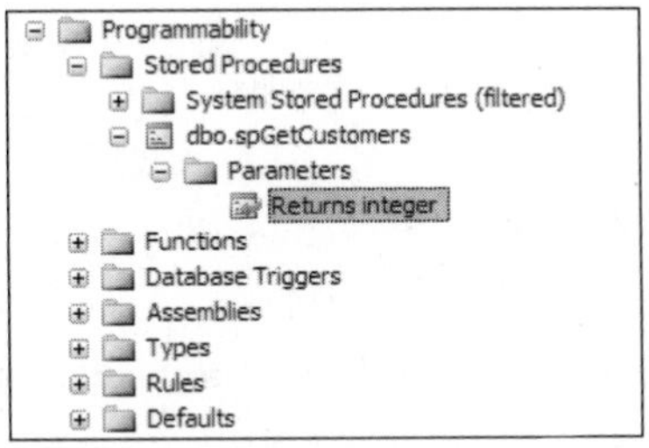

Figure 12-6:
Confirmation that you successfully created the spGetCustomers stored procedure.

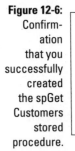

Notice in Figure 12-6 that a folder displays for any parameters that the stored procedure may take. A leaf also shows the return value of the stored procedure.

To execute the spGetCustomers stored procedure, type

```
EXECUTE spGetCustomers
```

or

```
EXEC spGetCustomers
```

Figure 12-7 shows the results of executing the spGetCustomers stored procedure.

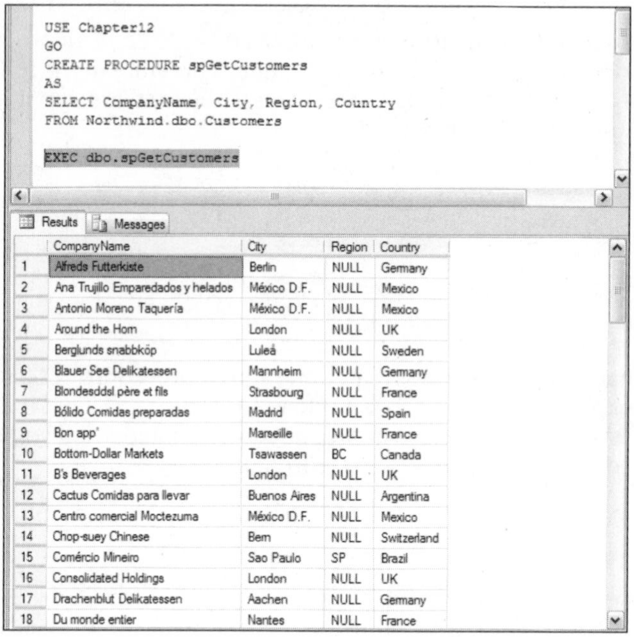

Figure 12-7:
Using
the spGet
Customers
stored
procedure
to retrieve
customer
data.

To run the spGetCustomers stored procedure from Object Explorer in SQL Server Management Studio, follows these steps:

1. **Expand the Stored Procedures node in the Chapter12 database.**

2. **Right-click the dbo.spGetCustomers stored procedure.**

3. **From the context menu, choose Execute Stored Procedure.**

   The Execute Procedure dialog box opens.

4. **In the Execute Procedure dialog box, click OK.**

In the query pane of SQL Server Management Studio, a new query is created with, assuming the grid is chosen for displaying results, the result of the query in one grid, and the value returned by the stored procedure in a separate grid. Figure 12-8 shows the appearance.

WARNING!

Don't name a stored procedure with the `sp_` prefix used in naming system stored procedures. If you happen to create a user-defined stored procedure that has the same name as a system stored procedure, it will never be executed if it is in the `dbo` schema or if an application uses non-schema qualified name references.

To illustrate the issue referred to in the preceding paragraph, create a stored procedure named `sp_who`, as in the following code:

```
CREATE PROCEDURE sp_who
AS
SELECT CompanyName, City, Region, Country
FROM Northwind.dbo.Customers
```

Figure 12-8: Executing a stored procedure from Object Explorer.

Notice that the preceding code is a simple `SELECT` statement of the same customer data used in the `spGetCustomers` stored procedure. If the stored procedure runs, you should see customer data, as shown in Figure 12-7.

A system stored procedure `sys.sp_who` can return information on processes. Type

```
EXEC sp_who
```

and inspect the results. As you can see in Figure 12-9, the expected customer data isn't displayed. Instead, data about current processes returned by the `sys.sp_who` stored procedure is displayed.

For user-defined stored procedures, I use `sp` (with no underscore) as a prefix for user-defined stored procedures. I then use an uppercase character as the next character in the name, as in `spGetCustomers`.

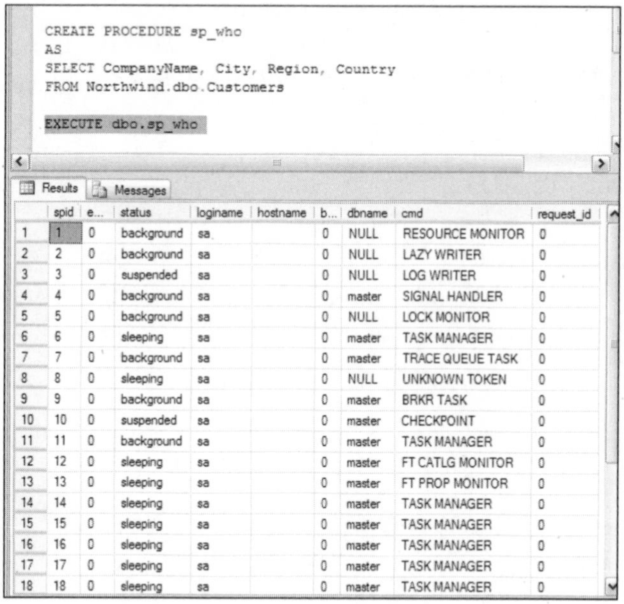

Figure 12-9:
The sys.sp_who stored procedure executes, not the dbo.sp_who stored procedure.

Using ALTER to Change a Stored Procedure

You can change an existing stored procedure in two ways. The less desirable option is to drop the stored procedure and then create a new stored procedure with the name of the stored procedure you just deleted. A significant disadvantage of that approach is that any permissions for the stored procedure are also deleted and need to be re-created from scratch.

To drop the `spGetCustomers` stored procedure, type

```
DROP spGetCustomers
```

You can then create a new stored procedure, `spGetCustomers`, with a different procedure definition.

The other option is to use an `ALTER PROCEDURE` statement. For example, to add the `PostalCode` column to the displayed customer information, use the following statement to alter the procedure:

```
ALTER PROCEDURE spGetCustomers
AS
SELECT CompanyName, City, Region, Country, PostalCode
FROM Northwind.dbo.Customers
```

To execute the stored procedure, type the following code:

```
EXECUTE spGetCustomers
```

Figure 12-10 shows that the `PostalCode` column is now included in the results.

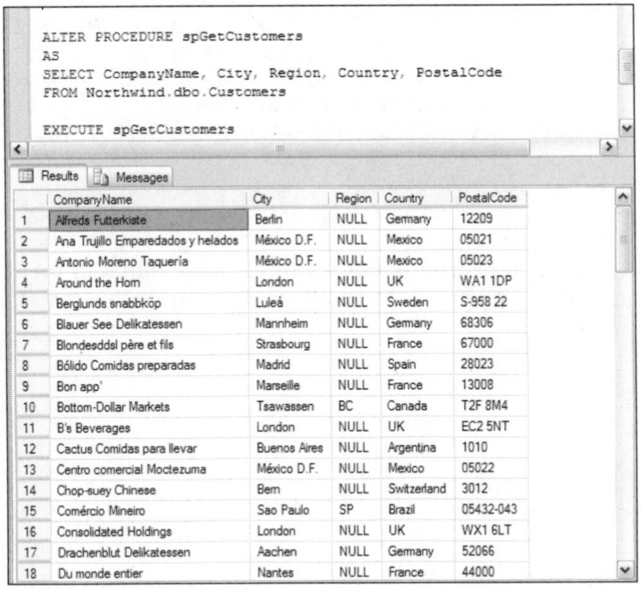

```
ALTER PROCEDURE spGetCustomers
AS
SELECT CompanyName, City, Region, Country, PostalCode
FROM Northwind.dbo.Customers

EXECUTE spGetCustomers
```


	CompanyName	City	Region	Country	PostalCode
1	Alfreds Futterkiste	Berlin	NULL	Germany	12209
2	Ana Trujillo Emparedados y helados	México D.F.	NULL	Mexico	05021
3	Antonio Moreno Taquería	México D.F.	NULL	Mexico	05023
4	Around the Horn	London	NULL	UK	WA1 1DP
5	Berglunds snabbköp	Luleå	NULL	Sweden	S-958 22
6	Blauer See Delikatessen	Mannheim	NULL	Germany	68306
7	Blondesddsl père et fils	Strasbourg	NULL	France	67000
8	Bólido Comidas preparadas	Madrid	NULL	Spain	28023
9	Bon app'	Marseille	NULL	France	13008
10	Bottom-Dollar Markets	Tsawassen	BC	Canada	T2F 8M4
11	B's Beverages	London	NULL	UK	EC2 5NT
12	Cactus Comidas para llevar	Buenos Aires	NULL	Argentina	1010
13	Centro comercial Moctezuma	México D.F.	NULL	Mexico	05022
14	Chop-suey Chinese	Bern	NULL	Switzerland	3012
15	Comércio Mineiro	Sao Paulo	SP	Brazil	05432-043
16	Consolidated Holdings	London	NULL	UK	WX1 6LT
17	Drachenblut Delikatessen	Aachen	NULL	Germany	52066
18	Du monde entier	Nantes	NULL	France	44000

Figure 12-10: The results of the stored procedure, including the Postal Code column.

In the preceding example, I made only a minor alteration to the Transact-SQL statement in the procedure definition. You can make any arbitrary change you wish in that code, bearing in mind the constraints on the Transact-SQL you can use in a stored procedure.

Using Parameters with Stored Procedures

Stored procedures that have no parameters can be useful. However, adding parameters to a stored procedure makes the stored procedure much more flexible.

The following stored procedure with no parameters retrieves credit card data for 2007 for the Vista credit card company from the AdventureWorks_new database:

```
USE AdventureWorks_new
GO
CREATE PROCEDURE VistaIn2007
AS
SELECT      Person.Contact.LastName,
            Person.Contact.MiddleName,
            Person.Contact.FirstName,
            Sales.CreditCard.CardType,
            Sales.CreditCard.CardNumber,
                        Sales.CreditCard.ExpYear,
            Sales.CreditCard.ExpMonth
FROM         Person.Contact INNER JOIN
                        Sales.ContactCreditCard ON
            Person.Contact.ContactID =
            Sales.ContactCreditCard.ContactID INNER JOIN
                        Sales.CreditCard ON
            Sales.ContactCreditCard.CreditCardID =
            Sales.CreditCard.CreditCardID
WHERE       (Sales.CreditCard.ExpYear = 2007) AND
            (Sales.CreditCard.CardType = N'Vista')
ORDER BY Sales.CreditCard.ExpYear,
            Sales.CreditCard.ExpMonth
```

That stored procedure is useful, but it can be made much more flexible by adding @Year and @CardType parameters, as in the following statement:

```
CREATE PROCEDURE CardByYearAndType
@Year int,
@CardType varchar(10)
AS
SELECT       Person.Contact.LastName,
             Person.Contact.MiddleName,
             Person.Contact.FirstName,
             Sales.CreditCard.CardType,
             Sales.CreditCard.CardNumber,
                        Sales.CreditCard.ExpYear,
             Sales.CreditCard.ExpMonth
FROM         Person.Contact INNER JOIN
                        Sales.ContactCreditCard ON
             Person.Contact.ContactID =
             Sales.ContactCreditCard.ContactID INNER JOIN
                        Sales.CreditCard ON
             Sales.ContactCreditCard.CreditCardID =
             Sales.CreditCard.CreditCardID
WHERE        (Sales.CreditCard.ExpYear = @Year) AND
             (Sales.CreditCard.CardType = @CardType)
ORDER BY Sales.CreditCard.ExpYear,
             Sales.CreditCard.ExpMonth
```

The CardByYearAndType stored procedure is much more flexible than the preceding VistaIn2007 stored procedure. You can substitute values for the parameters when executing the stored procedure.

The following command executes the stored procedure so that Vista cards expiring in 2008 are returned:

```
EXEC CardByYearAndType @Year = 2008, @CardType = 'Vista'
```

Figure 12-11 shows the results. Notice that the values in the ExpYear column are all 2008, and the values in the CardType column are all Vista.

Parameterized stored procedures offer protection against SQL injection attacks. If the value entered by a user contains malicious Transact-SQL code, it is highly unlikely that it is a valid value for a parameter for the underlying stored procedure. An error, therefore, occurs, and the malicious code does not execute on SQL Server.

```
CREATE PROCEDURE CardByYearAndType
@Year int,
@CardType varchar(10)
AS
SELECT          Person.Contact.LastName, Person.Contact.MiddleName, Per
                     Sales.CreditCard.ExpYear, Sales.CreditCard.E
FROM           Person.Contact INNER JOIN
                     Sales.ContactCreditCard ON Person.Contact.Co
                     Sales.CreditCard ON Sales.ContactCreditCard.
WHERE     (Sales.CreditCard.ExpYear = @Year) AND (Sales.CreditCard
ORDER BY Sales.CreditCard.ExpYear, Sales.CreditCard.ExpMonth

EXEC CardByYearAndType @Year = 2008, @CardType = 'Vista'
```

Results | Messages

	LastName	MiddleName	FirstName	CardType	CardNumber	ExpYear	ExpMonth
1	Cetinok	NULL	Baris	Vista	11118902196656	2008	1
2	Giakoumakis	NULL	Leo	Vista	11115037059446	2008	1
3	Huang	P	Laura	Vista	11112693724565	2008	1
4	Sanchez	S	Mayra	Vista	11114001076866	2008	1
5	Zeng	NULL	Cedric	Vista	11112007993253	2008	1
6	Anderson	J	Jeremy	Vista	11115307896822	2008	1
7	Tang	G	Kurt	Vista	11118100772217	2008	1
8	Nara	R	Terrence	Vista	11118198764165	2008	1
9	Carter	NULL	Xavier	Vista	11111269807878	2008	1
10	Collins	C	Xavier	Vista	11114190274106	2008	1
11	Xu	G	Carly	Vista	11119942122582	2008	1
12	Campbell	A	Richard	Vista	11114575780172	2008	1

Figure 12-11:
Using
parameter
values
when
executing
a stored
procedure.

Chapter 13

Using Triggers

A trigger is one way to enforce business rules and protect data integrity. (Triggers aren't the only way in which SQL Server 2005 enforces business rules and data integrity. Constraints, which I describe in Chapter 10, also provide an alternative way to enforce business rules and protect data integrity.)

Using triggers requires more thought than using constraints, but triggers also have capabilities that constraints lack. In this chapter, I discuss when you should use constraints and when you should consider using triggers. I also describe the different types of triggers that are available for you to use and show you how to create each type of trigger.

SQL Server 2005 provides support for two types of trigger — DML (Data Modification Language) and DDL (Data Definition Language). A DML trigger executes in response to INSERT, UPDATE, or DELETE events. A DDL trigger executes in response to a change in the structure of a database or table.

SQL Server 2005 allows you to create triggers that run after an event, and triggers that run instead of the intended Transact-SQL code. Not surprisingly, these kinds of triggers are called AFTER triggers and INSTEAD OF triggers, after the keywords that you use when you define the trigger.

Using Events That Execute Triggers

DML triggers execute in response to changes in data held in a table. Triggers can be also be created to fire on the execution of DDL (Data Definition Language) events. A DML trigger responds to the following events:

- ✔ INSERT
- ✔ DELETE
- ✔ UPDATE
- ✔ Any combination of the above

The preceding events can occur in a table or in a view. A DML trigger can be an AFTER trigger or an INSTEAD OF trigger. Earlier in this chapter, I show you how to create an AFTER DML trigger and an INSTEAD OF DML trigger.

Before creating a DML trigger, consider the following:

- ✔ The CREATE TRIGGER statement must be the first statement in a batch. All other statements in the batch are interpreted as the definition of the trigger.
- ✔ Permission to create a trigger defaults to a table owner.
- ✔ The names of DML triggers must follow the rules for identifiers because triggers are database objects.
- ✔ You can create a DML trigger in the current database only. The trigger can, however, reference another database.
- ✔ You can't create a trigger on a temporary table.
- ✔ A TRUNCATE TABLE doesn't cause a DELETE trigger to execute.

DML triggers were supported in SQL Server 2000, so you can create a DML trigger to run on a SQL Server 2000 database if you use the FOR version of the CREATE TRIGGER syntax. The AFTER version of the CREATE TRIGGER syntax is new in SQL Server 2005, so you can execute such a trigger only on a SQL Server 2005 database.

As already stated, triggers can also be created to fire on the execution of DDL (Data Definition Language) events. DDL triggers are new to SQL Server 2005. A DDL trigger responds to events that occur when metadata is changed. A DDL trigger responds to the following events:

✔ CREATE

✔ ALTER

✔ DROP

DDL triggers can also fire in response to some system stored procedures. In order to understand the behavior of your DDL triggers, you should test them against potentially relevant system stored procedures to see if the trigger is executed in response to running the stored procedure(s).

Both DDL and DML triggers can execute a managed code assembly loaded into SQL Server. I describe using managed code in Chapter 21.

Understanding Where and When to Use Triggers

A *trigger* is a specialized stored procedure that runs in response to an event in SQL Server. The event can be a change in data or a change in database structure. When the event is a change in data, a DML trigger runs, if you've created one to respond to the DML event. If the event is a change in the database structure, a DDL trigger runs, if you've created one to respond to the particular change in database structure.

A trigger differs from a stored procedure in that a trigger can be executed only in response to an event. No Transact-SQL statement executes a trigger equivalent to

```
EXECUTE <procedure_name>
```

To execute a trigger, you have to execute a Transact-SQL statement that causes an event to be fired for the trigger to respond to. The only way to execute a stored procedure, by contrast, is in response to an EXECUTE statement.

A trigger differs from a stored procedure in these respects:

✔ A trigger fires in response to an event. It can't be executed directly using a Transact-SQL statement. By contrast, a stored procedure is executed using a Transact-SQL EXECUTE statement and can't respond to a database event.

✔ A stored procedure may have one or more parameters. A trigger can't have parameters.

✔ A stored procedure has a return value. A trigger has no return value.

A trigger, although it responds to database engine events, isn't the same as an event notification. *Event notifications* execute in response to DDL events and some SQL Trace events by sending information about the events to a SQL Server Service Broker service. Service Broker is outside the scope of this book.

A trigger and its triggering statement are part of a single implicit transaction. That means that if the trigger contains a ROLLBACK TRANSACTION statement, not only the code in the trigger is rolled back, but the triggering Transact-SQL statement is also rolled back. The ability of triggers to rollback a transaction means that you need to give careful thought as to how to test conditions that determine the rollback. The later in the transaction process that the rollback occurs, the more provisional processing has to be undone. Particularly, if the processing is complex, this rollback can be time-consuming and lead to poor database performance.

Triggers are immensely flexible because you can write almost any arbitrary Transact-SQL code as part of the trigger. That means that a trigger can do anything that constraints can do and more. I described constraints in Chapter 10. A trigger is often not the best or most efficient tool to enforce data integrity. Unless you have strong reasons to consider a trigger in a particular situation, the following rules of thumb apply:

✔ To enforce domain integrity, use a CHECK constraint.

✔ To enforce entity integrity, use UNIQUE or PRIMARY KEY constraints.

✔ To enforce referential integrity, use FOREIGN KEY constraints.

Triggers can respond to the following situations that constraints can't handle:

✔ Unlike CHECK constraints, a trigger can reference data in another table. This allows you to, for example, compare inserted data to data in another table and perform an action, depending on the results of that comparison.

✔ Constraints use standard SQL Server 2005 error handling. If you require custom error messages, use a trigger.

✔ Triggers can evaluate values in a table before and after modification and respond, depending on that comparison.

If you decide that one of the preceding constraints isn't appropriate, you have two types of triggers available to you in SQL Server 2005. Triggers in SQL Server 2005 execute in response to two kinds of changes:

✔ **Changes in the database structure:** Data Definition Language, DDL, triggers

✔ **Changes in the database content:** Data Modification Language, DML, triggers

Triggers in SQL Server 2005 can occur at one of two times, relative to their triggering action:

✔ An AFTER trigger occurs after the triggering action.

✔ An INSTEAD OF trigger occurs instead of the triggering action. In other words, the triggering action isn't executed in the normal way, but it's substituted by the INSTEAD OF trigger.

In the following sections, I describe AFTER triggers, INSTEAD OF triggers, DDL triggers, and DML triggers and show you how you can use them.

Some triggers use internal SQL Server 2005 tables. When you INSERT a row into an existing table, SQL Server inserts a copy of that row into the Inserted table. If you DELETE a row from an existing table, SQL Server inserts a copy of the deleted row into the Deleted table. If you UPDATE a row in an existing table, SQL Server inserts a copy of that row into both the Inserted and Deleted tables.

Using AFTER Triggers

An AFTER trigger executes after a triggering action. A *triggering action* is the Transact-SQL statement, or statements, that produces the event to which the trigger responds. You can create one, or more than one, trigger to execute in response to a particular triggering action. For example, you can create multiple triggers that respond to a DELETE event, just at different points in time. More specifically, an AFTER trigger after the event has occurred, and an INSTEAD OF trigger executes in lieu of the triggering event. However, this is not a particularly sensible practice because it is easy to lose track of the execution path of too many triggers.

An AFTER trigger executes after the following:

- ✔ Constraint processing
- ✔ Declarative referential actions
- ✔ Creation of the Inserted and Deleted tables
- ✔ The triggering action

An AFTER trigger never executes if there's a constraint violation. An AFTER trigger can reference the Inserted and Deleted tables to execute, so an AFTER trigger with multiple triggering actions can execute differently for each triggering action.

You can create an AFTER trigger only on a table.

The syntax for an AFTER trigger is similar whether the trigger executes in response to an INSERT, a DELETE, or an UPDATE or a combination of those events.

The basic syntax to create an AFTER trigger is as follows:

```
CREATE TRIGGER <trigger_name>
ON <table_name>
AFTER <operation(s)>
AS
<define what the trigger does>
```

An alternate syntax using FOR, which works the same as AFTER, is shown here:

```
CREATE TRIGGER <trigger_name>
ON <table_name>
FOR <operation(s)>
AS
<define what the trigger does>
```

The name of the trigger follows the usual SQL Server 2005 naming rules. The operation(s) in the AFTER clause is either a single value or a comma-separated list. So to create a trigger that responds only to an INSERT event, use this form:

```
CREATE TRIGGER <trigger_name>
ON <table_name>
AFTER INSERT
AS
<define what the trigger does>
```

To create a trigger that responds to both INSERT and UPDATE events, use this form:

```
CREATE TRIGGER <trigger_name>
ON <table_name>
AFTER INSERT, UPDATE
AS
<define what the trigger does>
```

A common use of AFTER triggers that are also DML triggers is to audit who changed data in a database. The changes can be insertions, updates, or deletions. To create an AFTER trigger that responds to an INSERT statement, for example, follow these steps:

1. **Open a new query in SQL Server Management Studio.**

2. **Create a database, Chapter13, by executing this command:**

   ```
   CREATE DATABASE Chapter13
   ```

3. **Create a table, AuditedTable, that you want to audit for INSERT events:**

   ```
   USE Chapter13
   CREATE TABLE AuditedTable(
    MessageID int PRIMARY KEY IDENTITY,
    Message varchar(200)
    )
   ```

4. **Insert an example row into the AuditedTable table.**

   At this stage, there is no trigger, so you see only one message that one row is affected.

   ```
   INSERT INTO AuditedTable
   VALUES ('Hello trigger world!')
   ```

5. **Create the table that you store audit information in using the following command.**

   The Changed column contains a timestamp value that shows the order in which audit information is added to the AuditTable table. The WhenChanged column stores information about when the change was made. The TableName column stores data showing the table that was changed. The UserName column stores data about the user who made the change in the AuditedTable table. The Operation column stores data about what kind of operation was audited.

```
CREATE TABLE AuditTable
(
 Changed TIMESTAMP,
 WhenChanged DateTime,
 TableName char(40),
 UserName varchar(40),
 Operation char(6)
)
```

6. **Confirm that you created the `AuditTable` table using the following command:**

```
SELECT *
FROM AuditTable
```

7. **Insert a sample row into the `AuditTable` table:**

```
INSERT INTO AuditTable
( WhenChanged, TableName, UserName, Operation)
VALUES(
GetDate(), 'AuditedTable', 'John Smith', 'INSERT'
)
```

8. **Create the trigger, `AuditInserts`, using the following command:**

```
CREATE TRIGGER AuditInserts
ON dbo.AuditedTable
AFTER INSERT
AS
INSERT INTO dbo.AuditTable (WhenChanged, TableName,
        UserName, Operation)
SELECT GetDate(), 'AuditedTable', suser_name(),
        'INSERT'
```

Notice that the trigger executes only in response to an INSERT operation. Notice that there's nothing to insert data into the Changed column because that's a timestamp column. The GetDate() function is used to populate the WhenChanged column with the current date and time. The suser_name() function populates the UserName column with the name of the user who caused the INSERT operation to be executed. The string INSERT is supplied literally. That's possible because the trigger runs only in response to an INSERT operation. (See the AFTER clause.)

9. **Now that you've created the trigger, you can test that it works by inserting a row into the `AuditedTable` table:**

```
INSERT INTO AuditedTable
VALUES ('This should fire an INSERT trigger.')
```

Figure 13-1 shows that two rows have been affected when the preceding command executed. That is expected. The first message indicates a successful `INSERT` operation into the `AuditedTable`, as per the preceding command. The second message indicates that the `AuditInserts` trigger has executed and inserted a row into the `AuditTable` table.

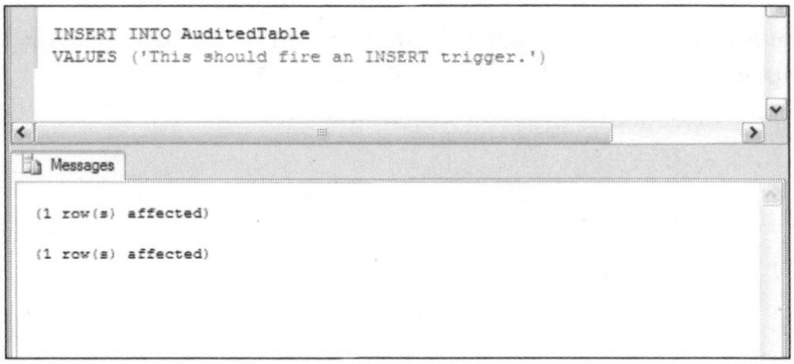

Figure 13-1:
A message
for each
of two
inserts,
the second
insert
produced by
the trigger.

```
INSERT INTO AuditedTable
VALUES ('This should fire an INSERT trigger.')
```

```
Messages

(1 row(s) affected)

(1 row(s) affected)
```

10. **You can test that the row in Step 9 inserted successfully and that the trigger executed successfully (and inserted a row into the `AuditTable` table) by using these commands:**

```
SELECT *
FROM AuditedTable

SELECT *
FROM AuditTable
```

Figure 13-2 shows the results of executing the commands in Step 10.

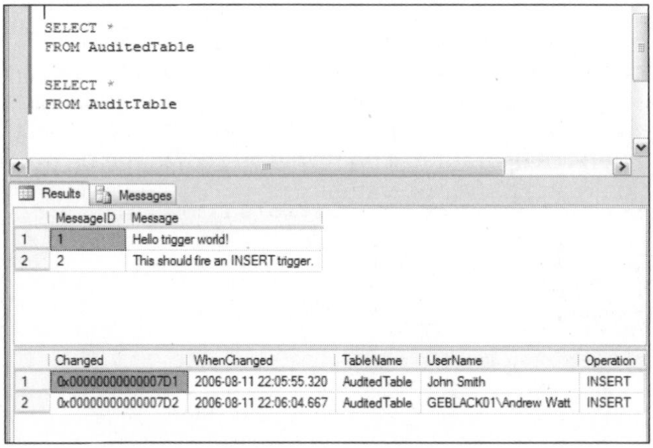

```
SELECT *
FROM AuditedTable

SELECT *
FROM AuditTable
```

Figure 13-2:
Successful
execution
of the
AuditInserts
trigger.

	MessageID	Message
1	1	Hello trigger world!
2	2	This should fire an INSERT trigger.

	Changed	WhenChanged	TableName	UserName	Operation
1	0x00000000000007D1	2006-08-11 22:05:55.320	AuditedTable	John Smith	INSERT
2	0x00000000000007D2	2006-08-11 22:06:04.667	AuditedTable	GEBLACK01\Andrew Watt	INSERT

When you want to create a trigger that responds to more than one event, you need to add some logic to correctly add data to the Operation column. To modify the trigger so that it responds to both INSERT and UPDATE events, follow these steps:

1. **Delete the AuditInserts trigger using this command:**

```
DROP TRIGGER AuditInserts
```

2. **Create a new AFTER trigger, AuditInsertsUpdates, which executes in response to INSERT and UPDATE events:**

```
CREATE TRIGGER AuditInsertsUpdates
ON dbo.AuditedTable
AFTER INSERT, UPDATE
AS
DECLARE @Operation char(6)
IF EXISTS (SELECT * FROM DELETED)
  SET @OPERATION = 'UPDATE'
ELSE
  SET @OPERATION = 'INSERT'
INSERT INTO dbo.AuditTable (WhenChanged, TableName,
        UserName, Operation)
SELECT GetDate(), 'AuditedTable', suser_name(),
        @Operation
```

Notice the code I added to correctly insert a value into the Operation column. First, I declare a variable @Operation:

```
DECLARE @Operation char(6)
```

Next, I use an IF statement to test whether a row exists in an internal SQL Server table called Deleted. If a row is present in the Deleted table, an UPDATE operation must have taken place (an update can be considered to be a deletion combined with an insertion). The AFTER clause of the CREATE TRIGGER statement

```
AFTER INSERT, UPDATE
```

tells you that the trigger only executes in response to INSERT operations or UPDATE operations. Only an UPDATE operation adds a row to the Deleted table, so if a row exists in the Deleted table, the operation was an UPDATE operation. If no row is present in the Deleted table, the operation is an INSERT operation.

```
IF EXISTS (SELECT * FROM DELETED)
  SET @OPERATION = 'UPDATE'
ELSE
  SET @OPERATION = 'INSERT'
```

The @Operation variable is used to populate the Operation column:

```
INSERT INTO dbo.AuditTable (WhenChanged, TableName,
        UserName, Operation)
SELECT GetDate(), 'AuditedTable', suser_name(),
        @Operation
```

3. **Now that the AuditInsertsUpdates trigger has been created, test that it works by inserting a row into the AuditedTable table and then updating an existing row in the AuditedTable table.**

```
INSERT INTO AuditedTable
VALUES ('This is an INSERTed message.')
UPDATE AuditedTable
SET Message = 'This row was updated'
WHERE MessageID = 1
```

Figure 13-3 shows the results when executing the preceding commands. Notice that there are four messages indicating that one row was affected. Two of those messages are due to successful execution of the preceding INSERT and UPDATE statements. Two of the messages are due to the AuditInsertsUpdates trigger executing, once for the INSERT statement and once for the UPDATE statement.

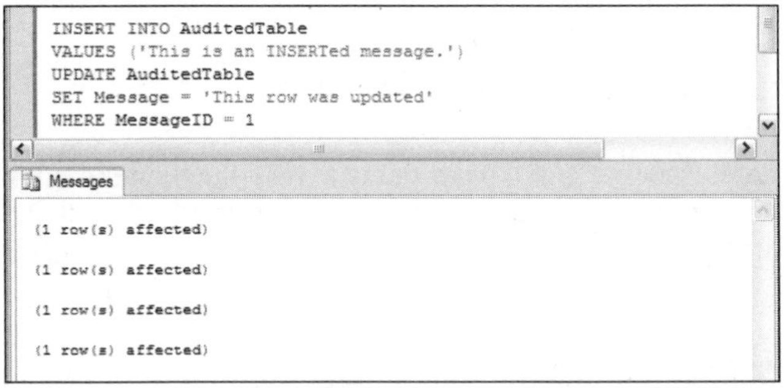

Figure 13-3:
Four messages due to execution of two statements and two executions of the trigger.

```
INSERT INTO AuditedTable
VALUES ('This is an INSERTed message.')
UPDATE AuditedTable
SET Message = 'This row was updated'
WHERE MessageID = 1
```

Messages

```
(1 row(s) affected)
(1 row(s) affected)
(1 row(s) affected)
(1 row(s) affected)
```

4. **Confirm that two rows have been inserted into the AuditTable table using these commands:**

```
SELECT *
FROM AuditedTable

SELECT *
FROM AuditTable
```

Figure 13-4 shows the result of executing the preceding commands. In the upper results, row 4 is the row inserted most recently. Notice too that row has the message created using the UPDATE statement in Step 3. In the lower part of the results, row 4 is the result of executing the INSERT statement in Step 3. Notice that the value in the Operation column is INSERT. Row 5 is the result of executing the UPDATE statement in Step 3. Notice that the value in the Operation column is UPDATE. Thus the @Operation variable has worked to correctly identify the operation that was audited.

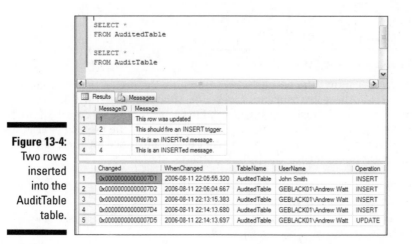

Figure 13-4:
Two rows inserted into the AuditTable table.

You can create a CLR AFTER trigger using a .NET language of your choice. I introduce Common Language Runtime, CLR, programming in SQL Server 2005 in Chapter 21.

Using INSTEAD OF Triggers

An INSTEAD OF trigger executes *instead of* the operation that was otherwise going to happen when a piece of Transact-SQL code executed. You can define only one INSTEAD OF trigger for any given triggering action, unlike AFTER triggers, where you can define multiple triggers for a single triggering action.

An INSTEAD OF trigger executes

- ✔ Before constraint processing.
- ✔ Instead of the triggering action.
- ✔ After creation of the Inserted and Deleted tables.

To update a view that references more than one table, you must use an INSTEAD OF trigger.

The following example shows you how you can use an INSTEAD OF trigger to prevent the data in a table being changed. Follow these steps:

1. **Create a table, CantChangeMe, for which you will create an INSTEAD OF trigger.**

   ```
   USE Chapter13
   CREATE TABLE CantChangeMe
   (MessageID int PRIMARY KEY IDENTITY.
    Message varchar(200))
   ```

2. **Insert a test row into the CantChangeMe table before you create the trigger:**

   ```
   INSERT
   INTO CantChangeMe
   VALUES ('This was inserted before the trigger was
           created.')
   ```

3. **Confirm successful insertion of the row.**

   ```
   SELECT *
   FROM CantChangeMe
   ```

4. **Create the INSTEAD OF trigger, PreventChanges, using this CREATE TRIGGER statement.**

   This statement prints a simple message telling the user that he or she can't change the database.

   ```
   CREATE TRIGGER PreventChanges
   ON CantChangeMe
   INSTEAD OF INSERT, UPDATE, DELETE
   AS
   Print 'You cannot change this table. Do not even try!'
   ```

5. **Attempt to insert a row into the CantChangeMe table.**

   This insert will now fail because you created the PreventChanges trigger in the preceding step.

   ```
   INSERT
   INTO CantChangeMe
   VALUES ('This INSERT will fail.')
   ```

Figure 13-5 shows the results of executing the preceding INSERT statement. Notice that the message from the PreventChanges trigger is displayed. Don't be misled by the

```
(1 row(s) affected)
```

message into thinking that the INSERT operation was successful. At least it wasn't successful in the normal sense. The trigger code ran instead of the INSERT statement. It was the trigger code that ran successfully.

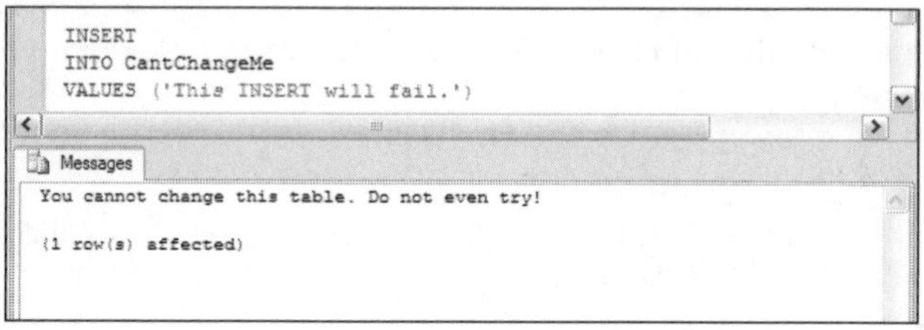

Figure 13-5:
An INSERT
operation
causes the
trigger's
message
to be
displayed.

```
INSERT
INTO CantChangeMe
VALUES ('This INSERT will fail.')
```

Messages
You cannot change this table. Do not even try!

(1 row(s) affected)

6. **Confirm that the INSERT operation into the CantChangeMe table didn't work.**

```
SELECT *
FROM CantChangeMe
```

Figure 13-6 shows that only the row inserted before the trigger was created is present in the CantChangeMe table.

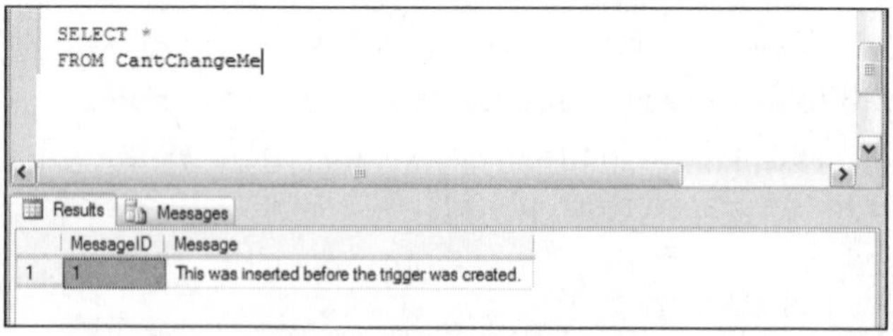

Figure 13-6:
The INSERT
statement in
Step 5 didn't
insert a row.

```
SELECT *
FROM CantChangeMe
```

Results | Messages
MessageID | Message
1 | 1 | This was inserted before the trigger was created.

7. **Confirm also that you can't delete a row from the CantChangeMe table:**

```
DELETE
FROM CantChangeMe
WHERE MessageID = 1
```

You see the same messages as in Figure 13-5. The INSTEAD OF trigger prevented you deleting a row.

8. **Confirm that the row wasn't deleted:**

```
SELECT *
FROM CantChangeMe
```

You see the same row as you saw in Figure 13-6 confirming that the DELETE statement did not affect the CantChangeMe table. The INSTEAD OF trigger prevented the row from being deleted.

Another use of INSTEAD OF triggers is to respond to DML statements attempted on a view that you created using a join from two or more base tables. The trigger definition can include Transact-SQL statements to insert or update rows in relevant tables that were used in the join that created the view. Successful execution of such an INSTEAD OF trigger depends on having enough data to successfully INSERT into or UPDATE each table. If you have no data to insert into a column in a base table that doesn't allow NULLs, has no defined default, and isn't an identity column, inserting the row fails.

Triggers and the Transact-SQL statement that fires them are part of a single transaction, so it is possible to rollback the trigger and the firing statement.

You can create a CLR INSTEAD OF trigger using a .NET language of your choice. I introduce Common Language Runtime, CLR, programming in SQL Server 2005 in Chapter 21.

Using DDL Triggers

DDL triggers are new to SQL Server 2005. The scope can be database or server level (all databases created for a particular SQL Server installation). DDL triggers are fired when a change occurs to a schema object.

For example, you can use a DDL trigger to prevent a user from executing CREATE TABLE, DROP TABLE, and DROP TABLE statements on a table. Effectively, you can use DDL triggers to prevent users from creating, dropping, or changing tables.

More specifically, a trigger executes in the security context of the user who executes the triggering action. This has potential for malicious use. Suppose a user, Fred, creates the following trigger:

```
CREATE TRIGGER ElevateFred
ON DATABASE
FOR ALTER_TABLE
AS
GRANT CONTROL SERVER Fred
```

If a sysadmin executes a Transact-SQL statement, the `ElevateFred` trigger executes as if the following statement were executed by a sysadmin:

```
GRANT CONTROL SERVER Fred
```

A sysadmin has permissions to grant this permission but almost certainly didn't intend to grant such extensive permissions to Fred. This kind of security problem can occur with `AFTER` triggers and `INSTEAD OF` triggers.

A primary way to avoid such malicious code is to be discerning in who you grant permissions on a database that would allow them to create triggers. Know your staff. Give permissions to staff on a need-to-have basis only.

Another level of protection is to review all existing triggers. The following code allows you to see all DML triggers in the `Chapter13` database:

```
USE Chapter13
SELECT *
FROM sys.triggers
```

To see DDL triggers, execute the following code:

```
SELECT *
FROM sys.server_triggers
```

To disable all database-level DDL triggers in the current database, execute this code:

```
DISABLE TRIGGER ALL ON DATABASE
```

To disable all server-level DDL triggers in the current SQL Server instance, execute this code:

```
DISABLE TRIGGER ALL ON SERVER
```

Debugging Triggers

As I mention earlier in the chapter, the code in a trigger executes in response to an event. This creates issues when you want to test the code in the trigger because only the relevant event, or events, causes the code in the trigger to execute.

One way to approach debugging is to create a stored procedure that contains a statement, or statements, that you know will fire the trigger. For example, the following stored procedure fires the AFTER trigger on the AuditedTable table that you create earlier in this chapter.

```
CREATE PROCEDURE TestInsertTrigger
AS
INSERT
INTO AuditedTable
VALUES ('This is from the test stored procedure.')
```

To run the stored procedure, execute this command:

```
EXEC TestInsertTrigger
```

You see two messages that one row has been affected. To confirm that the trigger has executed, execute these commands:

```
SELECT *
FROM AuditedTable
SELECT *
FROM AuditTable
```

Notice in Figure 13-7 that row 5 in the upper part of the results grid is the row inserted by the TestInsertTrigger stored procedure. Row 6 in the lower part of the results grid is the row inserted by the trigger into the AuditTable table.

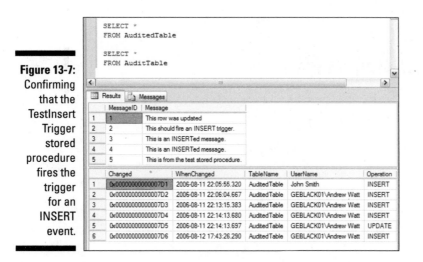

Figure 13-7: Confirming that the TestInsert Trigger stored procedure fires the trigger for an INSERT event.

Chapter 14

Creating Functions

*I*n this chapter, I introduce you to SQL Server functions. I explain what a SQL Server function is, and I discuss the two types of user-defined functions supported in SQL Server 2005: a Transact-SQL function or a CLR function created by a user who is using the CREATE FUNCTION statement.

I show you how to create user-defined functions with Transact-SQL and show you how they can be used in your Transact-SQL code. I don't discuss CLR user-defined functions in this chapter, however, I discuss CLR programming in SQL Server 2005 in Chapter 21.

I also introduce you to the built-in system functions available in SQL Server 2005. I show you examples of how you can use system functions in your own Transact-SQL code.

In SQL Server 2005, you can create user-defined functions using .NET languages, which run on the Common Language Runtime built into SQL Server.

What Is a Transact-SQL Function?

A Transact-SQL function resembles many other programming language functions. A *function* is a software module that can accept one or more parameters, performs some processing, and returns a value.

SQL Server has two types of functions:

- **Functions that return scalar values.** A scalar-valued function can return any scalar SQL Server 2005 value data type except `text`, `ntext`, `image`, `cursor`, or `timestamp`.

- **Table-valued functions.** A table-valued function returns a `table` data type. You can use table-valued functions in place of views.

A Transact-SQL scalar function can contain one or more Transact-SQL statements. If the code contains multiple statements, those statements are contained in a `BEGIN . . . END` block.

A function differs from a stored procedure in these respects:

- The value returned by a stored procedure indicates success or failure of execution of the function. The value returned by a function can be used in your Transact-SQL statements.

- A stored procedure cannot be used inline in, say, a `SELECT` statement. By contrast, you can use a function inline in a `SELECT` statement and other Transact-SQL statements.

Creating User-Defined Functions

As already stated, a user-defined function is a Transact-SQL or CLR function created by a user who is using the `CREATE FUNCTION` statement.

Several characteristics of a user-defined function determine whether SQL Server can index the results of a function:

- **Determinism** is whether the function always returns the same value given a particular state of the database.

- **Precision** is when a function is said to be precise if it doesn't use floating point arithmetic.

- **Data access** is when the SQL Server database engine can determine automatically whether a Transact-SQL user-defined function accesses data with the SQL Server in-process provider.

- **System Metadata Access** is whether the function accesses metadata held by SQL Server.

- **IsSystemVerified** is whether the function can be established by SQL Server to be deterministic. A deterministic function always produces the same result for given input. If the function accesses any function for which `IsSystemVerified = false`, the same value is set for `IsSystemVerified` for the current function.

A user-defined function can be used in the following ways:

- ✔ In a Transact-SQL statement, for example, a SELECT statement
- ✔ In an application that calls the function
- ✔ In the definition of another user-defined function
- ✔ To define a column in a table
- ✔ To define a CHECK constraint on a column
- ✔ To replace a stored procedure

In SQL Server 2005, you can create user-defined functions in the following languages:

- ✔ Transact-SQL
- ✔ Languages that create code that runs on the Common Language Runtime (CLR), such as Visual Basic .NET or Visual C#

Creating user-defined functions in your Transact-SQL code offers the following advantages:

- ✔ They let you code in a modular way and reuse your code. Store these functions in the database once and then call them as needed from your Transact-SQL code.
- ✔ Execution speed is improved. User-defined functions are parsed and the execution plan is cached. When called more than once, this saves parsing time and speeds up execution.
- ✔ Functions can reduce network traffic. For example, by using a user-defined function in a WHERE clause, you can significantly reduce the number of rows sent to a client.

A user-defined function consists of the following parts:

- ✔ The Head
- ✔ The Body

The head consists of the following parts:

- ✔ The function name, which might include a schema name
- ✔ The name(s) of input parameter(s) and their data types
- ✔ Any options that apply to the input parameter(s)
- ✔ The data type of the value returned by the function
- ✔ Any options that apply to the return value

The body of a function consists of one of the following parts:

✔ One or more Transact-SQL statements when the function is a Transact-SQL function

✔ A reference to a .NET assembly when the function is a CLR function

The following is a simple form of the syntax of the CREATE FUNCTION statement to return a scalar value. Notice that this form of the syntax doesn't take any parameters:

```
CREATE FUNCTION [schemaName.]<function_name>
RETURNS <return_datatype>
AS
BEGIN
 <Transact-SQL_statements>
 RETURNS <scalar_datatype>
END
```

The following example creates a user-defined function that returns the average price of products in the dbo.Products table in the Northwind database. The following instructions assume that you have the Northwind sample database installed:

1. **Create a new query in SQL Server Management Studio.**

2. **Execute the following command to ensure that you're working with the Northwind database:**

   ```
   USE Northwind
   ```

3. **Create the user-defined function dbo.FindAveragePrice() by executing the following code:**

   ```
   CREATE FUNCTION dbo.FindAveragePrice()
   RETURNS money
   WITH SCHEMABINDING
   AS
   BEGIN
     RETURN (SELECT avg(UnitPrice) FROM dbo.Products)
   END
   ```

4. **Use the function to display the average price for products in the table. Execute the following code. Notice that you use the dbo.FindAveragePrice() function inline in a SELECT statement:**

   ```
   SELECT dbo.FindAveragePrice() AS "Average Price"
   ```

5. **Display products with prices greater than the average price by using the following code:**

   ```
   SELECT ProductName, UnitPrice
   FROM dbo.Products
   WHERE UnitPrice > dbo.FindAveragePrice()
   ORDER BY UnitPrice
   ```

Figure 14-1 shows the results of executing this code.

```
SELECT ProductName, UnitPrice
FROM dbo.Products
WHERE UnitPrice > dbo.FindAveragePrice()
ORDER BY UnitPrice
```

	ProductName	UnitPrice
1	Uncle Bob's Organic Dried Pears	30.00
2	Ikura	31.00
3	Gumbär Gummibärchen	31.23
4	Mascarpone Fabioli	32.00
5	Perth Pasties	32.80
6	Wimmers gute Semmelknödel	33.25
7	Camembert Pierrot	34.00
8	Mozzarella di Giovanni	34.80
9	Gudbrandsdalsost	36.00
10	Gnocchi di nonna Alice	38.00
11	Queso Manchego La Pastora	38.00
12	Alice Mutton	39.00
13	Northwoods Cranberry Sauce	40.00
14	Schoggi Schokolade	43.90
15	Vegie-spread	43.90

Figure 14-1: Displaying products with an average price that is greater than the average for all products.

User-defined functions can take parameters. The following function, dbo.AmountAboveAverage(), uses the result of the dbo. FindAveragePrice() function as part of its definition.

The following code creates the dbo.AmountAboveAverage() function. Notice that the parameter (single in this function) is passed in the parentheses that follow the function name. Notice too, that the dbo. FindAveragePrice() function is used in calculating the value to be returned by the dbo.AmountAboveAverage() function.

```
CREATE FUNCTION dbo.AmountAboveAverage(@Price money)
RETURNS money
AS
BEGIN
  RETURN @Price - dbo.FindAveragePrice()
END
```

You can incorporate the values returned by both functions to display how much the unit price of each product differs from the average.

```
SELECT ProductName, UnitPrice, dbo.FindAveragePrice() AS
        "Average Price",
        dbo.AmountAboveAverage(UnitPrice) AS "Above
        Average"
FROM dbo.Products
WHERE UnitPrice > dbo.FindAveragePrice()
ORDER BY UnitPrice
```

Figure 14-2 displays the list of products, the average price, and the difference from the average of each unit price.

```
SELECT ProductName, UnitPrice, dbo.FindAveragePrice() AS "Average
FROM dbo.Products
WHERE UnitPrice > dbo.FindAveragePrice()
ORDER BY UnitPrice
```

	ProductName	UnitPrice	Average Price	Above Average
1	Uncle Bob's Organic Dried Pears	30.00	28.8663	1.1337
2	Ikura	31.00	28.8663	2.1337
3	Gumbär Gummibärchen	31.23	28.8663	2.3637
4	Mascarpone Fabioli	32.00	28.8663	3.1337
5	Perth Pasties	32.80	28.8663	3.9337
6	Wimmers gute Semmelknödel	33.25	28.8663	4.3837
7	Camembert Pierrot	34.00	28.8663	5.1337
8	Mozzarella di Giovanni	34.80	28.8663	5.9337
9	Gudbrandsdalsost	36.00	28.8663	7.1337
10	Gnocchi di nonna Alice	38.00	28.8663	9.1337
11	Queso Manchego La Pastora	38.00	28.8663	9.1337
12	Alice Mutton	39.00	28.8663	10.1337
13	Northwoods Cranberry Sauce	40.00	28.8663	11.1337
14	Schoggi Schokolade	43.90	28.8663	15.0337
15	Vegie-spread	43.90	28.8663	15.0337

Figure 14-2: Use two functions to display the average price and the difference from the average.

To create a function that returns a table, use this form of the syntax of the CREATE FUNCTION statement:

```
CREATE FUNCTION [schemaName.]<functionname>()
RETURNS TABLE
AS
RETURN  (<statement(s)_to_define_table)
```

The following function retrieves customers for a specified country:

```
CREATE FUNCTION dbo.GetCustomersByCountry(@Country
         nvarchar(15))
RETURNS TABLE
RETURN (
 SELECT CompanyName, ContactName, City, Country
 FROM dbo.Customers
 WHERE Country = @Country
 )
```

Notice that the dbo.GetCustomersByCountry() function takes a parameter, @Country, which is an nvarchar(15). You select the data type of the parameter based on the data type of the Country column in the Customers table. Notice that the @Country parameter is used in the WHERE clause in the SELECT statement that defines the table to be returned.

You can use the table-valued function as you would an ordinary table. For example, you can retrieve data from it by using a SELECT statement:

```
SELECT *
FROM dbo.GetCustomersByCountry('France')
```

Notice that the literal value, France, is supplied as a parameter to the function in the preceding code. Figure 14-3 shows the results of executing the preceding statement.

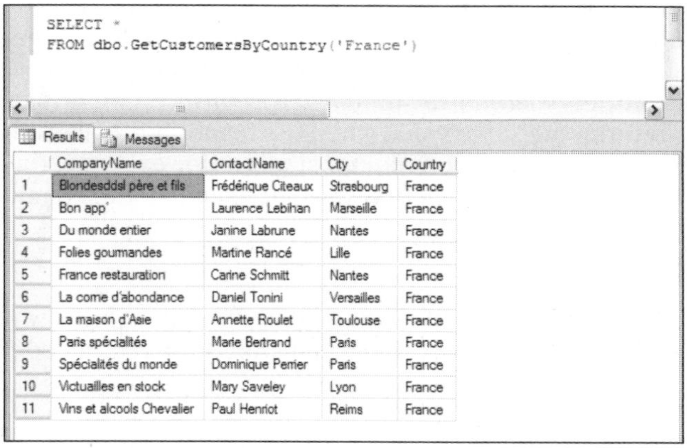

Figure 14-3: Selecting data from a table-valued function with a SELECT statement.

Altering and Dropping Functions

To alter a user-defined function, use the ALTER FUNCTION statement. To delete a user-defined function, use the DROP FUNCTION statement.

Altering a function has the advantages that permissions aren't changed and that any dependent stored procedures, functions, or triggers are unaffected. If you delete a function and create it again, you have to grant any necessary permissions and make any necessary alterations to dependent stored procedures, functions, or triggers. To alter a scalar-valued function, use the ALTER FUNCTION statement as follows.

```
ALTER FUNCTION [<schema_name>.]<function_name>
<parameter_name> [AS] <parameter_datatype>
RETURNS <return_datatype>
BEGIN
 <Transact-SQL statement(s)>
 RETURN <scalar_expression>
END
```

To delete a function, use the DROP FUNCTION statement with the function name:

```
DROP FUNCTION [<schema_name>.]<function_name>
```

Using System Functions

The built-in system functions in SQL Server 2005 provide a great range of functionality that you can use in your Transact-SQL code. However, that functionality, although very useful, is fixed. You cannot modify system functions, for example, by using the ALTER FUNCTION statement. SQL Server system functions are either *deterministic* or *non-deterministic*. A deterministic function always returns the same value when the function is called with the same input values, whatever the other circumstances (for example, the state of the database) at the time of the function call. For example, the command

```
SELECT Sum (1 + 1)
```

uses the Sum() function to add two integers. The command always returns the same result and is, therefore, deterministic. However, the command

```
SELECT GetDate()
```

uses the GetDate() function to return the current date and time and then returns a different time every time you run it (assuming that you don't run it twice in the same millisecond). Clearly, the date and time returned by GetDate() doesn't depend on database state. Therefore, the Sum() function is deterministic, and the GetDate() function is non-deterministic.

SQL Server 2005 provides an extensive range of system functions that you can use in your code. To explore the system functions available to you in any particular database, follow these steps:

1. **Start SQL Server Management Studio and open the Object Explorer if it isn't already visible by choosing View⇨Object Explorer.**

2. **Expand the Databases node and then expand the Northwind node.**

3. **Expand the Programmability, Functions, and System Functions nodes.**

   The appearance is similar to Figure 14-4.

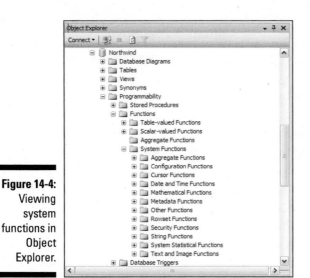

System functions are grouped under the following headings in Object Explorer:

- ✓ Aggregate functions
- ✓ Configuration functions
- ✓ Cursor functions
- ✓ Date and time functions
- ✓ Mathematical functions
- ✓ Metadata functions
- ✓ Other functions
- ✓ Rowset functions
- ✓ Security functions
- ✓ String functions
- ✓ System statistical functions
- ✓ Text and image functions

Aggregate functions perform a calculation of some kind on a set of values and return a single value. The aggregate functions supported in SQL Server 2005 are described in Table 14-1. Assume that *column* is a generic column name or expression, and that *table* is a generic table name.

Table 14-1	Aggregate Functions	
Function	*Description*	*Syntax/Example*
avg()	Returns the average of a groupof values.	SELECT AVG(column) FROM table
binary_ checksum()	Returns the binary check-sum over a row of a table or a list of expressions.	SELECT BINARY_ CHECKSUM(*) FROM table
checksum()	Returns the checksum over a row of a table or a list of expressions.	SELECT CHECKSUM(column) FROM table
checksum_ agg()	Returns the checksum of the values in a group.	SELECT CHECKSUM_ AGG(CAST(column)) FROM table
count()	Returns an int, which is the number of values in a group.	SELECT COUNT(*) FROM table
count_ big()	Returns a bigint, which is the number of values in a group.	SELECT COUNT_BIG(*) FROM table
max()	Returns the maximum value in an expression.	SELECT MAX(column) FROM table
min()	Returns the minimum value in an expression.	SELECT MIN(column) FROM table
stdev()	Returns the standard devi-ation of the values in an expression.	SELECT STDDEV(column) FROM table
sum()	Returns the sum of the values in an expression (optionally, the DISTINCT values).	SELECT SUM(column) FROM table
var()	Returns the variance of the values in an expression.	SELECT VAR(column) FROM table
varp()	Returns the variance for a population of values.	SELECT VARP(column) FROM table

Table 14-2 lists the configuration functions that are supported in SQL Server 2005.

Table 14-2	Configuration Functions	
Function	*Description*	*Syntax/Example*
@@DateFirst	Specifies the currently set first day of the week.	SELECT @@DATEFIRST
@@Dbts	Returns the value of the current timestamp for the database.	SELECT @@DBTS
@@LangId	Returns the language identifier of the language currently in use.	SELECT @@LANGID
@@Language	Returns the name of the language currently in use.	SELECT @@LANGUAGE
@@Lock_ Timeout	Returns the lock timeout, in milliseconds, for the current session.	SELECT @@LOCKTIMEOUT
@@Max_ Connections	Returns the maximum permitted number of user connections.	SELECT @@MAX_ CONNECTIONS
@@Max_ Precision	Returns the precision level of numeric and decimal data types.	SELECT @@MAX_ PRECISION
@@NestLevel	Returns the nesting level of the execution of the current stored procedure.	SELECT @@NESTLEVEL
@@Options	Returns information about currently set options.	SELECT @@OPTIONS
@@RemServer	Returns the name of a remote SQL Server.	SELECT @@REMSERV
@@Servername	Returns the name of the local SQL Server.	SELECT @@SERVERNAME
@@Servicename	Returns the name under which SQL Server is running.	SELECT @@SERVICENAME
@@id	Returns the process identifier of the current user process.	SELECT @@SPID
@@Textsize	Returns the current value of TEXTSIZE.	SELECT @@TEXTSIZE
@@Version	Returns the version, date and processor of SQL Server.	SELECT @@VERSION

SQL Server 2005 supports the cursor functions listed in Table 14-3.

Table 14-3	Cursor Functions	
Function	*Description*	*Syntax/Example*
@@Cursor_Rows	Returns the number of qualifying rows in the most recently opened cursor on a connection.	SELECT @@CURSOR_ROWS
@@Cursor_Status	Returns a scalar value that allows the caller of a stored procedure to determine whether a cursor was returned.	SELECT @@CURSOR_STATUS
@@Fetch_Status	Returns the status of the most recent cursor FETCH statement.	SELECT @@FETCH_STATUS

SQL Server 2005 supports the date and time functions listed in Table 14-4.

Table 14-4	Date and Time Functions	
Function	*Description*	*Syntax/Example*
Dateadd()	Returns a new datetime value after adding an interval to a datetime value. The example adds 5 days to the column in table.	SELECT (day, 5, column) FROM table
Datediff()	Returns the number of date and time boundaries crossed between two dates. The example finds the difference between the two dates, in days.	SELECT (day, date1, date2)
Datename()	Returns a string representing a specified part of a specified datetime value. The example finds the name of the day, for today's date, such as Monday, Tuesday, Wednesday, and so on.	SELECT DATENAME(day, GETDATE())

Function	Description	Syntax/Example
Day()	Returns an integer that represents the day part of a specified datetime value. The example finds the day of the month for today's date.	SELECT DAY (GETDATE())
Getdate()	Returns the current date and time. The example returns today's date.	SELECT GETDATE()
Getutcdate()	Returns the current date and time in Universal Coordinated Time (UTC). The example returns the current date and time, as per Greenwich Mean Time.	SELECT GETUTCDATE()
Month()	Returns the month part of a specified date. The example returns the month number, between 1 and 12, of today's date.	SELECT MONTH (GETDATE())
Year()	Returns the year part of a specified date. Returns just the year for the current date.	SELECT YEAR (GETDATE())

Table 14-5 lists the mathematical functions that are supported in SQL Server 2005.

Table 14-5	Mathematical Functions	
Function	**Description**	**Syntax/Example**
Abs()	Returns the absolute, positive value of an expression. The example returns 1, 0, and 1.	SELECT ABS(-1), ABS(0),ABS(1)
Acos()	Returns an angle, in radians, whose cosine is the given expression. The example returns 1.	SELECT ACOS(0)
Asin()	Returns an angle, in radians, whose sine is the given expression. The example returns 0.	SELECT ASIN(0)

(continued)

Table 14-5 *(continued)*

Function	Description	Syntax/Example
Atan()	Returns an angle, in radians, whose tangent is the given expression. The example returns 0.	SELECT ATAN(0)
Atn2()	Returns an angle, in radians, whose tangent is the quotient of two given expressions. The example returns 0.	SELECT ATN2(0,1)
Ceiling()	Rounds up to the nearest integer regardless of decimal value. The example returns 3.	SELECT CEILING(2.1)
Cos()	Returns the cosine of a specified angle. The example returns 1.	SELECT COS(0)
Cot()	Returns the cotangent of a specified angle. The example returns 0.642.	SELECT COT(1)
Degrees()	Returns an angle expressed in degrees, given an angle specified in radians. The example returns an angle very close to 180 degrees.	SELECT DEGREES (3.142)
Exp()	Returns the exponent value of a given expression. The example returns 1.	SELECT EXP(0)
Floor()	Rounds down to the nearest integer regardless of decimal value. The example returns 2.	SELECT FLOOR(2.9)
Log()	Returns the natural logarithm of a given expression. The example returns the number that the constant is raised to, to get 100.	SELECT LOG(100)
Log10()	Returns the base 10 logarithm of a given expression. The example returns 2, where 10 raised to the power of 2 equals 100.	SELECT LOG10(100)

Function	Description	Syntax/Example
Pi()	Returns the constant pi. The example returns the value of pi, which is approximately 3.142.	SELECT PI()
Power()	Returns the value of a given expression to a specified power. The example returns of 8 (2 raised to the power of 3).	SELECT POWER(2,3)
Radians()	Returns a value, in radians, for an angle expressed in degrees. The example returns 1 radian.	SELECT RADIANS(90)
Rand()	Returns a random value between 0 and 1.	SELECT RAND()
Round()	Returns a value that represents an expression rounded to a specified precision. The example returns 2.46.	SELECT ROUND (2.455,2)
Sign()	Returns the sign of an expression. The example returns −1, 0, and 1.	SELECT SIGN(-5), SIGN(0),SIGN(5)
Sin()	Returns the sine of an angle. The example returns 0.	SELECT SIN(0)
Sqrt()	Returns the square root of an expression. The example returns 1.	SELECT COS(0)
Square()	Returns the square of a given expression. The example returns 16 (4 raised to the power of 2).	SELECT SQUARE(4)
Tan()	Returns the tangent of an angle. The example returns 0.	SELECT TAN(0)

The metadata functions listed in Table 14-6 are supported in SQL Server 2005.

Table 14-6	Metadata Functions	
Function	*Description*	*Syntax/Example*
`Col_Length()`	Returns the length of a column in bytes.	`SELECT COL_LENGTH (table,column)`
`Col_Name()`	Returns the name of a column.	`SELECT COL_NAME (table_id,column_ id)`
`ColumnProperty()`	Returns a property value for a column or procedure parameter.	`SELECT COLUMNPROPERTY (ID,column,property)`
`DatabaseProperty()`	Returns the value of a database property.	`SELECT DATABASEPROPERTY (database,property)`
`Db_Id()`	Returns the identification number of a database.	`SELECT DB_ID (database)`
`Db_Name()`	Returns the name of a database.	`SELECT DB_NAME (database_id)`
`File_Id()`	Returns the file identification number for a given logical file name in the current database.	`SELECT FILE_ID (file)`
`File_Name()`	Returns the filename for a given file identification number in the current database.	`SELECT FILE_NAME (file_id)`
`Filegroup_Id()`	Returns the filegroup identification number for a given filegroup name.	`SELECT FILEGROUP_ID (filegroup)`
`Filegroup_Name()`	Returns a filegroup name for a given filegroup identification number.	`SELECT FILEGROUP_ NAME(filegroup_id)`
`Filegroup property()`	Returns the value of a specified filegroup property.	`SELECT FILEGROUPPROPERTY (filegroup,property)`

Function	*Description*	*Syntax/Example*
`Fileproperty()`	Returns the value of a specified file property.	`SELECT FILEPROPERTY (file,property)`
`Fulltextcatalog property()`	Returns the value of a specified full text catalog property.	`SELECT FULLTEXT CATALOGPROPERTY (catalog,property)`
`Fulltextservice property()`	Returns information about full-text service properties.	`SELECT FULLTEXT SERVICEPROPERTY (property)`
`Index_Col()`	Returns an indexed column name.	`SELECT INDEX_COL (database.schema. table, index, key)`
`Indexkey_ Property()`	Returns a property value given a table identification number, key identification number, and index identification number.	`SELECT INDEXKEY_ PROPERTY(object, index_id, key_id, property)`
`Indexproperty()`	Returns a property value, given a table and index.	`SELECT (object_id, index, property)`
`Object_Id()`	Returns the identification number of an object.	`SELECT (database. schema,object, object_type)`
`Object_Name()`	Returns the name of an object, given the object identification number.	`SELECT OBJECT_NAME (object_id)`
`Objectproperty()`	Returns the value of a specified object property.	`SELECT OBJECT PROPERTY(id, property)`
`Objectproperty ex()`	Returns information about properties of a schema-scoped object.	`SELECT OBJECT PROPERTYEX(id, property)`

(continued)

Table 14-6 *(continued)*

Function	Description	Syntax/Example
`@@Procid()`	Returns the stored procedure identification number of the current stored procedure.	`SELECT @@PROCID`
`Sql_Variant_ Property()`	Returns the values of the properties of a `Sql_variant` value.	`SELECT SQL_VARIANT_ PROPERTY ( expression , property )`
`Typeproperty()`	Returns the value of a property of a data type.	`SELECT TYPEPROPERTY (type , property)`

The "other" functions (Object Explorer terminology) in Table 14-7 are supported in SQL Server 2005.

Table 14-7   **"Other" Functions**

Function	Description	Syntax/Example
`App_Name()`	Returns the application name of the current session.	`SELECT APP_NAME()`
`Cast()`	Explicitly converts an expression from one data type to another.	`SELECT (expression AS datatype)`
`Coalesce()`	Returns the first not `NULL` expression in its arguments.	`SELECT COALESCE (expression, [, ... ])`
`Collation Property()`	Returns the value of a specified property of a collation.	`SELECT COLLATION PROPERTY(collation, property)`
`Columns_ Update()`	Returns a varbinary bit pattern, which indicates which columns of a table or view were inserted or updated.	`SELECT COLUMNS_ UPDATED()`
`Convert()`	Explicitly converts an expression from one data type to another.	`SELECT CONVERT (datatype, expression)`

Function	Description	Syntax/Example
Current_ Timestamp	Returns the current date and time. This is an ANSI equivalent to the GetDate() function.	SELECT CURRENT_ TIMESTAMP
Current_User	Returns the name of the current user.	SELECT CURRENT_ USER
Datalength()	Returns the number of bytes used to represent an expression.	SELECT DATALENGTH (expression)
@@Error	Returns the error number for the last Transact-SQL statement that was executed.	SELECT @@ERROR
fn_Help collations()	Returns a list of supported collations.	SELECT * FROM FN_ HELPCOLLATIONS()
::fn_Server shared drives()	Returns the names of shared drives used by a clustered server.	SELECT * FROM FN_ SERVERSHARED DRIVES()
::fn_Virtual server nodes()	Returns a list of nodes on which a virtual server can run.	SELECT * FROM FN_ VIRTUALSERVER NODES()
Format message()	Returns a formatted message from an existing message in sys.messages.	SELECT FORMAT MESSAGE(message#, parameters_list)
Getansinull()	Returns the default nullability of the database.	SELECT GETANSINULL (database)
Host_id()	Returns the identification number of a computer.	SELECT HOST_ID()
Host_name()	Returns the name of a computer.	SELECT HOST_NAME()
Ident_ Current()	Returns the last identity value generated for a table.	SELECT IDENT_ CURRENT(table)
Ident_Incr()	Returns the increment values specified for a column.	SELECT IDENT_ INCR(table)
Ident_Seed()	Returns the seed value used during creation of an identity column.	SELECT IDENT_ SEED(table)

(continued)

Table 14-7 *(continued)*

Function	Description	Syntax/Example
@@Identity	Returns the last inserted identity value.	SELECT @@IDENTITY
Isdate()	Finds out if an input expression is a valid date.	SELECT ISDATE (expression)
Isnull()	Replaces NULL with a specified value.	SELECT ISNULL (expression)
Isnumeric()	Finds out if an input expression is a valid numeric type.	SELECT ISNUMBERIC (expression)
Newid()	Creates a new value of type unique identifier.	SELECT NEWID()
Nullif()	Returns a NULL value if the two specified expressions are equivalent.	SELECT NULLIF (expression1, expression2)
Parsename()	Returns a specified part of an object name.	SELECT PARSENAME (object_name, object_piece)
Permissions()	Returns a bitmap, representing the permissions of the current user.	SELECT PERMISSIONS (object_id, column)
@@Rowcount()	Returns the number of rows affected by the preceding statement.	SELECT @@ROWCOUNT
Rowcount_ big()	Returns a bigint value, representing the number of rows affected by the preceding statement.	SELECT ROWCOUNT_ BIG()
Scope_ Identity()	Returns the last IDENTITY value inserted into an IDENTITY column in the same scope.	SELECT SCOPE_ IDENTITY()
Server property()	Returns the values of properties of a SQL Server instance.	SELECT SERVER PROPERTY(property)
Session property()	Returns the options for a session.	SELECT SESSION PROPERTY(option)

Function	Description	Syntax/Example
`Session_User`	Returns the name of the user in the current session.	`SELECT SESSION_ USER`
`Stats_Date()`	Returns the date when statistics for an index were last updated.	`SELECT STATS_DATE (table_id, index_id)`
`System_User`	Returns the name of the current login in the session.	`SELECT SYSTEM_USER`
`@@Trancount`	Returns the number of active transactions for a connection.	`SELECT @@TRANCOUNT`
`Update()`	Returns a `boolean` value that indicates whether an `INSERT` or `UPDATE` was made on a specified column.	`SELECT UPDATE (column)`
`User_Name()`	Returns a username for a specified identification number.	`SELECT USER_NAME(id)`

Table 14-8 lists the rowset functions that are supported in SQL Server 2005.

Table 14-8	Rowset Functions	
Function	**Description**	**Syntax/Example**
`Contains table()`	Returns a table of zero or more rows, which contain character-based data types that satisfy specified matching criteria.	`SELECT CONTAINSTABLE (table, column_list)`
`Freetexttable()`	Returns a table of zero or more rows, which contain character-based data types that satisfy specified meanings.	`SELECT FREETEXTTABLE (table, column_list)`
`Opendata source()`	Returns connection information.	`SELECT OPENDATA SOURCE(provider, init_string)`
`Openquery()`	Executes a specified query on a linked server.	`SELECT OPENQUERY (linked_server, query)`

(continued)

Table 14-8 *(continued)*

Function	Description	Syntax/Example
Openrowset()	Contains connection information sufficient to connect to remote data via an OLE DB source.	SELECT * FROM OPENROWSET (parameters ...)
Openxml()	Provides a rowset view of an XML document.	SELECT * FROM OPENXML (parameters ...)

Table 14-9 describes the security functions that are supported in SQL Server 2005.

Table 14-9   **Security Functions**

Function	Description	Syntax/Example
fn_Trace_Get eventinfo	Returns a table containing data about traced events.	SELECT FN_TRACE_ GETEVENTINFO (trace_id)
fn_Trace_Get filterinfo	Returns a table of the filters used in a specified trace.	SELECT FN_TRACE_ GETFILTERINFO (trace_id)
fn_Trace_Get info() -	Returns the values of properties of a specified trace or traces.	SELECT FN_TRACE_ GETINFO(trace_id)
fn_Trace_Get table()	Returns a table containing trace file information.	SELECT FN_TRACE_ GETTABLE(file, number of files)
Has_Dbaccess()	Returns a value indicating whether the current user has access to a specified database.	SELECT HAS_DBACCESS (database)
Is_Member()	Indicates whether the current user is a member of a SQL Server role or a specified Windows group.	SELECT IS_MEMBER (group, role)
Is_Srvrole member()	Indicates whether a login is a member of a specified server role.	SELECT IS_SERVROLE MEMBER(role, login)

Function	Description	Syntax/Example
Suser_Sid()	Returns the security identification number for a specified login.	SELECT SUSER_SID (login)
Suser_Sname()	Returns the login name for a specified security identification number.	SELECT SUSER_SNAME (server_user_sid)
User()	Returns a user's data-basename.	SELECT USER
User_Id()	Returns a user's identification number.	SELECT USER_ID(user)
User_Name()	Returns a user's username.	SELECT USER(id)

Table 14-10 lists which string functions are supported in SQL Server 2005.

Table 14-10	**String Functions**	
Function	*Description*	*Syntax/Example*
Ascii()	Returns the ASCII code for the leftmost character in an expression.	SELECT ASCII (expression)
Char()	Converts an integer ASCII code to a character.	SELECT ASCII (integer)
Charindex()	Returns the starting position of an expression in a string.	SELECT CHARINDEX (expression1, expression2 [,start])
Difference()	Returns the difference in Soundex values of two expressions as an integer.	SELECT DIFFERENCE (expression, expression)
Left()	Returns the leftmost specified number of characters from an expression.	SELECT LEFT (expression, integer)
Len()	Returns the number of characters in a string.	SELECT LEN (expression)

(continued)

Table 14-10 *(continued)*

Function	Description	Syntax/Example
Lower()	Returns a string expression with characters converted to lowercase.	SELECT LOWER (expression)
Ltrim()	Returns a string with leading spaces trimmed.	SELECT LTRIM (expression)
Nchar()	Returns the Unicode character for a specified integer.	SELECT NCHAR (integer)
Patindex()	Returns the start position of the first occurrence of a pattern in a specified expression.	SELECT PATINDEX (pattern, expression)
Quotename()	Returns a Unicode string with delimiters added in order to make a legal SQL Server delimited identifier.	SELECT QUOTENAME (string, quote)
Replace()	Returns a string with all occurrences of a specified sequence of characters replaced by the replacement sequence of characters.	SELECT REPLACE (expression1, expression2, expression3)
Replicate()	Returns a character expression repeated a specified number of times.	SELECT REPLICATE (expression, integer)
Reverse()	Returns a string with the character order reversed.	SELECT REVERSE (expression)
Right()	Returns the rightmost specified number of characters from a string expression.	SELECT RIGHT (expression, integer)
Rtrim()	Returns a character expression with any trailing spaces removed.	SELECT RTRIM (expression)
Soundex()	Returns a 4-character Soundex code for a specified string.	SELECT SOUNDEX (expression)

Function	Description	Syntax/Example
Space()	Returns a string of a specified number of space characters.	SELECT SPACE (integer)
Str()	Converts a numeric expression to a string expression.	SELECT STR (expression, length)
Stuff()	Returns a string in which a specified number of characters is replaced by another set of characters at a specified starting point.	SELECT STUFF (expression1, start, length, expression2)
Substring()	Returns part of a string.	SELECT SUBSTRING (expression, start, length)
Unicode()	Returns an integer, representing the Unicode value of the first character of a string.	SELECT UNICODE (expression)
Upper()	Returns a string expression with characters converted to uppercase.	SELECT UPPER (expression)

SQL Server 2005 supports the system statistical functions in Table 14-11.

Table 14-11	System Statistical Functions	
Function	**Description**	**Syntax/Example**
@@Connections	Returns the number of attempted connections since SQL Server was most recently started.	SELECT @@CONNECTIONS
@@Cpu_Busy	Returns the number of milliseconds of CPU usage since SQL Server was most recently started.	SELECT @@CPU_BUSY

(continued)

Table 14-11 *(continued)*

Function	Description	Syntax/Example
`::fn_Virtual filestats()`	Returns I/O (input/output) statistics for data and log files.	`SELECT FN_VIRTUAL FILESTATS(database_ id, file_id)`
`@@Idle`	Returns the number of milliseconds that SQL Server has been idle since SQL Server was most recently started.	`SELECT @@IDLE`
`@@Io_Busy`	Returns the number of milliseconds that SQL Server has spent carrying out I/O operations since it was most recently started.	`SELECT @@IO_BUSY`
`@@Pack_ Received`	Returns the number of network packet errors since SQL Server was most recently started.	`SELECT @@PACK_ RECEIVED`
`@@Pack_Sent`	Returns the number of packets sent to the network since SQL Server was most recently started.	`SELECT @@PACK_SENT`
`@@Packet_ Errors`	Returns the number of packet errors since SQL Server was most recently started.	`SELECT @@PACKET_ ERRORS`
`@@Timeticks`	Returns the number of microseconds per time tick.	`SELECT @@TIMETICKS`
`@@Total_Errors`	Returns the number of disk read/write errors since SQL Server was most recently started.	`SELECT @@TOTAL_ ERRORS`
`@@Total_Read`	Returns the number of disk reads since SQL Server was most recently started.	`SELECT @@TOTAL_READ`
`@@Total_Write`	Returns the number of disk writes since SQL Server was most recently started.	`SELECT @@TOTAL_WRITE`

SQL Server 2005 supports the text and image functions described in Table 14-12.

Table 14-12	Text and Image Functions	
Function	*Description*	*Syntax/Example*
Patindex()	Returns the starting position of a specified pattern in a given expression.	SELECT PATINDEX (pattern, expression)
Textptr()	Returns the text-pointer value that corresponds to a text, ntext, or image column.	SELECT TEXTPTR (column)
Textvalid()	Tests whether a text pointer is valid.	SELECT TEXTVAL (table.column, text_ptr)

You use the system functions in your T-SQL code where it makes sense. Often that will be in a SELECT statement. For example, in the pubs database the dbo.sales table has a qty column. Suppose you want to find the average quantity of books and the total quantity of books. You can use the avg() and sum() functions, using the column name as the argument for the function. The following code displays the average number of each book in an order and the total number of books ordered.

```
USE PUBS

SELECT avg(qty) "Average Sales"
FROM dbo.sales

SELECT sum(qty) "Total Sales"
FROM dbo.sales
```

Figure 14-5 shows the results of the queries. Notice that I have supplied a meaningful name for the results from each function.

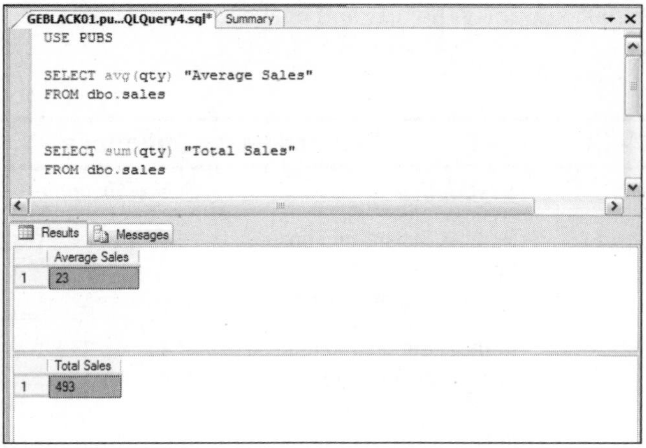

Figure 14-5: Using the avg() and sum() functions.

Chapter 15

Creating Indexes

*I*n this chapter, I introduce you to SQL Server indexes. An index in a database is just like an index in a book. A database index contains a sorted list of relevant items in a table, is much smaller, and is much easier to find something of relevance in, compared to scanning an entire table of rows. Indexes can help you achieve better performance from queries you execute against a database. However, creating a good combination of indexes for a particular table or tables isn't always straightforward. Creating the most useful indexes requires that you give significant thought to the indexes you create — and spend a good deal of time testing them.

SQL Server 2005 supports several types of index. I introduce these to you and discuss the clustered and nonclustered types of index in more detail.

I show you how to create an index using the CREATE INDEX statement. However, I emphasize that you need to think carefully about what indexes are appropriate for your database and how the database is used. In addition, you need to monitor how indexes are used in queries.

Getting a Handle on Why You Might Need Indexes

One of the most important characteristics you should aim for in a SQL Server application is that it runs quickly. Users, not surprisingly, dislike slow performance from an application. So, developers of database applications pay a lot of attention to trying to improve performance. You need to carefully consider the need for indexes for your database and how it is used.

A well-designed index reduces disk I/O operations. I/O operations are particularly costly in terms of time and have a particularly deleterious effect on performance. The more you can reduce disk access, the more likely it is that your database application will perform well. Then again, the more indexes you build on a table, the slower DML activity can become. Why? Every update to a row in a table must also update all indexes as well.

When introducing indexes, I find it helpful to compare SQL Server indexes with indexes in books. There are, obviously, differences in detail, but the analogy still works for a complex topic.

Think about how indexes are used — or not used — for books and other printed material, and you begin to see some of the issues that arise when you consider whether to create indexes for a SQL Server table or tables. In the following paragraphs, I walk you through a couple of scenarios that help shed some light on how SQL Server looks for data in a table or view.

Consider two printed publications, one 8-pages long and the other 1,000-pages long. If you were asked to find specific data in either publication, would you prefer to reference an index or quickly look over each page until you find the data? Assuming that each page contains topic headings, it might be simplest and possibly quickest to just scan the 8-page publication from beginning to end rather than go to the trouble of requesting that the author create an index. But if you're looking for specific data in the thousand-page book, you're going to want to look at an index rather than take the time to look at each page.

The SQL Server equivalent of scanning the document from beginning to end is the *table scan*. Essentially, SQL Server looks at every row in a table, one after the other, to find the data needed in, for example, a SELECT query. In retrieving data from a small table, a table scan might be the most effective and speedy way to retrieve the data. On the other hand, for the 1,000-page book, scanning headings on each page quickly becomes tedious and time-consuming. If you're going to need to find specific information from the book, a well-constructed index is clearly a good idea. The index contains a pointer (or pointers) to the location(s) where the desired information is stored. A SQL Server *nonclustered index* works in a similar way, containing a pointer to each desired piece of data. Once the pointer to desired data has been located, SQL Server knows where to retrieve the actual data from.

Consider the scenario of two publications, each 500-pages long. In one, the topics are ordered randomly. In the other, topics are arranged alphabetically. Suppose you want to find all topics that begin with C. This is like the following T-SQL query:

```
SELECT *
FROM Dictionary
WHERE Topic LIKE 'C%'
```

In the first book, topics are organized randomly, so without an index, the only way to find all the topics that begin with C is to look at every page of the book, which is obviously slow and time-consuming. By analogy, a table scan is also time-consuming in this scenario. In the longer book, however, when you find any topic beginning with C, you can look backwards or forwards to find other topics that begin with C. A clustered index resembles a dictionary. The data is ordered in the book. Likewise, in a clustered index, the data is ordered. A clustered index also resembles the dictionary in that once you find the desired topic, you also have found the data. Contrast that with the nonclustered index, where you find only a pointer to the data and then have to retrieve the desired data.

Both clustered and nonclustered indexes use an approach that makes use of B-trees, binary tree indexes. A binary tree index looks a little like an upside tree, with a single root node, connected to branches (intermediate), which in turn are connected to other branches or leaves. Each page in an index B-tree is called an *index node*. The three types of index nodes are

  ✔ **Root node:** The root node is the entry point for the tree.

  ✔ **Intermediate node:** Nodes between the root node and the leaf nodes.

  ✔ **Leaf node:** This is the node that either contains the desired data (in a clustered index) or has a pointer to the desired data (nonclustered index).

In a clustered index, the root node and intermediate nodes contain *index rows*. Each index row contains a key value and a pointer to an intermediate node or to a *data row* in a leaf node of the index.

You can store the data rows in a clustered index in only one order, as determined by the key columns. As a result, a table can have only a single clustered index because, for any given key columns, data rows can be ordered in only one way.

When you create a PRIMARY KEY constraint on a column, you, by default, create a clustered index on the column or columns that define the primary key.

When you create a PRIMARY KEY constraint or a UNIQUE constraint on a column, there is, by definition, a unique value or combination of values for each row. If a table has no PRIMARY KEY or UNIQUE constraint, SQL Server adds a 4-byte, unique identifier to each data row to ensure that each row can be distinguished from all other data rows in the table. That value is stored in a uniqueifier column for internal use only.

If no index exists on a table and you want to retrieve a row (or multiple rows) of data from that table, SQL Server is likely to carry out a *table scan* to find the data.

A table scan can be the most efficient approach when

- ✔ The number of rows in a table is small.
- ✔ A large percentage of the rows in a table are retrieved to satisfy a query.

On larger tables, a table scan is likely to be slower than using an index. However, if the table is frequently updated, having the table unindexed improves the performance of INSERT and UPDATE operations compared to an indexed table.

Considering the Types of Indexes

In this section, I introduce you to the different types of index that SQL Server 2005 supports. Later in this section, I examine a fuller list of the index types.

SQL Server 2005 supports the following types of index:

- ✔ **Clustered:** Creates an index from all columns in a table.
- ✔ **Nonclustered:** Indexes one or more specified columns in a table.
- ✔ **Unique:** Enforces uniqueness for an index.

✔ **Indexed views:** Views can be indexed, as well as tables.

✔ **Full-text index:** Used to create textual searching indexes into large text documents.

✔ **XML index:** Indexes the XML data type.

As well as deciding what type of index is appropriate for you to create, you also need to consider *whether* an index is appropriate for the tables that you want to query. There is an unavoidable trade-off between the potential for improved query performance when you create a well-designed index and the cost in terms of more time-consuming updates: Not only the table, but the index (or indexes) needs to be updated as well.

If the database is an online transaction processing (OLTP) database with frequent inserts and updates, the impact of creating multiple indexes on insert and update performance can be significant. On the other hand, if you're querying a data warehouse or decision support system where the data is effectively read-only — or almost read-only — the issue of increased time for inserts and updates is much less important.

Clustered indexes are particularly appropriate for these situations:

✔ The query includes a WHERE clause with operators such as BETWEEN, >, >=, <, and <=.

✔ The query returns large result sets.

✔ The query uses JOIN clauses.

✔ The query accesses values in a column sequentially. For example, a query on OrderIDs between 920 and 940 or OrderDates between 2006/01/01 and 2006/01/31.

✔ The query uses an ORDER BY clause or a GROUP BY clause. The index might remove the need to sort the data because the data is already ordered.

Clustered indexes should use as few columns as possible. Ideally, you should create a clustered index on columns that have the following characteristics:

✔ Contain unique values or, failing that, contain mostly distinct values.

✔ Are defined as IDENTITY. Each value in the column is known to be unique.

✔ Are often used to sort data returned by a query. Having data in a clustered index that is already sorted in a desired order can save the cost of sorts during the query.

Clustered indexes aren't well-suited for the following situations:

- ✔ There is a wide key for each data row.
- ✔ Values in the key columns undergo frequent changes. Because data in a clustered index is sorted on key column values, a change in those values means that data rows have to be moved into their correctly sorted positions after any changes.

You can create multiple, nonclustered indexes on a table or indexed view. A nonclustered index is similar to an index in a book. The index contains a pointer to the data but doesn't contain the data itself. Use nonclustered indexes to support frequently executed queries not supported by the clustered index on the table.

Multiple, nonclustered indexes are useful on tables that are infrequently updated but that contain large volumes of data. When tables are frequently updated, be careful to keep indexes to a minimum and keep the columns as narrow as practicable.

Creating an Index

You create an index using the CREATE INDEX statement. However, before creating an index, you need to think carefully about these issues:

- ✔ The characteristics of your database and its tables
- ✔ The types of query that are executed against the database
- ✔ The data columns that are accessed in queries

Indexes on small tables might reduce rather than improve performance. Traversing an index might take more time than doing a simple table scan if the table is small. If you need to execute inserts or updates on the table, you might get the worst of both worlds with potentially slower queries and inserts, which are slower due to the need to update the index or indexes when an insert or update is executed. In general, however, queries on small tables are not likely to be particularly time-consuming.

If you create a clustered index on a very large table, consider using the ONLINE option in the CREATE INDEX statement if you're using the Enterprise Edition of SQL Server 2005. The ONLINE option allows users to access data in the table during the time that the index is being created. So, if you have a table that is accessed online or is used by branch offices around the world, it might need to be in use almost continuously. In that kind of situation where you cannot afford for the table to be unavailable, the ONLINE option is likely the way to go.

You cannot create an index on columns of the following data types as key columns:

- ✔ ntext
- ✔ text
- ✔ image
- ✔ varchar(max)
- ✔ nvarchar(max)
- ✔ varbinary(max)

You can use an xml data type as a key only in an XML index. I discuss XML programming in Chapter 20.

The CREATE INDEX statement looks like the following:

```
CREATE [ UNIQUE ] [ CLUSTERED | NONCLUSTERED ] INDEX
        <index_name>
    ON <table_or_view> ( <column_list> )
    [ INCLUDE ( <column_list>) ]
    [ WITH ( <relational_index_options> ) ]
    [ ON { partition_scheme_name ( column_name ) |
          filegroup_name
          | default
```

The CREATE INDEX statement supports several options, as described in Table 15-1.

Table 15-1	Options Supported by CREATE INDEX
Option	_Description_
PAD_INDEX	Sets the percentage of free space in intermediate-level pages during index creation.
FILLFACTOR	Sets the percentage of free space in leaf-level pages during index creation.
SORT_IN_TEMPDB	Specifies whether intermediate search results generated during index creation are stored in the tempdb database.

(continued)

Table 15-1 (continued)

Option	Description
IGNORE_DUP_KEY	Specifies the error response to duplicate key values in a multiple-row INSERT transaction on a unique clustered or a unique nonclustered index.
STATISTICS_NORECOMPUTE	Specifies whether out-of-date index statistics should be automatically recomputed.
DROP_EXISTING	Specifies that an existing index should be deleted and recreated.
ONLINE	Specifies whether users can access data while the index is being created. The ONLINE option is available only in SQL Server 2005 Enterprise Edition.
ALLOW_ROW_LOCKS	Specifies whether row locks are used when accessing data.
ALLOW_PAGE_LOCKS	Specifies whether page locks are used when accessing data.
MAXDOP	Specifies the maximum number of CPUs that can be used in the indexing operation. Use of multiple CPUs is available only in SQL Server 2005 Enterprise Edition.

The maximum number of bytes in key columns in an index is 900. Columns with Unicode characters, such as an nvarchar column, use two bytes per character. There are a couple of ways that you can find out the number of bytes in each column you use in a key. Suppose you want to find out the number of bytes used by each column in the dbo.Employees table in the Northwind database. You can expand the nodes in Object Explorer so that you can see the data types in each column in the dbo.Employees table. Remember that Unicode data uses two bytes per character when you calculate the total number of bytes used by your key columns. Alternatively, run the following code in the query pane in SQL Server Management Studio, when Northwind is the current database.

```
SELECT name, max_length
FROM sys.columns
WHERE Object_ID = OBJECT_ID('dbo.Employees')
```

Figure 15-1 shows the appearance after executing the preceding code. Notice that the column data types in Object Explorer are shown in the left part of the figure.

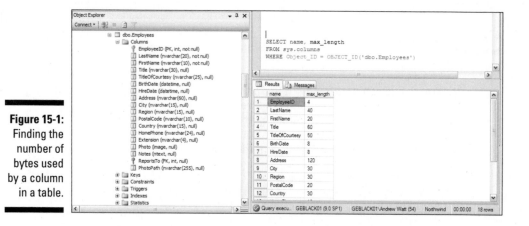

Figure 15-1:
Finding the number of bytes used by a column in a table.

The code displays the name and number of bytes used by each column in the Employees table. The OBJECT_ID() system function takes the name of a table or view as its argument and returns its object_id. The sys.columns catalog view contains information about columns in the database. The WHERE clause filters the results so that only information about columns in the desired table is returned.

You can have SQL Server calculate the number of bytes for you using the following approach. The following example finds the number of bytes used when the LastName and FirstName columns in the dbo.Employees table in the Northwind database are being considered for use in key columns in an index.

```
USE Northwind
GO
SELECT SUM(Max_Length) As TotalIndexKeySize
FROM sys.columns
WHERE name IN (N'LastName', N'FirstName')
```

Figure 15-2 shows the result of running the preceding statement. Notice that a number of bytes used is displayed.

```
USE Northwind
GO
SELECT SUM(Max_Length) As TotalIndexKeySize
FROM sys.columns
WHERE name IN (N'LastName', N'FirstName')
```

	TotalIndexKeySize
1	60

You can create indexes with included columns. An *included column* is a column that is part of a nonclustered index and is not a key column. An included column is created using the INCLUDE keyword in the CREATE INDEX statement. The CREATE INDEX statement to create an index that has an included column has this general form:

```
CREATE INDEX <index_name>
ON <table_name> (<column_list>)
INCLUDE (<included_column_name>)
```

When you consider creating an index with one or more included columns, the following considerations apply:

✔ You can define an included column on a nonclustered index for a table or for an indexed view. You cannot define an included column in a clustered index.

✔ The text, ntext, and image data types are not allowed. An included column can be of any other SQL Server 2005 data type.

✔ If a computed column is deterministic, it can be an included column.

✔ A column cannot be both a key column and an included column.

Altering an Index

To alter an index, use the ALTER INDEX statement. To execute the ALTER INDEX statement, you must have at least ALTER permissions on the table or view whose index is to be altered.

```
ALTER INDEX { <index_name> | ALL }
    ON <table_name>
    REBUILD
    [ WITH ( <rebuild_index_options> ) ]
```

Rebuilding an index deletes and recreates the index. This can be beneficial by removing fragmentation and reordering index rows so that they're in contiguous pages. You can expect improved performance compared to the preceding fragmented index state.

To rebuild the `PK_Employees` index on the `dbo.Employees` table in the `Northwind` database, use these commands:

```
USE Northwind
GO
ALTER INDEX PK_Employees
ON dbo.Employees
REBUILD
```

To rebuild all indexes on the `dbo.Employees` table in the `Northwind` database, use these commands:

```
USE Northwind
GO
ALTER INDEX ALL
ON dbo.Employees
REBUILD
```

You can use the `ALTER INDEX` statement to disable an index. When used with that intention, the `ALTER INDEX` statement takes the following form:

```
ALTER INDEX <index_name> ON <table_name>
DISABLE
```

You can use the `ALTER INDEX` statement to disable a `PRIMARY KEY` constraint. When used to do that, the `ALTER INDEX` statement takes the following form:

```
ALTER INDEX <PK_index_name> ON <table_name>
DISABLE
```

When you use the `ALTER INDEX` statement to disable a `PRIMARY KEY` constraint, you see an error message like the following:

```
Warning: Foreign key <foreign_key_name> on table
         <table_name> referencing table
         <other_table_name> was disabled as a result of
         disabling the index <PK_index_name>.
```

Dropping an Index

If you invest time and effort to find an optimal combination of indexes for a table, it's likely that you will, during that exploration, create indexes that aren't very useful. However, even if those indexes aren't used in queries, they still add a cost for each INSERT or UPDATE operation on the table on which you created the index. So, make a point of looking at each of the indexes you create and ask yourself if all the indexes are necessary. Sometimes, perhaps often, you'll find at least one index that you can usefully delete.

To delete an index, use the DROP INDEX statement. To drop an index, you often use the DROP INDEX statement as follows:

```
USE <database_name>
GO
DROP INDEX <index_name>
ON <table_name>
```

You can drop multiple indexes in a single statement. For example, to drop two indexes on different tables, you can use a statement of the following form:

```
DROP INDEX
  <index1_name> ON <table1_name>,
  <index2_name> ON <table2_name>
```

Chapter 16

Handling Errors Using TRY . . . CATCH

*I*nevitably, if you work extensively with SQL Server, you'll need to be able to handle errors. Errors can arise from several sources. If you write enough Transact-SQL code, you make mistakes. And, if you work with Transact-SQL code written by other developers, you find that they make mistakes, too. In addition, users do things that you don't anticipate that cause your code not to work, or not to work in the way you expect. Any of these possibilities can occur and mean that errors can adversely affect the user experience if you don't take steps to handle such errors effectively.

In this chapter, I review error-handling techniques available to you in SQL Server 2000. I do that because you're likely to find code written for SQL Server 2000 that you might have to review or adapt. These techniques are based on the @@ERROR function.

In addition, I introduce you to the TRY...CATCH construct, which is new in SQL Server 2005. The TRY...CATCH construct allows you to process certain types of errors in ways similar to those available in other programming languages. In addition, within the context of a TRY...CATCH construct, you can use several new system functions that return information about errors.

Error Handling in Transact-SQL

Error severity in SQL Server is ranked on a scale from 0 to 24. You can write code to handle errors in the range 10 through 16. Errors of severity 17 or above can't be handled by the developer. Errors of severity 20 or above are fatal errors. The following list briefly describes each error severity and some likely causes of errors:

- **0–9:** When the severity is in this range, SQL Server produces information messages or indicates that a minor error has occurred.

- **10:** SQL Server displays informational messages containing status information or reporting errors that aren't severe.

- **11:** Indicates that an object or entity doesn't exist.

- **12:** Relates to errors occurring during queries that rely on query hints and that don't apply locking.

- **13:** Indicates transaction deadlock errors.

- **14:** Indicates security-related errors.

- **15:** Indicates Transact-SQL syntax errors.

- **16:** Indicates other errors that the developer can correct.

- **17:** Indicates that SQL Server ran out of resources or exceeded some limit set by an administrator.

- **18:** Indicates a problem in the database engine, but execution of the Transact-SQL statement completes, and the connection to the database is maintained.

- **19:** Indicates that a nonconfigurable limit in the database engine has been exceeded, and the current batch has been terminated.

- **20:** Indicates that a Transact-SQL statement has encountered a problem. It's unlikely that the underlying database has been damaged.

- **21:** Indicates that all current tasks have been affected. However, it's unlikely that the database has been damaged.

- **22:** Indicates that a table or index specified in the relevant error message has been damaged.

- **23:** Indicates that the integrity of the entire database is in question.

- **24:** Indicates a media failure.

Errors of severity 22 through 24 are uncommon. However, they can occur. When a table or database has been damaged, your backup and restore strategy is tested.

Using the @@ERROR Function

The @@ERROR system function is the system function that you would have used in SQL Server 2000 to capture information about an error. The value returned by the @@ERROR function changes after the execution of each Transact-SQL statement. If the Transact-SQL statement executes without error, the value returned by @@ERROR is 0. If an error occurs during execution of the Transact-SQL statement, @@ERROR contains the relevant error number.

The fact that the value returned by @@ERROR changes after each Transact-SQL statement means that you need to add a lot of error-handling code to your Transact-SQL scripts if you want your code to respond to the occurrence of an error throughout the code.

Look at how you can use @@ERROR. Suppose you divide 1 by 0. You get an error. But that error number is accessible only from @@ERROR on the next line of Transact-SQL code, as you can see by running the following code:

```
SELECT 1/0
PRINT 'The value of @@ERROR is ' + CAST(@@ERROR AS
         NVARCHAR(8))
PRINT 'The value of @@ERROR is ' + CAST(@@ERROR AS
         NVARCHAR(8))
```

The value of @@ERROR is an INT. In the PRINT statements, I cast it to an NVARCHAR(8) for display. Notice in Figure 16-1 that the system error message is displayed in the first line on the Messages tab. The result of the first PRINT statement is displayed in the second line in the figure, and the value of @@ERROR is 8134. However, in the second PRINT statement, shown in the third line in the figure, the value of @@ERROR is 0 because the previous Transact-SQL statement (the first PRINT statement) ran without error.

Figure 16-1:
The value in
@@ERROR
can change
after each
Transact-
SQL
statement.

The temporary nature of the value stored in @@ERROR means that you must use one of two strategies if you want to create error-handling code that's compatible with SQL Server 2000:

✔ Test or use @@ERROR immediately after a Transact-SQL statement completes.

✔ Save the value of @@ERROR in a variable and use that variable later.

The IF statement allows you to test the value returned by @@ERROR. Often, you use a simple IF statement with no ELSE clause, but you can use the ELSE clause, if you like. The following code tests the value of @@ERROR after dividing 1 by 0 and after dividing 1 by 2.

```
SELECT 1/0
IF @@ERROR <> 0
  PRINT 'There was an error. The error number was ' +
        CAST(@@ERROR AS NVARCHAR(8))
ELSE
  PRINT 'The statement executed successfully.'

SELECT 1/2
IF @@ERROR <> 0
  PRINT 'There was an error. The error number was ' +
        CAST(@@ERROR AS NVARCHAR(8))
ELSE
  PRINT 'The statement executed successfully.'
```

Figure 16-2 shows the result of executing the preceding commands. Notice that when 1 is divided by 0, the custom error message that uses @@ERROR is displayed. Importantly, notice that the value returned by @@ERROR has been reset to 0. When no error occurs, the PRINT statement in the ELSE clause is executed.

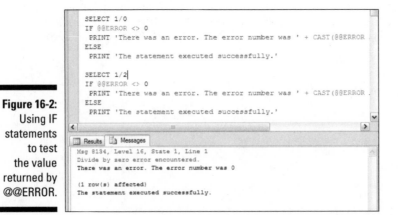

Figure 16-2:
Using IF
statements
to test
the value
returned by
@@ERROR.

A widely used approach to get around the temporary nature of @@ERROR is to add multiple assignment statements where the value contained in @@ERROR at any point during the code is assigned to another variable. You can then use that variable in your code to retrieve the error number at a later time.

In the following code, I declare a variable @ERROR (one at sign) before attempting to divide by zero. In the statement after the attempt to divide by zero, I assign the value of @@ERROR to @ERROR. Notice that the PRINT statements now refer to @ERROR (not @@ERROR).

```
DECLARE @ERROR INT
SELECT 1/0
SET @ERROR = @@ERROR
PRINT 'The value of @ERROR is ' + CAST(@ERROR AS
        NVARCHAR(8))
PRINT 'The value of @ERROR is ' + CAST(@ERROR AS
        NVARCHAR(8))
```

Figure 16-3 shows the result of executing the preceding code.

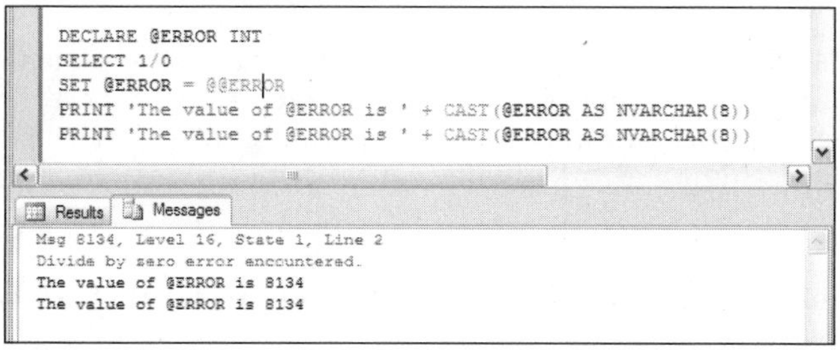

Figure 16-3: Assigning the value returned by @@ERROR to a variable.

Often, you'll use the value of the variable you create in an IF statement because the value of the variable is stable, unlike the value of @@ERROR.

You can use @@ERROR together with the TRY . . . CATCH construct that I discuss later in this chapter. Again, the value of @@ERROR is available only in the first line of the CATCH block. The following code illustrates that.

```
BEGIN TRY
SELECT 1/0
END TRY
BEGIN CATCH
  PRINT 'The value of @@ERROR is ' + CAST(@@ERROR AS
          NVARCHAR(8))
  PRINT 'You shouldn''t have done that!'
  PRINT 'The value of @@ERROR is now ' + CAST(@@ERROR AS
          NVARCHAR(8))
END CATCH
```

Figure 16-4 illustrates the results of running the preceding code.

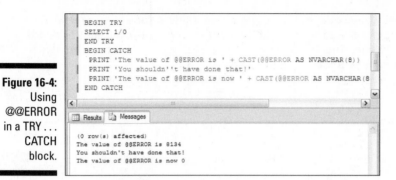

```
BEGIN TRY
SELECT 1/0
END TRY
BEGIN CATCH
  PRINT 'The value of @@ERROR is ' + CAST(@@ERROR AS NVARCHAR(8))
  PRINT 'You shouldn''t have done that!'
  PRINT 'The value of @@ERROR is now ' + CAST(@@ERROR AS NVARCHAR(8
END CATCH
```

| Results | Messages |

```
(0 row(s) affected)
The value of @@ERROR is 8134
You shouldn't have done that!
The value of @@ERROR is now 0
```

Figure 16-4:
Using
@@ERROR
in a TRY . . .
CATCH
block.

Using RAISERROR

RAISERROR returns a message to an application using the same format as a system error or warning message. It lets you create custom error messages to complement system error messages and warnings. RAISERROR is also a useful tool to generate errors of different severities to test your application code.

There is only one *E* in RAISERROR. If you spell it with two *E*s, you'll see an error message.

Use RAISERROR for the following:

- ✔ Debugging and troubleshooting your Transact-SQL code.
- ✔ Returning error messages with custom text.
- ✔ Making execution jump from a TRY block to the corresponding CATCH block.
- ✔ Returning error information from a CATCH block.

There are two syntax forms for using RAISERROR in your Transact-SQL code.

- ✔ Create a new message using the sp_addmessage system stored procedure and reference that using RAISERROR.
- ✔ Specify a message in the RAISERROR statement.

The following code illustrates the first syntax form. First, add a new message using the sp_addmessage system stored procedure.

```
sp_addmessage @msgnum = 88888,
               @Severity = 16,
               @msgtext = 'You cannot divide by zero. It is
            not allowed.'
```

The value of the @msgnum parameter must be 50000 or greater. The message to be returned to an application is the value of the @msgtext parameter. In the following code, the value of the @Numerator variable is tested before the division is carried out, thereby avoiding the system error message.

```
DECLARE @Numerator INT
SET @Numerator = 0
IF @Numerator = 0
 RAISERROR (88888, 16, 1)
ELSE
 SELECT 1 / @Numerator AS RESULT
```

Figure 16-5 shows the result of executing the preceding commands.

Figure 16-5:
Using
RAISERROR
to produce
a custom
error
message.

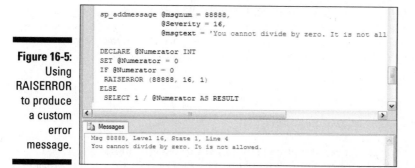

The other syntax form for RAISERROR specifies an error text in the RAISERROR statement:

```
DECLARE @Numerator INT
SET @Numerator = 0
IF @Numerator = 0
 RAISERROR ('This is different message.', 16, 1)
ELSE
 SELECT 1 / @Numerator AS RESULT
```

Notice in the preceding code that the first argument to RAISERROR is the message text. As before, you can specify an error severity. By default, the message number is 50000, as you can see in Figure 16-6.

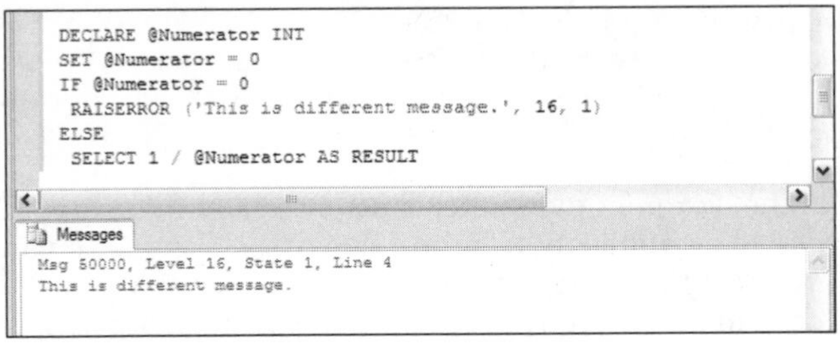

Figure 16-6:
Specifying
an error
message
in the
RAISERROR
statement.

```
DECLARE @Numerator INT
SET @Numerator = 0
IF @Numerator = 0
  RAISERROR ('This is different message.', 16, 1)
ELSE
  SELECT 1 / @Numerator AS RESULT
```

```
Messages
Msg 50000, Level 16, State 1, Line 4
This is different message.
```

I show you how to use RAISERROR in a TRY...CATCH block in the next section after I introduce TRY...CATCH and the error functions new in SQL Server 2005.

Using TRY . . . CATCH

Prior to SQL Server 2005, error-handling in SQL Server was a pretty clumsy process involving the extensive use of @@ERROR using the techniques I show you earlier in this chapter. In SQL Server 2005, you have two new tools that help you write more succinct and more easily maintained error-handling code:

✔ The TRY...CATCH construct

✔ New, error-related functions

The TRY...CATCH construct has similarities to exception-handling techniques in other programming languages. The TRY...CATCH construct takes the following general form:

```
BEGIN TRY
<Transact-SQL_statement_or_statement_block>
END TRY
BEGIN CATCH
<Transact-SQL_statement_or_statement_block>
END CATCH
```

The CATCH block must immediately follow the TRY block to which it corresponds. However, one, or more, blank line between the END TRY and BEGIN CATCH lines is allowed.

When an error occurs in the TRY block — that is, after the BEGIN TRY line and before the END TRY line — control passes to the CATCH block. If no error occurs in the TRY block, the code in the CATCH block isn't executed.

The following code shows a very simple TRY . . . CATCH construct with no error in the TRY block. The code in the CATCH block never executes.

```
BEGIN TRY
  PRINT 'Hello'
END TRY
BEGIN CATCH
  PRINT 'CATCH entered.'
END CATCH
```

In the following code, an attempt to divide by zero takes place in the TRY block, so control passes to the CATCH block and the code there is executed — in this case, a simple PRINT statement.

```
BEGIN TRY
  PRINT 'Hello'
  SELECT 1/0
END TRY
BEGIN CATCH
  PRINT 'CATCH entered.'
END CATCH
```

Figure 16-7 shows the results of executing the preceding two pieces of code. The first Hello in the Messages tab is from execution of the first TRY...CATCH block. The code in the CATCH block isn't executed. The second Hello comes from the PRINT statement in the second TRY block. When the attempt to divide by zero occurs, control passes to the CATCH block, and the PRINT statement there is executed.

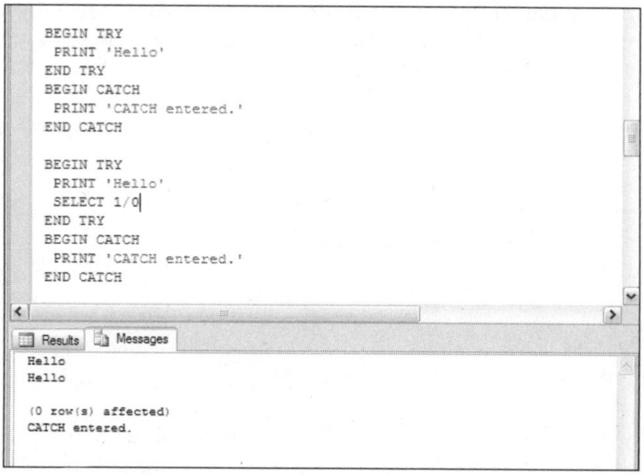

Figure 16-7: Simple TRY . . . CATCH constructs.

In the CATCH block, you can find and display additional information about errors that occur using the following new functions:

✔ ERROR_LINE — Returns the line number at which an error occurs. If the error occurs in the TRY block, the line number in the TRY block is returned. If the error occurs in a stored procedure or trigger, the line number in the stored procedure or trigger is returned. It returns NULL if it's used outside a CATCH block. The return type is int.

✔ ERROR_MESSAGE — Contains information about the occurrence of the error. It returns NULL if it's used outside a CATCH block. The return type is nvarchar(4000).

✔ ERROR_NUMBER — Each SQL Server error message has its own number. The ERROR_NUMBER() function returns the error number that occurs in a TRY block. It returns NULL if it's used outside a CATCH block. The return type is int.

✔ ERROR_PROCEDURE — Returns the name of the stored procedure or trigger in which an error occurs, if the stored procedure or trigger executes from inside a TRY block and ERROR_PROCEDURE() is executed in the corresponding CATCH block. It returns NULL if it's used outside a CATCH block or if the error in the TRY block doesn't occur in a stored procedure or trigger. The return type is nvarchar(126).

✔ ERROR_SEVERITY — Indicates how severe the error is that occurs in the TRY block. It returns NULL if it's used outside a CATCH block. The return type is int.

✔ ERROR_STATE — Returns the state number of an error that occurs in a TRY block if ERROR_STATE() is executed in the corresponding CATCH block. It returns NULL if it's used outside a CATCH block. The return type is int.

All of the preceding functions return the relevant error information wherever you use them in a CATCH block. You're no longer constrained as you were with @@ERROR to find the error information in the first line of the CATCH block.

The following example shows how you can use all the error-related functions in a CATCH block.

```
BEGIN TRY
PRINT 'The error is going to occur on Line 2.'
SELECT 1/0
PRINT 'This line is never reached.'
END TRY
BEGIN CATCH
PRINT 'The error occurred on line ' + CAST(ERROR_LINE() AS
        NVARCHAR(8))
PRINT 'The error message is ' + CAST(ERROR_MESSAGE() AS
        NVARCHAR(80))
PRINT 'The error number is ' + CAST(ERROR_NUMBER() AS
        NVARCHAR(8))
```

```
PRINT 'The error procedure is ' + CAST(ERROR_PROCEDURE()
        AS NVARCHAR(8))
PRINT 'The error severity is ' + CAST(ERROR_SEVERITY() AS
        NVARCHAR(8))
PRINT 'The error state is ' + CAST(ERROR_STATE() AS
        NVARCHAR(8))
END CATCH
```

Figure 16-8 shows the results on the Messages tab of executing the preceding code. Notice that int values are type cast to nvarchar(8) data types for display. Notice too that the line,

```
PRINT 'The error procedure is ' + CAST(ERROR_PROCEDURE()
        AS NVARCHAR(8))
```

is blank. Because the error doesn't occur in a stored procedure or trigger, the value returned by ERROR_PROCEDURE() is NULL. Adding anything to NULL is NULL. So the PRINT statement prints NULL on the line. You see a blank line.

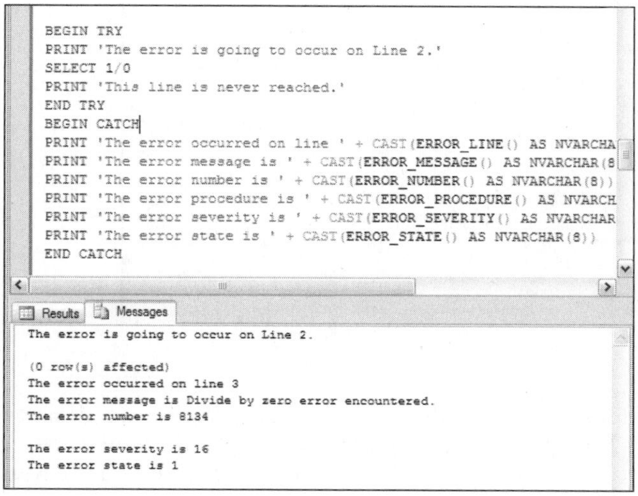

Figure 16-8: Displaying the values returned by the new, error-related functions.

The following example shows how the ERROR_LINE() and ERROR_PROCEDURE() functions work when the error arises in a stored procedure. First, create a stored procedure, procDivideByZero, using the following code:

```
CREATE PROCEDURE procDivideByZero
AS
    SELECT 1/0
GO
```

Then, execute the stored procedure in a TRY...CATCH construct.

```
BEGIN TRY
  EXECUTE procDivideByZero
END TRY
BEGIN CATCH
  PRINT 'The error occurred on line ' + CAST(ERROR_LINE()
        AS NVARCHAR(3))
  PRINT 'The error occurred in this stored procedure: ' +
        ERROR_PROCEDURE()
END CATCH
```

Notice in Figure 16-9 that the value returned by ERROR_LINE() is 3. This is because in the CREATE PROCEDURE statement, the SELECT statement that contains the divide by zero error is on line 3 (including the CREATE PROCEDURE line and the AS line).

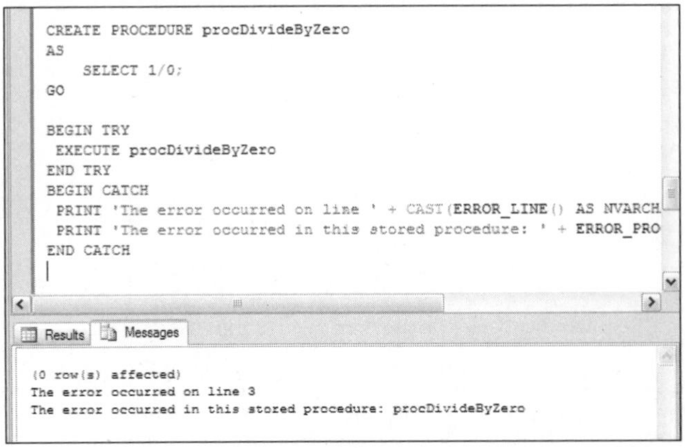

Figure 16-9:
Displaying
the line
number and
procedure
when a
stored
procedure
gives an
error.

In the previous example, I show error information on the Messages tab in SQL Server Management Studio. The following code, which uses the SELECT statement, allows you to display the error information on the Results tab in SQL Server Management Studio.

```
BEGIN TRY
  SELECT 1/0;
END TRY
BEGIN CATCH
  SELECT ERROR_NUMBER() AS ErrorNumber,
         ERROR_SEVERITY() AS ErrorSeverity,
         ERROR_STATE() AS ErrorState,
         ERROR_PROCEDURE() AS ErrorProcedure,
         ERROR_LINE() AS ErrorLine,
         ERROR_MESSAGE() AS ErrorMessage
END CATCH
```

Figure 16-10 shows the results of executing the preceding code. Notice that the value in the ErrorProcedure column is NULL.

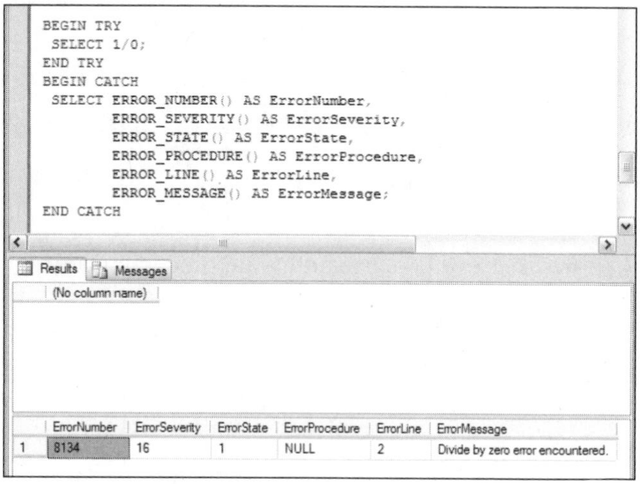

```
BEGIN TRY
 SELECT 1/0;
END TRY
BEGIN CATCH
 SELECT ERROR_NUMBER() AS ErrorNumber,
        ERROR_SEVERITY() AS ErrorSeverity,
        ERROR_STATE() AS ErrorState,
        ERROR_PROCEDURE() AS ErrorProcedure,
        ERROR_LINE() AS ErrorLine,
        ERROR_MESSAGE() AS ErrorMessage;
END CATCH
```

	ErrorNumber	ErrorSeverity	ErrorState	ErrorProcedure	ErrorLine	ErrorMessage
1	8134	16	1	NULL	2	Divide by zero error encountered.

Figure 16-10: Displaying error information in the Results tab.

The Transact-SQL code in the CATCH block can be of arbitrary complexity, making use of the new, error-related functions and if you choose, the @@ERROR function, too.

Nesting TRY . . . CATCH Statements

You can nest TRY . . . CATCH statements to produce error-handling routines of significant complexity. A nested TRY . . . CATCH construct is situated inside the TRY block of the outer TRY . . . CATCH construct.

The following example illustrates how to construct nested TRY . . . CATCH constructs and shows error information from each TRY . . . CATCH construct. The nested (inner) TRY . . . CATCH construct attempts a divide by zero operation. The outer TRY . . . CATCH construct attempts to cast a string to a datetime value.

```
BEGIN TRY
 BEGIN TRY
  SELECT 1/0
 END TRY
 BEGIN CATCH
  PRINT 'Inner TRY error number: ' +  CAST(ERROR_NUMBER()
          AS NVARCHAR(8))
  PRINT 'The Inner TRY error occurred on line: ' +
          CAST(ERROR_LINE() AS NVARCHAR(8))
```

```
      PRINT 'The Inner TRY error message is ' +
            ERROR_MESSAGE()
  END CATCH
    SELECT CAST('This is not a datetime value.' AS datetime)
  END TRY
BEGIN CATCH
  PRINT 'Outer TRY error number: ' + CAST(ERROR_NUMBER() AS
        NVARCHAR(8))
  PRINT 'The Outer TRY error occurred on line: ' +
        CAST(ERROR_LINE() AS NVARCHAR(8))
  PRINT 'The Outer TRY error message is ' + ERROR_MESSAGE()
END CATCH
```

Figure 16-11 shows the results of executing the preceding code.

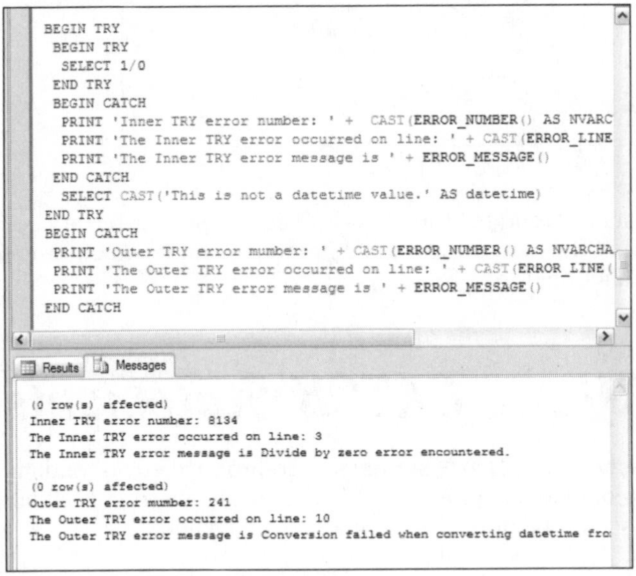

Figure 16-11:
Using
nested
TRY . . .
CATCH
constructs.

Part IV

Programming SQL Server Security

"You ever get the feeling this project could just up and die at any moment?"

In this part . . .

This part introduces you to SQL Server 2005 security. A database uses certain specialized features to ensure that data in your database can be made secure from prying eyes. Security features include logins, users, permissions, roles, and encryption.

Database security comprises various parts and layers. The top layer is the login or user. A user is an access portal into a database, validated by the name of a user (or login), and password. The database is protected from the outside world because nobody knows what the login names are. You can't even connect to a database without knowing a user's name. Additionally, users cannot log in to each other's accounts because they don't have each other's passwords.

The next layer is the permissions layer, where a logged-in user is granted permission (or *not* granted permission) to be able to read and change a specific object, such as a table owned by another user. Permissions can also be allocated for specific functions, such as the ability to create a new table, allowing or prohibiting a user to create tables. A role is a grouping mechanism containing one or more permissions. Granting a role to a user grants all permissions contained within a role to the granted user, in a single statement.

Modern databases commonly contain encryption mechanisms allowing various levels of automating encryption and decryption of data. This means that when data is stored in a database, it is stored in encrypted form. The only way to make sense of data as it is read is to decrypt it just before reading.

Chapter 17

Adding Logins and Users

*K*eeping your data secure is one of the most important tasks that you have to carry out as a SQL Server administrator or developer. The tasks you need to carry out depend, in part, on how you use SQL Server in your organization. Inside the organization, you're likely to principally be concerned with ensuring that users get access to data which they legitimately have a right to access. Of course, you also want to ensure that internal users don't get access to data they're not authorized to see. Although, in general terms, fellow employees should be trustworthy, you need to assume that they're not.

After you open access to your database(s) to users outside your organization, you need to give even more careful thought to security. Someone out there will, in time, try to access data that he has no right to see or try to damage your data. An understanding of how SQL Server 2005 security works helps you design your applications to minimize the chances of a successful malicious attack.

In this chapter, I first give an overview of security in SQL Server 2005. I review the information you can retrieve from security catalog views to show you how security is currently configured. I also examine the differences between the concepts of logins and users.

Introducing SQL Server 2005 Security

Microsoft has made significant changes to security in SQL Server 2005 compared to SQL Server 2000. Therefore, even if you're familiar with SQL Server 2000 security, you need to get up to speed on security features and how to achieve an appropriate security configuration in SQL Server 2005.

SQL Server 2005 security works only in a setting where you have carefully considered other security issues and features. Among the factors outside SQL Server that you should consider are

- Reviewing physical security of your server(s).

- Using firewalls between SQL Server and the Internet and separating your intranet into appropriate security zones.

- Isolating services. For example, don't run SQL Server on a domain controller. Run separate SQL Server services under separate accounts. Then again, separation may not always be possible. Unless network services access is required, execute as LocalSystem.

- Creating service accounts that have the minimum necessary privileges. If those accounts are compromised, the damage a hacker can do is minimal.

- Disabling unnecessary protocols. For example, disable NetBIOS in a server in a perimeter network.

Other general security measures you should consider for SQL Server are

- Associating SQL Server services with Windows accounts.

- Where possible, requiring Windows authentication for connections to SQL Server.

- Assigning a strong password for the sysadmin SQL Server account.

- Enabling password policy for SQL Server logins.

- Requiring strong passwords for SQL Server logins.

After you install SQL Server 2005, you can configure many general security settings using the SQL Server Surface Area Configuration tool. To run the SQL Server Surface Configuration tool, choose Start⇨All Programs⇨ Microsoft SQL Server 2005⇨Configuration Tools⇨SQL Server Surface Area Configuration. Figure 17-1 shows the SQL Server 2005 Surface Area Configuration initial window.

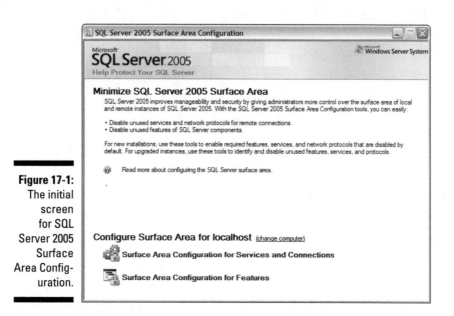

Figure 17-1:
The initial
screen
for SQL
Server 2005
Surface
Area Config-
uration.

In the SQL Server 2005 Surface Area Configuration initial window, you have options to

 ✔ Link to the Books Online information about how to use the tool.

 ✔ Link to the Surface Area Configuration dialog box for Services and Connections.

 ✔ Link to the Surface Area Configuration dialog box for Features.

Each of the latter two configuration dialog boxes gives you an extensive range of aspects of SQL Server 2005 database engine that you can configure. Figure 17-2 shows the dialog box that allows you to specify whether remote connections are accepted and which protocol(s) are used.

Remote connections are disabled by default and must be explicitly enabled in a fresh installation of SQL Server 2005. On the other hand, when performing an upgrade from SQL Server 2000 to SQL Server 2005, remote connections are left enabled as they were. In other words, when upgrading the underlying configuration files are left intact.

With a new install of SQL Server 2005, many features are turned off by default. However, if you upgrade from SQL Server 2000, more features might be enabled (either because SQL Server 2000 defaults were retained or features were turned on). As a result, an upgraded install of SQL Server 2005 might have more potential security vulnerabilities than a new install.

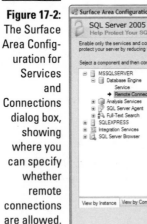

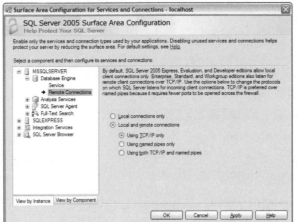

Catalog views allow you to retrieve and display metadata about many aspects of SQL Server 2005. Among the catalog views are several that allow you to access information relevant to security. You can access server-level and data-base-level security catalog views in SQL Server 2005.

In the rest of this section, I present a compressed summary of information about permissions and other security data available from catalog views. If you're unfamiliar with SQL Server security, you might need to refer to SQL Server Books Online (http://msdn2.microsoft.com/en-us/library/ms130214.aspx) or other documentation for complementary information.

The server-level security catalog views are

✔ sys.server_permissions   A list of server-level permissions

✔ sys.server_principals   A list of server-level principals

✔ sys.server_role_members   A list of members for each server role

✔ sys.sql_logins   A list of SQL logins

✔ sys.system_components_surface_area_configuration

   A list of the system objects whose configuration can be changed from a Surface Area Configuration component

The security catalog views allow you easily to find out many of the current security settings for a server or database.

Understanding Logins and Users

In SQL Server 2005, a login and a user are two distinct things. A *login* is a server-level security principal. A *user* is a database-level principal.

To view logins on an instance of SQL Server 2005, open Object Explorer in SQL Server Management Studio. Expand the node for the instance of interest and then expand the `Security` node for the instance. Expand the `Logins` node.

You won't find logins in the `Security` nodes under each database in Object Explorer. Logins are server-level (that is, *instance-level*) principals.

To retrieve information about existing logins for a SQL Server 2005 instance, use the `sys.sql_logins` catalog view. The following command displays all logins on an instance of SQL Server 2005:

```
SELECT *
FROM sys.sql_logins
```

The following information is available for each SQL Server login:

- ✔ `name`   The name of the principal — for example, `sa` — or the roles available in each server.

- ✔ `principal_id`   The unique identification number for the principal. The ID is unique for any principal in that server.

- ✔ `type`   The type of principal. The data type is `char(1)`. Allowed values are `S` (SQL Server login), `U` (Windows login), `G` (Windows group), `R` (server role), `C` (login mapped to a certificate), and `K` (login mapped to an asymmetric key).

- ✔ `type_desc`   A short description of the type of the principal. The data type is `nvarchar(60)`. Allowed values are `SQL_LOGIN`, `WINDOWS_LOGIN`, `WINDOWS_GROUP`, `SERVER_ROLE`, `CERTIFICATE_MAPPED_LOGIN`, and `ASYMMETRIC_KEY_MAPPED_LOGIN`.

- ✔ `is_disabled`   Indicates whether the principal is disabled. The data type is `int`. A value of `1` indicates that the principal is disabled.

- ✔ `create_date`   Indicates the date and time when the principal was created. The data type is `datetime`.

- ✔ `modify_date`   Indicates the date and time when the principal was last modified. The data type is `datetime`.

- ✔ default_database_name   The default database for the principal. The data type is sysname.

- ✔ default_language-name   The default language for the principal. The data type is sysname.

- ✔ credential_id   The ID of any credential associated with the principal. The data type is int. If no credential is associated with the principal, the value is NULL.

- ✔ is_policy_checked   Specifies whether the password policy is checked. The data type is bit.

- ✔ is_expiration_checked   Specifies whether expiration of the password is checked. The data type is bit.

- ✔ password_hash   A hash of the password for the SQL Server login.

I discuss users in more detail in Chapter 19.

Adding Logins

To add a login to a SQL Server 2005 instance, use the CREATE LOGIN statement or use Object Explorer in SQL Server Management Studio.

The simplest form of the CREATE LOGIN statement supplies the login name and a password:

```
CREATE LOGIN <login_name>
WITH PASSWORD = 'somePassword'
```

For example, to create a login, Alan, with a password, execute the following command:

```
CREATE LOGIN Alan
WITH PASSWORD = 'abc123!"'
```

To specify that the login must change the password when first logging in, add MUST CHANGE:

```
CREATE LOGIN Alan
WITH PASSWORD = 'abc123!"' MUST_CHANGE
```

To create a login from a Windows domain account, use this form:

```
CREATE LOGIN [DomainName\UserName]
FROM WINDOWS
```

To create a login using Object Explorer in SQL Server Management Studio, follow these steps:

1. **Open Object Explorer in SQL Server Management Studio and choose View⇨Object Explorer.**

2. **Expand the node for the relevant SQL Server 2005 instance and expand the `Security` node under the node for the server instance.**

3. **Right-click the `Logins` node and select New Login from the context menu.**

   The Login – New dialog box shown in Figure 17-3 opens.

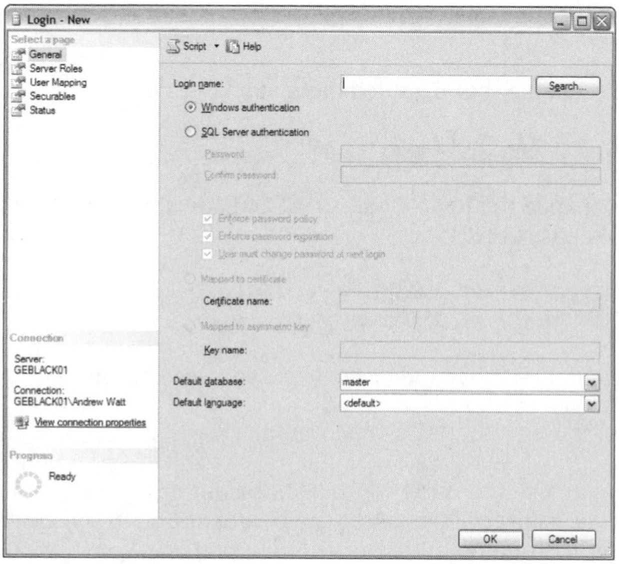

Figure 17-3:
The Login – New dialog box.

4. **Specify a name for the login in the Login Name text box.**

5. **Specify whether Windows authentication or SQL Server is to be used.**

   SQL Server authentication in reality applies a mix of both Windows and SQL Server security. This is called *mixed-mode.* Mixed-mode is more secure because it utilizes both Windows logins and SQL Server database logins. You have to know both login-password combinations to connect to a SQL Server database.

   If mixed-mode authentication is to be used, specify a password for the login. Also, decide whether the Enforce Password Policy, Enforce Password Expiration, and User Must Change Password at Next login check boxes are selected.

6. **Optionally, specify a default database and default language for the login. Click OK to close the dialog box.**

The Login – New dialog box contains a check box called User Must Change Password at Next Login. Microsoft uses the word *user* in the name of this check box, but they mean *login,* in my view. The term *login* refers to the mixed-mode login through Windows, SQL Server, or both.

To alter a login, use the ALTER LOGIN statement or use the Properties dialog box accessible from Object Explorer for an existing login. The ALTER LOGIN statement can be used to change login properties, as shown in the following syntax. For example, you can disable a login to prevent the person from logging in to SQL Server:

```
ALTER LOGIN <login_name> DISABLE
```

And you can reenable that disabled login at a later date:

```
ALTER LOGIN <login_name> ENABLE
```

You can also change the login's password and specify the new password against the old password:

```
ALTER LOGIN WITH PASSWORD = 'password'
   [OLD PASSWORD = 'oldpassword']
```

You can even change the name of the login you are altering:

```
ALTER LOGIN WITH NAME = <login_name>
```

To delete a login, use the DROP LOGIN statement or right-click an existing login in Object Explorer. Then select the Delete option in the context menu. The DROP LOGIN statement has very simple syntax:

```
DROP LOGIN <login_name>
```

Understanding Schemas and Users

Schemas and users are both database-level principals. In SQL Server 2005, there is a significant change from SQL Server 2000 — schemas and users are no longer interchangeable. In SQL Server 2005, a schema is a namespace that exists independently of the user who created it. A schema is, essentially, a container for objects in a database.

The separation of schemas from users has the following characteristics:

- ✔ The owner of a schema can be changed.
- ✔ Objects can be moved between schemas.
- ✔ One schema can contain objects owned by multiple users.
- ✔ Multiple users can share a single default schema.
- ✔ A schema can be owned by any database principal.
- ✔ A user can be dropped without dropping objects in the corresponding schema.

The user who creates a schema is the initial owner of the schema. However, ownership of the schema can be transferred to another user. This helps avoid the awkward scenarios in SQL Server 2000, where a user created a schema and then left the company. Before, when objects in the schema were used in several applications, you couldn't transfer ownership of the schema from the defunct user. With the separation of schemas and users in SQL Server 2005, if a user who owns a schema leaves the company, all that you need to do is transfer that ownership of the schema to a current user.

Beware of the following potential problems if you use code from SQL Server 2000:

- ✔ If code assumes that a user and schema are synonymous, incorrect results may be returned.
- ✔ Catalog views designed for SQL Server 2000, such as sysobjects, can return incorrect results.

The sys.database_principals and sys.schemas catalog views in SQL Server 2005 replace the sys.users system table in SQL Server 2000. Similarly, use the sys.server_principals catalog view in SQL Server 2005 instead of the syslogins system table in SQL Server 2000.

Using Schemas

Schemas are a new security feature in SQL Server 2005. Schemas are namespaces that distinguish database objects from similarly named objects in another schema.

The dot notation is used when referring to a table in a specific schema. For example, the `TestTable` table in the `dbo` schema is referred to as `dbo.TestTable`, as shown here:

```
SELECT *
FROM dbo.TestTable
```

To create a schema in the current database, use the `CREATE SCHEMA` statement, as follows:

```
CREATE SCHEMA <schema_name>
```

To create a schema in the current database and specify its owner by using the `CREATE SCHEMA` statement, use the following form:

```
CREATE SCHEMA <schema_name> AUTHORIZATION <owner_name>
```

Each user has a *default schema*. Objects referred to are assumed to be in the default schema for a user unless the name of another schema is explicit. For example, if the user, `FredUser`, has a default schema, `accounts`, a reference to a table name that exists in the accounts schema and another schema is assumed to come from the `accounts` schema. For example, if the `accounts` schema and `purchases` schema both had tables named `orders`, the following code is assumed by SQL Server 2005 to refer to `accounts.orders` (if `FredUser` is the relevant user):

```
SELECT *
FROM orders
```

To select data from the `orders` table in the `purchases` schema, the code is:

```
SELECT *
FROM purchases.orders
```

To change the default schema of an existing user, use the `ALTER USER` statement, as in the following command:

```
ALTER USER
FredUser WITH DEFAULT_SCHEMA = TestSchema
```

To execute the preceding command, you need to create a schema called `TestSchema` by using this command:

```
CREATE SCHEMA TestSchema
```

If you worked through the examples earlier in this chapter and see the error message,

```
Msg 15151, Level 16, State 1, Line 1
Cannot alter the user 'FredUser', because it does not
         exist or you do not have permission.
```

you need to execute the REVOKE statement to execute as a user with appropriate permissions.

To change the ownership of a schema, use the ALTER AUTHORIZATION statement. The general form of the ALTER AUTHORIZATION statement to change ownership of a schema is

```
ALTER AUTHORIZATION
ON SCHEMA::<schema_name>
TO <user_name>
```

Use the DROP SCHEMA statement to delete a schema from a database. To remove the TestSchema schema from the current database, use the following command:

```
DROP SCHEMA TestSchema
```

You can't drop a schema that contains objects. To drop a schema that contains objects, you must first drop the objects. For example, to drop the TestSchema schema that contains a TestTable table, use the following commands:

```
DROP TABLE TestSchema.TestTable
DROP SCHEMA TestSchema
```

Adding Users

In SQL Server 2005, a *user* is a database-level principal. If no permissions were explicitly granted or denied to a user, that user has the permissions of the public database role. In general, a role is a grouping of privileges and permissions, allowing a user to connect to a database, see things like tables, create tables, change tables, and so on. The public database role simply groups these permissions and privileges, making it easier to grant essential privileges such as the permission to connect to a SQL Server database. (Roles are discussed in more detail in Chapter 18.)

To create a new user in the current database, use the CREATE USER command or use the Object Explorer in SQL Server Management Studio.

The sp_adduser system stored procedure is deprecated in SQL Server 2005. Use the CREATE USER statement instead.

To create a new user with Object Explorer in SQL Server Management Studio, follow these steps:

1. **Open SQL Server Management Studio.**

   If the Object Explorer isn't visible, choose View➪Object Explorer.

2. **Expand the node for the database of interest; for example, the Chapter17 database.**

3. **Expand the Security node for the database.**

4. **Right-click the Users node and choose New User from the context menu.**

   The Database User – New dialog box, as shown in Figure 17-4, opens.

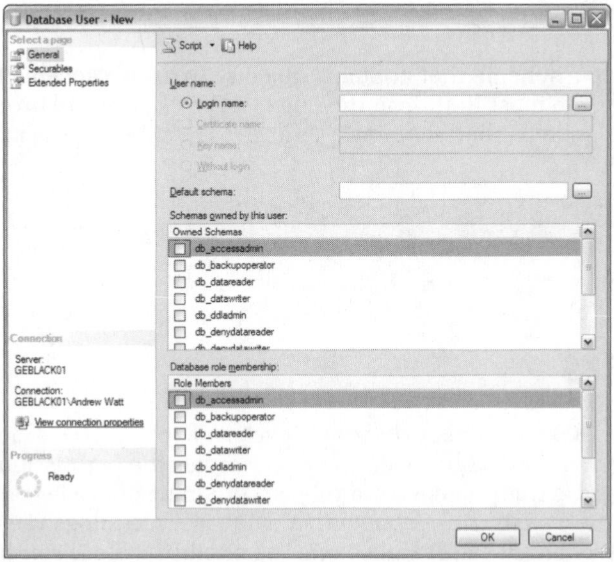

Figure 17-4: The Database User – New dialog box.

5. **Type a name for the new user in the User Name text box.**

6. **If you know the login that you want to associate the new user with, type a login name in the Login Name text box.**

   If you're unsure of the login name, click the ellipsis button to the right of the Login Name text box. The Select Login dialog box opens.

7. **(Optional) In the Select Login dialog box, click the Browse button.**

   The Browse for Objects dialog box, as shown in Figure 17-5, opens.

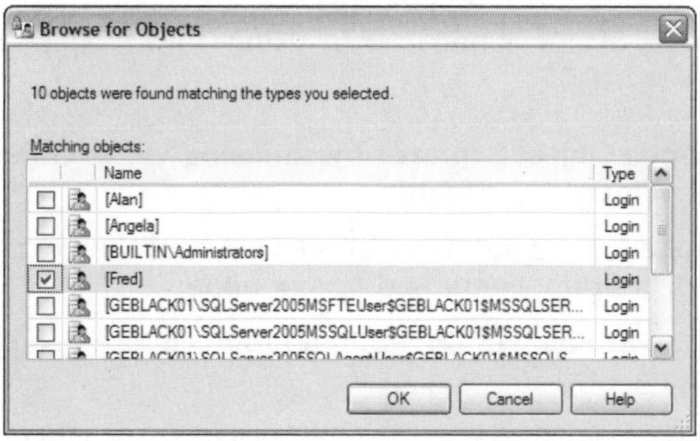

Figure 17-5:
The Browse
for Objects
dialog box.

Browse for Objects

10 objects were found matching the types you selected.

Matching objects:

	Name	Type
☐	[Alan]	Login
☐	[Angela]	Login
☐	[BUILTIN\Administrators]	Login
☑	[Fred]	Login
☐	[GEBLACK01\SQLServer2005MSFTEUser$GEBLACK01$MSSQLSER...	Login
☐	[GEBLACK01\SQLServer2005MSSQLUser$GEBLACK01$MSSQLSER...	Login
☐	[GEBLACK01\SQLServer2005SQLAgentUser$GEBLACK01$MSSQLS...	Login

OK   Cancel   Help

8. **If necessary, scroll down the list of logins displayed in the Browse for Objects dialog box and then select the desired login to associate with the user by selecting the check box beside the name of the login, and then click OK.**

9. **Click OK in the Select Logins dialog box.**

   You return to the Database User – New dialog box.

10. **If you know the schema that you want as the default schema for the user, type the schema name in the Default Schema text box.**

    If you need to find the name of the desired schema, click the ellipsis button to the right of the Default Schema text box. The Select Schema dialog box opens. Click the Browse button to open the Browse for Objects dialog box.

11. **In the Browse for Objects dialog box, scroll down, if necessary, to locate the desired schema name. Select the desired schema by selecting the check box next to the schema name. Click OK to close the Browse for Objects dialog box.**

12. **In the Select Schema dialog box, click OK to close it and return to the Database User – New dialog box.**

13. (Optional) Specify any schemas to be owned by the new user by selecting one or more check boxes in the Schemas Owned by This User area of the Database User – New dialog box.

14. (Optional) Specify any database roles to which the new user is to be a new member by selecting one or more check boxes in the Database Role Membership area of the Database User – New dialog box.

15. Review your selections. If satisfied, click OK to create the new user and close the Database User – New dialog box.

To alter the properties of an existing user by using Object Explorer, follow these steps:

1. If necessary, open Object Explorer by choosing View⇨Object Explorer in SQL Server Management Studio.

2. Expand the node for the database of interest, and then expand its `Security` node and the contained `Users` node.

3. Right-click the user name of interest and then choose Properties from the context menu.

   The Database User – User Name dialog box opens. You can't change the user's name or the name of the associated login from the dialog box.

4. On the General pane, you can alter the user's default schema, specify schemas owned by the user, and specify which roles the user is a member of.

Chapter 18

Creating Database-Level Security

· ·

In This Chapter

▶ Assigning database object permissions

▶ Using roles

▶ Working with application roles

▶ Using security functions

· ·

*I*n SQL Server 2005, you can consider security at the server and database levels. In this chapter, I discuss the database-level principals — schemas, users, and roles.

In addition, I discuss application roles and available security functions in SQL Server 2005.

Assigning Permissions on Database Objects

In SQL Server 2005, three statements allow you to GRANT, REVOKE, or DENY permissions on SQL Server objects.

A complete description of the GRANT statement syntax is beyond the scope of this chapter. However, the following description illustrates how you can use the GRANT statement.

The GRANT statement grants permission(s) on a *securable* (an object such as a table) to a user (a principal). To GRANT an extensive range of permissions, use the ALL argument:

```
GRANT ALL
ON <securable>
TO <principal>
```

The GRANT ALL statement doesn't grant all possible permissions. The permissions granted depend on the securable. The GRANT ALL statement grants the following permissions:

- ✔ When the securable is a database, the BACKUP DATABASE, BACKUP LOG, CREATE DATABASE, CREATE DEFAULT, CREATE FUNCTION, CREATE PROCEDURE, CREATE RULE, CREATE TABLE, and CREATE VIEW permissions are granted.

- ✔ When the securable is a scalar function, the EXECUTE and REFERENCES permissions are granted.

- ✔ When the securable is a table-valued function, the DELETE, INSERT, REFERENCES, SELECT, and UPDATE permissions are granted.

- ✔ When the securable is a stored procedure, the EXECUTE permission is granted.

- ✔ When the securable is a table, the DELETE, INSERT, REFERENCES, SELECT, and UPDATE permissions are granted.

- ✔ When the securable is a view, the DELETE, INSERT, REFERENCES, SELECT, and UPDATE permissions are granted.

The GRANT ALL statement has a synonym, GRANT ALL PRIVILEGES, which has the same semantics.

The principals you can grant privileges to vary, depending on the securable in the ON clause. When the securable is a table, you can grant a permission to the following principals:

- ✔ Database user mapped to a SQL Server login

- ✔ Database role

- ✔ Application role

- ✔ Database user mapped to a Windows user

- ✔ Database user mapped to a Windows group

- ✔ Database user mapped to an asymmetric key

- ✔ Database user mapped to a certificate

- ✔ Database user with no login

Add the WITH GRANT OPTION to the GRANT ALL statement to allow the grantee to grant the specified permissions:

```
GRANT ALL
ON <securable>
TO <principal>
WITH GRANT OPTION
```

The following examples assume the existence of a database, Chapter18, a login, FredLogin, and a user, FredUser. Execute the following statements to set up the desired database, login, and user. Depending on how your SQL Server instance treats password policy, you may need to provide a more complex password.

```
CREATE DATABASE Chapter18
GO
USE Chapter18
GO
CREATE LOGIN FredLogin
WITH PASSWORD = 'abc123'
GO
CREATE USER FredUser
FOR LOGIN FredLogin
```

Confirm in Object Explorer that the login and user were created successfully. You may need to choose Refresh on the context menu to display the newly created principal. If you've followed along to this point, the user, FredUser, has only the public role permissions on the Chapter18 database.

Create a table, TestTable, and populate one row by using the following commands:

```
CREATE TABLE TestTable
(MessageID int IDENTITY,
 Message varchar(200))
GO
INSERT
INTO TestTable
VALUES('This is a test message.')
```

Confirm that your current user can execute a SELECT statement from the TestTable table with this command:

```
SELECT *
FROM TestTable
```

To execute Transact-SQL commands as the user, FredUser, use the following command:

```
EXECUTE AS USER = 'FredUser'
```

To attempt to execute a SELECT statement, use the following statement:

```
SELECT *
FROM TestTable
```

The following error message displays:

```
Msg 229, Level 14, State 5, Line 1
SELECT permission denied on object 'TestTable', database
        'Chapter18', schema 'dbo'.
```

The user, FredUser, has no permissions on the TestTable table. To allow FredUser to SELECT data from the TestTable table, GRANT at least SELECT permission to the user.

If you attempt to execute the following statement,

```
GRANT SELECT ON dbo.TestTable TO FredUser
```

you see the following error message:

```
Cannot grant, deny, or revoke permissions to sa, dbo,
        information_schema, sys, or yourself.
```

This error occurs because you're executing as FredUser. To grant a permission to FredUser, REVERT to the dbo or other role with relevant permissions. Execute this statement:

```
REVERT
```

You can grant a SELECT permission to FredUser by executing the following statement:

```
GRANT SELECT
ON OBJECT::dbo.TestTable
TO FredUser
```

Figure 18-1 shows the successful execution of a SELECT statement.

Figure 18-1: Successful execution of a SELECT statement after the SELECT permission is granted.

```
REVERT

GRANT SELECT
ON OBJECT::dbo.TestTable
TO FredUser

EXECUTE AS USER = 'FredUser'

SELECT *
FROM TestTable
```

Results Messages

	MessageID	Message
1	1	This is a test message.

If you're running as `dbo` or another user with appropriate permissions, you can grant `INSERT` permission to `FredUser` by using the following statement:

```
GRANT INSERT
ON OBJECT::dbo.TestTable
TO FredUser
```

The `REVOKE` statement is used to revoke previously granted permissions. To revoke the `SELECT` permission from `FredUser`, you need to revert to `dbo`.

```
REVERT
GO
REVOKE SELECT
ON OBJECT::dbo.TestTable
To FredUser
```

If you then execute as `FredUser` and attempt to execute a `SELECT` statement on the `TestTable` table, you see an error message:

```
Msg 229, Level 14, State 5, Line 1
SELECT permission denied on object 'TestTable', database
        'Chapter18', schema 'dbo'.
```

The `DENY` statement prevents a principal being granted a permission on a securable. However, denying access to a user should be an exceptional circumstance because tracking down an error at a later stage could be awkward. The `DENY` statement operates on the following securables, which are members of the `OBJECT` class:

- Tables
- Views
- Table-valued functions
- Stored procedures
- Extended stored procedures
- Scalar functions
- Aggregate functions
- Service queues
- Synonyms

The following example explores how the `DENY` statement works with the `SELECT` permission for `FredUser`. First, revert to `dbo` (or user with equivalent permissions) because `FredUser` can't grant or deny a permission to himself:

```
REVERT
```

Grant the SELECT permission again to the user FredUser:

```
GRANT SELECT
ON OBJECT::dbo.TestTable
TO FredUser
```

Execute as FredUser and then confirm that he can now execute a SELECT statement successfully. Then revert to dbo.

Execute the following DENY statement for FredUser:

```
DENY SELECT
ON OBJECT::dbo.TestTable
TO FredUser
```

Execute as FredUser and then confirm that he now can't execute a SELECT statement successfully. This is because the previous denial using the DENY statement takes priority. The error message is as follows:

```
Msg 229, Level 14, State 5, Line 1
SELECT permission denied on object 'TestTable', database
        'Chapter18', schema 'dbo'.
```

Using Roles

A *role* is a grouping of permissions and privileges. Rather than granting a gazillion and one different privileges to lots and lots of users, why not use a role? A role allows you to assign all the myriad of permissions and privileges to a role, which groups all of those privileges. Then all you have to do is to assign the role to a user.

Roles are granted and revoked to and from users, just like any other permission or privilege — that is, by using the GRANT and REVOKE statements.

Each SQL Server 2005 database has the following fixed database roles:

- ✔ db_accessadmin   Members can add or remove access for Windows logins, Windows groups, and SQL Server logins.
- ✔ db_backupoperator   Members can back up the database.
- ✔ db_datareader   Members can read all data from all user tables in the database.
- ✔ db_datawriter   Members can add, delete, or update all data in all user tables in the database.
- ✔ db_ddladmin   Members can execute any Data Definition Language (DDL) command in the database.

> ✔ db_denydatareader   Members can't read any data in user tables in the database.
>
> ✔ db_denydatawriter   Members can't add, delete, or update data in any user table in the database.
>
> ✔ db_owner   Members can execute any configuration or maintenance action on the database.
>
> ✔ db_securityadmin   Members can manage permissions for the database, including modifying membership of roles.

To create a user-defined role, use the CREATE ROLE statement. To create a role called MyReadOnlyRole, use this command:

```
CREATE ROLE MyReadOnlyRole
```

Use the ALTER ROLE command to modify the name of a role. The statement takes the following form:

```
ALTER ROLE <existing_name_of_role>
WITH NAME = <new_name_of_role>
```

Changing the name of a role doesn't change its ID number, its owner, or its permissions.

To drop a role for the current database, use the DROP ROLE statement in the following form:

```
DROP ROLE <role_name>
```

Using Application Roles

An application role is a database-level principal. An *application role* enables an application to run as if it is a user of a database. As for a normal user, you can GRANT, REVOKE, or DENY permissions for an application by using an application role.

The existence of an application role enables users of the associated application to connect to a predefined set of data. For example, if the Human Resources department had a need to connect to specific, sensitive employee information, you could create an appropriate application role to allow users of that Human Resources application to connect to the sensitive data. Of course, in parallel, you or an administrator colleague need to ensure that access to the Human Resources application is available only to properly authorized users.

To create an application role, use the CREATE APPLICATION ROLE statement.

```
CREATE APPLICATION ROLE <application_role_name>
WITH PASSWORD = 'password'
```

(Optional) You can specify a default schema as follows:

```
CREATE APPLICATION ROLE <application_role_name>
WITH PASSWORD = 'password', DEFAULT SCHEMA =
          <default_schema_name>
```

When you create an application role, it has no members and is inactivated by default. Enable the application role with the sp_setapprole system stored procedure.

The sp_setapprole stored procedure activates permissions associated with an application role in the current database.

Using Security Functions

SQL Server 2005 provides several functions that return useful information when you manage SQL Server security. The security functions are

- ✔ CURRENT_USER   Returns the name of the current user. This function is equivalent to USER_NAME().

- ✔ Has_Perms_By_Name   Returns the effective permissions of a user on a securable.

- ✔ IS_MEMBER   Tests whether the current user is a member of a specified Windows group or SQL Server database role.

- ✔ IS_SRVROLEMEMBER   Tests whether a SQL Server 2005 login is a member of a specified fixed server role.

- ✔ PERMISSIONS   Returns a bitmap, indicating the permissions of the current user.

- ✔ SCHEMA_ID   Returns the ID of a schema given the schema name.

- ✔ SCHEMA_NAME   Returns the name of a schema, given its identifier.

- ✔ SESSION_USER   Returns the user name of the current context in the current database.

✔ SETUSER   Allows a member of the sysadmin fixed server role or the db_owner fixed database role to impersonate another user. You can use the SETUSER function with SQL Server users but not with Windows users. The SETUSER function is deprecated in SQL Server 2005, but you may see legacy code using it. In SQL Server 2005, use the EXECUTE_AS function instead.

✔ SUSER_ID   Returns the login ID of the user. In SQL Server 2005, the value returned is the value of principal_id in the catalog view sys.server_principals.

✔ SUSER_NAME   Returns the name of the login.

✔ SUSER_SNAME   Returns the name of the login associated with a specified security ID.

✔ SUSER_SID   Returns the security ID of the specified login.

✔ sys.fn_builtin_permissions   Returns data about the hierarchy of permissions on a SQL Server server instance.

✔ SYSTEM_USER   Returns the currently executing context. Returns the login name if the name of the user and login are different.

✔ USER_ID   Returns the identification number for a database user.

✔ USER_NAME   Returns the name of a database user, given the identification number.

Detailed descriptions of all these functions are beyond the scope of this chapter. The following examples illustrate the kind of things you can do with such functions.

The Has_Perms_By_Name function has several uses. For example, to find out if you have permissions on the current database, use this command:

```
SELECT has_perms_by_name(db_name(), 'DATABASE', 'ANY')
```

Use the SUSER_ID function by supplying the login of a user. To find the login ID of the user, Fred, use the following command:

```
SELECT SUSER_ID('Fred')
```

The sys.fn_builtin_permissions function returns the following information for each permission:

✔ class_desc   A brief description of the type of securable. The data type is nvarchar(60).

✔ permission   The name of the permission. The data type is sysname.

✔ type   The code for the compact permission type. The data type is char(4). Several dozen codes exist, which you can look up in SQL Server 2005 documentation, either in your SQL Server 2005 software installation or online on the Microsoft Developer Network Web site at msdn.com.

✔ covering_permission_name   If not NULL, the name of the permission on this class that implies the other permissions on the class. The data type is sysname.

✔ parent_class_desc   If not NULL, the name of the parent class of the current class. The data type is sysname.

✔ parent_covering_permission_name   If not NULL, the name of the permission on the parent class that implies the other permissions on that parent class.

You can use the CURRENT_USER function to discover which user carried out a certain action in relation to data. The following example shows how you can use the CURRENT_USER function to capture information about which operative handled a particular call at a call center. Create a simple CallCenter table by using the following code:

```
USE Chapter18
CREATE TABLE CallCenter
(CallID int IDENTITY NOT NULL,
 CustomerLastName varchar(30),
 CustomerFirstName varchar(30),
 CallInformation varchar(200),
 CallOperative varchar(50) NOT NULL DEFAULT CURRENT_USER
)
```

Insert a sample row of data with the following code.

```
INSERT
INTO CallCenter (CustomerLastName, CustomerFirstName,
        CallInformation)
VALUES ('Smith', 'John', 'Problem with recently purchased
        widget.')
```

Because a DEFAULT was specified for the CallOperative column in the CREATE TABLE statement, you capture that information automatically by executing the following command:

```
SELECT *
FROM CallCenter
```

Chapter 19

Securing Data Using Encryption

Security in SQL Server 2005, as in other contexts, depends on several components. In Chapters 17 and 18, I discuss features such as logins, users, and roles, which are designed to allow legitimate users to access data they're entitled to and prevent illegitimate users from having access to data. Using such mechanisms well gives you a high degree of confidence that unauthorized access to data is unlikely.

For some types of highly confidential data, an additional layer of security makes good sense. Consider a scenario where a bank or other financial institution holds credit card and other sensitive financial data on large numbers of individuals. Encryption essentially can be used to turn sensitive information into something that can't be read by prying eyes. Those prying would have to have the decryption algorithm to read the encrypted data, adding that extra layer of security.

Introducing Encryption

Encryption is useful because it adds an additional layer of security. When it comes down to the details, there really isn't much that can be added. Encryption is just like military coding of sensitive signals: It gets encrypted at one end, transmitted, and decrypted at the other end. The coding algorithm is just that — either you know it or you don't. All encryption does is to prevent people from reading something, be it a secret military message or credit card numbers in your database (unless of course someone has the time and energy to crack the code, which is possible but very difficult).

In this section, I introduce you to several ways of looking at encryption as it relates to SQL Server 2005.

You can look at encryption in SQL Server 2005 as a hierarchy at the following levels:

- ✔ Windows level
- ✔ SQL Server 2005 level
- ✔ Database level

At a Windows level, the data protection API (DPAPI) is used to encrypt the service master key. The DPAPI has two methods, `CryptProtectData` and `CryptUnprotectData`. The DPAPI generates a key from the user's credentials (for example, a password). It then generates a master key, which it encrypts using the key generated from the user's credentials. In addition, a session key is generated for each call to `CryptProtectData`. The session key is then used to carry out encryption.

The master key expires every few months. This, in effect, compartmentalizes encryption from different time periods. This adds to security because breaking encryption for one time period (itself an unlikely event) doesn't allow encryption from other time periods to be unencrypted.

The output from `CryptProtectData` is a binary large object (BLOB). It contains information including the encrypted data, the GUID for the master key, and an HMAC signature of the BLOB to allow any tampering to be detected. For most practical purposes, treat the output from `CryptProtectData` to be input for `CryptUnprotectData`.

At the SQL Server 2005 level, the service master key is stored. The service master key is generated automatically the first time that it's needed to encrypt another (lower, that is, database level) key or generate a key for a linked server. By default, the service master key is generated using the DPAPI and the local machine key. The service master key can be opened by using the service account used to create it or using a principal that has access to the service account name and its password.

Regenerating or restoring the service master key is a resource-intensive operation. If the service master key has been compromised, it's urgent that you take remedial action. Otherwise, it's sensible to carry out regenerating or restoring the service master key at a time of low resource demand.

The service master key is a crucial item in encryption for that SQL Server instance. Back it up and store the backup copy in a secure location offsite. Storing a backup offsite makes sense to allow for disaster scenarios where the machine itself is destroyed by fire, for example, but backup copies of data including important encrypted data exist offsite. With both pieces of data, you can access the encrypted data after successful restoration of data from the offsite backups.

To alter the service master key, use the ALTER SERVICE MASTER KEY statement.

To regenerate the service master key, use this command:

```
ALTER SERVICE MASTER KEY REGENERATE
```

If you change the service account under which SQL Server 2005 runs without using SQL Server Configuration Manager, you need to enable decryption of the service master key that is encrypted with the credentials of the old account.

To enable decryption of the service master key by the new account while still running SQL Server under the old account, use this form of the ALTER SERVICE MASTER KEY statement:

```
ALTER SERVICE MASTER KEY
    WITH NEW_ACCOUNT = 'someAccount',
    NEW_PASSWORD = 'somePassword'
```

Don't use the preceding form if the new service account is network service, local service, or localsystem.

To enable decryption of the service master key by the new account while running SQL Server under the new account, use this form of the ALTER SERVICE MASTER KEY statement:

```
ALTER SERVICE MASTER KEY
    WITH OLD_ACCOUNT = 'someAccount',
    OLD_PASSWORD = 'somePassword'
```

Use the preceding form if the new service account is network service, local service, or localsystem.

If you change the service account for SQL Server 2005, use the SQL Server Configuration Manager. Using SQL Server Configuration Manager carries out any necessary encryptions and decryptions.

To back up the service master key, use the BACKUP SERVICE MASTER KEY statement of the following form:

```
BACKUP SERVICE MASTER KEY
TO FILE = 'pathToFile'
ENCRYPTION BY PASSWORD = 'somePassword'
```

The password is used to encrypt the service master key in the backup. The password should — due to the importance of the service master key — be a complex one. A note of the password should be stored carefully in a secure place offsite.

Given the importance of the service master key for encrypted data, you should carry out backing it up soon after you install SQL Server 2005.

To restore the service master key, use the RESTORE SERVICE MASTER KEY statement of the following form:

```
RESTORE SERVICE MASTER KEY
FROM FILE = 'pathToFile'
DECRYPTION BY PASSWORD = 'somePassword'
```

When the service master key is restored, SQL Server 2005 decrypts all the keys that had been encrypted with the current service master key. SQL Server then encrypts the keys using the copy of the service master key from the backup file. If any of the decryption operations fail, the restore fails. However, you can use the option that follows to force the service master key to be replaced during restoration, even at the risk of data loss:

```
RESTORE SERVICE MASTER KEY
FROM FILE = 'pathToFile'
DECRYPTION BY PASSWORD = 'somePassword' FORCE
```

Data whose key cannot be decrypted will be lost if you use the FORCE option.

At the database level, encryption relies on a database master key. The *database master key* is a symmetric key that is used to protect the private keys of certificates and asymmetric keys in a database. Once created, the database master key is encrypted using the Triple DES algorithm and a user-specified password. To enable automatic decryption, a copy of the key is encrypted using the service master key and stored in the current database and in the master database.

You create a database master key manually using the CREATE MASTER KEY statement.

Ensure that you're in the correct database by executing the following command:

```
USE <database_name>
```

Then, execute the following statement to create the database master key in the current database:

```
CREATE MASTER KEY
ENCRYPTION BY PASSWORD = 'somePassword'
```

Once you create the database master key, ensure that you back it up securely at an offsite location. If the database master key is deleted or corrupted, SQL Server will probably be unable to decrypt the other keys and certificates in the database. As a result, the data encrypted using those keys or certificates won't be accessible.

Choose a password to use when the copy of the database master key is stored on the backup media. That password should be different from the password used when you created the database master key.

If you have multiple databases with encrypted data in a SQL Server instance, be sure that you accurately note the passwords used to encrypt the database master key and to encrypt the backup. Be sure that you know which password is used for which purpose.

Backup the database master key using the following command:

```
BACKUP MASTER KEY
TO FILE = 'pathToFile'
ENCRYPTION BY PASSWORD = 'somePassword'
```

Store the backup file in a folder with very restrictive Access Control Lists on an appropriate hard disk. After you create the backup file, copy it to removable media. Verify the copy and store it offsite in a secure place.

Use the ALTER MASTER KEY statement to alter the properties of a database master key. One form of the ALTER MASTER KEY statement is used to regenerate the database master key:

```
ALTER MASTER KEY
REGENERATE WITH ENCRYPTION BY PASSWORD = 'somePassword'
```

Also, you can use the ALTER MASTER KEY statement to change how the encryption of the database master key is carried out.

If the encryption is currently by password, use the following statement to drop the password encryption:

```
ALTER MASTER KEY
DROP ENCRYPTION BY PASSWORD = 'somePassword'
```

Alternatively, you can drop encryption by the service master key by executing this statement:

```
ALTER MASTER KEY
DROP ENCRYPTION BY SERVICE MASTER KEY
```

To alter the database master key, use one of the following statements. To encrypt using a password, use this form:

```
ALTER MASTER KEY
ADD ENCRYPTION BY PASSWORD = 'somePassword'
```

To encrypt using the service master key, use this form:

```
ALTER MASTER KEY
ADD ENCRYPTION BY SERVICE MASTER KEY
```

If the database master key is encrypted using the service master key, encryption and decryption are carried out automatically.

Use the OPEN MASTER KEY statement to open the database master key of the current database:

```
OPEN MASTER KEY
DECRYPTION  BY PASSWORD = 'somePassword'
```

To close the database master key of the current database, execute the following statement:

```
CLOSE MASTER KEY
```

SQL Server 2005 supports the following mechanisms for encryption:

- ✔ **Certificates:** A certificate associates a value with a particular person, computer, or service. When two endpoints communicate with each other, they match the certificate to ensure that the two same endpoints are talking to each other, as they were when the certificate was first established. The benefit of using certificates is in their simplicity, establishing a level of trust between two endpoints in a communication.

- ✔ **Symmetric keys:** This method utilizes a single key for both encryption and decryption of communications. Only a single key is used, so this method is a little faster than asymmetric keys, but slightly less secure.

- ✔ **Asymmetric keys:** This is the most secure form of key in that there are two keys: a private key and a public key. Both keys can decrypt what is encrypted by the other key, but they can only encrypt using the private key. So each endpoint in a communication can encrypt its own originating data, but not the data from any other person or computer. As a result, asymmetric keys create more work than symmetric keys, and thus increase demand on resources. However, slightly more security is enabled. One of the best uses for an asymmetric key is for encrypting a symmetric key.

SQL Server 2005 supports the following security catalog views:

- ✔ `sys.asymmetric_keys`   Returns a row for each asymmetric key.
- ✔ `sys.certificates`   Returns a row for each certificate in the database.
- ✔ `sys.credentials`   Returns a row for each credential.
- ✔ `sys.crypt_properties`   Returns a row for each cryptographic property associated with a securable.
- ✔ `sys.key_encryptions`   Returns a row for each symmetric key specified using the `ENCRYPTION BY` clause of the `CREATE SYMMETRIC KEY` statement.
- ✔ `sys.symmetric_keys`   Returns a row for each symmetric key created using the `CREATE SYMMETRIC KEY` statement.

You can retrieve information about each asymmetric key from the `sys.asymmetric_keys` catalog view using the following statement:

```
SELECT *
FROM sys.asymmetric_keys
```

The following information is available about each asymmetric key:

- ✔ `name`   The name of the asymmetric key. It's unique in a database. The data type is `sysname`.
- ✔ `principal_id`   The ID of the database principal that owns the key.
- ✔ `asymmetric_key_id`   The ID of the asymmetric key. It's unique in the database.
- ✔ `pvt_key_encryption_type`   Specifies how the key is encrypted. The data type is `char(2)`. Allowed values are `NA` (not encrypted), `MK` (key is encrypted by the master key), `PW` (the key is encrypted using a user-defined password), and `SK` (the key is encrypted using the service master key).
- ✔ `pvt_key_encryption_type_desc`   A brief description of the encryption type. The data type is `nvarchar(60)`. Allowed values are `NO_PRIVATE_KEY`, `ENCRYPTED_BY_MASTER_KEY`, `ENCRYPTED_BY_PASSWORD`, and `ENCRYPTED_BY_SERVICE_MASTER_KEY`.
- ✔ `thumbprint`   A SHA-1 hash of the key. The data type is `varbinary(32)`.
- ✔ `algorithm`   The algorithm used with the key. The data type is `char(2)`. Allowed values are `1R` (512-bit RSA), `2R` (1024-bit RSA), and `3R` (2048-bit RSA).

✔ algorithm_desc   A brief description of the algorithm used with the key. Allowed values are RSA_512, RSA_1024, and RSA_2048.

✔ key_length   The length of the key in bits. The data type is int.

✔ sid   The login security identifier for this key. The data type is varbinary(85).

✔ string_sid   A string representation of the login security identifier for the key. The data type is nvarchar(128).

✔ public_key   The public key. The data type is varbinary(max).

✔ attested_by   For system use.

To display database certificates, use this command:

```
SELECT *
FROM sys.certificates
```

To display the cryptographic properties, use this command:

```
SELECT *
FROM sys.crypt_properties
```

Working with Asymmetric and Symmetric Encryption

SQL Server 2005 supports two types of key — asymmetric and symmetric. An *asymmetric key* includes a private key and the corresponding public key.

An asymmetric key's private key is 512-, 1024-, or 2048-bits long. By default, the database master key is used to protect the asymmetric key, assuming that a database master key exists for that database. Otherwise, a password is used.

To create an asymmetric key, use the CREATE ASYMMETRIC KEY statement:

```
CREATE ASYMMETRIC KEY <asymmetric_key_name>
FROM <asymmetric_key_source>
ENCRYPTION BY PASSWORD = 'somePassword'
```

or

```
CREATE ASYMMETRIC KEY <asymmetric_key_name>
WITH ALGORITHM = <algorithm_name>
ENCRYPTION BY PASSWORD = 'somePassword'
```

The allowed key sources are

- ✔ A strong name file (`FILE = 'pathToStrongNameFile'`)
- ✔ An executable file (`EXECUTABLE FILE = 'pathToExecutableFile'`)
- ✔ An assembly (`ASSEMBLY <assemblyName>`)

To alter an asymmetric key, use the `ALTER ASYMMETRIC KEY` statement. There are several ways to use the `ALTER ASYMMETRIC KEY` statement. For example, to change the password for the private key, use this form:

```
ALTER ASYMMETRIC KEY <asymmetric_key_name>
    WITH PRIVATE KEY (
    DECRYPTION BY PASSWORD = 'oldPassword',
    ENCRYPTION BY PASSWORD = 'newPassword')
```

To drop an asymmetric key, use the `DROP ASYMMETRIC KEY` statement:

```
DROP ASYMMETRIC KEY <asymmetric_key_name>
```

To create a symmetric key, use the `CREATE SYMMETRIC KEY` statement:

```
CREATE SYMMETRIC KEY
WITH <key_options>
ENCRYPTION BY <encrypting_mechanism>
```

The key options are

- ✔ `KEY_SOURCE = 'somePassword'`
- ✔ `ALGORITHM = <some_supported_Algorithm>`
- ✔ `IDENTITY VALUE = <identity_phrase>`

The encrypting mechanisms are

- ✔ `CERTIFICATE <certificate_name>`
- ✔ `PASSWORD = 'somePassword'`
- ✔ `SYMMETRIC_KEY <symmetric_key_name>`
- ✔ `ASYMMETRIC_KEY <asymmetric_key_name>`

The supported algorithms are

- ✔ DES
- ✔ Triple DES
- ✔ RC2

- ✔ RC4
- ✔ RC4_128
- ✔ DESX
- ✔ AES_128
- ✔ AES_192
- ✔ AES_256

To drop a symmetric key, use the DROP SYMMETRIC KEY statement:

```
DROP SYMMETRIC KEY <symmetric_key_name>
```

Using Certificates

Certificates are created in order to establish a level of trust between two end-points in a communication. When you visit a new Web site on the Internet and try to download a new goodie, sometimes your browser asks you if you really trust the content from that site. That means that there is no certificate established between your computer (or your computer's browser) and the site in question.

To create a certificate, use the CREATE CERTIFICATE statement.

The following example shows how to create a self-signed certificate called Test:

```
CREATE CERTIFICATE Test
    ENCRYPTION BY PASSWORD = 'abc123'
    WITH SUBJECT = 'A self-signed certificate',
    EXPIRY_DATE = '12/31/2007'
```

To confirm that you've successfully created the certificate called Test, execute the following statement:

```
SELECT *
FROM sys.certificates
WHERE name = 'Test'
```

Figure 19-1 shows the result of executing the preceding statement.

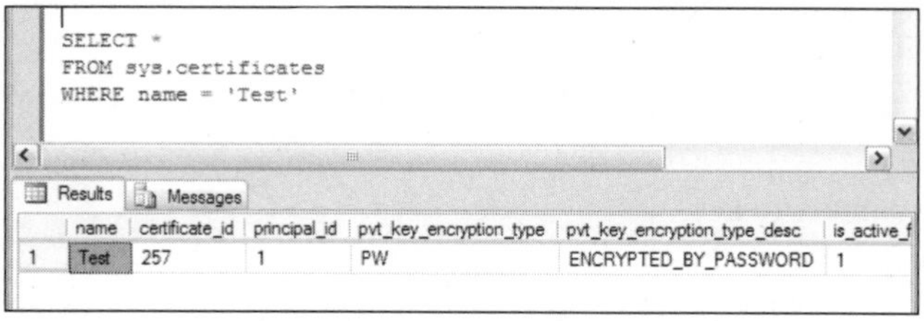

Figure 19-1:
Retrieving
information
from
sys.certifi-
cates about
the Test
certificate.

```
SELECT *
FROM sys.certificates
WHERE name = 'Test'
```

	name	certificate_id	principal_id	pvt_key_encryption_type	pvt_key_encryption_type_desc	is_active_f
1	Test	257	1	PW	ENCRYPTED_BY_PASSWORD	1

Encrypting Data

The following example illustrates how you can encrypt data in a specified
column. First, create a database called Chapter19.

```
USE master
CREATE DATABASE Chapter19
```

Make Chapter19 the current database.

```
USE Chapter19
```

Create a database master key.

```
CREATE MASTER KEY ENCRYPTION BY
    PASSWORD = 'abcd1234DEFG??'
```

Create a certificate called Chapter19TestCertificate.

```
CREATE CERTIFICATE Chapter19TestCertificate
   WITH SUBJECT = 'Test for Chapter 19'
```

Create a symmetric key called TestSymmetricKey to be encrypted by the
newly created certificate Chapter19TestCertificate.

```
CREATE SYMMETRIC KEY TestSymmetricKey
    WITH ALGORITHM = DES
    ENCRYPTION BY CERTIFICATE Chapter19TestCertificate
```

Create a table called WithEncryptedColumn that contains unencrypted and
encrypted messages.

```
CREATE TABLE WithEncryptedColumn
(MessageID int IDENTITY,
 OpenMessage varchar(200),
 EncryptedMessage varbinary (256)
)
```

Open the symmetric key.

```
OPEN SYMMETRIC KEY TestSymmetricKey
 DECRYPTION BY CERTIFICATE Chapter19TestCertificate
```

Insert unencrypted data into the OpenMessage column.

```
INSERT
INTO WithEncryptedColumn (OpenMessage)
VALUES ('Hello world.')
```

Update the WithEncryptedColumn table so that the value stored in the OpenMessage column is stored, in an encrypted form, in the EncryptedMessage column.

```
UPDATE WithEncryptedColumn
SET EncryptedMessage =
           EncryptByKey(Key_GUID('TestSymmetricKey'),
           OpenMessage)
```

Confirm that the data has been successfully inserted into the EncryptedMessage column in an encrypted form.

```
SELECT *
FROM WithEncryptedColumn
```

Figure 19-2 shows the result of executing the preceding command. Notice that the simple message is shown unencrypted in the OpenMessage column but is encrypted in the EncryptedMessage column.

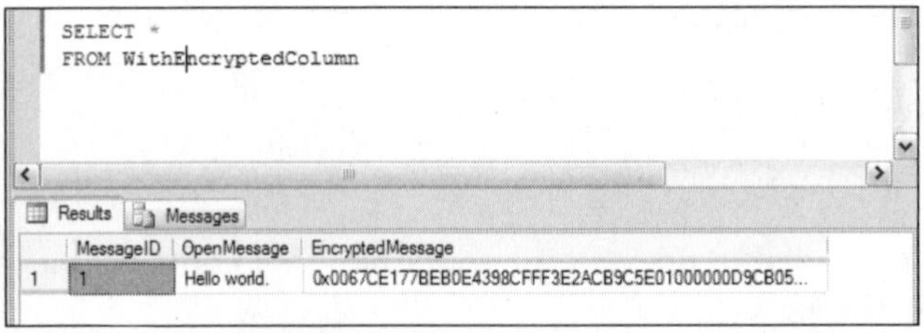

Figure 19-2: Unencrypted and encrypted data.

Part V

Beyond Transact-SQL Programming

The 5th Wave

By Rich Tennant

BEAL & BEAL
DATABASE
CONSULTANTS

"Your database is beyond repair, but before I tell you our backup recommendation, let me ask you a question. How many index cards do you think will fit on the walls of your computer room?"

In this part . . .

This part introduces some programming features that you can take advantage of, including XML, the Common Language Runtime (CLR), Visual Studio, and SQL Server Management Objects (SQL-SMO).

XML is an acronym for the eXtensible Markup Language. XML is essentially a data file, which contains both data and metadata. A single XML document can act just like a database and, in fact, is a database in itself (because it contains both data and metadata — it's self-descriptive). Additionally, XML documents are a universal standard that can be automatically interpreted and displayed in an Internet Web browser, such as Internet Explorer. SQL Server 2005 allows storage of embedded and executable XML documents inside SQL Server databases. This means you can execute standardized XML functionality directly on an XML document, which is stored in a database.

The CLR is essentially the .NET Framework inside SQL Server 2005. The .NET Framework allows programming of executable objects in any compatible programming language. Those compiled executables can then be executed from within SQL Server 2005 as .NET Framework objects. In other words, you can write stored procedures in any compatible programming language.

Microsoft Visual Studio is a Microsoft Software Development Kit (SDK), which, like many Microsoft products, is well integrated with SQL Server 2005. The Management Server is entirely constructed using the SQL-SMO. SQL Server 2005 programming gives you access to the SQL-SMO.

Chapter 20

Working with XML

*I*n previous editions of SQL Server, the only way to store data was in relational form. XML data had to be shredded into a relational form for storage and had to be reassembled for display or other uses. With the increasing interchange of data using XML, creating relational structures for the XML data isn't always easy. In addition, converting data from XML to relational data for storage in SQL Server and converting it back again to XML for display or other output can be resource intensive. As a result of such considerations, SQL Server 2005 supports the storage of XML documents as XML.

In this chapter, I introduce the approach to storing and manipulating XML data taken in SQL Server 2005. I show you how to store and retrieve untyped and typed XML data and discuss how to use XML schema documents.

I introduce the XML Query Language, XQuery, which you can use in SQL Server 2005 to retrieve XML data when it's stored using the xml data type. SQL Server 2005 also supports extensions to XQuery that allow you to carry out insert, update, and delete operations on data stored as the xml data type.

I show you how to create an index on an XML column. I also discuss how you can expose relational data as XML using the FOR XML clause.

XML in SQL Server 2005

You might wonder why XML should be stored in a relational database. After all, there are specialized XML databases. Several reasons support the storage of XML in relational databases, including the following:

- ✔ Relational databases have the capacity to back up data manually or on a schedule.
- ✔ In a relational database, you can break data into file groups or partitions.
- ✔ Relational databases have well-tested security mechanisms.
- ✔ Relational databases can index data.
- ✔ Relational databases that can store XML provide a "one-stop shop" for storing all your data.

In SQL Server 2005, Microsoft has made several improvements in the support for XML, compared to SQL Server 2000. The new or improved features are

- ✔ An xml data type to allow you to store XML documents and fragments
- ✔ Support of a subset of the XQuery (XML Query) language under development at the W3C (World Wide Web Consortium)
- ✔ Support of an XML Data Modification Language to allow you to insert, update, or delete XML data
- ✔ Support of the indexing of XML data
- ✔ Extension of the FOR XML clause
- ✔ The introduction of XML Web Services, which is outside the scope of this book

You can use the xml data type to store XML documents in a column in a relational table or as a Transact-SQL variable. In addition, you can use the xml data type for parameters of stored procedures or functions. You can store XML documents as complete documents (that is, *well-formed XML documents*) or document fragments. A *well-formed XML document* has a single document element with all other elements in the document being descendants of that element (as well as satisfying other technical criteria). An *XML document fragment* may have multiple document elements and strictly speaking, isn't a well-formed XML document.

You can store XML fragments only if the XML is typed. I describe how to store typed XML later in this chapter.

The following document is a well-formed XML document. It has a single document element, books, with all other elements in the document (in this case, book elements) being descendants of the books element.

```
<books>
  <book>
    <title>SQL Server 2005 for Dummies</title>
    <author>Andrew Watt</author>
  </book>
  <book>
    <title>SQL Server 2005 Programming for Dummies</title>
    <author>Andrew Watt</author>
  </book>
</books>
```

The following is an XML fragment. There are two book elements that are not enclosed in a single document element. An XML parser would not accept the fragment as a well-formed XML document.

```
<book>
  <title>SQL Server 2005 for Dummies</title>
  <author>Andrew Watt</author>
</book>
<book>
  <title>SQL Server 2005 Programming for Dummies</title>
  <author>Andrew Watt</author>
</book>
```

One of the characteristics of an XML fragment is that if you wrap it in a single document element, the result is well-formed XML.

XQuery was designed by the World Wide Web Consortium as a general-purpose query language for XML. In SQL Server 2005, XQuery is incorporated into the Transact-SQL language to allow you to query data stored using the xml data type.

The FOR XML clause is used with the Transact-SQL SELECT statement to generate XML output.

Using Typed and Untyped XML

When you use the XML data type in a table column, you can store the XML as *typed* or *untyped* XML. *Typed XML* is XML that conforms to an XML schema document in a collection of XML schema documents. Untyped XML need not conform to a schema.

The stored representation of an XML document, whether typed or untyped, must not exceed 2GB.

The examples in this chapter use the Chapter20 database. Execute the following commands to create the Chapter20 database and set it as the current database:

```
USE master
CREATE DATABASE Chapter20

USE Chapter20
```

To store XML data in an untyped XML column, you use the CREATE TABLE statement in the usual way and specify the data type of the column as xml. The following CREATE TABLE statement for the Books table creates a column, BookInfo, of data type xml:

```
CREATE TABLE Books
(
BookID int IDENTITY PRIMARY KEY,
BookInfo xml
)
```

Then insert two rows into the Books table using the following statements:

```
INSERT
INTO Books
VALUES ('<book>
    <title>SQL Server 2005 for Dummies</title>
    <author>Andrew Watt</author>
  </book>')

INSERT
INTO Books
VALUES ('<book>
    <title>SQL Server 2005 Programming for Dummies</title>
    <author>Andrew Watt</author>
  </book>')
```

Notice that the XML content is shown as a string inside paired apostrophes in the VALUES clause, as with any other string value.

Confirm that the two rows have been successfully inserted using the following command:

```
SELECT *
FROM Books
```

Figure 20-1 shows the results.

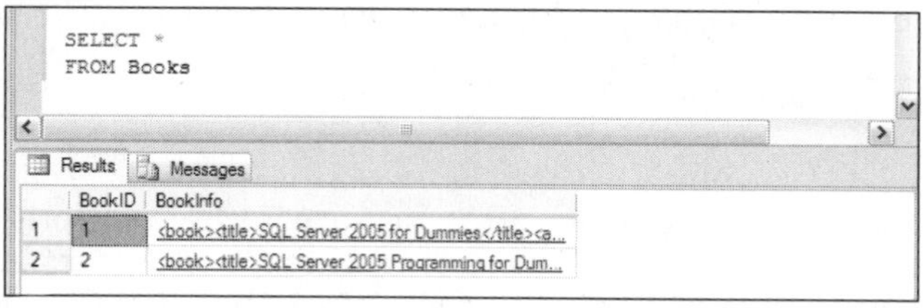

Figure 20-1:
Reading XML data from a string.

The XML returned from the `BookInfo` column is a hyperlink. You can click on the data returned in each row and open the XML document in a separate tab in SQL Server Management Studio. Figure 20-2 shows the XML data from the first row in Figure 20-1. As you can see, even with a short XML document, the display in a separate tab makes it easier to see the structure and content of an XML document, as compared to the display in Figure 20-1.

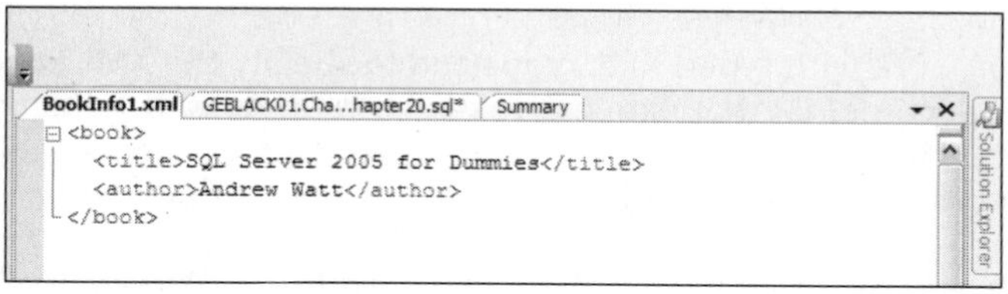

Figure 20-2:
Displaying an XML document from the BookInfo column in a separate tab.

The XML that you insert into the `BookInfo` column is checked for well-formedness. (In other words, it's checked to ensure that it's actually technically correct XML.) But it isn't checked for whether it conforms to an XML schema document because it's untyped XML.

If you attempt to insert a string that looks like XML but isn't well-formed, an error message is displayed. The following statement attempts to insert a document that superficially looks like XML but isn't well-formed. Notice in the last line of the code the `<book>` start tag that should be `</book>` (an end tag).

```
INSERT
INTO Books
VALUES ('<book>
    <title>SQL Server 2005 Express Edition for
           Dummies</title>
  <author>Robert Schneider</author>
  <book>')
```

If you execute the preceding code, the following error message appears:

```
Msg 9400, Level 16, State 1, Line 1
XML parsing: line 4, character 8, unexpected end of input
```

If you're unfamiliar with XML, the error message might be surprising. From the XML parser's point of view, you have two <book> start tags but no end tag. So it's unexpected that the document ends without the two end tags to correspond to the two <book> start tags that are present. If you correct the preceding code so that it reads:

```
INSERT
INTO Books
VALUES ('<book>
    <title>SQL Server 2005 Express Edition for
          Dummies</title>
    <author>Robert Schneider</author>
  </book>')
```

it will insert correctly into the Books table.

When you work with typed XML, you need to specify the XML schema document (or documents) that data has to conform to. An XML schema document can contain information about the structure of XML elements and can specify the data type for data in specific elements in an XML document.

To create an XML schema collection, you need to have created a W3C schema document — sometimes called an *XSD schema document* — because the file extension is .xsd. You either need to have an understanding of the W3C XML Schema standard or use a tool or colleague who can create a schema document for you.

To create an XML schema collection, use the CREATE XML SCHEMA COLLECTION statement. The following statement creates an XML schema collection, SingleBookSchemaCollection. After you paste the schema from Visual Studio 2005, you need to change the encoding from utf-8 to utf-16. If you don't do that, you will see an error message.

```
CREATE XML SCHEMA COLLECTION SingleBookSchemaCollection AS
N'<?xml version="1.0" encoding="utf-16"?>
<xs:schema attributeFormDefault="unqualified"
          elementFormDefault="qualified"
          xmlns:xs="http://www.w3.org/2001/XMLSchema">
        <xs:element name="book">
                                        <xs:complexType>
```

```
                                        <xs:sequence>

        <xs:element name="title" type="xs:string" />

        <xs:element name="author" type="xs:string" />

                                        </xs:sequence>

                                    </xs:complexType>
            </xs:element>
</xs:schema>'
```

The schema document specifies that the XML document contains a book element with two child elements, title and author.

Be careful that the first characters in the schema are `<?xml`. In the following code, a newline character is at the end of the second line before the `<?xml`, and an error message is displayed.

```
CREATE XML SCHEMA COLLECTION SingleBookSchemaCollection AS
N'
<?xml version="1.0" encoding="utf-8"?>
<xs:schema attributeFormDefault="unqualified"
        elementFormDefault="qualified"
        xmlns:xs="http://www.w3.org/2001/XMLSchema">
        <xs:element name="book">
                                    <xs:complexType>

                                    <xs:sequence>

        <xs:element name="title" type="xs:string" />

        <xs:element name="author" type="xs:string" />

                                    </xs:sequence>
                                    </xs:complexType>
            </xs:element>
</xs:schema>'
```

To view the XML Schema collection that you created, use the following SELECT statement:

```
SELECT
            xml_schema_namespace(N'dbo',N'SingleBookSchemaC
            ollection')
```

Figure 20-3 shows the result when there is a single XML schema document in the collection.

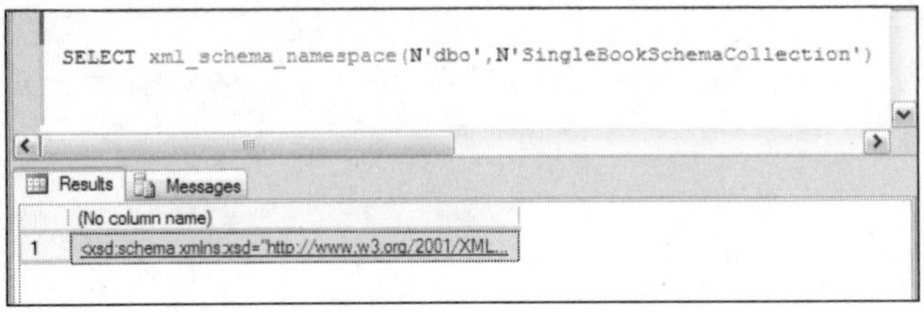

Figure 20-3:
Viewing the
document(s)
in an XML
schema
collection.

An alternative way to view XML schema collection information is to execute

```
SELECT *
FROM sys.xml_schema_collections
```

You need to associate the XML schema collection with a column (or variable) of xml data type. The following statement creates a table, BooksTyped, where the BookInfo column is the xml data type, which is typed according to the SingleBookSchemaCollection XML schema collection.

```
CREATE TABLE BooksTyped
(
BookID int IDENTITY PRIMARY KEY,
BookInfo xml (dbo.SingleBookSchemaCollection)
)
```

To insert a row, use the same syntax as for untyped XML data:

```
INSERT
INTO BOOKS
VALUES ('<book>
    <title>SQL Server 2005 for Dummies</title>
    <author>Andrew Watt</author>
  </book>')
```

If you attempt to insert a row that doesn't conform to the schema document, an error message is displayed. The following statement attempts to insert an XML document that contains a publisher element not specified in the schema document:

```
INSERT
INTO BooksTyped
VALUES ('<book>
    <title>SQL Server 2005 Programming for Dummies</title>
    <author>Andrew Watt</author>
    <publisher>Wiley Publishing</publisher>
  </book>')
```

The following error message is displayed. The `Location` indicates that a `publisher` element is present and wasn't expected, according to the schema. The final line of the error message is an XPath (XML Path language) *location path,* which specifies where the unexpected element occurs.

```
Msg 6923, Level 16, State 1, Line 1
XML Validation: Unexpected element(s): publisher.
        Location: /*:book[1]/*:publisher[1]
```

If you remove the `publisher` element, the XML document inserts as expected. However, you might want to accept XML documents that also have a `publisher` element.

One approach is to add another XML schema collection, by executing the following code:

```
CREATE XML SCHEMA COLLECTION SingleBookSchemaCollection2
AS
N'<?xml version="1.0" encoding="utf-16"?>
<xs:schema attributeFormDefault="unqualified"
        elementFormDefault="qualified"
        xmlns:xs="http://www.w3.org/2001/XMLSchema">
        <xs:element name="book">
                                <xs:complexType>

                                <xs:sequence>

        <xs:element name="title" type="xs:string" />

        <xs:element name="author" type="xs:string" />
                <xs:element name="publisher"
        type="xs:string" minOccurs="0" maxOccurs="1" />

                                </xs:sequence>
                                </xs:complexType>

        </xs:element>
</xs:schema>'
```

Notice in the `xs:element` element the `minOccurs` and `maxOccurs` attributes that define the minimum and maximum allowed occurrences of the `publisher` element.

You then use the `ALTER TABLE` statement to alter the `BookInfo` column to use the `SingleBookSchemaCollection2` XML schema collection:

```
ALTER TABLE BooksTyped
ALTER COLUMN BookInfo xml(SingleBookSchemaCollection2)
```

You can then insert the row that includes a `publisher` element by executing the following code:

```
INSERT
INTO BooksTyped
VALUES ('<book>
    <title>SQL Server 2005 Programming for Dummies</title>
    <author>Andrew Watt</author>
    <publisher>Wiley Publishing</publisher>
  </book>')
```

In addition, you can insert a row that has no `publisher` element in the XML document:

```
INSERT
INTO BooksTyped
VALUES ('<book>
    <title>SQL Server 2005 Express Edition for
          Dummies</title>
    <author>Robert Schneider</author>
  </book>')
```

To alter an XML schema collection, use the `ALTER XML SCHEMA COLLECTION` statement. The `ALTER XML SCHEMA COLLECTION` statement allows you to add new schema components to an existing XML schema collection.

To delete an XML schema collection, use the `DROP XML SCHEMA COLLECTION` statement. For example, execute this command if you want to delete the `SingleBookSchemaCollection` XML schema collection:

```
DROP XML SCHEMA COLLECTION SingleBookSchemaCollection
```

Querying XML Data

SQL Server 2005 includes a subset of the XQuery language, which is under development by the World Wide Web Consortium (W3C). The syntax of XQuery is based on a nonfinal draft of the XQuery specification. However, it's hoped that the final XQuery syntax and the syntax in the subset used in SQL Server 2005 will be the same.

In the context of SQL Server 2005, XQuery is a language for querying data stored using the `xml` data type. The full syntax of XQuery is complex. Detailed consideration of its syntax is beyond the scope of this chapter.

To retrieve data from a column of `xml` data type, you append `query` to a column name using dot notation. So, to retrieve information from the `BookInfo` column in the `BooksTyped` table, use the following query:

```
USE Chapter20
SELECT BookInfo.query('/book')
FROM dbo.BooksTyped
```

Figure 20-4 shows the result of executing the preceding command in SQL Server Management Studio. The content of the paired parentheses is an XQuery expression. In this case, it's also an XPath 2.0 expression, meaning start at the `root` node (indicated by the forward slash) and find a `book` element.

Figure 20-4:
Retrieving
data from
an XML
column.

```
USE Chapter20
SELECT BookInfo.query('/book')
FROM dbo.BooksTyped
```

	(No column name)
1	\<book>\<title>SQL Server 2005 for Dummies\</title>\<author>Andrew Watt\</author>\</book>
2	\<book>\<title>SQL Server 2005 Programming for Dummies\</title>\<author>Andrew Watt\</author>\<publishe...
3	\<book>\<title>SQL Server 2005 Express Edition for Dummies\</title>\<author>Robert Schneider\</author>\</...

You can combine data from relational columns and XML columns in a single `SELECT` statement. For example, the following statement retrieves both the ID of a book and the data from the `BookInfo` column.

```
USE Chapter20
SELECT BookID, BookInfo.query('/book')
FROM dbo.BooksTyped
```

The XQuery expression inside the parentheses can focus the query. For example, the following query retrieves the `author` element and its content.

```
USE Chapter20
SELECT BookID, BookInfo.query('/book/author')
FROM dbo.BooksTyped
```

Figure 20-5 shows the results of executing the preceding code.

Figure 20-5:
Retrieving
information
in the author
element.

You can combine an XQuery query with other clauses in the SELECT statement. For example, the following statement uses the WHERE clause to filter the results returned by the SELECT statement.

```
USE Chapter20
SELECT BookID, BookInfo.query('/book')
FROM dbo.BooksTyped
WHERE BookID = 3
```

DML on XML data

The official version of XQuery available at the time that SQL Server 2005 was being designed had no support for operations such as INSERT, UPDATE, and DELETE. Microsoft added proprietary extensions to the XQuery language to allow data to be inserted, updated, and deleted.

The DML supports three operations:

✔ insert
✔ delete
✔ replace value of

When inserting into an xml data type, you have the following options:

✔ as first
✔ as last
✔ into
✔ after
✔ before

The following UPDATE statement shows how to add a publisher element as last.

```
UPDATE Books
SET BookInfo.modify('insert <publisher>Wiley
          Publishing</publisher>
 as last
 into (/book)[1]')
```

Execute the following statement to show the modified rows in the Books table.

```
SELECT *
FROM Books
```

Figure 20-6 shows the XML document returned for one row in the results.

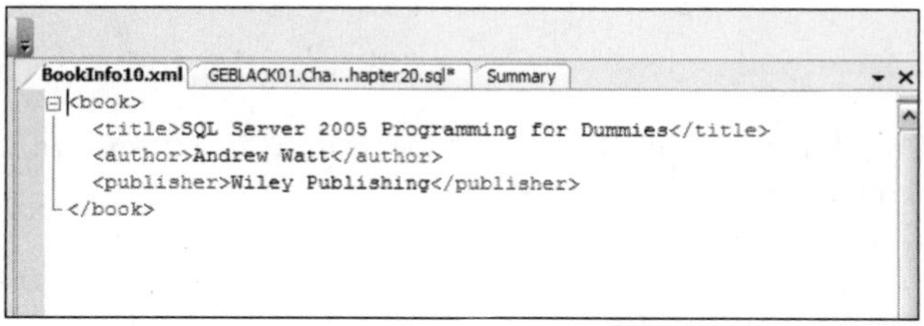

Figure 20-6: A publisher element added to an XML document.

```
BookInfo10.xml   GEBLACK01.Cha...hapter20.sql*   Summary
<book>
    <title>SQL Server 2005 Programming for Dummies</title>
    <author>Andrew Watt</author>
    <publisher>Wiley Publishing</publisher>
</book>
```

To insert an ISBN element after the author element, use the following command:

```
UPDATE Books
SET BookInfo.modify('insert <ISBN>Not yet known.</ISBN>
 after (/book/author)[1]
 ')
```

Confirm the successful inserts using the following command:

```
SELECT *
FROM Books
```

Figure 20-7 shows the XML document with an ISBN element added.

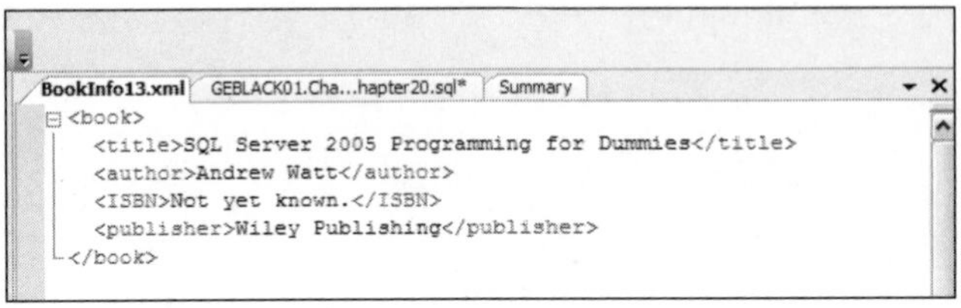

Figure 20-7:
An ISBN
element has
been added
after the
author
element.

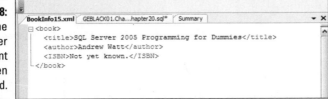

```
BookInfo13.xml   GEBLACK01.Cha...hapter20.sql*   Summary                    ▼ ✕
⊟ <book>                                                                      ⌃
     <title>SQL Server 2005 Programming for Dummies</title>
     <author>Andrew Watt</author>
     <ISBN>Not yet known.</ISBN>
     <publisher>Wiley Publishing</publisher>
   └ </book>
```

To delete the `publisher` element, use the following statement:

```
UPDATE Books
SET BookInfo.modify('delete /book/publisher')
```

Confirm the successful deletion by executing the following code:

```
SELECT *
FROM Books
```

Click the XML document in the second row. Figure 20-8 shows that the `publisher` element has been deleted.

Figure 20-8:
The
publisher
element
has been
deleted.

```
BookInfo15.xml   GEBLACK01.Cha...hapter20.sql*   Summary                    ▼ ✕
⊟ <book>                                                                      ⌃
     <title>SQL Server 2005 Programming for Dummies</title>
     <author>Andrew Watt</author>
     <ISBN>Not yet known.</ISBN>
   └ </book>
```

To replace the value of the `ISBN` element for all rows in the `Books` table, execute this statement:

```
UPDATE Books
SET BookInfo.modify('replace value of
(/book/ISBN/text())[1]
with "07645774227" ')
```

Execute the following statement to confirm that the data has changed:

```
SELECT *
FROM Books
```

Click on the XML document in the second row. Figure 20-9 shows that the value of the ISBN element has been changed.

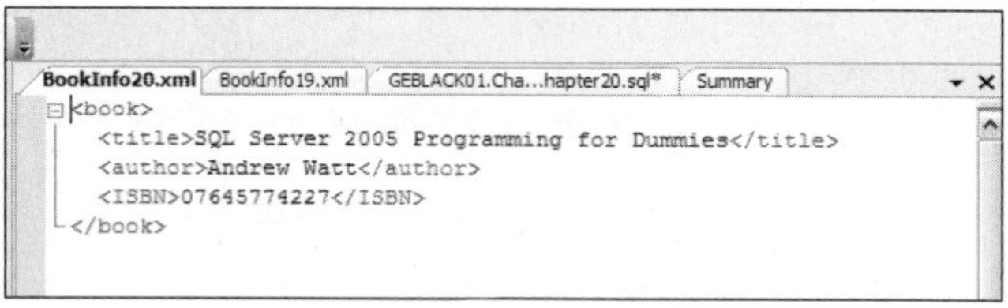

Figure 20-9:
The value of
the ISBN
element
has been
changed.

```
BookInfo20.xml   BookInfo19.xml   GEBLACK01.Cha...hapter20.sql*   Summary        ▾ ✕
<book>
    <title>SQL Server 2005 Programming for Dummies</title>
    <author>Andrew Watt</author>
    <ISBN>07645774227</ISBN>
</book>
```

These examples give you an example of how you can insert, delete, and replace the values of parts of an XML document in a column of xml data type. XQuery provides control structures to let you apply, for example, conditional logic to modify() operations.

Indexing XML

XML data stored as the xml data type is stored internally as *binary large objects* (BLOBs). These BLOBs are allowed to be up to 2GB in size. In the absence of an index, the relevant BLOBs are shredded at runtime to evaluate a query. There are similarities to a table scan on relational data. If the BLOB is large, the query can be slow. If an index has been created on a column of data type xml, associated queries execute more quickly.

As with all indexes, consider the potential trade-off of improving query speed when an index exists, compared to the additional processing overhead each time that data is added to the table that contains the column of data type xml.

On a column of data type xml, SQL Server 2005 supports the following indexes:

✓ **Primary XML index:** Indexes an XML column
✓ **Secondary XML index:** Indexes values within an XML document

To create a primary XML index, BookInfoIndex, on the BookInfo column in the Books table, use this command:

```
USE Chapter20
CREATE PRIMARY XML INDEX BookInfoIndex
ON dbo.Books (BookInfo)
```

To confirm the successful creation of the primary XML index, execute the following command:

```
SELECT *
FROM sys.indexes
WHERE name = 'BookInfoIndex'
```

SQL Server 2005 supports the following types of secondary XML indexes:

- ✔ PATH   If your queries frequently use XPath paths

- ✔ VALUE   If your queries use values

- ✔ PROPERTY   If your queries frequently use the values() method of the xml data type

Exposing Relational Data as XML

SQL Server 2005 provides a lot of support for storing data as XML using the XML data type. An alternative approach is to store data as relational data and to expose that relational data, when appropriate, as XML.

You can use the following modes in a FOR XML clause in SQL Server 2005:

- ✔ RAW   The RAW mode returns a single row element for each rowset returned. To generate an element hierarchy, use nested SELECT statements.

- ✔ AUTO   The AUTO mode produces hierarchical XML automatically, as the mode's name suggests. You have little control over the structure produced.

- ✔ EXPLICIT   The EXPLICT mode is extremely complex to use. I suggest you avoid it unless no other mode can give you the results you want.

- ✔ PATH   You can use the PATH mode with nested FOR XML clauses to flexibly produce XML structures.

Exposing relational data as XML means that you can use simple queries to read tables and produce XML documents. The following query uses RAW mode to return the rows of a single table as XML data:

```
USE AdventureWorks
SELECT * FROM Person.CountryRegion FOR XML RAW
```

This is a partial result, showing each row converted to a single XML element:

```
<row CountryRegionCode="AD" Name="Andorra" ModifiedDate="1998-06-01T00:00:00" />
<row CountryRegionCode="AE" Name="United Arab Emirates"
            ModifiedDate="1998-06-01T00:00:00" />
<row CountryRegionCode="AF" Name="Afghanistan"
            ModifiedDate="1998-06-01T00:00:00" />
<row CountryRegionCode="AG" Name="Antigua and Barbuda"
            ModifiedDate="1998-06-01T00:00:00" />
<row CountryRegionCode="AI" Name="Anguilla" ModifiedDate="1998-06-01T00:00:00"
            />
```

And you can change the name of the element using this query:

```
SELECT * FROM Person.CountryRegion FOR XML RAW('region')
```

And this is another partial result, with the element name now set to *region:*

```
<region CountryRegionCode="AD" Name="Andorra" ModifiedDate="1998-06-01T00:00:00"
            />
<region CountryRegionCode="AE" Name="United Arab Emirates"
            ModifiedDate="1998-06-01T00:00:00" />
<region CountryRegionCode="AF" Name="Afghanistan"
            ModifiedDate="1998-06-01T00:00:00" />
<region CountryRegionCode="AG" Name="Antigua and Barbuda"
            ModifiedDate="1998-06-01T00:00:00" />
<region CountryRegionCode="AI" Name="Anguilla"
            ModifiedDate="1998-06-01T00:00:00" />
```

The next example uses the ELEMENTS clause to convert all attributes into child elements:

```
SELECT * FROM Person.CountryRegion FOR XML RAW('region'), ELEMENTS
```

Now as you can see, the region element contains elements of what were attributes in the previous example:

```
<region>
  <CountryRegionCode>AD</CountryRegionCode>
  <Name>Andorra</Name>
  <ModifiedDate>1998-06-01T00:00:00</ModifiedDate>
</region>
<region>
  <CountryRegionCode>AE</CountryRegionCode>
  <Name>United Arab Emirates</Name>
  <ModifiedDate>1998-06-01T00:00:00</ModifiedDate>
</region>
```

Now to make things interesting, join two tables together:

```
SELECT * FROM Person.CountryRegion c
    INNER JOIN Person.StateProvince s
ON(c.CountryRegionCode=s.CountryRegionCode)
FOR XML RAW('region'), ELEMENTS
```

This is a partial result, showing both country and state elements, all contained within the region element, as elements themselves:

```
<region>
  <CountryRegionCode>AS</CountryRegionCode>
  <Name>American Samoa</Name>
  <ModifiedDate>1998-06-01T00:00:00</ModifiedDate>
  <StateProvinceID>5</StateProvinceID>
  <StateProvinceCode>AS </StateProvinceCode>
  <CountryRegionCode>AS</CountryRegionCode>
  <IsOnlyStateProvinceFlag>1</IsOnlyStateProvinceFlag>
  <Name>American Samoa</Name>
  <TerritoryID>1</TerritoryID>
  <rowguid>255D15E1-9F6E-4CF8-9E5F-6B3858AD9B6A</rowguid>
  <ModifiedDate>2004-03-11T10:17:21.587</ModifiedDate>
</region>
```

So that's RAW mode. Now I'll discuss AUTO mode, which is a little more sophisticated than RAW mode. Here's the join again but this time in AUTO mode:

```
SELECT * FROM Person.CountryRegion c
    INNER JOIN Person.StateProvince s
ON(c.CountryRegionCode=s.CountryRegionCode)
FOR XML AUTO
```

This is another partial result, showing that AUTO mode has produced a hierarchically structured XML document:

```
<c CountryRegionCode="AS" Name="American Samoa"
            ModifiedDate="1998-06-01T00:00:00">
  <s StateProvinceID="5" StateProvinceCode="AS " CountryRegionCode="AS"
            IsOnlyStateProvinceFlag="1" Name="American Samoa" TerritoryID="1"
            rowguid="255D15E1-9F6E-4CF8-9E5F-6B3858AD9B6A"
            ModifiedDate="2004-03-11T10:17:21.587" />
</c>
<c CountryRegionCode="AU" Name="Australia" ModifiedDate="1998-06-01T00:00:00">
  <s StateProvinceID="50" StateProvinceCode="NSW" CountryRegionCode="AU"
            IsOnlyStateProvinceFlag="0" Name="New South Wales" TerritoryID="9"
            rowguid="9910DD7E-A4C5-4599-86F5-9F581B53A92D"
            ModifiedDate="2004-03-11T10:17:21.587" />
```

```
    <s StateProvinceID="64" StateProvinceCode="QLD" CountryRegionCode="AU"
            IsOnlyStateProvinceFlag="0" Name="Queensland" TerritoryID="9"
            rowguid="152658FA-AD59-4FA0-82A6-F76980F0183F"
            ModifiedDate="2004-03-11T10:17:21.587" />
    <s StateProvinceID="66" StateProvinceCode="SA " CountryRegionCode="AU"
            IsOnlyStateProvinceFlag="0" Name="South Australia" TerritoryID="9"
            rowguid="DCAE37CD-FD8D-41FE-90ED-EDAD22B63DC8"
            ModifiedDate="2004-03-11T10:17:21.587" />
    <s StateProvinceID="71" StateProvinceCode="TAS" CountryRegionCode="AU"
            IsOnlyStateProvinceFlag="0" Name="Tasmania" TerritoryID="9"
            rowguid="2DB59B03-9F19-4D12-ACEF-974016827BE1"
            ModifiedDate="2004-03-11T10:17:21.587" />
    <s StateProvinceID="77" StateProvinceCode="VIC" CountryRegionCode="AU"
            IsOnlyStateProvinceFlag="0" Name="Victoria" TerritoryID="9"
            rowguid="6A683928-8F1F-4369-A64A-60979E216824"
            ModifiedDate="2004-03-11T10:17:21.587" />
</c>
```

Next add the ROOT and ELEMENTS clauses as follows:

```
SELECT * FROM Person.CountryRegion c
   INNER JOIN Person.StateProvince s
ON(c.CountryRegionCode=s.CountryRegionCode)
FOR XML AUTO,ROOT,ELEMENTS
```

You get further improvement as a result:

```
<root>
  <c>
    <CountryRegionCode>AS</CountryRegionCode>
    <Name>American Samoa</Name>
    <ModifiedDate>1998-06-01T00:00:00</ModifiedDate>
    <s>
      <StateProvinceID>5</StateProvinceID>
      <StateProvinceCode>AS </StateProvinceCode>
      <CountryRegionCode>AS</CountryRegionCode>
      <IsOnlyStateProvinceFlag>1</IsOnlyStateProvinceFlag>
      <Name>American Samoa</Name>
      <TerritoryID>1</TerritoryID>
      <rowguid>255D15E1-9F6E-4CF8-9E5F-6B3858AD9B6A</rowguid>
      <ModifiedDate>2004-03-11T10:17:21.587</ModifiedDate>
    </s>
  </c>
```

And here's XML PATH in a query:

```
SELECT CountryRegionCode, Name, ModifiedDate
FROM Person.CountryRegion
FOR XML PATH('country'),ROOT
```

This example changes the *region* element into a *country* element. This is once again, a partial result:

```
<root>
  <country>
    <CountryRegionCode>AD</CountryRegionCode>
    <Name>Andorra</Name>
    <ModifiedDate>1998-06-01T00:00:00</ModifiedDate>
  </country>
  <country>
    <CountryRegionCode>AE</CountryRegionCode>
    <Name>United Arab Emirates</Name>
    <ModifiedDate>1998-06-01T00:00:00</ModifiedDate>
  </country>
  ...
</root>\
```

Chapter 21

Working with the Common Language Runtime

Microsoft invested a lot in the .NET Framework as its fundamental programming model and platform. The .NET Framework provides numerous classes that support a broad range of programming tasks, which can allow you to program applications that would be difficult, time-consuming, or even impossible to code in Transact-SQL.

In this chapter, I introduce the Common Language Runtime (CLR) and describe some of its characteristics.

I also discuss how security is implemented in the Common Language Runtime and how this can improve on the security of existing approaches, such as extended stored procedures.

I show you how to configure SQL Server 2005 to enable the Common Language Runtime. I also show you how to create an assembly and execute it inside the SQL Server 2005 database engine.

Introducing the CLR

SQL Server 2005 is the first version of SQL Server to include the .NET Framework and its Common Language Runtime inside the database engine. The Transact-SQL language is a very powerful data access and data manipulation language, but it lacks constructs and facilities that are present in many general-purpose programming languages, including those languages you can use to write code for the CLR.

The *Common Language Runtime* is the execution environment for managed code. It has similarities to the Java Virtual Machine on which Java runs. The CLR provides various services to managed code, such as just-in-time compilation, memory management, handling of exceptions, enforcing type safety, and security. Executing well-written managed code on the CLR provides robust, scalable code execution.

The CLR offers the following potential advantages:

- ✔ CLR languages have a greater range of general-purpose programming constructs — such as arrays, collections, and FOR EACH loops — than does Transact-SQL.

- ✔ The .NET Framework class library offers an extensive range of high-quality, pre-written code that you can use in your own code.

- ✔ The .NET Framework supports string handling and the use of regular expressions.

- ✔ Managed code is object-oriented, so you can take advantage of functionality such as encapsulation, inheritance, and polymorphism. Creating a namespace and class hierarchy can help to organize the large amounts of code used in large projects.

- ✔ Safety of coding is improved because you no longer need to use extended stored procedures where code safety is potentially problematic.

- ✔ You can use a standardized development environment, Visual Studio 2005, for database application development and for other application development.

- ✔ The CLR languages can provide improved performance in some, nondata-access uses, as compared to Transact-SQL.

Not all classes of the .NET Framework are supported in SQL Server 2005, because some classes aren't appropriate to server-based code execution. The following .NET Framework libraries or namespaces are supported in SQL Server 2005:

- ✔ CustomMarshalers

- ✔ Microsoft.VisualBasic

- ✔ Microsoft.VisualC

- ✔ mscorlib

- ✔ System

- ✔ System.Configuration

- ✔ System.Data

- ✔ System.Data.OracleClient

✔ System.Data.SqlXml

✔ System.Deployment

✔ System.Security

✔ System.Transactions

✔ System.Web.Services

✔ System.Xml

It's possible, using the CREATE ASSEMBLY statement, to incorporate code from unsupported namespaces in your SQL Server 2005 programming. However, you should carefully review the security and reliability of including such code with SQL Server 2005.

To get the most benefit from CLR programming, install the .NET Framework 2.0 SDK, which includes copious documentation of the classes in the .NET Framework class library.

You can use the CLR (as an alternative to Transact-SQL) when creating the following SQL Server objects:

✔ Stored procedures

✔ Triggers

✔ User-defined types

✔ User-defined functions (both scalar and table-valued)

✔ User-defined aggregates

You must use one of the many versions of Visual Studio 2005 to write applications that use version 2.0 of the .NET Framework in SQL Server 2005. You can't use Visual Studio 2003.

When creating CLR managed code, you write the source code in a high-level language such as Visual Basic.NET. Often, you'll write that code in the Visual Studio 2005 environment although you can write it in any text editor and compile it separately. The Visual Studio 2005 environment is designed to support writing and debugging code written in Visual Basic.NET and Visual C# (and other languages). This can make coding in the Visual Studio 2005 environment the easiest way to create managed code, although—for newcomers to the Visual Studio environment—the complexity and the flexibility of the interface can initially be daunting.

The source code is likely to contain several classes, each of which might have multiple properties and methods. When you compile the source code, a file called an *assembly* is produced. The assembly contains the compiled code, plus a *manifest* that contains references to dependent assemblies. In addition, the manifest contains metadata about the assembly, including the permissions required for the assembly to run correctly.

The compiled code is MSIL (Microsoft Intermediate Language), whether the source code is Visual Basic.NET, Visual C#, or some other language. The Common Language Runtime can execute MSIL. When it executes MSIL code, the CLR automatically carries out type checking, memory management, security, and other support services.

The following rules of thumb suggest when to use .NET Framework code and when to use Transact-SQL. Use .NET code when you want to carry out intensive computation or use programming logic not easily expressed or not expressible in Transact-SQL. Also, use managed code to replace extended stored procedures to improve safety and security. Use Transact-SQL when data access or data manipulation is dominant.

Understanding CLR Permissions

The Common Language Runtime supports a security model called Code Access Security.

Code Access Security is defined in three places:

- **Machine policy:** The policy for all managed code on the machine.
- **User policy:** For SQL Server 2005, this is the policy for the account on which the SQL Server service is running.
- **Host policy:** The policy set up for the CLR by its host, in this case, SQL Server 2005.

An assembly is accessed only if the relevant permissions are present in all three policies.

The host policy levels set by SQL Server 2005 are

- **Safe:** Only internal computation and local data access by the assembly are allowed. An assembly with SAFE permissions cannot access the file system, the network, the registry, or environment variables. This is the safest of the three permission sets.
- **External access:** The permissions granted by SAFE permissions plus access to the file system, the network, the Registry, and environment variables.
- **Unsafe:** Allows access to all resources, both inside and outside SQL Server 2005. This is the least safe of the three permission sets.

Configuring SQL Server for the CLR

By default, the Common Language Runtime is disabled when you install SQL Server 2005. In order to run managed code, you need to enable the CLR, using either Transact-SQL code or the Surface Area Configuration tool.

To enable the CLR using Transact-SQL, follow these steps:

1. **Open SQL Server Management Studio by choosing Start⇨ All Programs⇨Microsoft SQL Server 2005⇨SQL Server Management Studio.**

2. **In SQL Server Management Studio, click the New Query button.**

3. **Execute the following code:**

```
sp_configure 'show advanced options', 1;
GO
RECONFIGURE;
GO
sp_configure 'clr enabled', 1;
GO
RECONFIGURE;
GO
```

If the code executes successfully, you should see the following messages:

```
Configuration option 'show advanced options' changed from
        1 to 1. Run the RECONFIGURE statement to
        install.
Configuration option 'clr enabled' changed from 0 to 1.
        Run the RECONFIGURE statement to install.
```

Because you include the RECONFIGURE statement in the code, you don't need to do any more to configure the option. You can confirm that the CLR has been enabled by executing the following code:

```
sp_configure
```

Figure 21-1 shows the result. Notice, in row 9 of the results, that the value in the config_value for clr enabled is 1.

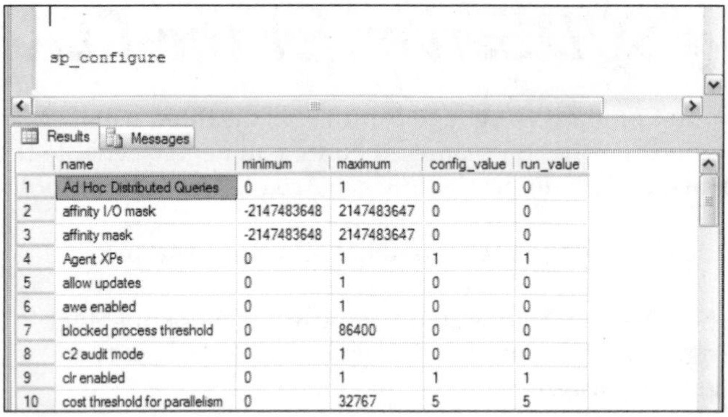

Figure 21-1:
Confirming
that the CLR
has been
enabled.

When you use the `sp_configure` stored procedure to enable CLR integration, you don't need to restart SQL Server. The new setting takes effect immediately.

If, at some later time, you want to disable the CLR, execute the following code:

```
sp_configure 'show advanced options', 1;
GO
RECONFIGURE;
GO
sp_configure 'clr enabled', 0;
GO
RECONFIGURE;
GO
```

To enable or disable CLR integration as I have just described, you need `ALTER SETTINGS` permissions at the server level. Members of the sysadmin and serveradmin roles have those permissions.

To enable CLR integration using the Surface Area Configuration tool, follow these steps:

1. **Open the Surface Area Configuration tool by choosing Start⇨All Programs⇨Microsoft SQL Server 2005⇨Configuration Tools⇨SQL Server Surface Area Configuration.**

2. **Click Surface Area Configuration for Features.**

   The Surface Area Configuration for Features dialog box, shown in Figure 21-2, opens.

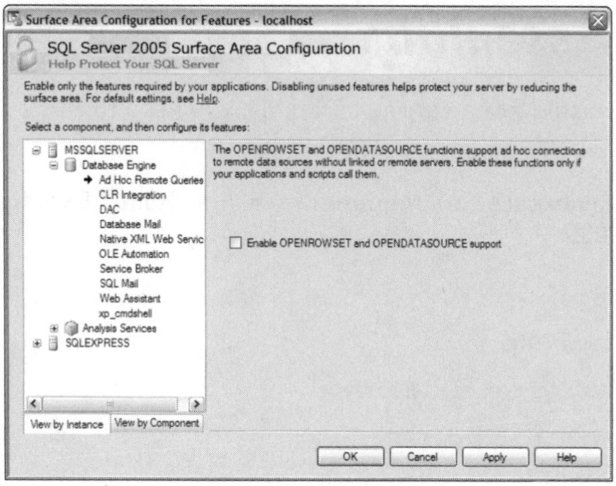

Figure 21-2:
The Surface
Area Config-
uration for
Features
window.

3. **Click the CLR Integration option in the left pane of the Surface Area Configuration for Features dialog window.**

   If CLR integration is already enabled, the check box on the CLR Integration screen is selected, as shown in Figure 21-3.

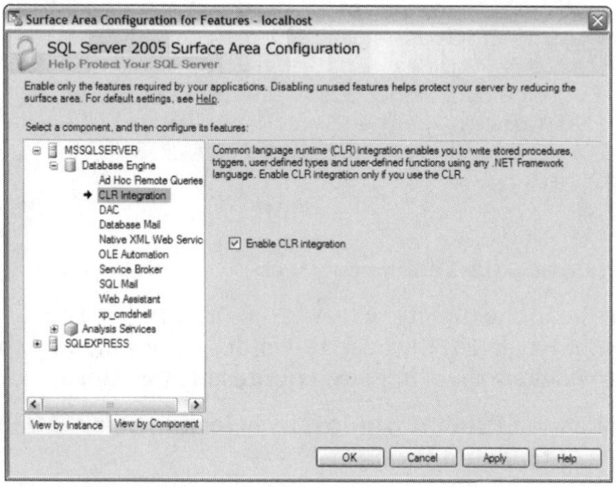

Figure 21-3:
The Enable
CLR
Integration
option
selected.

4. **If you checked the CLR Integration check box, click Apply and then click OK.**

Creating an Assembly

To create and be able to execute an assembly, you need to carry out several steps.

The following namespaces are required when you create CLR-targeted code in SQL Server 2005:

- ✔ System.Data
- ✔ System.Data.Sql
- ✔ Microsoft.SqlServer.Server
- ✔ System.Data.SqlTypes

To create a simple assembly that contains a stored procedure, follow these steps:

1. **In a text editor, type the following source code:**

```
Imports System
Imports System.Data
Imports Microsoft.SqlServer.Server
Imports System.Data.SqlTypes

Public Class ShowMessageProcedure
    <Microsoft.SqlServer.Server.SqlProcedure> _
    Public Shared  Sub ShowMessage()
        SqlContext.Pipe.Send("A simple CLR stored
        procedure has executed.\n")
    End Sub
End Class
```

2. **Save the code as SimpleAssembly.vb.**

   I saved the file in the directory C:\SQL 2005 Prog for Dummies\Chapter 21. Because the folder names include spaces, you need to enclose them in paired quotes in later steps.

3. **Open a Command Prompt window by selecting Start⇨All Programs⇨ Accessories⇨Command Prompt.**

4. **In the Command Prompt window, navigate to the directory that contains the .NET Framework version 2.0.**

   The original release of version 2.0 of the .NET Framework is located in C:\WINDOWS\Microsoft.NET\Framework\v2.0.50727, assuming that drive C: is your system drive.

5. **Type the following command to compile Visual Basic code.**

```
vbc /target:library "C:\SQL 2005 Prog for
        Dummies\Chapter 21\SimpleAssembly.vb"
```

If you stored the Visual Basic source file in a different directory, modify the command accordingly.

If you want to compile C# code, use the `csc.exe` C# compiler that's located in the same directory as `vbc.exe`.

6. **If the code compiles correctly, you see a response similar to Figure 21-4.**

If you see an error message about a missing Sub Main, check to make sure that you used the `/target:library` switch in the command.

Figure 21-4:
Compiling
the Visual
Basic
source.

7. **In Windows Explorer, navigate to the folder you stored the Visual Basic source code file in and confirm that a new file `SimpleAssembly.dll` has been added there by the Visual Basic compiler.**

You now need to load the assembly into SQL Server 2005. To do that, you use the `CREATE ASSEMBLY` statement.

8. **In SQL Server Management Studio, create a new query by clicking the New Query button. Type the following code:**

```
CREATE ASSEMBLY showMessage from 'C:\SQL 2005 Prog for
        Dummies\Chapter 21\SimpleAssembly.dll'
WITH PERMISSION_SET = SAFE
```

If the code executes correctly, the assembly now exists in SQL Server 2005.

9. **Now use the CREATE PROCEDURE statement to create a stored procedure called showMyMessage.**

```
CREATE PROCEDURE showMyMessage
AS
EXTERNAL NAME
        showMessage.ShowMessageProcedure.ShowMessage
```

10. **Execute the showMyMessage stored procedure using the following command:**

```
EXEC showMyMessage
```

If you omitted enabling the CLR integration, you see the following error message:

```
Msg 6263, Level 16, State 1, Line 1
Execution of user code in the .NET Framework is
        disabled. Enable "clr enabled" configuration
        option.
```

11. **To enable CLR integration (if it isn't already enabled), execute this code:**

```
sp_configure 'show advanced options', 1;
GO
RECONFIGURE;
GO
sp_configure 'clr enabled', 1;
GO
RECONFIGURE;
GO
```

If you want to modify the message (or otherwise alter the Visual Basic source code), you need to recompile the source and add the assembly to SQL Server 2005 again. If you want to use the same assembly name, you need to execute the following two statements before you can execute the CREATE ASSEMBLY statement again:

```
DROP PROCEDURE showMyMessage
DROP ASSEMBLY showMessage
```

Chapter 22

Using Visual Studio 2005

*V*isual Studio 2005 is Microsoft's premier general application development environment for version 2.0 of the .NET Framework and for SQL Server 2005. In addition to using Visual Studio 2005 to develop general .NET 2.0 applications, you can use the Business Intelligence Development Studio (BIDS) to develop SQL Server 2005 business intelligence applications based on SQL Server Analysis Services, SQL Server Integration Services, and SQL Server Reporting Services. BIDS is, in effect, a version of Visual Studio 2005 focused only on business intelligence projects.

A great place to access downloads of Visual Studio 2005 and find further information is `http://msdn2.microsoft.com/en-us/vstudio/ default.aspx`.

If you install Visual Studio 2005 and Business Intelligence Development Studio on one machine, the features of the two products are merged so that both general programming project templates and SQL Server 2005 business intelligence project templates are available when you start to create a new project.

Visual Studio 2005 has several features that support developers in creating applications that are based on relational databases. Microsoft describes these parts of Visual Studio 2005 as *visual database tools*. The *visual database tools* are the parts of Visual Studio 2005 that help you create relational databases, maintain those databases, and create parts of your applications that manipulate data.

Visual Studio 2005 supports the following visual designers:

▸ **Database Diagram Designer:** Allows you to visually create, edit, and display the tables and relationships in a database. It works with SQL Server 2005 and SQL Server 2000 databases.

> ✔ **Table Designer:** Allows you to design an individual table.
>
> ✔ **Query and View Designers:** Allow you to SELECT (View Designer) or SELECT, INSERT, UPDATE and DELETE data (Query Designer).

There are several editions of Visual Studio 2005 and multiple configuration options that you can set. As a result, the appearance you see in your own edition of a Visual Studio 2005 product might differ from the appearance shown in some of the figures in this chapter.

The available versions of Visual Studio 2005 include the following:

> ✔ Visual Studio 2005 Professional
>
> ✔ Visual Studio 2005 Standard
>
> ✔ Visual Basic Express
>
> ✔ Visual C# Express
>
> ✔ Visual Web Developer

For a detailed feature comparison of these versions, visit http://msdn2. microsoft.com/en-us/vstudio/aa700921.aspx.

In addition, some versions of Visual Studio are designed specifically for enterprise architects: these include functionality to facilitate the design of complex enterprise applications.

Using Server Explorer

Server Explorer allows you to work with database connections. These database connections allow you to read and write data and create objects in the database.

Solution Explorer, which I introduce in the next section, lets you work with database references. Be careful not to confuse Server Explorer and Solution Explorer.

Server Explorer allows you to carry out several database-related tasks during application development.

In the Express Editions of Visual Studio 2005, Server Explorer is called Database Explorer.

The following assumes that you created a database called Chapter22 by executing the following statements in SQL Server Management Studio:

```
USE master
CREATE DATABASE Chapter22
```

To connect to an existing database, in this case the Chapter22 database, follow these steps:

1. **Open Server Explorer by choosing View⇨Server Explorer.**

   Figure 22-1 shows the initial appearance in Server Explorer.

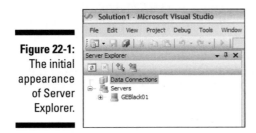

Figure 22-1: The initial appearance of Server Explorer.

2. **In Server Explorer, right-click the Data Connections node. From the context menu, choose Add Connection.**

   The Add Connection dialog box shown in Figure 22-2 opens.

Figure 22-2: The Add Connection dialog box.

The default setting for the data source is Microsoft SQL Server (SqlClient). If you need, on occasion, to connect to a different type of database, click the Change button and make an appropriate choice from the Change Data Source dialog box.

3. **Type a name for the SQL Server instance in the Server Name text box or use the drop-down list to make a selection from the available SQL Server instances.**

   Use . (the period character) to connect to a local default SQL Server instance. To connect to a different instance of SQL Server, use the *MachineName\InstanceName* form for a named instance and the *MachineName* form for a default instance of SQL Server on a remote machine.

4. **Once you enter a valid name for a server instance, the Select or Enter a Database Name drop-down list becomes available. Select the Chapter22 database, as shown in Figure 22-3.**

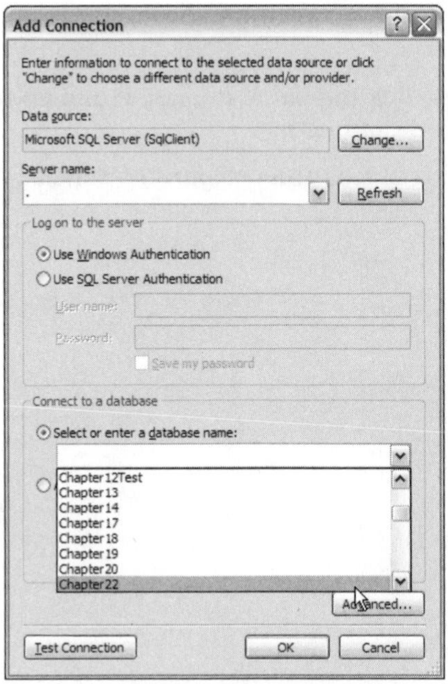

Figure 22-3:
Select a
database to
connect to.

5. **Click the Test Connection button to test that the connection to the Chapter22 database is working correctly.**

   If it's working, a dialog box with the message Test connection succeeded. appears. Click OK to dismiss that dialog box.

6. **If you want to set or inspect advanced properties for the connection to the database, click the Advanced button. If not, skip ahead to Step 7.**

The Advanced Properties dialog box shown in Figure 22-4 appears.

7. Make any changes you want in the Advanced Properties dialog box. Click OK to confirm your changes.

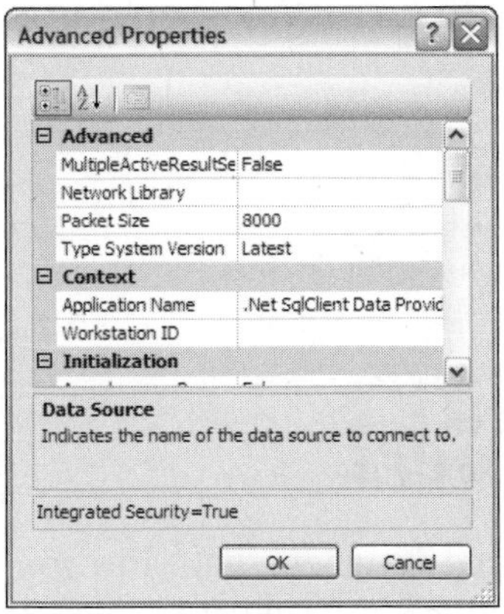

Figure 22-4:
The
Advanced
Properties
dialog box.

8. Click OK to confirm your selections from the Add Connection dialog box.

A new data connection to the `Chapter22` database is displayed in the Server Explorer, as shown in Figure 22-5.

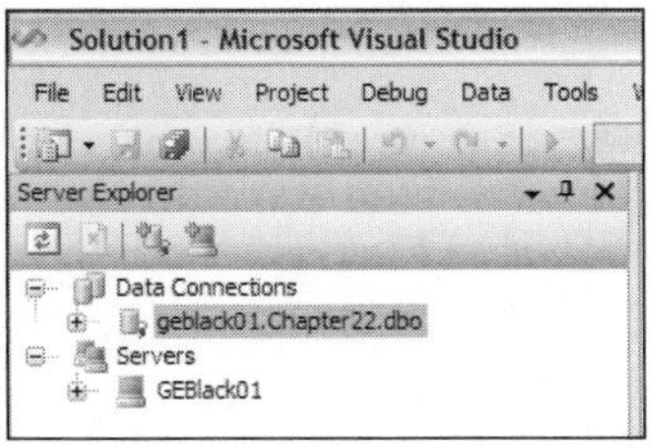

Figure 22-5:
The new
connection
is added to
the data
connections
in Server
Explorer.

9. Click the node for the `Chapter22` database and you see additional nodes, as shown in Figure 22-6.

The available nodes are similar to those you've seen earlier in this book in SQL Server Management Studio's Object Explorer. They give you access to the visual designers that I describe in the next section.

Some database connection features of Visual Studio Express editions and Visual Web Developer Express edition operate with local connections only.

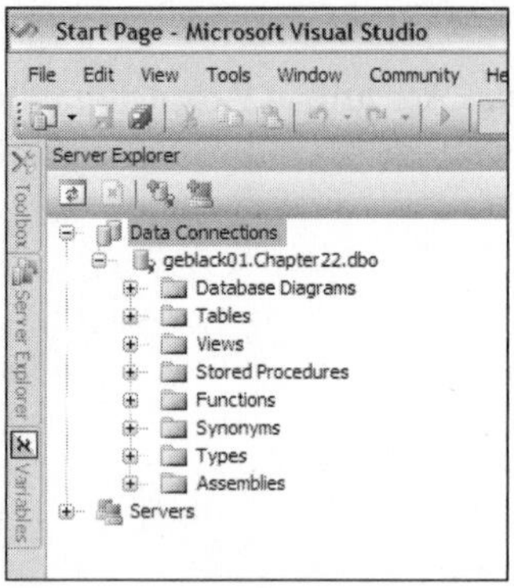

Figure 22-6:
The available nodes for a database connection in Server Explorer.

Using the Visual Designers

Visual Studio 2005 supports three visual designers that allow you to carry out tasks relevant to working with databases. As already stated, the three designer tools are the Database Diagram Designer, the Table Designer, and the Query and View Designer.

The Database Diagram Designer allows you to display the tables, with their relationships, as they exist in a database.

The following example uses the pubs database, which already has multiple tables with suitable relationships. To create a connection to the pubs database, follow the steps described in the previous section. To access the Database Diagram Designer, follow these steps:

1. **In Server Explorer, right-click the `Database Diagrams` node for the connection to the `pubs` database and choose the Add New Diagram option in the context menu, as shown in Figure 22-7.**

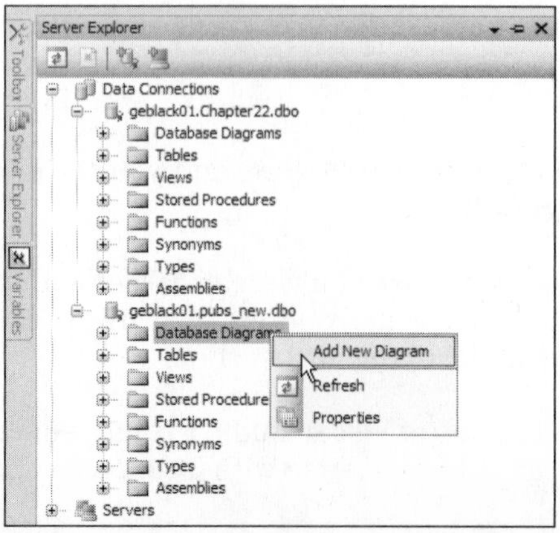

Figure 22-7:
Launching the Database Diagram Designer.

The Add Table dialog box opens.

2. **Select the `titles` table and click Add. Select the `authors` table and click Add. Select the `titleauthors` table and click Add. Click Close to close the Add Table dialog box.**

After moving the table shapes in the Database Diagram Designer, you see an appearance like Figure 22-8. It allows you to visualize the relationships between the `authors`, `titleauthor`, and `titles` tables in the `pubs` database.

Figure 22-8:
A database diagram for the `titles`, `title author`, and `authors` tables.

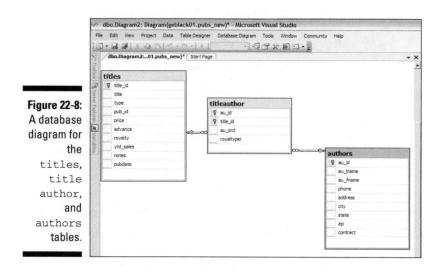

You can, for complex databases, create multiple diagrams to help you understand how tables in the database are related and what the relevant keys are.

The Table Designer allows you, from Visual Studio 2005, to design a new table in a SQL Server database. To add a `Messages` table to the `Chapter22` database, follow these steps.

1. **In Server Explorer, right-click the `Tables` node in the `Chapter22` database. From the context menu, choose the Add New Table option.**

The Table Designer opens, looking like Figure 22-9.

2. **In the `Column Name` column, type** MessageID.

3. **In the `Data Type` column, type int. In the Column Properties tab, which appears automatically after you specify a data type, scroll down until you see the `Identity Specification` node. Expand that node. In the right column for the (`Is Identity`) property, select Yes, as shown in Figure 22-10.**

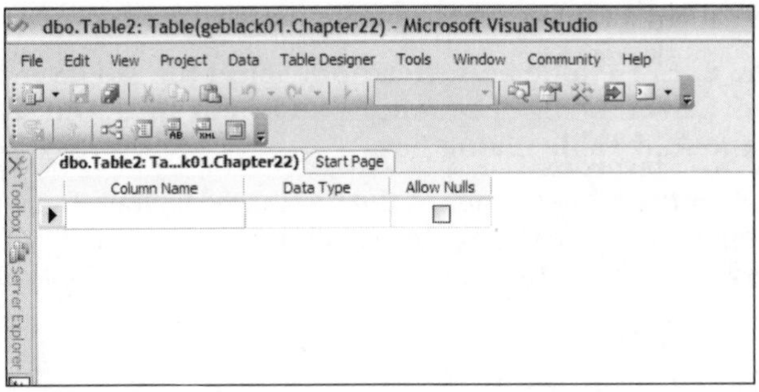

Figure 22-9:
The initial
appearance
of the Table
Designer.

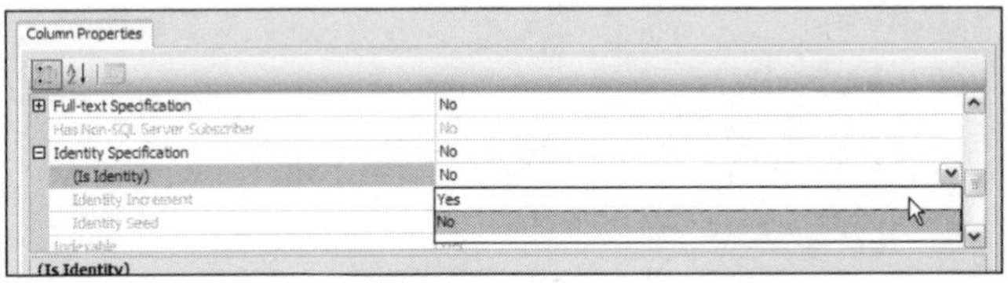

Figure 22-10:
Specifying
that the
MessageID
column is
an identity
column.

4. **Ensure that the check box in the `Allow Nulls` column is not selected.**

5. **In the second row of the Table Designer, type** Message **in the `Column Name` column.**

6. **In the `Data Type` column, type** varchar(200).

7. **Ensure that the check box in the Allow Nulls column is not selected.**

   The appearance should be like Figure 22-11.

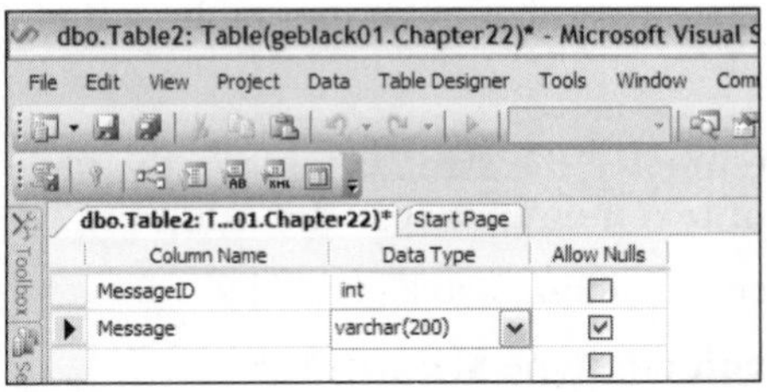

Figure 22-11:
Specifying
the columns
in the
Messages
table.

8. **Press Ctrl+S to save the new table. In the Choose Name dialog box, name the table `Messages` and click OK to save the `Messages` table.**

9. **Expand the `Tables` node in Server Explorer and confirm that the `Messages` table is displayed. Expand the `Messages` node and confirm that the `MessageID` and `Message` columns are displayed.**

After you've created a table — or using another existing table — you can view its data from Server Explorer. To view the data in the Messages table, follow these steps:

1. **In Server Explorer, expand the `Chapter22` node and expand the `Tables` node.**

2. **Right-click the `Messages` node and choose the Show Table Data option in the context menu.**

   The appearance should be like Figure 22-12. Because you haven't yet added data to the Messages table, no data appears.

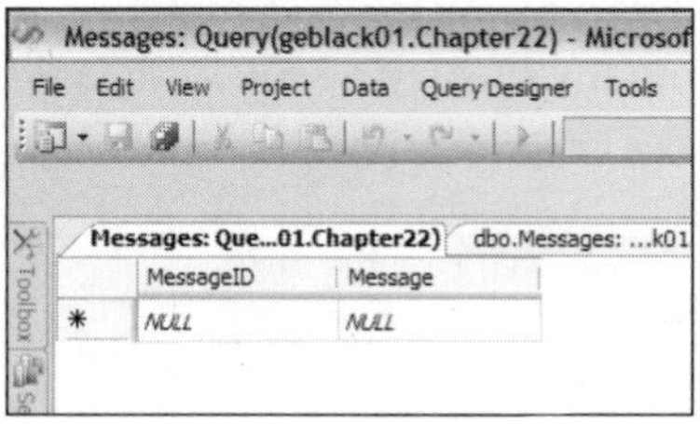

Figure 22-12:
Viewing the data for a newly created table.

3. **Increase the width of the `Message` column and type** Hello world!.

   Don't type anything in the MessageID column. Because that's an identity column, SQL Server provides a value automatically.

4. **Click the `Message` column in the second row. Notice that the value 1 has been automatically supplied for the first row. Type** This is a second message.

   The appearance should be like Figure 22-13. Notice that MessageID in the second row currently doesn't have a value. If you click in the third row or close the table, that value is added.

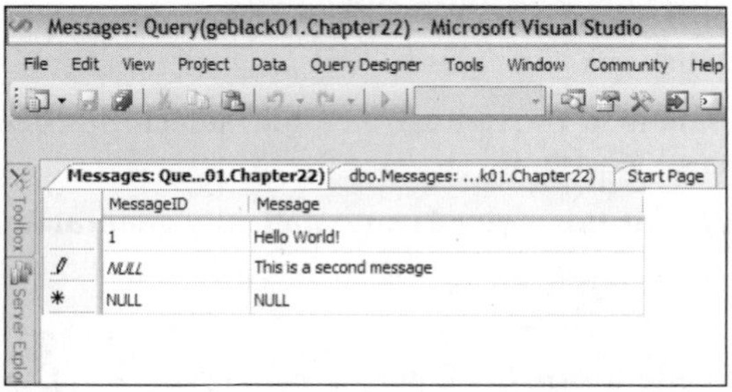

Figure 22-13:
Adding data to the Messages table.

To delete a table from a database, follow these steps:

1. **Expand the node for the database in Server Explorer.**

2. **Expand the Tables node.**

3. **Select the table you want to delete. Right-click and choose Delete from the context menu.**

To create a new query on the Messages table from Server Explorer, follow these steps:

1. **Right-click the Chapter22 node.**

2. **Choose the New Query option from the context menu.**

   The Query Designer opens, initially displaying the Add Table dialog box, shown in Figure 22-14.

   The Messages table is already highlighted.

3. **Click the Add button to add the Messages table to the design surface. Click Close to close the Add Table dialog box.**

   Your screen should look like Figure 22-15.

4. **To select all columns in the Messages table, select the check box with * (All columns) beside it.**

5. **The Transact-SQL for the query is automatically generated:**

```
SELECT      Messages.*
FROM        Messages
```

6. **To execute the code inside the Query Designer, choose Query Designer⇨Execute SQL.**

   The results are displayed in the results pane, shown in Figure 22-16.

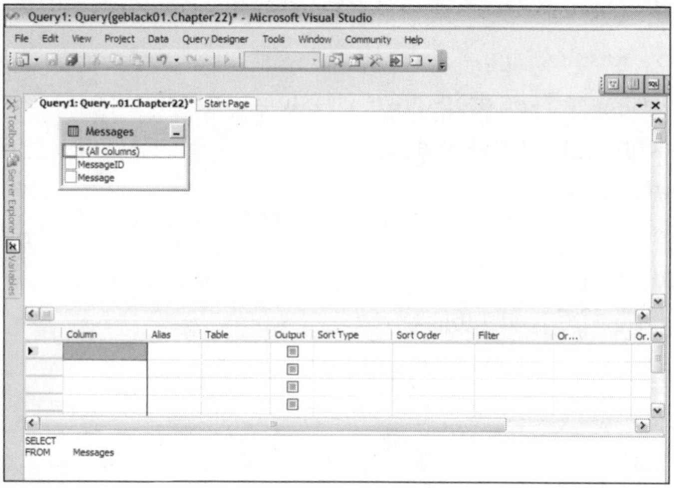

Figure 22-15:
The initial
appearance
of the Query
Designer.

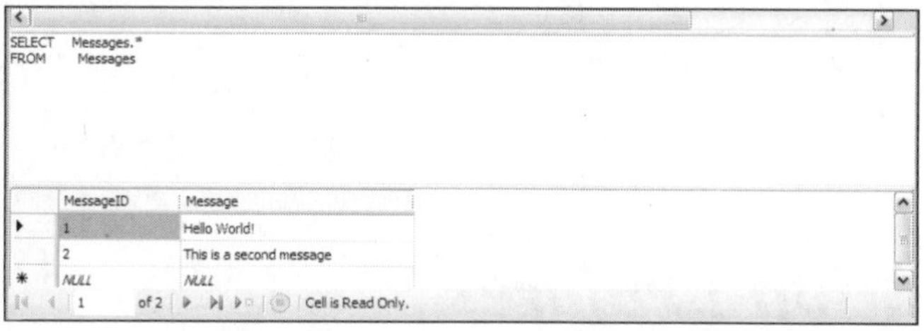

Figure 22-16:
Executing
Transact-
SQL inside
the Query
Designer.

7. **Right-click the tab for the query and select Close from the context menu to close it.**

    A Query Designer toolbar is usually visible by default. If it isn't visible, choose View➪Toolbars➪Query Designer. The Query Designer toolbar is shown in Figure 22-17.

Figure 22-17:
The Query
Designer
toolbar.

The Query Designer toolbar has the following buttons (from left to right in Figure 22-17):

✔ Show Diagram Pane

✔ Show Criteria Pane

✔ Show SQL Pane

✔ Show Results Pane

✔ The Change Type drop-down list (shown in Figure 22-18)

✔ Execute SQL (shows as a !)

✔ Verify SQL Syntax

✔ Add Group By

✔ Add Table

✔ Add New Derived Table

Figure 22-18:
The Change
Type drop-
down list in
the Query
Designer
toolbar.

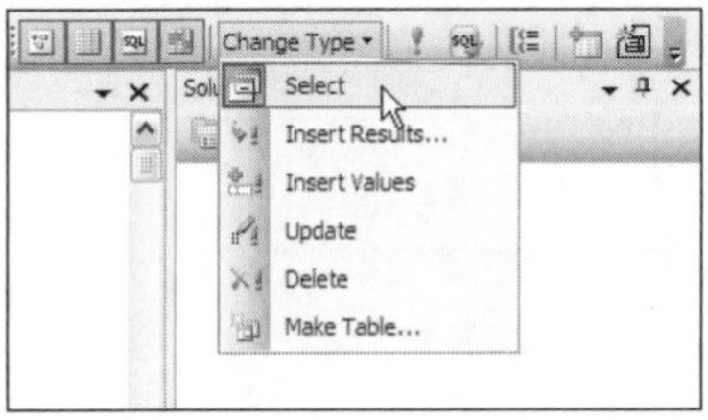

Using Solution Explorer

In Solution Explorer, you can work with databases using database references. These database references differ a little from the database connections that you work with using Server Explorer/Database Explorer. In Solution Explorer, you can't expand a database reference and work with objects in the database, which (as you saw in the previous section) is something you can do if you expand a database connection in Server Explorer.

In Solution Explorer, you can have database references to multiple databases used during the development of a project. For example, you might initially use only a database reference to a test database situated locally on your client computer (the computer you perform development on).

When you create a database reference in Solution Explorer, you also create a database connection in Server Explorer. You can create a database reference using a connection that already exists in Server Explorer or create a new connection. Either way, a database reference in Solution Explorer must have a corresponding database connection in Server Explorer.

To create a database reference in Solution Explorer for a new database project, follow these steps:

1. **Open Visual Studio 2005 by choosing Start⇨All Programs⇨ Microsoft Visual Studio 2005⇨Microsoft Visual Studio 2005.**

2. **To create a new project, choose File⇨New⇨Project.**

   The New Project dialog box opens.

3. **In the New Project dialog box, choose Other Project Types⇨Database in the left pane.**

4. **Choose the Database Project option in the right pane.**

5. **In the Name text box, type** Chapter22DatabaseProject. **If you want, alter the path in the Location text box.**

   The New Project Dialog box should look like Figure 22-19.

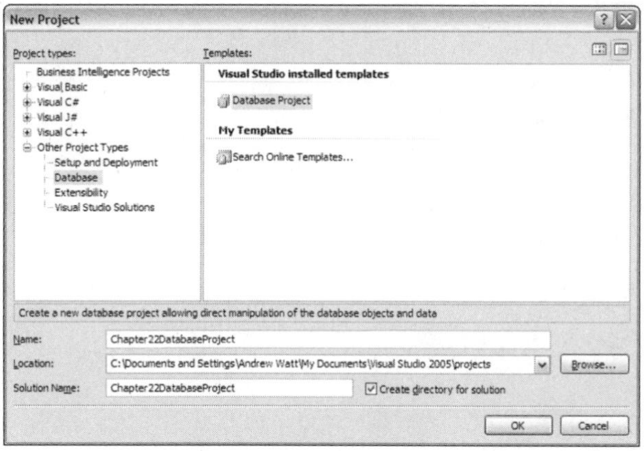

Figure 22-19:
The
completed
New Project
dialog box.

6. **Click the OK button to create the new project.**

   The New Database Reference dialog box appears.

7. **Select the server instance in the New Database Reference dialog box. Select the `Chapter22` database from the drop-down list shown in Figure 22-20.**

8. **Click OK to create the database reference to the `Chapter22` database.**

9. **Choose View⇨Solution Explorer to confirm that a database reference to the `Chapter22` database has been added to the project. The appearance will be similar to Figure 22-21.**

The database project isn't the type of project template that you'll use most often if you create custom applications as front ends for SQL Server databases. In the next section, I show you how to create a simple Windows Forms application.

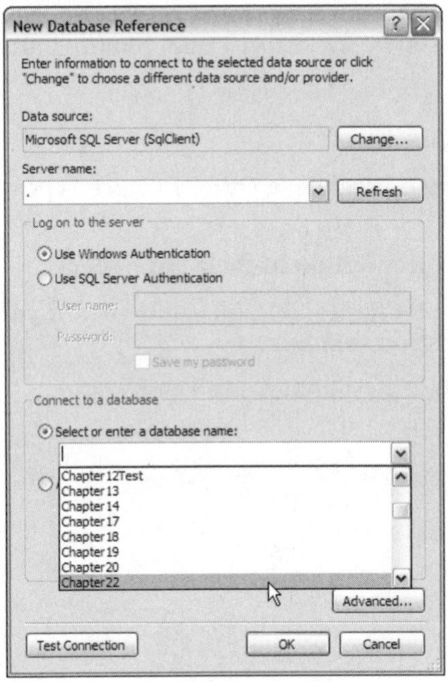

Figure 22-20:
The New
Database
Reference
dialog box.

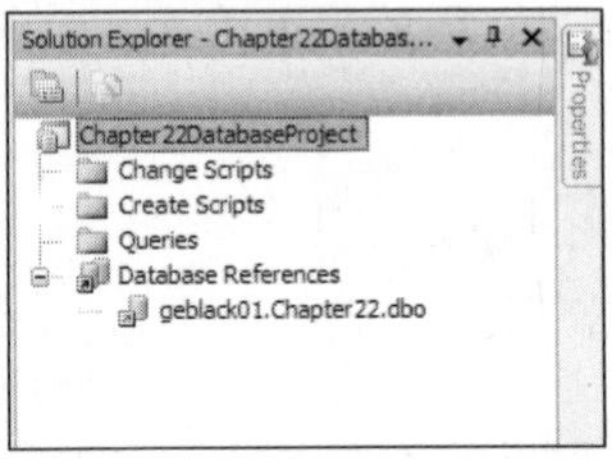

Figure 22-21:
The
database
reference in
Solution
Explorer.

Creating a Project

In Visual Studio 2005, you create applications as solutions or projects. You can create a project using either Visual Basic.NET or Visual C#. Including access to a SQL Server database is, of course, not part of every Visual Studio 2005 project, but accessing relational data is certainly a common use of a Windows Forms project.

Visual Studio 2005 supports the following forms controls that relate specifically to the display of data. Other forms controls, such as labels, might also be data-bound but often display literal data rather than data dynamically retrieved from a database.

✔ `DataGridView`   Replaces and improves on the `DataGrid` control. It displays data in rows and columns. You can customize the appearance and behavior of the control.

✔ `DataGrid`   Still available in Visual Studio 2005, although it's been replaced by the `DataGridView`.

✔ `DataSet`   Provides temporary storage for your application's data.

If you're programming in ASP.NET rather than Windows Forms, the broadly equivalent control to the `DataGridView` control is the `GridView` control.

To create a new Visual Basic Windows Forms project that uses a data-bound `DataGridView` control, follow these steps:

1. **To start Visual Studio 2005, choose Start⇨All Programs⇨ Visual Studio 2005⇨Visual Studio 2005.**

2. **To create a new project, choose File⇨New⇨Project.**

   The New Project dialog box (refer to Figure 22-19) appears.

3. **Choose Visual Basic⇨Windows in the left pane. Select Windows Application in the right pane. In the Name text box, type the project name** Chapter22WinFormsProject.

   If you want to, you can change the location for the project by editing the path in the Location text box. Your screen should resemble Figure 22-22.

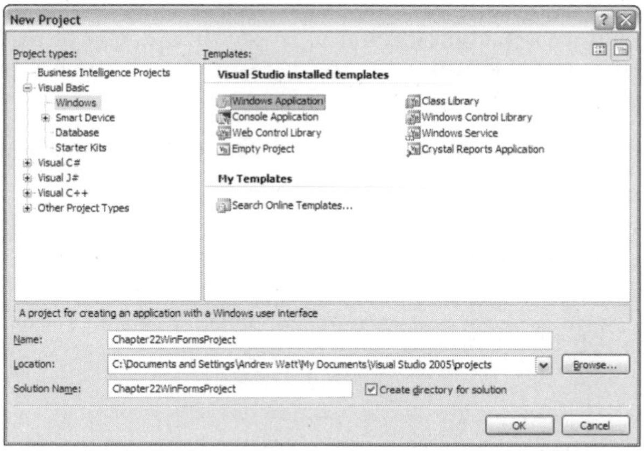

Figure 22-22: The New Project dialog box completed for the Chapter22 WinForms Project project.

4. **Click OK to create the new Windows Forms project.**

   The appearance is similar to Figure 22-23, but it might vary depending on the edition of Visual Studio 2005 and your configuration settings. If necessary, to display Server Explorer, choose View⇨Server Explorer. If necessary, to display Solution Explorer, choose View⇨Solution Explorer.

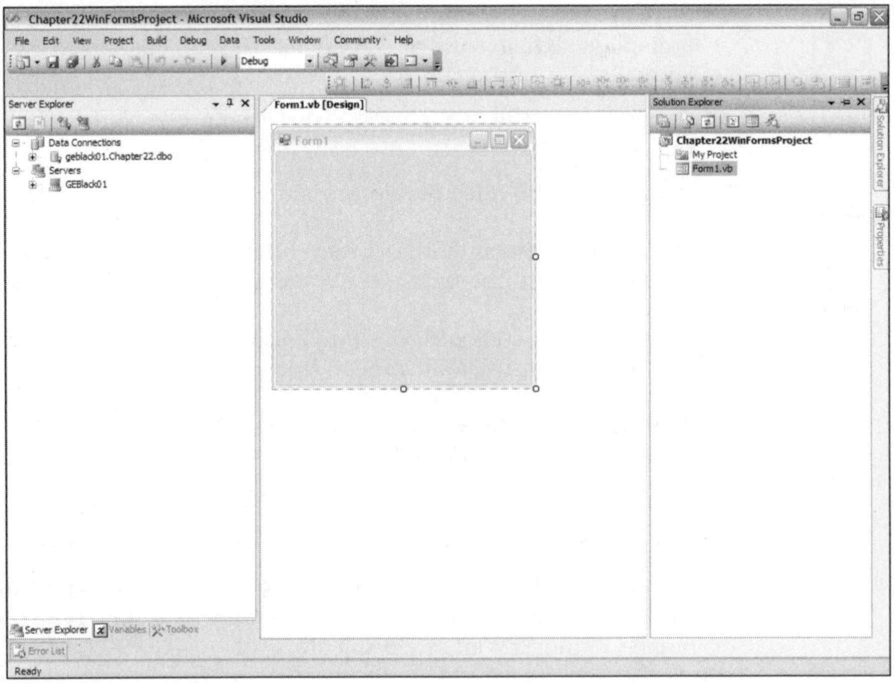

Figure 22-23:
A newly
created
Windows
Forms
project.

In Server Explorer (Database Explorer), you can see the connection to the `Chapter22` database created earlier in this chapter.

5. **To create a data set, right-click the project name, `Chapter22Win` `FormsProject`, in Solution Explorer. From the context menu, choose Add⇨New Item.**

The Add New Item dialog box, shown in Figure 22-24, appears.

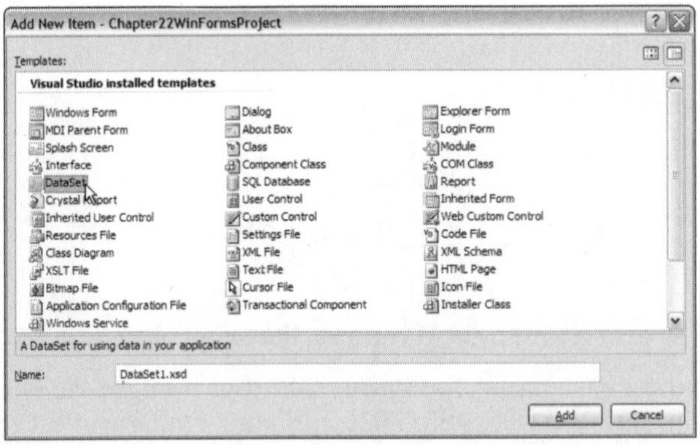

Figure 22-24:
The Add
New Item
dialog box.

6. **Click the DataSet option in the Add New Item dialog box. Name the data set** MessagesDataSet **and click OK to close the Add New Item dialog box.**

A new item, `MessagesDataSet.xsd`, is added to Solution Explorer. A design interface for you to design the data set is displayed in the main part of the Visual Studio design surface.

7. **In Server Explorer, expand the nodes for the Chapter22 database and the Tables node. Hover the mouse pointer over the node for the Messages table (as shown in Figure 22-25).**

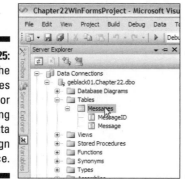

Figure 22-25: Mouse the Messages table prior to dragging it to the data set design surface.

8. **Drag the table to the design surface for the data set. On the data set design surface, you should see a shape like the one shown in Figure 22-26.**

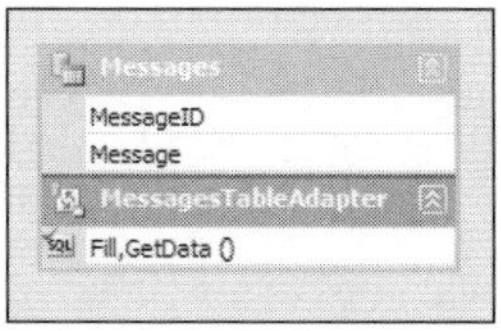

Figure 22-26: The data set and the data table adapter on the data set design surface.

9. **Click the tab labeled Form1.vb[Design] to return to the Windows Form design surface.**

10. **Click the Windows Form, if necessary, to display the handles on the outer edge of the form. Drag the handle on the right edge of the form to the right.**

11. From the Toolbox (choose View➪Toolbox to make it visible, if necessary), drag a `DataGridView` control to the Windows Form.

The appearance should resemble Figure 22-27. Notice that, by default, the check boxes that specify support for inserting (Enable Adding), updating (Enable Editing), and deleting (Enable Deleting) are selected.

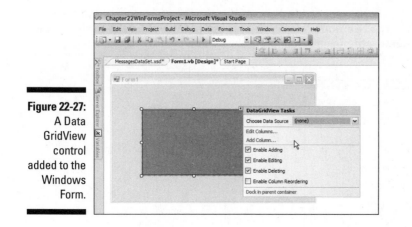

Figure 22-27:
A Data GridView control added to the Windows Form.

12. To specify where the data to be displayed in the `DataGridView` comes from, you need to specify a data source. One way to do that is to press F4 to display the Properties window and scroll down until the `DataSource` property is displayed.

Figure 22-28 shows the dialog box that appears when you click the drop-down list for the `DataSource` property.

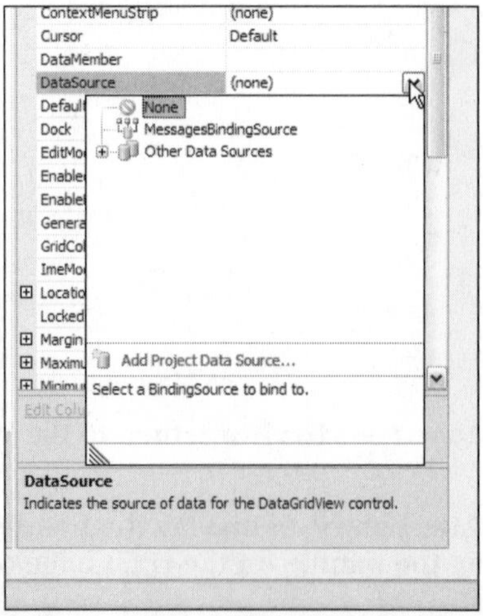

Figure 22-28:
The dialog box for selecting a value for the DataSource property.

13. **Expand the nodes for** `Other Data Sources`, `Project Data Sources`, **and** `MessagesDataSet` **as shown in Figure 22-29. Select the** `Messages` **table.**

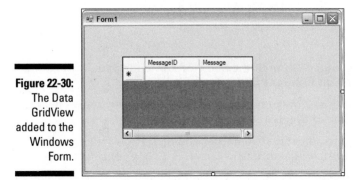

The form now looks like Figure 22-30.

14. **Click the form to show its handles. Drag the right handle to the right to increase the width of the form. Click the** `DataGridView` **control to display its handles. Drag the right handle to the right to increase the width of the** `DataGridView` **control.**

15. **Change the width of the** `Messages` **column. Click the arrow button, as shown in Figure 22-31.**

16. **Click the Edit Columns option in the DataGridView Tasks dialog box.**

The Edit Columns dialog box shown in Figure 22-32 appears.

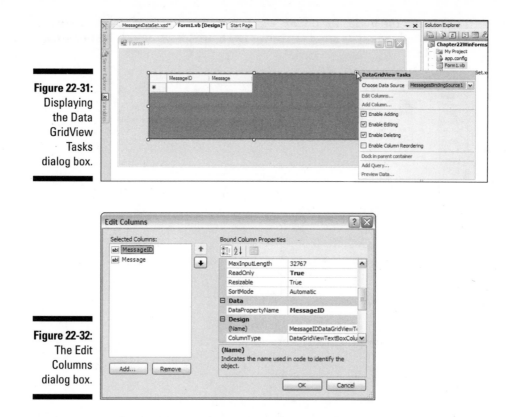

Figure 22-31:
Displaying the Data GridView Tasks dialog box.

Figure 22-32:
The Edit Columns dialog box.

17. **Select the Message column in the Selected Columns pane toward the left side of the Edit Columns dialog box.**

18. **Scroll down in the right column so that the Width property appears. Change the value of the Width property to 240.**

    You might need to adjust that value, depending on how much you increased the width of the form and DataGridView control in Step 15.

19. **Click OK to close the Edit Columns dialog box and apply the change in width of the Message column.**

    The form now looks like Figure 22-33.

20. **Before testing the form, save everything by choosing File⇨Save All.**

21. **Press F5 to test the form in debug mode. If the Windows Form executes correctly, you should see a result like Figure 22-34.**

    To be able to edit data in the data source, you need to take a couple of steps.

Figure 22-33:
The width
of the
Message
column
in the Data
GridView
control
has been
increased.

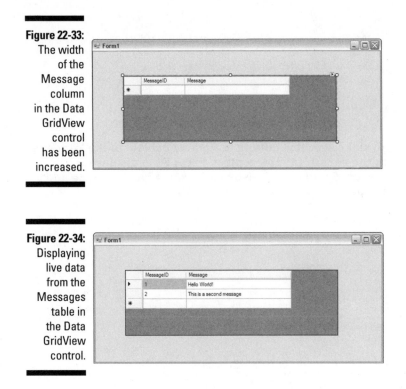

Figure 22-34:
Displaying
live data
from the
Messages
table in
the Data
GridView
control.

22. **In Solution Explorer, right-click `Form1.vb` and choose View Code from the context menu. Edit the Visual Basic code so that it reads as shown in this step.**

Notice the two `Imports` statements for relevant namespaces. Save your changes by choosing File⇨Save All.

```
Imports System
Imports System.Windows.Forms


Public Class Form1

    Private Sub Form1_Load(ByVal sender As
        System.Object, ByVal e As System.EventArgs)
        Handles MyBase.Load
        'TODO: This line of code loads data into the
        'MessagesDataSet.Messages' table. You can
        move, or remove it, as needed.
```

```
            Me.MessagesTableAdapter.Fill(Me.MessagesDataSe
            t.Messages)
            Me.DataGridView1.EditMode =
            DataGridViewEditMode.EditOnEnter

        End Sub
End Class
```

23. **To check to make sure that editing has been enabled, in the Windows Form, click the `DataGridView` control. Press F4 to display the Properties pane. Scroll down so you can inspect the `EditMode` and `Enabled` properties, as shown in Figure 22-35.**

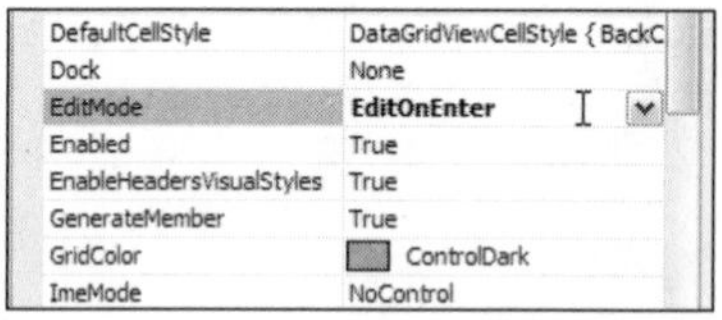

Figure 22-35:
Inspect the EditMode and Enabled properties of the Data GridView control.

If you find that you can't edit values in the form, check to be sure that you didn't disable editing on the `DataGridView` control or on the `Message` column.

The preceding example gives you an indication of how you can use the `DataGridView` control in a Windows Form project. In Visual Studio 2005, you have tons of flexibility to create Windows Forms or ASP.NET applications, depending on which edition of Visual Studio 2005 you have. Binding a control to a data source is straightforward.

Chapter 23

Working with SQL Server Management Objects

*O*ne of the uses for SQL Server programming is to create applications that allow you, or administrator colleagues, to carry out administrative tasks in a way that's customized for your business needs. SQL Server Management Objects (SMO) is the SQL Server 2005 object model that you use to create applications for administering SQL Server.

In this chapter, I introduce you to SQL Server Management Objects and show you the basics of using them to create administration-oriented applications. A full description of SMO would be about the length of this entire book; therefore, the following description serves only to introduce the topic.

Getting Started with SQL-SMO

SQL Server Management Objects, SMO, is new in SQL Server 2005. SMO replaces SQL-DMO (SQL Server Distributed Management Objects), which was the object programming model used in SQL Server 2000 for management of SQL Server. Unlike SQL-DMO, SMO is a managed code object model.

An SMO application is created in Visual Studio 2005. You can use either Visual Basic.NET or Visual C# to create applications that use SMO. In addition, you can use any other language that's supported on version 2.0 of the Common Language Runtime.

To create an SMO application, you need to import at least some of the following namespaces. Which namespaces you need to import depends on the functionality you want from your application.

- ✔ `Microsoft.SqlServer.Management.Smo` contains objects that represent core SMO objects such as instances and utility classes. The `Server` object is a member of this namespace.

- ✔ `Microsoft.SqlServer.Management.Common` contains classes that are common to SQL Server Management Objects (SMO) and Replication Management Objects (RMO).

- ✔ `Microsoft.SqlServer.Management.Smo.Agent` contains classes that represent SQL Server Agent.

- ✔ `Microsoft.SqlServer.Management.Smo.Wmi` contains classes that represent the WMI (Windows Management Instrumentation) provider.

- ✔ `Microsoft.SqlServer.Management.Smo.RegisteredServers` contains classes that represent registered servers.

- ✔ `Microsoft.SqlServer.Management.Smo.Mail` contains classes that represent Database Mail.

- ✔ `Microsoft.SqlServer.Management.Smo.Broker` contains classes that represent SQL Server Service Broker.

- ✔ `Microsoft.SqlServer.Management.Nmo` contains classes that represent SQL Server Notification Services.

I don't cover Replication Management Objects in this book.

Discovering the SQL-SMO Object Model

In this section, I introduce the SMO object model and briefly compare its characteristics to those of its predecessor, SQL-DMO. I then look at part of the hierarchy of objects in the SMO object model.

The SMO model provides several improvements, compared to SQL-DMO:

- ✔ SMO improves performance by loading objects only when they are specifically referenced.

- ✔ Transact-SQL statements can be captured and sent over the network as a batch.

- ✔ You can manage the SQL Server services using a WMI provider. This feature allows you to start, stop, or pause SQL Server–related services programmatically.

✔ Transact-SQL scripts can be generated to recreate objects and their relationships.

✔ Use of Unique Resource Names (URNs) that allow objects to be uniquely identified.

The top-level object in the SMO object model that represents an instance of SQL Server is the `Server` object. All other instances of class objects are descendants of the `Server` object. The `Server` object represents an instance of SQL Server and is a member of the `Microsoft.SqlServer.Management.Smo` namespace. When you create a `Server` object variable, you establish a connection to an instance of SQL Server 2005 or 2000. If you don't specify a name for the instance, the connection is to the local, default instance of SQL Server.

The top-level object is called the `Server` object. This object might better be called the `Instance` object because the `Server` object relates to a SQL Server instance.

Using the `Server` object, you can carry out the following tasks:

✔ Create a connection to a SQL Server instance.

✔ Modify settings for a connection to a SQL Server instance.

✔ Execute Transact-SQL statements.

✔ Capture Transact-SQL output from an SMO program.

✔ Manage transactions.

✔ View information about the operating system.

✔ View and modify SQL Server settings, user options, and configuration options.

✔ Register the SQL Server instance in a Windows Active Directory service.

✔ Reference databases, endpoints, credentials, logins, linked servers, system messages, DDL triggers, system data types, and user-defined messages.

✔ Regenerate the service master key.

✔ Detach and attach databases.

✔ Stop processes.

✔ Grant, deny, or revoke permissions.

✔ Read the error log.

✔ Create endpoints.

Also, a ManagedComputer object with a separate object hierarchy represents SQL Server services and network settings available through a Windows Management Instrumentation (WMI) provider. I don't describe the ManagedComputer object in this book.

The values of Server object properties can be retrieved by members of the public fixed server role. To set values of Server object properties (where that is possible), you need to be a member of the sysadmin fixed server role.

Table 23-1 lists the properties for the Server object.

Table 23-1	Server Object Properties
Property	**Description**
ActiveDirectory	The Register() method allows a SQL Server instance to be registered in the Active Directory directory service.
BackupDevices	Represents a collection of BackupDevice objects. Each BackupDevice object represents a backup device associated with the SQL Server instance.
Configuration	Gets or sets configuration information on a SQL Server instance. Modifying a Configuration object is equivalent to executing the sp_configure system stored procedure.
ConnectionContext	Gets the current server connection information for a SQL Server instance.
Credentials	Represents a collection of Credential objects. Each Credential object represents a credential associated with a SQL Server instance.
Databases	Represents a collection of Database objects. Each Database object represents a database associated with a SQL Server instance.
DefaultTextMode	Gets or sets a Boolean value, which determines whether or not the default text mode is set for an instance of SQL Server.
Endpoints	Represents a collection of Endpoint objects. Each Endpoint object represents an endpoint defined on a SQL Server instance.
Events	Gets the server events associated with an instance of SQL Server.
FullTextService	Allows access to the full-text search settings for an instance of SQL Server.

Property	Description
Information	Allows access to read-only properties of an instance of SQL Server, such as the operating system or SQL Server version.
InstanceName	Gets the instance name of an instance of SQL Server.
JobServer	Gets the SQL Server Agent associated with an instance of SQL Server.
Languages	Represents a collection of Language objects, which represent the languages associated with an instance of SQL Server.
LinkedServers	Represents a collection of LinkedServer objects. Each LinkedServer object represents a linked server associated with an instance of SQL Server.
Logins	Represents a collection of Login objects. Each Login object represents a login associated with an instance of SQL Server.
Mail	Gets the Microsoft SQL Mail service associated with an instance of SQL Server.
Name	Gets the name of an instance of SQL Server.
NotificationServices	Gets the Notification Services associated with an instance of SQL Server.
Properties	Gets a collection of Property objects.
ProxyAccount	Gets the proxy account associated with an instance of SQL Server.
ReplicationServer	Gets the replication service associated with an instance of SQL Server.
Roles	Represents a collection of ServerRole objects. Each ServerRole object represents a role associated with an instance of SQL Server.
ServiceMasterKey	Gets the Service Master Key associated with an instance of SQL Server.
Settings	Gets modifiable settings associated with an instance of SQL Server.
State	Gets the state of a referenced object.

(continued)

Table 23-1 *(continued)*

Property	Description
SystemDataTypes	Represents a collection of SystemDataType objects. Each SystemDataType object represents a system data type associated with an instance of SQL Server.
SystemMessages	Represents a collection of SystemMessage objects. Each SystemMessage object represents a system message associated with an instance of SQL Server.
Triggers	Represents a collection of ServerDdl Trigger objects. Each ServerDdl Trigger object represents a DDL (Data Definition Language) trigger associated with an instance of SQL Server.
Urn	Gets the Uniform Resource Name that uniquely identifies an instance of SQL Server.
UserData	Gets or sets user-defined data.
UserDefinedMessages	Represents a collection of UserDefined Message objects. Each UserDefined Message object represents a user-defined message associated with an instance of SQL Server.
UserOptions	Gets user options for the connection to an instance of SQL Server.

The Server object has the public methods listed in Table 23-2.

Table 23-2	Server Object Public Methods
Public Method	**Description**
Alter()	Updates any Server object property changes on an instance of SQL Server
AttachDatabase()	Attaches an existing database to an instance of SQL Server
CompareUrn()	Compares two URNs
DeleteBackupHistory()	Deletes the backup history for an instance of SQL Server up to a specified date and time

Public Method	*Description*
`Deny()`	Denies specified permissions to specified grantee(s) for an instance of SQL Server
`DetachDatabase()`	Detaches a database from an instance of SQL Server
`DetachedDatabaseInfo()`	Gets information about a detached database file
`EnumAvailableMedia()`	Gets an enumeration of media available on the local network to an instance of SQL Server
`EnumCollations()`	Gets an enumeration of the collations available on an instance of SQL Server
`EnumDatabaseMirror WitnessRoles()`	Gets an enumeration of database witness roles associated with an instance of SQL Server
`EnumDetachedDatabase Files()`	Gets an enumeration of detached database files
`EnumDetachedLogFiles()`	Gets an enumeration of detached log files
`EnumDirectories()`	Gets an enumeration of directories relative to a specified path
`EnumErrorLogs()`	Gets an enumeration of error log files associated with an instance of SQL Server
`EnumLocks()`	Gets an enumeration of current locks on an instance of SQL Server
`EnumMembers()`	Gets an enumeration of server roles and database roles associated with an instance of SQL Server
`EnumObjectPermissions()`	Gets an enumeration of permissions on objects associated with an instance of SQL Server
`EnumPerformanceCounters()`	Gets an enumeration of performance counters supported by an instance of SQL Server
`EnumProcesses()`	Gets an enumeration of running processes associated with an instance of SQL Server
`EnumServerAttributes()`	Gets an enumeration of server attributes for an instance of SQL Server

(continued)

Table 23-2 *(continued)*

Public Method	Description
EnumServerPermissions()	Gets an enumeration of server permissions associated with an instance of SQL Server
EnumStartupProcedures()	Gets an enumeration of startup procedures associated with an instance of SQL Server
EnumWindowsDomainGroups()	Gets an enumeration of Windows group accounts defined on a domain
EnumWindowsGroupInfo()	Gets an enumeration of Windows groups that have been granted access to an instance of SQL Server
EnumWindowsUserInfo()	Gets an enumeration of Windows users that have been granted access to an instance of SQL Server
Equals()	Tests whether two objects are equal
GetActiveDBConnectionCount()	Gets a count of the current number of active connections for a database
GetDefaultInitFields()	Returns property types initialized by default
GetHashCode()	Serves as a hash function
GetPropertyNames()	Returns the names of initialized properties for a specified object type
GetSmoObject()	Returns an object specified by a URN (Uniform Resource Name) address
GetType()	Gets the type of the current instance
Grant()	Grants specified permission(s) to a specified grantee(s) on an instance of SQL Server
Initialize()	Initializes an object and forces its properties to be loaded
IsDetachedPrimaryFile()	Tests whether a specified file is or is not a primary database file (.mdf file extension)
IsWindowsGroupMember()	Tests whether a specified Windows user account is a member of a specified Windows group

Public Method	Description
KillAllProcesses()	Stops all processes associated with a specified database
KillDatabase()	Deletes a specified database and drops any active connections to it
KillProcess()	Stops a specified process
PingSqlServerVersion()	Retrieves the version number of an instance of SQL Server
ReadErrorLog()	Reads information from a SQL Server instance's error log
ReferenceEquals()	Tests whether two instances of the Object object are equal
Refresh()	Refreshes the objects and properties of the Server object
Revoke()	Revokes previously granted permission(s) from a specified grantee(s) on an instance of SQL Server
SetDefaultInitFields()	Specifies whether or not all properties are fetched when an object is initialized
ToString()	Returns a string that represents a specified object

There are several dozen other classes in the Microsoft.SqlServer. Management.Smo namespace — for example, an asymmetric key, a column in a database, a certificate, a foreign key, or an index. To take your SMO programming beyond the basics described in this chapter, you need to familiarize yourself with the objects in the Microsoft.SqlServer.Management. Smo namespace.

If you want to work programmatically directly with databases, you need to understand the properties and methods of the Database object. It has several dozen properties and methods.

Creating a SQL-SMO Program

In this section, I show you how to create a basic, console-based, SMO application. You can use similar techniques to create a Windows Forms–based SMO application.

The instructions refer to a Visual Basic.NET application. If you want to program in Visual C#, substitute Visual C# for Visual Basic in Step 3 of the instructions. Where the Visual Basic instructions mention Imports statements, replace those with Using statements when you program in Visual C#. In addition, you need to edit the code to reflect the differences in syntax between Visual Basic and C#.

To create a console-based Visual Basic SMO application, follow these steps:

1. **Start Visual Studio 2005 by choosing Start⇨All Programs⇨ Visual Studio 2005⇨Visual Studio 2005.**

2. **To create a new project, choose File⇨New⇨Project.**

3. **In the left pane of the New Project dialog box, choose Visual Basic⇨Windows. In the right pane of the New Project dialog box, select Console Application. Name the project** SMOConsoleApp.

   The New Project dialog box should look like Figure 23-1.

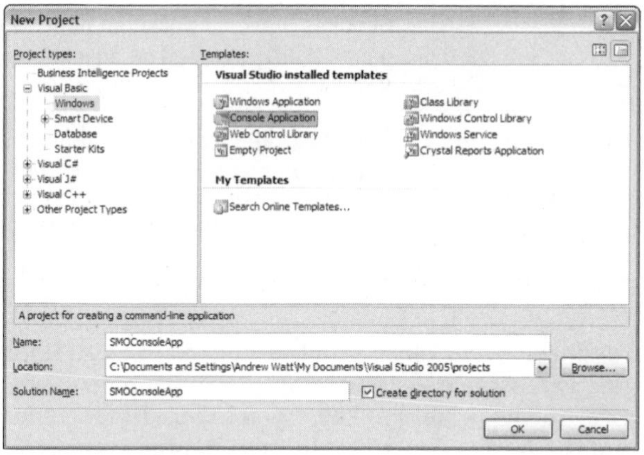

Figure 23-1:
The New Project dialog box to create a Visual Basic console application.

4. **Click OK.**

   Visual Studio creates a project from the Console Application project template.

5. **To add references to the SMO assemblies, choose Project⇨ Add Reference, as shown in Figure 23-2.**

   The Add Reference dialog box opens.

6. **Click the Browse tab. Navigate to the folder**

```
C:\Program Files\Microsoft SQL
        Server\90\SDK\Assemblies
```

7. **Select the following assemblies by holding down the Ctrl key and clicking each of the assemblies.**

   - `Microsoft.SqlServer.ConnectionInfo.dll`

   - `Microsoft.SqlServer.ServiceBrokerEnum.dll`

   - `Microsoft.SqlServer.Smo.dll`

   - `Microsoft.SqlServer.SmoEnum.dll`

   - `Microsoft.SqlServer.OlapEnum.dll`

   - `Microsoft.SqlServer.SqlEnum.dll`

   - `Microsoft.SqlServer.WmiEnum.dll`

   The appearance should be similar to Figure 23-3 when you've selected the assemblies.

8. **Click OK to add the references.**

9. **Verify that you've successfully added the references. Choose View⇨ Solution Explorer to display the Solution Explorer. Click the Show All Files button near the top of Solution Explorer. Expand the `References` node.**

   All the assemblies are visible under the `References` node, as shown in Figure 23-4.

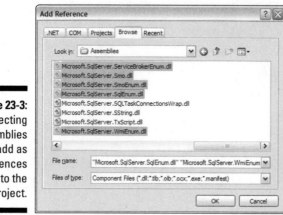

Figure 23-3:
Selecting
assemblies
to add as
references
to the
project.

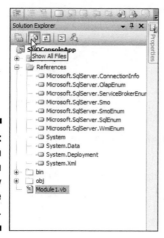

Figure 23-4:
Confirm
that you
successfully
added the
references.

10. **If the coding window for Module1.vb isn't displayed, choose View⇨ Code.**

11. **On the first lines of the code for Module1.vb, add the following Imports statements:**

```
Imports Microsoft.SqlServer.Management.Smo
Imports Microsoft.SqlServer.Management.Common
```

12. **Add the following code, which connects to the local default instance of SQL Server:**

```
Dim srv As Server
srv = New Server
```

13. Add the following code to display the version number of the default instance of SQL Server to which you've just connected.

The final line simply acts to keep the console open until you press the Enter key.

```
Console.Write("The SQL Server version is: ")
Console.WriteLine(srv.Information.Version)
Console.ReadLine()
```

The full code is

```
Imports Microsoft.SqlServer.Management.Smo
Imports Microsoft.SqlServer.Management.Common

Module Module1
  Sub Main()

  Dim srv As Server
  srv = New Server

  Console.Write("The SQL Server version is: ")
  Console.WriteLine(srv.Information.Version)
  Console.ReadLine()



  End Sub

End Module
```

14. Choose File⇨Save All to save the project.

15. Press F5 to execute the code in debug mode.

Figure 23-5 shows the result of executing the code in the Visual Basic module. If you wish, you can confirm the version number for the local default instance in Object Explorer in SQL Server Management Studio.

Figure 23-5: A simple console application that displays the version of the local instance of SQL Server.

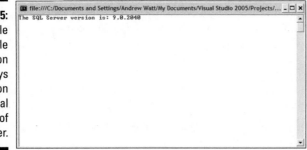

```
file:///C:/Documents and Settings/Andrew Watt/My Documents/Visual Studio 2005/Projects/...
The SQL Server version is: 9.0.2040
```

16. **Press the Enter key to close the console application's window.**

17. **Add the following code to display information about a configuration setting of the SQL Server instance (whether the CLR is enabled) and how many logins there are for the instance.**

```
Console.Write("Is CLR enabled?: ")
Console.WriteLine(srv.Configuration.IsSqlClrEnabled.Co
        nfigValue)
Console.Write("The number of Logins is: ")
Console.WriteLine(srv.Logins.Count.ToString)
```

18. **Press F5 to execute the code in debug mode.**

Figure 23-6 shows the results. As you can see in the SQL Server instance on my machine, the CLR is enabled, and there are 11 logins.

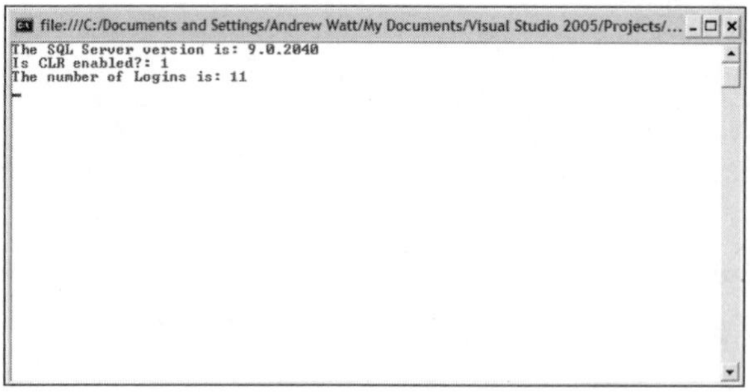

Figure 23-6:
Displaying information about CLR configuration and logins for the SQL Server instance.

```
file:///C:/Documents and Settings/Andrew Watt/My Documents/Visual Studio 2005/Projects/...
The SQL Server version is: 9.0.2040
Is CLR enabled?: 1
The number of Logins is: 11
```

The following example allows you to enumerate databases in a SQL Server instance. Follow these steps:

1. **Start Visual Studio 2005 by choosing Start⇨All Programs⇨ Visual Studio 2005⇨Visual Studio 2005.**

2. **To create a new project, choose File⇨New⇨Project.**

3. **In the left pane of the New Project dialog box, choose Visual Basic⇨ Windows. In the right pane of the New Project dialog select Console Application. Name the project** SMOConsoleApp2.

4. **Click OK.**

   Visual Studio creates a project from the Console Application project template.

5. **To add references to the SMO assemblies, choose Project⇨ Add Reference.**

6. **If you created the preceding example, in the Add Reference dialog box, select the Recent tab and add the references I listed on the Recent tab. Hold down Ctrl and select each namespace.**

    Your screen should look like Figure 23-7.

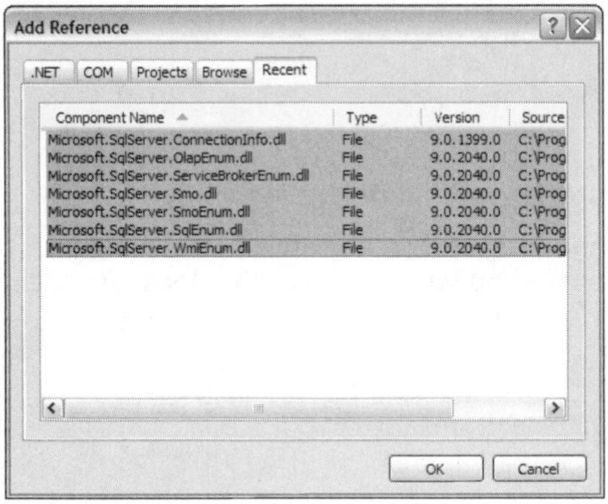

Figure 23-7:
Using name-
spaces on
the Recent
tab in
the Add
Reference
dialog box.

7. **Click OK in the Add Reference dialog box to add the references.**

8. **If the coding window for `Module1.vb` isn't displayed, choose View⇨ Code.**

9. **Edit the code to read as follows:**

    (Notice that you add an additional namespace, `Imports Microsoft. SqlServer.Management.SqlEnum`. The `For each` loop iterates through `Database` objects. The name of each database is output on a separate line.)

```
Imports Microsoft.SqlServer.Management.Smo
Imports Microsoft.SqlServer.Management.SqlEnum
Imports Microsoft.SqlServer.Management.Common


Module Module1

    Sub Main()

        Dim srv As Server
        srv = New Server
        Dim DBs As DatabaseCollection
        DBs = srv.Databases
        Dim DB As New Database
```

```
        Console.Write("The SQL Server version is: ")
        Console.WriteLine(srv.Information.Version)
        For Each DB In DBs
            Console.WriteLine(DB.Name)
        Next DB

        Console.ReadLine()

    End Sub
End Module
```

10. Press F5 to execute the code in debug mode.

The appearance should resemble the one shown in Figure 23-8, depending on what databases you've created on your local instance of SQL Server.

Figure 23-8:
Displaying databases in a SQL Server instance.

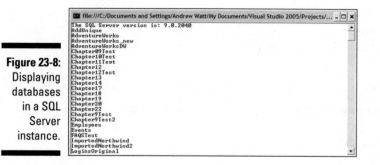

11. Press the Enter key to close the console window.

You can create SMO applications using Visual Basic or Visual C#. To create a Windows Forms SMO application, use the Windows Application project template in Visual Studio 2005.

Part VI
The Part of Tens

The 5th Wave
By Rich Tennant

"We're researching molecular/digital technology that moves massive amounts of information across binary pathways that interact with free-agent programs capable of making decisions and performing logical tasks. We see applications in really high-end doorbells."

In this part . . .

*T*his book focuses on programming tasks directly relevant to Transact-SQL and numerous other related programming tasks. Chapter 24 reminds you of some broader issues that, if you master them, can help you to program like a pro. Chapter 25 gives you a list of further reading resources.

Listening is very important. If you don't listen to what a client wants out of a computer system, you have very little chance of getting it right. You have to have some understanding of a potential client's business in order to build not only a robust computer system but also a usable one.

You can find a plethora of information on the Internet and in other books on all sorts of topics. Computer topics, and specifically Microsoft products and SQL Server database, are not excluded from this list. The best source of information for SQL Server 2005 is the Microsoft documentation, both with the software and on Microsoft Web sites. However, a simple text string search in an Internet search engine can often yield fruitful results.

Chapter 24

Ten Tips to Program Like a Pro

*I*n this book, I introduce you to many techniques you can use to program SQL Server 2005 using Transact-SQL. A good understanding of how to use the Transact-SQL language is essential to create complex, real-life applications based on SQL Server. However, you need a range of other skills and accomplishments to program like a pro.

In this chapter, I describe ten (plus one) approaches that help you program like a pro.

Listen to Your Clients' Needs

You might be great at designing a database, but if that database doesn't meet the needs of your clients and how they work (or would prefer to work), the database you design won't be much good to them.

One of the most difficult and time-consuming phases of creating an application based on a SQL Server database (or databases) can be the phase where you spend time listening to clients. In part, this phase can be lengthy because the clients aren't technically literate and don't know what would help them work more efficiently.

Listening to your clients helps you design a better database. The reason why is because your clients know their business a lot better than you do. You're the computer person. You have to interpret how your clients express their needs, into some form of computer program. It is prudent and in your best interest to assume your own ignorance of client needs before beginning the process of design. That way you are more likely to pay attention to small details.

Document the Project

Even on small database projects, take the time to document what you're doing. Even the simple act of writing down the aims of the project—and what the client needs the application for—can help you think more clearly.

Document the client's needs and get the client to sign off on the project. That's important whether the client is another department or group in your own company or you're writing applications commercially. Making sure that everybody wants the same things from the project can avoid a lot of hassle later in the project and avoid disagreements about cost and time overruns.

Budget Enough Time for the Project

To successfully create a database project, you'll invest a lot of time in the various phases of the project. Make sure that you make realistic estimates of the time you need to do the necessary work. If the client's timescale makes achieving the project impossible (in your judgment), either increase the number of appropriately skilled staff or discuss with the client which aspects of the application can be put off to a later version of the application.

Agreeing to a schedule that you can't deliver can get you a bad reputation for failing to deliver on time—and can be costly if there are penalty clauses in any contract for the project.

Think about Long-Term Needs

We live in a rapidly changing world. Your client's business needs next year might be very different from her current needs. Don't design an application that won't scale or can't be adapted to take into account changes in business practices.

Think Carefully about Relations in the Database

Take time to determine how you should create the tables of the database and their relationships. Aim to create a data model that keeps a single idea to a single table.

What you really need to do is to break down the business you are modeling from a business perspective (how the business operates). This is a little like a data warehouse design. If you are building an Internet (OLTP) database and it needs extensive normalization, you take that step after you have a clear picture in your mind, or on paper, of how your client's business functions.

Handle Many-to-Many Relationships Appropriately

Some real-life relationships are many-to-many. For example, in the pubs database, you see how the fact that a title can have multiple authors and an author can write (at least part of) multiple books means that an additional table is needed to express the notion of a many-to-many relationship as two one-to-many relationships.

Think about Performance

Your clients will want your application to perform well. You might need to denormalize some relations to improve performance. Denormalization is the opposite of normalization. Normalization is the approach to relational database design, unless you are building a data warehouse. Normalization sacrifices performance for data integrity by dividing all your data into the most granular (smallest) pieces possible.

When running things like reports, a highly granular structure requires lots of join queries, which can take a long time to run. Denormalization can be necessary after normalization in order to speed up reporting functionality if a client is dissatisfied with over performance or the performance of specific things such as time-critical reports.

Creating indexes can enable queries to retrieve data more quickly. But be careful about the cost for updating, inserting, and deleting operations. Take time to find an appropriate balance for your clients' needs.

Design and Test on Development Hardware

You should develop your application on a developer machine that is entirely separate from your production databases. Attempting to develop an application that, at an early stage, accesses production data is asking for trouble. It's more than asking for trouble. A production server provides software that your client's clients are using — right at this moment! Software development makes sweeping changes, requires constant down time, and even when tested is very unpredictable. If you want to keep your clients happy, avoid anything but production software in a production environment. If your client insists otherwise, either get him or her to sign off on liability or just run for the hills.

Test Your Application Carefully

Take time to test the application you create. Users can try to do odd things when working with an unfamiliar application. To anticipate this, try to break the application by clicking at potentially silly places in the interface. Sometimes you will be surprised by the effect of what you do.

Think about Which Edition of SQL Server to Use

Think about the edition of SQL Server 2005 you need to deliver the performance and throughput that your client wants.

How will the database be loaded? Will there be clear times of peak demand? Will there be times when the database can be taken offline?

Questions like these determine whether, at one end of the scale, you might need only SQL Server 2005 Express Edition or whether, to scale to enterprise levels, you need the much more costly Enterprise Edition.

Do you need to create business intelligence applications that relate to the database? If so, you need to check whether the functionality in Integration Services, Analysis Services, and Reporting Services is available in the edition of SQL Server 2005 that you initially plan to use.

Think about the Hardware You Need

The hardware that you use for your production server is important. Think carefully about demands on the application and things that can go wrong.

What's the peak demand on the application? Can your hardware handle that? If it can't, where's the bottleneck?

In real life, a huge number of things can go wrong. Plan for things to go wrong. If the hard drive crashes on your production machine, do you have a recent, full backup of your data? If the server room burns down, will all your backups go up in smoke with it? You need to think about these and other questions for every business application. The data is, for many modern businesses, critical for survival of the business.

Think about the time to get up and running after a disaster. If you take days to get up and running after, say, a hardware failure, will your business survive?

Chapter 25

Ten Sources for More Information on SQL Server 2005

. . . .

*I*n this book, I introduce you to many topics relevant to programming SQL Server 2005. Inevitably, because of its sheer size, I can't cover everything that you might need to know to program SQL Server. There are several components of SQL Server 2005, each of which is itself enormous. In this book, I focus primarily on programming the database engine. But, depending on your business needs, you might also need to program SQL Server Integration Services and SQL Server Analysis Services.

In this chapter, I list and describe ten (plus one) sources where you can find additional information about SQL Server 2005.

Books Online

Books Online (`http://msdn2.microsoft.com/en-us/library/ms130214.aspx`) is the official Microsoft documentation for SQL Server 2005. It is affectionately referred to as *BOL*. Despite its name, you will very likely use it mostly offline.

Microsoft is now issuing downloadable updates to Books Online. Be sure to visit the Microsoft site to find out if there are updates for BOL that supersede the version you installed when you installed SQL Server 2005. Do a Google search of *SQL Server Books Online site:microsoft.com* and you have a good chance of finding any updates that might be available.

If you've used SQL Server 2000 Books Online, you'll notice huge changes in Books Online for SQL Server 2005. The interface has been completely redesigned—which can, at first, make finding information difficult.

You can install Books Online separately from the rest of SQL Server 2005 or install it together with other SQL Server components, such as the database engine, on a development machine.

In the Index pane and Contents pane of BOL, you can filter content by major topics such as Integration Services and Reporting Services. Filtering makes it very much easier to find the information that you want.

The Search functionality has been redesigned. There is a Search button in the toolbar. You can filter searches by technology and content type.

If you also install Visual Studio 2005 and MSDN, you'll find all BOL content is added to MSDN. Using the filters mentioned in the preceding paragraphs is a huge help if you want to reduce the chance of being overwhelmed with information.

The Public Newsgroups

The public SQL Server newsgroups are a great place to get help with specific problems.

SQL Server has a broad range of public newsgroups where you can get support from Microsoft MVPs, Microsoft staff, and other users of SQL Server.

The news server is `msnews.microsoft.com`. Use a newsreader such as Outlook Express, Thunderbird, or Agent to access the SQL Server newsgroups. The SQL Server newsgroups are in the stack `microsoft.public.sqlserver.*`. You don't need a password to access the public newsgroups.

Newsgroups you might want to look at specifically include `microsoft.public.sqlserver.newusers` and `microsoft.public.sqlserver.programming`.

The Public Fora

Microsoft has created several *fora* (forums) that allow users to ask questions about SQL Server 2005. To access them, go to `http://forums.microsoft.com/msdn/default.aspx?ForumGroupID=19`.

If the link has changed at the time you read this, try `http://forums.microsoft.com/msdn/default.aspx` or `http://forums.microsoft.com`. It's likely that you'll find a link from there to the SQL Server fora.

To get full benefit from the public fora, you'll need to have a Passport or Live identity.

The SQL Server 2005 Web Site

Microsoft's main Web site for information about SQL Server 2005 is located at `http://www.microsoft.com/sql/2005/default.mspx`. This provides overview information with links to many sources of more detailed information, including technical white papers.

If the preceding URL doesn't work when you read this, try `http://www.microsoft.com/sql/`. You should be able to find links to SQL Server 2005 information from there.

The SQL Server Developer Center

The SQL Server Developer Center, located at `http://msdn.microsoft.com/sql/`, contains a lot of useful information for anyone carrying out development tasks on SQL Server 2005.

The SQL Server 2005 TechCenter

The SQL Server 2005 TechCenter located at `http://www.microsoft.com/technet/prodtechnol/sql/default.mspx` has information about administration of SQL Server 2005.

The Business Intelligence Site

A dedicated SQL Server 2005 Business Intelligence Web site is located at `http://www.microsoft.com/sql/bi/default.mspx`. Here you can find useful information about SQL Server Integration Services, SQL Server Analysis Services, and SQL Server Reporting Services.

The Integration Services Developer Center

As I mention earlier, SQL Server Integration Services is an extensive program that is outside the scope of this book. However, you can do lots of things to program Integration Services, and it has its own Developer Center located at `http://msdn2.microsoft.com/en-us/sql/aa336312.aspx`. Here you can find technical white papers, information about webcasts, blogs, and a host of other information to help you with Integration Services development.

The Reporting Services Web Site

The Reporting Services Web site has information about SQL Server 2000 Reporting Services and SQL Server 2005 Reporting Services. It's located at `http://www.microsoft.com/sql/reporting/default.mspx`.

You can find downloads of sample reports, service packs, white papers, and a range of other relevant information.

Channel 9

Channel 9, `http://channel9.msdn.com`, has a host of interesting information on a range of Microsoft products. A few videos include interviews with SQL Server 2005 team members.

It can be difficult to find content on Channel 9. Often, the best way to find specific topics is to use the tool I suggest in the final section of this chapter.

Other Web Sites

A huge number of additional Web sites are available on SQL Server 2005. I could attempt to list some here. Instead, I am going to recommend one of the best tools for finding additional information about SQL Server 2005 — Google (`www.google.com`).

If you want to find information on any SQL Server 2005 topic, a Google search of the form *SQL Server 2005* topic words *site:microsoft.com* (replace the phrase *topic words* with the top you're interested in) is often the quickest and most effective way to find any information about SQL Server 2005 on the Microsoft site.

Of course, a simple *SQL Server 2005 Integration Services* search term in Google can turn up some very interesting material on sites other than the Microsoft ones.

If you're not familiar with Google syntax for searches, use the Advanced Search option, which you can access (at the time of this writing) from the Google home page.

Remember you can use Google to search Usenet newsgroups by clicking the Groups link above the Search text box in the Google interface.

Index